Female Genesis

Female Genesis

Creativity, Self and Gender

NICOLE WARD JOUVE

Polity Press

First published in 1998 by Polity Press
in association with Blackwell Publishers Ltd.

Editorial office:
Polity Press
65 Bridge Street
Cambridge CB2 1UR, UK

Marketing and production:
Blackwell Publishers Ltd
108 Cowley Road
Oxford OX4 1JF, UK

ISBN 0-7456-1681-X
ISBN 0-7456-1682-8 (pbk)

A CIP catalogue record for this book is available from the British Library.

Typeset in 10 on 11.5 pt Palatino
by Wearset, Boldon, Tyne and Wear.
Printed and bound in Great Britain by MPG Books Ltd, Bodmin, Cornwall

This book is printed on acid-free paper.

Contents

Acknowledgements   vii

Introduction   Male and Female Made (S)he Them   ix

IN FATHER'S LACK

Part I   Gendering the Female: Good/Bad Daughters   33

 1 Balzac's *A Daughter of Eve* and the Apple of Knowledge   35
 2 Maleness in the Act: The Case of the Papin Sisters   64

**Part II   Masculine/Feminine: The Battle of the Sexes
              and the First World War**   85

 3 The Missing Men and the Women's Sentence   87
 4 D. H. Lawrence: Womb Envy or A Womb of his Own?   103
 5 Virginia Woolf: Penis Envy and the Man's Sentence   119

TROUBLESOME MOTHERS

Part III   The Female Creator   139

 6 'Mother is a Figure of Speech . . .': Angela Carter   141
 7 'No One's Mother': Can the Mother Write Poetry?   163

Part IV   Creation, Gender and the Imaginary   183

8 Metaphors and Narrative: Of Tongues, Shells, Boats, Oranges . . .
  and the Sea   185

Conclusion   New Directions   227

9 The Name of the Father   229
10 Male and Female Made They Them   245

Index   251

Acknowledgements

This book has been born of much questing, listening and exchange. I could not possibly list all those who have helped me and inspired me, so will thank but a few: the 'team' of Women's Studies teachers and researchers and students at York University, UK, richly creative and fostering over the years, but also full of lively dissent; the teams in Women's Studies and in the Institute for Advanced Studies in the Humanities at UMass, Amherst, so generous and supportive – Lee R. Edwards, Jules Chametsky, Anne Halley and others; Helen Carr and the South Bank team for getting me to reflect on the 1920s; and Anne Digby at Oxford for encouraging me to carry it through; Helen Birch for directing me so perceptively towards the Papin sisters; Lorna Sage for her encouragement and dashing, irreverent love for Angela Carter; Vicki Bertram and all the 'Kicking Daffodils' poets and contributors for making such a feast of women's poems; Suniti Namjoshi and Gillian Hanscombe for sustaining me with their flair and originality and fun; Ros Coward for talking about fathers at a time when I was also thinking about them; Michael Wood, for intellectual grace and acumen; Simon Archer for listening, and being who he is; Susan Sellers and Sue Roe, for sharing with me their interest in women and creativity, leme van der Poël, for her provocative knowledge of French feminisms both sides of the Atlantic. The shortcomings are all my own.

The author and publishers wish to thank the following for permission to use copyright material:

Allison & Busby for Michèle Roberts, 'After my grandmother's death' in *Touch Papers*; Carcanet Press Ltd for an excerpt from Sujata Bhatt, 'White Asparagus' in *Brunizem*, 1988; Rosica Colin Ltd on behalf of the Estate of the author for an extract from Richard Aldington, 'In the

Trenches'. Copyright © The Estate of Richard Aldington; Elaine Feinstein for 'Patience' in *Some Unease and Angels*, Hutchinson; The Gallery Press for Paul Muldoon, 'The Language Issue' in *Pharaoh's Daughter*, tr., Nuala Nì Domhnaill, 1990; Karnak House for Grace Nichols, 'In My Name' from *I Is a Long Memoried Woman*. Copyright © 1983, 1996 Karnak House; Oxford University Press for Anne Stevenson, 'Generations' in *Travelling Behind Glass*, 1974; Laurence Pollinger on behalf of the Estate of Frieda Lawrence Ravagli and Viking Penguin, a division of Penguin Books USA Inc, for excerpts from D. H. Lawrence, 'Song of a Man Who is Loved' in *The Complete Poems of D. H. Lawrence*, edited by V. de Solo Pinto and F. W. Roberts. Copyright © 1964, 1971 by Angelo Ravagli and C. M. Weekley, Executors of the Estate of Frieda Lawrence Ravagli; George T. Sassoon and Viking Penguin, a division of Penguin Books USA Inc, for extracts from Siegfried Sassoon, 'Glory of Women' and 'Counter-Attack' from *Collected Poems of Siegfried Sassoon*. Copyright © 1918, 1920 by E. P. Dutton. Copyright © 1936, 1946, 1947, 1948 by Siegfried Sassoon; The University of Massachusetts Press for excerpts from Anne Halley, 'Prayer to the Mother' in *The Bearded Mother*, 1979. Copyright © 1979 by Anne Halley; A. P. Watt Ltd on behalf of Professor Anthony Clare for an excerpt from a review by him of Kay Jamieson's book *An Unquiet Mind* in *The Sunday Times*, 5th May 1996.

Every effort has been made to trace the copyright holders but if any have been inadvertently overlooked the publishers will be pleased to make the necessary arrangement at the first opportunity.

Introduction
Male and Female Made (S)he Them

> So God created man in his own image, in the image of God created he him;
> male and female created he them. (Genesis 1: 27)

It is the sixth day, the crowning day of creation. God blesses 'them', tells 'them' to 'be fruitful and multiply', gives 'them' dominion 'over every living thing'. 'Them'?

Male and FEMALE?

Men and women? The King James's translation of the Bible spells early and symptomatic trouble for women. On the one hand Genesis says 'them'. They, male and female, are equally included in the blessing, the bid to be fruitful, the dominion over every living thing. On the other, the translation says 'he' for God. 'He' created 'man', 'him', 'in his own image'. The masculine gender is associated with the creator, and the main name of the created human, Adam. Never mind that 'Adamah' means earth, soil, that Adam means the earthy, the clayey one, which applies as much to female as to male. That we are all, males and females, whether in the symbolic six days of the biblical creation, or through millions of years of evolution, made of matter. The Adam of chapter 2, the first human being, the one who is formed from the dust of the ground and breathed life into, is firmly male. Eve is created second, shaped from a rib from Adam's side, as a companion for Adam: for it is not good that man be alone. We all know the sequel: how Eve, not Adam, is seduced by the serpent, how she wants to taste of the fruit of knowledge, how the fall ensues. Countless prior, parallel or derived mythic stories follow:

from Pandora releasing all evils upon the world by opening the fatal box, to Eve in the medieval *Roman de Renart* stealing the rod God has given Adam to lash the sea and bring out of it all kinds of goodly animals. Adam has worked in the daytime. Eve creeps in at night, while Adam is asleep. She wants to be a creator too. She lashes the sea in her turn: out of it come all the evil beasts, lion and tiger and wolf and finally, last, fox ...

Since that first chapter of Genesis, 'they' have not been equal sharers in the blessing of creation, in dominion over all living things. Full identity as a human being, in the act of knowing and in the creative act, have been firmly aligned with the male of the species, at least within the classical Greek and the Judeao-Christian civilizations and their European offspring. The female creator has been a deviant, the stealer of the rod. Man has been the universal category. Woman the endless problem, the one who would not stay in her place, whose deviancy lost Eden. The one whose existence has needed continuous definition in relation to the male: as companion, as begetter ... For in that relation is her place, and if she tries again to have a direct relation to knowledge, to creation – well – we all know what evils will follow. Only when 'alone of all her sex' (as Marina Warner has stressed) she is both virgin and mother can she have power. The power of absolute humility. God's servant, God's mother: procreator, not creator. At least in the Christian tradition.

For there are earlier myths, earlier civilizations, in which there are goddesses, mother-centred societies. Is Judeo-Christianity, along with classical Greek and Roman thought, the expression of a male-centred, Arian era, succeeding a female-centered, Taurean one? Is the Judaeo-Christian privileging of the male a phase through which humankind has been going for quite a while, but that will change in its turn? Can we imagine a further evolution to yet other types of relationship, beyond the splendours but also appalling imbalances and excesses of the Piscean age? What difference would it make if it was a 'She' who created? Can we imagine such a state? Can we go back to it, as seventies feminisms dreamt to do?

Male and female made *she* them. But of course: all human beings are, as Adrienne Rich put it, 'of woman born'. All children, whether male or female, have come out of a woman. For human societies to move from a mother-centred to a male-centred state, for the male to become *the* maker, all sorts of structures have to move into place: taboos, kinship systems ... all the power structures which anthropology has described in the past hundred years or so, down to the religious and philosophical or scientific systems which have been analysed in the last thirty. Such as Aristotle's notion that the semen was the source of the embryo, the womb merely a vessel in which it developed, which neatly made the father into the key maker ... Or such as Freud's notion that the little boy's sexuality was the point of reference, the little girl a complicated set of deviations from it, so that femininity itself appeared to be a disorder ...

Male and Female Created (S)he Them. Introducing an 'S' into th
tion, making the creating subject either female or male, is my
putting the question of the female knower, the female creator, fi　　ᴀ
the centre of this book. The essays here gathered ponder *her*. Historically
grounded her: in the recent past, or today. She both mutates as contexts
and civilizations mutate, *and* finds the same questions recurring: by
virtue of her being a 'she'. Thus the first chapter asks how, at a particular
moment in western civilization, in nineteenth-century Restoration
France, a writer as aware of sexual difference as Balzac perceives the
human and social contradictions deriving from the education given to
young women, aimed at preserving them from knowledge, both intellectual and sexual. Each moment in history, each place, each class, makes
something else of Eve, alters her *gender*: yet Eve clings on . . .

A number of the chapters are concerned directly with the woman creator, especially in her relation to motherhood, presented throughout the
patriarchal ages as woman's true vocation, and the obstacle to her creativity: she is a procreator, she cannot be a creator. Will getting rid of the
Mother help women become more creative? Must the 'Angel in the
House', as Woolf called her, be murdered before women can be artists?
How crucial to her specific, irreverent creativity, her subversion of the
codes of femininity, is Angela Carter's hostility to the figure of the
Mother? Can the Mother be a poet? Or if a mother happens to be a poet,
is it another part of her that creates?

What is the female genesis?

Male AND Female?

'Male and female created He them.' Does that mean that all created
beings, both males and females, were made with masculine and feminine
components, with both principles active in them, the offspring of both?
Or that He made one male and one female, but as related components of
His creation? Male relative to female, female to male, each finding itself
and its fulfilment in relation to the other? There are, again over the ages,
countless human mediations and variations on this theme, from Pausa-
nias' story of the androgyne in Plato's *Symposium*, the double beings having been forcibly separated, each half seeking forever after for its other
half – to Virginia Woolf's notion that the true, the full creator is both
male and female, needs to achieve a lyrical state of balance – to Jung's
ascription of an inner anima figure to men, an animus figure to women:
it is in finding a relation to the inner other, the inner figure of the other
sex, that each sex achieves integration.

Several of the chapters here meditate on this relation of male to
female. The essays on the 'Battle of the Sexes and the First World War'
look at some of the damage, lived and imaginary, which the experience

of the war did to the sexes' relations to each other. They also suggest that there was, in the 1920s, an attempt on the part of both male and female writers to go beyond anger and mourning – an attempt at reparation, a seeking for balance which took the form of writing through, and out of, the imagined other sex. The essays seek to go beyond the terms, coined and bandied in these same 1920s, of penis envy for women and of womb envy for men, to the inner relation each sex can have with the complementary, imaginary organs.

Chapter 8 is concerned with image-related forms of creativity. This essay on metaphors looks at how both men and women writers imagine the creative act. It reflects on the differences and similarities between the ways in which each sex uses images of the sea, and of the boat or bark or shell, to figure the work of art: here again, the relation to the mother (as sea, or container) turns out to be central, this time to *both sexes*. The interesting question becomes, where do the differences appear, and at what stage: image-making (metaphor) or pattern-making (narrative)?

Though the lion's share of the book is given over to the female figure, creator or knower, archetypal or real mother, metaphor or figure of speech, the question of the male creator and knower is also posed, either through the figures of Balzac, Breton, the war poets, Lawrence, Ponge, Freud or Lacan, or through reflexions on their imagined relation to femininity. But it is only in the conclusion that the question of the Father, present mostly till then through his deficiencies or absence, manages to become, however briefly and in extremis, centre stage . . .

Feminisms: Where To Now?

There are born, periodically, movements that call themselves or are in the orbit of what today we call feminisms. They shake the obstacles that lie in the path of women's full access to humanity. They question the ways in which societies construct femininity. Obviously, at such times passionate, apposite and also excessive or skewed things are said and done. And less obviously, things that make one miserable by virtue of the complex business of being human, and not by virtue of the specific constraints placed upon one's sex, get mixed up with the question of one's sex. Movements build up, have an impact. There are angry, hostile, as well as positive, reactions. Some things change for the better. Others don't, like the dragon disturbed in its sleep, that stirs and shakes itself, then goes back to sleep on its mound of gold. Some things go back to what they were before, or worse. But then new subtle changes for the better timidly appear. In the process everybody, men and women, gets rattled. Other problems than the question of one's sex come to the fore, new and old, that seem more urgent, that are seen, rightly or wrongly, as unrelated: wars, poverty, unemployment, nuclear and environmental threats ... Or else it seems that the problem has been solved. Feminist issues are forgotten. Till women, somewhere and often in several places at once, begin to chafe at what they feel to be unjust and counterproductive or downright oppressive constraints. And the whole thing gets moving again.

Since 1968, we have been going through such a phase.

In the early days of what has been called second-wave feminism, a conspiracy of the evil Ps, the emanations of the Pater Familias, was seen to rule the empire. The Patriarchy was the enemy: a universal system of oppression to which men, by virtue of their sex, were all somehow party. Politics and Philosophy, the preserves of the males. Power: the realm of the Patriarchs. Phallogocentrism, privileging the Phallus and rationality, was the empire's system of thought. Based upon binaries it always placed one term, associated with the male, above the other, associated with the female. Man above woman, form above matter, mind over body, culture over nature. The One, Simone de Beauvoir had already said, above the Other, the second, sex. Subject (male) above (the sexual, female) object.

Feminism analysed the inequalities – economic, cultural. It pointed out that women owned 1 per cent of the world's wealth, did vast quantities of the world's work, were at the receiving end of battering and of legal discrimination, committed one-tenth of violent crimes. It proposed many ways to liberation. Equality was demanded. Let women have the same things as men. The same laws. And other laws too, abortion rights or affirmative rights that would put them on a par with men. Give them equal opportunities, rights. Equal pay. Let them have access to power: in politics, in the judiciary, the church, the media, finance ... Philosophical, cultural and psychoanalytic avenues were diversely pursued. Feminism proposed to revalue the Other, woman, in all that she was and had done as artist, thinker, politician. To revalue 'womanly' things and activities, the female body, quilt-making, nature, the subconscious, the mother and mothers. To analyse (as Luce Irigarary did) how the western subject had always been constructed in the masculine, and to make room for a feminine subject. To stop subsuming, to foreground the maternal body and those early impulses connected with it, as Kristeva has kept doing. Or else, as Cixous, in agreement with Derrida, did, to refuse hierarchized differences in favour of *différance*, of sexual difference as an interplay of masculine and feminine, endlessly renegotiable, endlessly deferring meaning. To write the repressed feminine body and in so doing to give a voice to what has never been heard. Or else again, following Deleuze, to propose 'becoming-woman' as a necessary, otherizing passage towards a new subjectivity, a minority experience as it were, relevant to both men and women. To disbelieve, shake, subvert the law, in language as in the polity always seen as the Law (and Name) of the Father. To argue (as Judith Butler does, following Foucault) that everything, matter, the body, is discursive – that gender itself is a repressive construct. The task then is to 'denaturalize' it, in order to expose its fundamental unnaturalness.[1]

But that was, it gradually became clear, mostly well-to-do white western women talking. Feminisms had denounced the ways in which 'man' had been taken as a universal term, made to mean all human beings, but had in fact specifically meant men: so men had always been privileged, even though they might not have felt it. Now it appeared that white Western feminists had done the same, had universalized 'woman'. They had been talking *for* others – subsuming women of colour, poor women, women from other cultures and parts of the world. How dare white Western feminists claim that what they wanted, from their privileged position, their liberal, generally atheistic system of values, was right for others? That was another form of oppression, African-American, African, Muslim, Asian, Hispanic women now forcefully pointed out. Post-colonial studies concurred. White feminisms were neocolonialist. Who had dared say that sisterhood was global?

Meanwhile many men saw how much women had gained, in their sense of self, their understanding, from all the shaking up, the questioning of the givens of femininity. Being a man was no picnic either, especially in a world full of uncertainties, unemployment, crumbling family patterns ... Let masculinity be questioned too. Masculinity studies came about. One now talked about gender, not women. While on one level, that is, a new awareness of the racial and cultural diversities of women's experiences shattered the notion that you could talk about women, on the other the specificities of women's plights became dissolved in the larger reflexion on the impact of socially constructed sexual difference.

And what about same-sex desire? Bisexual desire? What about compulsive heterosexuality, continuous with – expressive of? – phallogocentrism? Gay and lesbian studies, queer theory, bisexual studies grew. There again, through new alliances, new questionings, the terms women, woman, ceased to represent a focus, a locus, for liberation calls.

The enemy had multiplied (rather like Foucault's power). It had initially been the system, the empire, call it the patriarchy or capitalism or phallocracy – whoever was in charge (your man or your boss or father or prime minister would do). Now the enemy could be white women, Western women, affluent women, women from the north, heterosexual women, homophobia, racism, binaries, women who liked men, women you didn't agree with ... There were studies of violent women, women criminals, which shook the notion that there might be such things as feminine gentleness, maternal impulses which might be held up as models for a less violent world. Debates about the more emotional issues, violence, pornography, abuse, became polarized. It could now be seen that women were as aggressive as men (even though, in effect, they were less violent: but few were interested in that, unless it be as an argument in the continuing battle with the patriarchy). The women's movement split, and split again. Being a woman was no longer an identity. It was precisely sexual difference, biological differences made into an alienating bugbear, that came to be seen as the root of the trouble, binding women to motherhood. The very term Woman, which had been a rallying call, rather like 'workers of all countries unite' in the old Internationale, came under attack: the job to do, it now seemed, was to unmoor women from that body that had always been the pretext for their suppression. The body had to be mastered, shown to be changeable, malleable (the new clay, as it were, but it was the masterful ego that was to mould it, not the Spirit of God). Identity had to be tactical, forever reinvented, a mask put on, and cast off. Guerrilla tactics became the order of the day in a world in which the old iron curtains had fractured, then been shattered: alliances with other oppressed groups, theoretical wizardry, deconstruction, imaginary geometries, transvestism, transsexuality, endless transformations of your body, your image ... All to do with representations, scenarios in which you felt you had been an object: now you became the subject and agent and Pygmalion of your own body, your own sexuality. You had to be nimble. Question, and question again. You had to 'position' yourself before you talked. Swiftly slot into opposition: you were aware of the relativism of what you were saying. You were linking up in cyberspace.

This book stems from this context. Ending with dialogues, it is aware of contradictions, full of questioning and self-questioning. It continuously seeks to revise its positions, leaves issues in mid-air, 'to be continued' in some other space. A collection of 'essays', essayings of thought on this, that and the other, whatever happened to preoccupy me at a given moment, this is a book on the hop, shifting its terrain as it goes. It searches for a voice as it listens to voices.

But it is neither relative nor provisional. Though its answers change and are often contradictory, the contradictions are the fruit of necessity – not scepticism, or doubt that answers may be found. It believes that the apparent bewilderment and splitting of the women's movement are, as well as a symptom of contemporary crises, the sign of its coming of age. A much greater awareness of complexities is being arrived at. Genuinely diverse thinking is being done, and the intricate realities revealed by fine scholarship have made us more modest and tentative in what we say, but also thereby more far-reaching. Truly mature thinking is being produced, and through interdisciplinarity subtler perspectives are opening. Relations are being perceived that once would have been made invisible by the partitioning between disciplines. I hope that there are at least signs of such maturity in the diversity of my own approaches, and sources. I have certainly learned, and keep learning, a great deal from psychoanalysis, and not just those versions of it that have become fashionable. This book attempts to listen to voices which are not 'in' voices: thus in my essay on 'The Battle of the Sexes' I question the prominence given to Freud's and Lacan's views of femininity in feminist debates on psychoanalysis. Orthodoxies have formed in feminism as everywhere else, and they create blinkers which are difficult to remove, but which it is important to get out of the way.

Against Gender Trouble

If I belong to the 1990s in my awareness of the complexities of gender, I am very much against what seems to be at present, in feminist circles, the spirit of the decade. My sense is that the way to progress lies, not in making 'gender trouble', as Judith Butler has famously called it, in destabilizing the terms 'masculine' and 'feminine', but on the contrary – as my title suggests – in making more room for the female alongside the male genesis. In not letting the trees – the realization of the infinite diversities of women in their diverse cultures, of the complexities of power, of the difficulties in finding lasting answers to women's suppression and sometimes oppression (not to mention homophobia, ethnic or race or class hatred) – prevent one from seeing the wood: which is, that (as I see it) the end of life is to find fulfilment as a human being, male or female, male and female. Working to understand better how gender works, where it begins and ends, how masculinity relates to femininity and vice versa, can gain more than anarchic or theatrical processes of destabilization. For once things have got destabilized, what new formation is going to take their place except one made of the very ingredients you'd got there to start with? What human beings are made of won't go away: ambivalence ... Fear and anger and hatred and tenderness and love, those conflicting impulses which are the human lot and which for want of containment, of shapes and structures that might help them conflict in healthy, in bearable ways, can so easily erupt into psychopathological formations ... That the women's movement, philosophically so critical of binaries, should have become embattled in so many either/or positions (Women against Pornography/Women Against Women Against Pornography, defenders versus attackers of 'Essentialism') should be a lesson in humility. There may be more future in patiently learning about projections than in seeking for an endlessly border-hopping self. Long gone, it seems to me, in these Rwanda-torn times, are the Fanon days in which one could believe that the uprising of the wretched of the earth and their expulsion of the colonizers would lead to new-found identities and singing tomorrows. Carnival – wonderful as its subversiveness can be – has its limits too: for it to erupt a few days in the year, there have to be power structures in place all the other days. And you can only be a nomad if you are lucky enough to have the wherewithal – in a large and plentiful land or in your bank account – to sustain you in your wanderings ...

It is one of the immense merits of feminism in the last quarter of a century or so to have brought to light how much gender is constructed, how relative – and ideologically charged – our gender valuations and expectations are, how much economics, and custom, and ethnicity, and period and place, enter into it. But because it is so, there is no vantage-point from which all this could be inclusively thought out. Concepts like masculine and feminine can only be examined fruitfully within precise parameters: looking, for instance, at how the femininity of a young girl in aristocratic Restoration France is explored and critiqued by Balzac.

My own parameters are close to home. Like Marion Milner it seems to me that 'knowing is no good unless you feel the urgency of the thing.'[2] Thinking for me needs to be rooted in experience and not just abstract knowledge. My range is the literature I have lived with all my life, some nineteenth, some twentieth century, some by male, some by female authors, some in French and some in English. I grew up in France, have spent most of my adult life in English-speaking countries, and the divides and the differences have long exercised me: they were central to my previous book, concerned with bilingualism and being caught in the middle, between two cultures, *White Woman Speaks with Forked Tongue*. My growing interest in the psyche has taken me more and more into areas of literary and psychoanalytic theory. A long-lasting concern with feminist issues makes me revisit areas of feminist debates, particularly those which are alive to writing as flesh, as life: so-called French feminisms . . . For issues to have meaning for me, they have to be embodied.

Embodied: in texts. In speaking human beings, with their history, their agenda. And so I am uncomfortable with the more recent debates that analyse gender as technological, think that theory will produce *the* right answer (always the latest, the most dramatic = newsworthy; and always the only one). They discuss its geometries and geographies, praise the endlessly invented 'sexual personae' of art, costume, extol transvestism, self-modelling surgery, as if gender were removable at will, a thing of surface rather than one that plunges deep into our social and psychic histories, at once individual and collective. To my mind, writing *on* the body as opposed to French feminist seventies notions of writing the body subsumes that very body that is at present so fashionable. It makes it a thing that came out of nowhere, a materiality without an underground, used for a narcissistic show whose sole destination is the theatre of the gaze.

There *is* gender confusion – in all of us. And a good thing too; and probably a good thing, Andrew Samuels remarks, if there came to be more. For where there is most gender certainty on the surface is probably when there is most confusion beneath.[3] The worst homophobe may be the one who has least faced up to his or her leanings towards people of the same sex, and uses an aggressive show of certainty to protect herself or himself. Colette talks of the 'grave courage' that it takes for a woman to come to terms with 'ce qui l'incline vers la femme', her attraction to woman, Andrew Samuels of gender confusion and gender certainty as uncomfortable 'warring elements in the formation of gender identity'.

But that there is, and should be, and will continue to be, gender confusion does not mean that making gender confusion worse can in itself improve matters. The aim is to discover who one is, a complex thing, in which a lot more than questions of sexual identity enters. The aim is to come to terms with who one is over time, negotiate one's way between desire, compulsion and respect for others. Find whatever balance one can between one's own need for fulfilment and the multiple calls and demands of the social world in which one lives. Seeking to make 'gender trouble', as Judith Butler called it in her 1990 study of 'feminism and the subversion of identity', seeking to render the 'category ... "sex" ... in whatever form, permanently problematic'[4] may usefully add to the (already existing) gender confusion (although it will also increase the aggression of those who feel threatened by it). But the claim that there is in effect no distinction between sex and gender, that both are discursive formations, that both need to be exposed as such and, through parody and pastiche, displaced, is to refuse reality. Without the much-denounced so-called binaries – male and female, masculine and feminine – there would be nothing: no generation (the root is the same as for gender). No meaning.

There is a need for difference. All human beings have a relation, however mediated, however symbolical, to the mother and the father (of whatever sex, as Andrew Samuels adds). Where binaries go wrong is when they gell, are made into icons: when adjectives (male, female, masculine, feminine) coined to give form to the complexities inside us become nouns, hard formations that define, dictate, condemn. They do harm when they become hierarchized, used as instruments of power, the means to control, to superiority. It is power that is, or goes, wrong. Not human beings' need for difference. To throw out the binaries themselves as the discursive form that makes for suppression or oppression is to throw out the baby with the bathwater. Butler's ideas carry such authority at present, are taken as so normative almost, that I feel the need to spell out my disagreement.

Though interested in Foucault's 'figure of history as a relentless writing instrument' 'relentlessly' inscribing meaning on the body so that culture can emerge (as in Kafka's fable of *The Penal Colony*), Butler critiques the assumption that there *is* a body prior to its cultural inscription, a materiality prior to signification and form.[5] She argues that there are instead discursive acts or configurations which constitute the body: it does not exist prior to these. *Gender Trouble* quotes anthropologist Mary Douglas on taboos about purity and pollution, ways in which boundaries are established, and the fact that ' "it is only by exaggerating the difference between within and without, above and below, *male and female* ... that a semblance of order is created" ' (my italics). This suggests, Butler comments, that 'the limit of the body is never merely material ... the

boundaries of the body become ... the limits of the social *per se.*' Pollution (which goes with being in the wrong) is, Douglas is further quoted
as saying, ' "a type of danger which is not likely to occur except where
the lines of structure, cosmic or social, are clearly defined" '. ' "Why
should bodily margins be thought to be specifically invested with power
and danger?" '6

Butler finds confirmation of Douglas's stance in Kristeva's work, in
The Powers of Horror, on abjection and the expulsion of alien elements
which are in fact oneself (for instance, in vomiting) as if they were not:
this leads to the constitution of the 'not-me'. There is a direct link with
'homophobia and racism' (and metaphorics of expulsion and pollution
from Aids): 'The boundary of the body as well as the distinction between
internal and external is established through the ejection and transvalu-
ation of something originally part of identity into a defiling otherness'.7
The soul is (as Foucault had already argued) constituted through 'the
same processes, by the same 'punishing power' that constitutes the body,
produced ' "*around, on, within* the body'.8 The gendered body is constructed, Butler concludes, 'through a series of excursions and denials,
signifying absences' – in the body politic, by the incest taboo and the
homosexuality taboo. Compulsory heterosexuality is its name. It is
essentially repressive. Indeed, gender itself is a repressive act: 'an identity tenuously constituted in time, instituted in an exterior space through
a *stylized repetition of acts*'.9

Butler's following book, *Bodies That Matter* (1993) extends the argument from the body to matter itself: neither 'site nor surface', matter is *'a
process of materialization that stabilizes over time to produce the effect of boundary, fixity, surface we call matter'.*10 Discourse itself as performance constitutes it. It is the same repressive discourse, the 'symbolic' in fact, 'a series
of normativizing injunctions that secure the borders of sex through the
threat of psychosis, abjection, psychic unlivability',11 that do the consti-
tuting. Male and female, masculine and feminine, it seems, are concepts
whose very formation bespeaks oppression.

Butler's arguments are well put together. She moves between various
powerful voices with such confidence that it is difficult not to be carried
away by the skill. But her thesis rests upon enormous elisions, picking
and choosing from a narrow selection of theorists, and texts. Thus only a
little bit of Mary Douglas is wheeled in. Where Douglas says that ideas
about separating and purifying work by *exaggerating* the differences
between within and without, male and female, Butler concludes that the
taboos actually *constitute* male and female etc., as if there were *no
differences to start with*. Furthermore, the structural generality of the
taboos about pollution is left aside in favour of *particular cases*,
racism and homophobia – and it is homophobia Butler is actually interested in: she goes on to discuss homophobic reactions to Aids. She leads
up to the notion that taboos, discourse, gender, the symbolic – all somehow equated with each other – spring into being in order to exclude

homosexuals (Butler is not interested in the incest taboo either). Why this should be so, and why culture should constitute itself to exclude homosexuals (rather than slaves, or Yahoos) is not explained. (What about the urge of the species to reproduce, so often wheeled in by biological sociologists these days?) That no explanation should be offered is all the more weird as the culture that, through its philosophers Plato and Aristotle, most forcefully elaborated the binaries Butler attacks in *Bodies That Matter*, classical Athens, was a society in which male homosexuality was regarded as the noblest form of love: why not place *The Symposium* next to *Timaeus*? Plato's *Republic* excludes women and slaves from the body politic, but not homosexuals (the question is not even posed). What Butler does is that she turns a case in point, one particular form of exclusion – the exclusion of homosexuals, that is – into the be-all and end-all, the rule itself that constitutes gender. Under such dispensation, what else could one want to do but subvert it?

Gender is portrayed as if it were nothing *but* repression and exclusion, not just in the ways it might work, privileging one sex over the other, but as discourse itself. Everything in it is seen as inscription (of a torturing kind: Foucault's use of Kafka's *The Penal Colony* is drawn upon); as punishment, as discipline. Early feminists had been concerned, Simone de Beauvoir first of all, contending as she did with Lévi-Strauss's *Elementary Structures of Kinship*, by the structuralist suggestion that societies were symbolically founded upon the exchange of women. In Butler's version of things, discourse itself becomes structure, and it is founded upon the rejection and exclusion of homosexuals *by means of gender*. Which I must confess, rather strains my powers of belief. Men and women couldn't guess which were which, folks, though the monkeys they were descended from had always been able to find out. They invented exclusionary gender rules to throw out those who, liking people of the same sex, weren't procreating according to the needs of the tribe. And that is why we have societies, language, money ... But they were even cleverer than that. They invented discourse all at once, and they made it the gulag.

The other element which I find hard to assent to in Butler's method is the way in which psychoanalysis is drawn on when it suits, and left aside when it doesn't. On the one hand she seems to accept that gender is constituted over time, by a series, as she puts it, of repetitive acts. She puts it rather bleakly: what would happen if some version of this did not come about (would the child not go mad if it were made 'both', or alternately, into a girl and into a boy?). But this could be true of the way all sorts of factors – parental expectations and relating, peer group pressures – constitute us as male or female. On the other she writes as if things – discourse – materialized out of thin air, without a prior history, collective or individual. *Timaeus* is treated like an Ur-text, its being about beginnings – creation – somewhat taken to mean that it *is a beginning*. Western discourse appears born like Athena, motherless, out of Plato's skull, and

Western logos – discourse with its exclusion of women and slaves from the Republic – all at once with it. *Bodies That Matter* keeps referring to the 'matrix', the 'heterosexual matrix', as if some vile womb had produced the child. 'Matrix' was Irigaray's word in *Speculum of the Other Woman*: 'the speculative matrix of the subject'. She was accusing Freud, and beyond him Plato, of devising a thoroughly masculine subject which 'stands erect' upon the 'pressed down/repressed earth', 'the body/sex of the mother/nature'. An explanation of sorts was implied: fear and desire of the womb, a ban upon regressing to the womb, the drive for power, for possession of territory that has to be wrenched from the mother.[12] Butler's 'heterosexual matrix', far from being about subsuming the mother's body, imagines that the mother's body, and matter, are produced out of the discourse that divides them. It offers no sense of how it all came about. Were there no people before fifth-century Athens, and Plato? No other civilizations? India (and Buddha?)? China? Egypt? No mother-centred or matrilinear societies, no alternative myths of creation, no powerful goddesses? Isn't the 'gender' that *Timaeus* may be witness to bound up with the history and particularities of Athenian politics, and if so what do we do with the notion that gender is (ahistorical) discourse, full stop? (And if they excluded the *women*, as well as the slaves, the foreigners, etc., what does this do to the notion that gender is all about the taboo on homosexuality and incest? How did they know the women were women?)

Furthermore, if we return to the purity/pollution rules, to Kristeva on abjection, it seems to me that here again something which has a profound psychic dimension, making psyche and body part and parcel of each other, is twisted, by means of the (admittedly crucial) notion of boundaries into a constitutive, but arbitrary, means of exclusion. Talk about faeces, not vomit: the child's anal stage, the potty-training serves many purposes in socializing the child, not just training him to reject the not-me. It goes with separation – with mobility: Freud said, with money; other analysts stress, with the ability to create. It has eventually to do with self-discipline, respect for others, the ability to live culturally. And a host of other things. It *is* very important for human beings to learn to distinguish between me and not-me. If I don't eat, if I don't defecate, if I don't sweat, don't breathe – I die. What is outside (air, food) *has to* come in. What is inside (faeces, toxins) has to get out. Human societies may, on that model, create ostracisms, ritual exclusions. But my body is not something 'constituted' by means of an exclusionary discourse. It is there, growing up, continuously socialized, caught in the meshes of how my mother, father, etc., treat me. I am born it, it never ceases to change, it is part and parcel of my 'soul' – how I feel, what I feel. Blood goes to my heart and I go white if I am frightened. Whether I am male, or female . . .

Me/not-me. Inside/outside. The ways in which these differences are *exaggerated* (I feel the need to use and stress again the Mary Douglas word) varies almost infinitely from culture to culture. But it is not as if as human beings (rather than wild children, who might drop their faeces as wolves do, but then would not learn speech) we had a choice. The ability to distinguish me from not-me is the fruit (good *and* bitter?) of socialization, arrived at by successful negotiation of the various stages of separation (oral, anal, mirror, Oedipal . . .). It does entail repression, pushing under. What gets repressed, excluded, is not just desires that come to be seen as wrong (incestuous, same sex), but whole dimensions of ourselves, that go into making our shadow side – the unconscious. Though gendered (what gets repressed might be different in men and in women, different in one society and in another), it is not constituted by gender. It is at the root of our problems as human beings, in our individual and our collective relationships. Accessing the unconscious, whether with the hope of gradually working towards wholeness, as in the Jungian model, or with the more modest aim of achieving some sort of balance or playfulness or resilience, as in other models (Freud or Winnicott or Kristeva), is central to what psychoanalysis attempts to do in the way of healing. For our shadow side can erupt, individually or collectively, in terrifyingly destructive ways. Repressed impulses gone evil and then burst from their bonds can drive individuals to rape or murder, and a collectivity – national or ethnic – to massacre the 'others' in their midst: holocaust or genocide. The impulses to reject, to feel superior to, another, in a racist situation, can drive people to project their own fear of exclusion on to an emissary goat: as is profoundly perceived in Toni Morrison's *The Bluest Eyes*. The black community, rejected and made to feel worthless by the white, internalize their exclusion from the good things of life as ugliness, self-hatred: they are black, not white; black-eyed, not blue-eyed, which would entitle you to love and privilege. They off-load their own sense of pollution on to Pecola, the most rejected of them all:

> All of our waste which we dumped on her and which she absorbed. And all of our beauty, which was hers first and which she gave to us. All of us – all who knew her – felt so wholesome after we cleaned ourselves on her. We were beautiful when we stood astride her ugliness.[13]

What I am arguing is that exclusion through a system of value judgements, and the perpetuation and internalization of that exclusion, is a phenomenon much larger than gender. It is rooted in the paradoxes that make us human. It may be that as in the biblical loss of Eden, the capacity to know is bought at the price of the constitution of good and evil. Know: the Indo-European root Kn is the same as the Gn of Genesis, generation, gender, gnosis . . . Knowledge is a larger and more integral thing than discourse, and its relation to generation – to gender – is also more integral than Butler would like. However that may be, systems of values – of exclusion – take many forms, internal, racial, political as well as sexual. They are power-ridden – and no amount of *subversion* would fundamentally alter them. Only the long, painful coming to terms with the inner (as well as the outer) forces moving us (which is what the female narrator of *The Bluest Eyes* attempts) can make a difference. It does not make for rousing slogans, but for detailed hard work. The Papin sisters were *gendered* as male by the Surrealists because of the kind of murder they had committed. Maleness, that is, was projected on to them by men of a deeply troubled generation who identified with their deed on account of their own public and private history. It did not have much to do with the sisters' own gendering, with their own incestuous and homophiliac desires which sprang, not from a brilliant bit of subversiveness, but from a damaged family history, from a claustrophobic class situation. The absence, weakness or bad behaviour of the males in that episode was part of the problem, not a lucky escape from binaries or the patriarchy.

We are traversed, possessed in our depths, by past demons: those of the generations before us, parents, grandparents ... the history that preceded us, that surrounds us, the exploitations and destructions of the natural world and of other human beings by which, often without even knowing it, we have profited, the wars that have acted themselves out before us and in our own time, and every form of interchange that has made us. Our sexuality is shot through with it. What we do, above all what we are, like the celebrated ripples activated by the flutter of a butterfly's wings, affect others as others affect us. Most immediately, our relation to our mother and our father, or the persons in our childhood who embodied them for us, is foundational, and remains an integral part of our sexual selves: out of those relations, of the ways we have found or not found inner safety, have experienced and continue to experience love and hate, is our sexuality constructed. Though many – countless – other elements come into it – expectations, stereotypes, prejudices, role models, each of these different according to country, milieu, moment – the relation to the figures of Father and Mother (and siblings if we have them), the relation to the real father and mother, and their relation to their own father and mother, and beyond, are and remain fundamental. To think that technological or theoretical solutions can be found that could eliminate what we see as negative in femininity seems to me idealistic – unless it is conceived as provocation, as stirring, as a way of keeping the ball in play – of fostering a useful bit of gender *confusion*.

For WOMAN

Being a woman has been a prominent question in my life – in terms of my relations to men, often problematic, in terms of the excitement and pleasure, the sense of empowerment, that the women's movement has given me. Unfashionably in the 1990s, I find myself at odds with the main trends, which want to dispose of the very word, woman, as one which is tarred by the ways femininity has been constructed.

There is – as has always been recognized in the plural mode of 'the women's movement' or the choice of the French publishing house to call itself 'des femmes', or by Kristeva's oft quoted 'A woman cannot be; it is something which does not even belong in the order of being'[14] – a crucial 'hiatus between *Woman* and women', as Rosi Braidotti puts it.[15] But from early recognition that woman was a tricky term (What did one put in there? Was it loaded with all sorts of hidden agendas?), and preference being given to the plural as a way of acknowledging that there were women, many, diverse, speaking and living subjects, there has been escalation to the point where the word woman itself cannot be used. From Monique Wittig, who wants to substitute lesbian thinking for the 'straight' mind, for heterosexual forms of thought according to which there are men and there are women, to Denise Riley who refuses to be 'That Name', Woman, to Donna Haraway who hails the cyborg as half technological, half human, 'a creature in a post-gender world', who has 'no truck' with 'seductions of wholeness', organic or otherwise, and is without an 'origin story',[16] to Teresa de Lauretis who substitutes the term 'feminist' for the worn and discredited term woman – a formidable array of theorists aims to subvert and even dispose of, the very ... reality? ... which makes me want to call myself a feminist. Linda Alcoff asks very pertinently, it seems to me, 'What can we demand in the name of women if "women" do not exist and demands in their name simply reinforce the myth that they do? How can we speak out against sexism as detrimental to the interests of women if the category is a fiction?'[17]

Teresa de Lauretis's answer that we must recognize the difference 'between woman as representation ("Woman" as cultural imago) and woman as experience (real women as agents of change)'[18] and her assumption that the feminist position places one at the vanguard of that distinction does not make me happy. For thereby a superior category of 'aware' females is created, to which others might graduate if they live long enough or get educated enough to become enlightened. I am made as uncomfortable by that claim as by Donna Haraway's sense that her cyborg somehow represents the likes of Audre Lorde, the black lesbian 'sister outsider' position and is the subversive figurehead for 'young Korean women hired in the sex industry and in electronics assembly', who are often selected from high school, therefore quite literate, and maybe able one day to use their literacy for empowerment: 'Cyborg writing is about the power to survive, not on the basis of original innocence, but on the basis of seizing the tools to mark the world that marked them as other.'[19] An attractive piece of rhetoric, perhaps not fundamentally different from Cixous's call to 'women' to 'write' in 'The Laugh of the Medusa', all those years ago;[20] and a recognition of the empowerment there is in writing. But what 'tools of production' are we talking about? Computers? What about the textile industry and the sex industry? How many cyborgs will emerge from the subjection to those machines? Will only those who emerge, who become 'agents of change', deserve the name of – what? Women? Feminists?

I am happier with Alice Walker's term, 'Womanism' (though mainly directed at black feminisms and women who love women sexually), in that at least it sounds open, non-selective.[21] For in the name of what higher form of (female?) humanity, of speaking for the freest and boldest or most promisingly educated Third World females (I dare not say, women), of being at the vanguard of the revolution to come, are a few chosen, the rest excluded? Are the rest mere women – who do not change their lives, who just feel, do, live, rich or poor, free or unfree? Aren't they worth one's respect – and one's doing a little something – one's using what skill one has to make the world a little more aware of how difficult it may be to be – a woman?

Contemporary feminist theory's rejection of the term woman, made to carry an impossible charge, makes me want to say that if feminism is not about doing something for women, and myself in the process, then I am not a feminist. I certainly am not a feminist if by that is meant that I thereby belong to a superior category, or think that women are innately, or by virtue of having been or being oppressed, better than men (though they can happen to be so in practice, for particular reasons). I am persuaded that a women-only society would, in practice, soon recreate inside itself all the evils of humankind. *Lord of the Flies* would, I fear, rapidly overtake *Herland*. The amount of passionate in-fighting there has been in the women's movement bodes ill if it is harmony we are after.

I do however also think that being a woman, and what is variously called femininity, has been sadly and damagingly downgraded in our western societies, and that it is important to learn to revalue what they stand for. I see the various 1990s attacks against 'Woman' as unconsciously part of the same downgrading: an overvaluation of things male, the request that women be somehow more male – through an adjunction of technology, a mastering of machines, the adoption of male-authored scripts, of male-centred pornographic scenarios ... Haraway's cyborg is pure male, freed from all (sullying?) traces of the maternal, differentiation incarnate: 'an ultimate self untied at last from all dependency', without memory of the Garden of Eden or the cosmos, unlike Adam without any link with mud or dust. 'The main trouble with cyborgs, of course, is that they are the illegitimate offspring of militarism and patriarchal capitalism ... But illegitimate offspring are often exceedingly unfaithful to their origins. Their fathers, after all, are inessential.' A witty dig, since 'essentialism' is seen as the trouble with 'woman'. How Haraway can move from there to Audre Lorde who uses very un-cyborg language in *Sister Outsider* I fail to see: the erotic in women, Lorde writes for instance, is 'a source within each of us that lies in a deeply female and spiritual plane, firmly rooted in the power of our unexpressed and unrecognized feeling'.[22] Source, origin, female, feeling? Surely no cyborg would use these terms?

Certainly, all traces of femininity have been excised from the cyborg dream of the future, and this seems symptomatic: the women's movement seems to me to have exploded and imploded at once. Where it once stood for the empowerment of women, it now both rejects any idea of a common cause and wants to get rid of 'Woman' altogether ... Though the cyborg claims to be self-invented, its relation to the patriarchy, its *genealogy*, makes it firmly male. (Genealogies *are* patriarchal, whichever ways Foucault may claim to use the term: the most famous of them all is Matthew 1, that illustrates Christ's direct descent from Abraham.) The cyborg is descended from those romantic heroes, the illegitimate sons or sons rebelling against wicked fathers, who boasted like Rousseau 'if I am not better [than other men], at least I am other.' Always the same story, Antoinette Fouque would say, the reign of the *filiarcat*, power to the *sons*. 'To the slogan "A man out of two is a woman" there now succeeded the slogan "a woman is a man like any other".'[23]

Feminists' hostility to Woman stems from hostility to the mother: the reproductive female body and (as Adrienne Rich has called it) the 'institution of motherhood' are, as Simone de Beauvoir had abundantly argued, what deprives women of full humanity. Are there deep reasons for it?

In *XY: De l'identité masculine*, Elizabeth Badinter posits that what is 'proper to masculine identity' lies in 'differentiation from the maternal feminine, the *sine qua non* condition for men feeling that they belong to the group of men'. It is hard to achieve: even when successfully repressed, 'maternal symbiosis haunts the masculine unconscious. Because men have been for millennia brought up by women, they have to expend treasures of energy preserving the borders.'[24] Elizabeth Badinter usefully summarizes and convincingly documents much contemporary Anglo-American research into masculinity. She does not look at Jung, however, who would have produced a different emphasis. Though *Symbols of Transformation* has a chapter called 'The Battle for the Deliverance from the Mother', and though Jung produces prolific examples of the 'Terrible Mother', he insists on seeing the persecuting mother (such as Hera) as the one through whose creative enmity the hero is pushed towards achievements. Unlike Butler, for instance, Jung is alert to the unifying dimension of the world-soul, in Plato's *Timaeus*, the mother-imago. The matrix, for him, is not the source of all evils. Drawing on many mythologies and varied literary sources, he sees the womb as not just a place to be left behind, but one to be reunited with:

[Goethe's *Faust's*] 'realm of the Mothers' has not a few connections with the womb ... with the matrix, which frequently symbolizes the creative aspect of the unconscious. This libido is a force of nature, good and bad at once, or morally neutral. Uniting himself with it, Faust succeeds in accomplishing his life's work.[25]

If the hero has initially to gain victory over the 'mother' or her daemonic representative (the dragon), that is, if he must become differentiated from the mother, still 'in the second half of life' he must become 'feminized', assimilate 'contrasexual tendencies'. The mother then becomes a figure for the unconscious:

> The task consists in integrating the unconscious, in bringing together 'conscious' and 'unconscious'. I have called this the individuation process. At this stage the mother-symbol no longer connects back to beginnings, but points towards the unconscious as the creative matrix of the future.[26]

Jung is perhaps unusual in his capacity to own that fusional states appeal to him. But he is not alone, and is the living proof that a male, while acknowledging the need for masculine identity to be forged through an initial distanciation from the mother, does not have to end up in a state of total repudiation.

But what can lead females to want to repudiate the mother? Winnicott, in a highly interesting 1964 paper called 'This Feminism', written fifteen years after the publication of De Beauvoir's *The Second Sex* and several years before the appearance of second wave feminism, points out that *both* males and females were initially '*absolutely* dependent upon a woman, and then relatively dependent'. It is very difficult, he says, either 'for a man or woman to reach to a true acceptance of this fact of absolute and then relative dependence'. 'For this reason there is a separated-out phenomenon that we call WOMAN which dominates the whole scene, and affects all our arguments. WOMAN is the unacknowledged mother of the first stages of the life of every man and woman.' Somehow, he adds, 'a hatred of this has to be transformed into a kind of gratitude if full maturity of personality is to be reached.'[27]

Is this the key to recent feminist hostility to that very word, WOMAN?

Coming from a very different position, and in real, though unacknowledged agreement with Luce Irigaray, Antoinette Fouque strangely tallies with Winnicott (without knowing it). She sees the 'unconscious root of misogyny' as lying in the 'foreclosing [*forclusion*] of the mother's body as the place of origin of the living'. As long, she argues, as there is no recognition of our relation to origins, we are 'in a monosexed, therefore lobotomized, humanism'.[28] The cancelling out of origins is precisely what the cyborg is about – as is De Lauretis's notion that only women who are 'agents of *change*' (my italics) are worth retrieving. Feminist heroines of the 1990s are also about the cancelling out of origins. Angela Carter's New Eve, anticipating the cyborg and 1990s works on transexuality and transvestism by a decade (and at present so topical she has, in England at least, almost turned into an icon), is a man made female by surgery. As if Eve were only acceptable when she has no origins – not the slightest link with the maternal feminine: *no genesis*. As if, for 1990s feminists, it was even more important than for men to repudiate the maternal. Even fashion, Antoinette Fouque contends, follows that rule of 'pseudo-difference of the sexes'. 'A woman must look like a transvestite man. We haven't come out of the category of the double: A and A' rather than A and B.'[29]

The root of this refusal of femininity is, Fouque contends, in what Freud has called the 'primacy of the phallus' for both sexes, 'essentially Narcissistic' in its origin. The woman, finding herself deprived of her own libido, must either follow Echo's fate, or *become* the phallus (through such devices as *self-building* . . .).[30]

Provocatively, Winnicott's paper on feminism (mentioned above) produces a similar diagnostic, though the emphasis and aims are different. About to begin, he acknowledges to his audience that 'this is the most dangerous thing I have done in recent years,' and proposes that 'man and woman are not exactly the same as each other, and that each male has a female component, and each female has a male component'.[31] He then pauses, in case some of the audience wanted to claim that *'there are no differences'*. Which they don't. One wonders what the response would have been in post-1970 feminist circles – and I shudder at the thought of possible reactions to what I am about to relay.

The paper eventually gets to a discussion of envy of the opposite sex, and in particular men's envy of women going through the risk of childbirth, their own courting of dangers to emulate this. Or men's envy of the fact women do not have to 'solve the problem of an individual relationship to WOMAN'[32] (which, much 1990s feminist theory would tell him, is highly contentious). But, though he doesn't use the term 'penis envy', he first gets on to the 'detail' of 'the male organ's quality of being obvious, contrasted with the female organ's quality of being hidden'. He picks his words with care: 'There is no doubt that girls do have a bit of bother when going through this phase.... Just for a while they feel inferior, or maimed.' He hastens to add that at the next phase of genitality, 'the girl is equalized.' She becomes important 'because she can attract father, because she can have babies', at puberty has breasts and periods, etc. But the 'trauma' sustained by girls at the phallic phase can lead to 'over-valuation of the erect penis', envy of males, fantasies of a hidden or lost penis, and the 'delusion' that a penis exists, and that there are no differences between male and female at the phallic stage. The delusion can be shared by both men and women, and the worst part of it is that 'it makes men emphasize the "castrated" aspect of the female personality, and this makes for a belief in female inferiority that infuriates females.'[33] Winnicott makes it quite clear that he does not hold with such supposed inferiority, and that 'logic can be brought on the side of much of what feminism does and says.' He however sees being stuck at the phallic stage as 'a root of feminism'. It happens when there has been some early form of deprivation. It is lack of fostering in boys as well as girls, 'at the breast, for instance', that makes it crucial. 'The phallic phase has exaggerated importance for those who come up to it already deprived.'[34]

I am not qualified to comment on the validity of this analysis or otherwise, except to say that it fits my own case up to a point (that is, for a long time my feminism *was* rooted in difficulties with the maternal and an overvaluation of the phallic ... I hope it isn't any more). Winnicott may be wrong to connect the phallic stage so closely to feminism since he himself recognizes that much of feminism has logic for it. The lack of a historical dimension here is certainly a drawback. It still strikes me, none the less, how suggestive what he says is about the otherwise bewildering combination, in so much 1990s theory by women, of a repudiation of the mother and an overvaluation of things male.

Strangely, an antifeminist like Paglia, keen to attack feminist villains, produces a reverse mirror-image of, for instance, Butler and Haraway. True, where they are into discourse, science and technology, she wallows in daemonic destructiveness. Where Butler attacks the boundaries set up by classical discourse, Paglia celebrates 'Apollonialism, cold and absolute', the West's 'sublime refusal' of a Dionysiac, Darwinian nature,[35] aligned with woman, 'who is nature's proxy'.[36] But the enemy is very much the same: idealistic or nurturing visions of (mother) nature. The values that are being defended are very similar at bottom: the artificial, rebellious hero *son*, cyborg, transvestite or queer, who, through his repudiation of a 'Pandemonium' Mother Nature 'waiting at society's gate to dissolve us in her chthonian bosom',[37] acts as the ... erect phallus. Even Paglia's sentences act the part: 'all cultural achievement is a projection, a swerve into Apollonian transcendence ... men are anatomically destined to be projectors ...'; 'The Apollonian is a male line drawn against the dehumanizing magnitude of female nature'; 'Our hard personalities are imagistic projections from the Apollonian higher cortex.'[38]

No wonder so many male readers loved Paglia: at last someone was putting them back in the saddle. Here was a *woman* licensing them to see and say how terrifying, how threatening the maternal (the WOMAN?) was, how important it was to hold the line against her, how heroic the attempt to conquer her. Paglia never wonders about how *both* idealizing (Rousseauist) and demonizing (Nietzschean or Baudelairean) versions of nature historically came about. She seems to have no awareness that the meanings of 'nature' shift with each age – as I tried to show in my book on Baudelaire, and as Keith Thomas powerfully demonstrates in *Man and the Natural World*.[39] Nor does it occur to her that perhaps nature is, as Jung suggests, 'good and bad at once, or morally neutral'. Greek gods were richly ambivalent: Apollo was wolf as well as sun-god ... What it does not seem to have occurred to her admirers to wonder is why in the 1990s, while there are such anxieties among men about masculinity, such timid or brave attempts to negotiate men's relation to the feminine, there is among women, both pro- and antifeminists, such a disparagement of the feminine, such an overvaluation of the phallic ... Or why, in the battle of the sexes, they (the men) should need an Amazon to strike blows for them: fight fire with fire, WOMAN with woman – even though that woman acts the honorary male? It's like something out of a saga novel –

or like the Athenians' need for the goddess Athena, born fully armed from Zeus' forehead: a goddess without genesis . . .

Masculine AND Feminine

A number of voices this century – philosophers, spiritual or religious thinkers, psychoanalysts – have pleaded in favour of feminine values, argued for a better balance of masculine and feminine in society at large and in all of us. But feminism itself has been deeply divided. Where Adrienne Rich, so-called French feminisms, some contemporary and some feminist theologians, supporters of 'differences' and the proponents of maternal thinking advocated a revaluation of the feminine, campaigners for equality have tended the other way. Recent theorists in particular – those I have been countering – have gone for wholly masculine sets of values. They are much in the limelight now: in the critique and downgrading of the word Woman, in Butler's critique of gender, in Haraway's praise of the cyborg. But *equally* in antifeminist Paglia's advocacy of a violent androgyny, in which the women creators are congratulated for their masculine, angry, qualities, and the only femininity allowed to exist is that which is mediated by males: Donatello's coquettish David, standing over Goliath's severed head . . .

The pendulum always swings. Is this book a sign that the pendulum has begun to swing the other way? Yet there is such societal resistance to the valuing of femininity, the pendulum needs a bit of help. My 1980s study of the Yorkshire Ripper case, of the profound misogyny of which it was the sign, had quoted Freud on men's dread and repudiation of femininity: he claims it is so deep it is 'rock-bottom'. Well, in quite a few quarters this end-of-the-century, it seems, it still is rock-bottom. And so, there may be some value to my wanting to help it climb back up . . . to the spirit level?

Masculine versus feminine. What do I mean? Activity versus – not passivity as the yielding to superior force, but what Wordsworth called a 'wise passiveness'; or versus receptivity. Courage versus love: Mars and Venus. Or else courage versus faith, trust. Action versus contemplation. Talking, expressing oneself, versus listening, being able to hear others. Intellect versus understanding from the heart, intuition. Animus, to use the suggestive Jungian terms again, versus anima: categories of *the relation to the other*, figures and dramatizations, inner and projected, of our relation to the other sex.[40] Narrowness versus breadth. Penetration versus containment. The couples one can suggest are many. Both masculine and feminine pertain in infinite combinations to men and women, and the ways in which they are embodied, felt, acted out, by men and women depend on many things – temperament, inherited and acquired traits, how the milieu in which one grows up constructs us as males and females, how we emerge from that formation as desiring beings, societal and cultural valuations, role models, vested power interests . . .

Masculine, feminine. Adjectives, not nouns. Always metaphoric. Movable and dynamic, as metaphors are. Always *relational*. 'For the individual woman or man,' Andrew Samuels writes, 'anatomy is a metaphor for the richness and potential of the "other".'[41]

What makes masculine/feminine into the binary opposition it has been denounced as, is polarization. Either/or. Wanting human beings to incarnate attributes, and making the embodied qualities into identities. Caricatures ensue: men think, women feel; men are rational, women intuitive; men are extravert, ergo go out to work; women are intravert and naturally domestic, therefore they stay at home. Masculinity and femininity are thus set up as the exclusive attributes of males or females, as in the Victorian period and its aftermath, and hierarchized: masculine is seen as superior to feminine. This is what I call gender, its formations enormously complex, bewildering: whom you've grown up thinking you are is of course part of who you are. They mutate from age to age and place to place and class to class. They can be interrelated: the southern belle is part and parcel of the tough, outdoor working black woman slave whose exploited labour supports her own luxurious leisure, but also whose dire alienation is constructed as a complement to her own mild one: two interlinked forms of *gendered* femininity. And they are ridden with contradictions. Balzac's 'Daughter of Eve' is faced with impossibly conflicting demands. So is her author.

But, to my mind, masculine and feminine, though caught up in gender formations, are not gender. Power and notions of superiority and inferiority are at work if you oppose – as was, for instance, the case for those late nineteenth-century hysterical women whom Charcot and then Freud treated – speech and silence, knowing mind and symptomatic body, doctor who knows and patient who cannot know what she is suffering from. But if you think of speech as activity (self-expression, communication), silence as *chosen* meditation, contemplativeness (another form of communication); and if you further think of them as masculine and feminine, then both cease to be power-laden. Both are human modes of communication available to both men and women, and the degree to which they choose the one or the other, develop their capacity for the one or the other, is expressive of who they are. Though there is an opposition, it is not one which constitutes gender. Gender enters into it, shades or twists it. The opposition of masculine and feminine can instead be seen as a dialectic, a relationship.

Both exist in relation to each other – in creativity as in anything else. Call it bisexuality, as Freud and others did, or androgyny: which does not necessarily lead to Paglia's model of the androgyne. Paglia is right to stress how many artists have been homosexual. Women creators tend to be those who can best access their animus, have the 'virile' qualities that make action possible, and men creators are often those who can access

Constantin Brancusi, *Princesse X*, 1916, Musée national d'art moderne, Centre Georges Pompidou,
© ADAGP, Paris and DACS, London 1997

their anima, are receptive, sensitive, able to let ideas gestate. But Paglia
twists the androgyne into an almost transsexual or transvestite persona
that makes things all one way, denies that here is a matter of relation, of
complex inner and outer energizing. She makes an ambiguous unit out
of what is a dialectical relationship: as evidenced by the collage, on the
cover of *Sexual Personae*, of the half faces of Nefertiti and Emily Dickinson – striking, but how true? What do Nefertiti and Dickinson *actually*
have in common except the overgeneral idea that there was artifice in
both? I think instead of Brancusi's sculpture *Princesse X*. It is a living,
dynamic form (not a unit, not a collage). It makes one see both difference
and similarity. It is startling, subversive if one likes, in its ability to combine suggested femininity and masculinity to such a provocative degree:
an erect penis and balls comes across as a delicate, stately, gently bowing
female. It works, because each possibility is powerful, is active and is
complete, and there is a dialectic tension between them. Male and
female, pulling against each other, yet one.

Paglia is important and I keep returning to her because in her taste for
a mix-up of the sexes, for sexual *personae*, she has captured something of

the spirit of the nineties: as evidenced by a 1995 exhibition at the Museum of Modern Art in Paris, *Fémininmasculin*,[42] where the Brancusi was shown, and which, through its exhibits and the collection of essays accompanying it, focused (as its one-word title emphasized) on inversions and mixings of the sexes, turning things inside out.[43] Of course, some of the exhibits did not necessarily verify the intention: the Brancusi to my mind did not.

Creativity and Self

It is neither to Paglia nor to *Fémininmasculin* that I want to turn, but to the bisexual model proposed by Winnicott. It makes sense to me in that it links creativity and self. Winnicott stresses that he is not interested in the special creativity of artists, but in human creativity. This holds for me: though the more insight I have into artists, the more I admire the power, intelligence, nouse, inventiveness, skill that I perceive, and that are so beyond me; I am not interested in genius *per se*, or in basking in its reflected glory, but in what of common, of recognizable humanity, of joy and desire, of rage and grief artists express. My essays reflect on writers and artists, wonderful books or pictures: but it is with the desire to find common meanings.

Winnicott talks about BEING and DOING. Humans cannot do, create, unless first of all they are. A sense of self is bound up with the ability to be creative (which after the event, as it were, explains to me why some of my essays insisted on posing questions of identity, whereas others were more clearly about creation). This sense of self, of individuality, the problem the individual may have with who he or she is, Winnicott connects with the modern world, though he gives no precise date (who could?) – one, two thousand years? He briefly refers to Foucault, but more precisely to a Freud footnote in *Moses and Monotheism* (1939) that refers to Moses as ' "the first individual in human history" '. Unlike Moses, dialoguing with God in solitude, forging ahead towards an unknown future, humans in earlier times were so identified with the community they did not have to seek for a sense of self, or explanations for life and the world, in their own heads and hearts. Modern human beings do. They succeed in finding life meaningful when, as Melanie Klein showed, they, as infants, learn to recognize and deal with conflict, find an inner balance between their erotic and their destructive impulses. For Winnicott, 'either individuals live creatively and feel that life is worth living or else they cannot live creatively and are doubtful about the value of living.'[44] He anchors this capacity or non-capacity in the quality of the early environment for the baby.

Winnicott has been much criticized, in both feminist and non-feminist circles, for making the mother the unique provider of the good-enough environment that enables the individual to develop a sense of being. His

views may need to be reformulated in the light of changing and more
varied forms of parenting, as Andrew Samuels suggests. But what he
says about *environment*, whichever parent, carer, combination of carers
provide it, seems to me to be profoundly true. Marie's bewilderment in
Balzac's story (see chapter 1), the Papin sisters' murderousness, are
rooted in a faulty, or tragically deficient, early familial environment.
Conversely, despite the many shortcomings and downright tragedies in
their familial histories, there was enough 'good enough' in the childhoods of D. H. Lawrence and Virginia Woolf (chapters 4 and 5) for them
to become creative. To those who, like the scientists I evoke at the end of
chapter 8 on metaphor, or like Paglia, stress nothing but the psychopathology or daemonic urges of modern writers, I want to say that these
writers must have had balance enough to sit down and *construct* all those
elaborate fabrics of words. They had the BEING that enabled them to
DO.

The value of Winnicott's thinking, for my purposes, is that he insists
on distinguishing male and female elements from boys and girls, men
and women, and on the *lack of symmetry* of these elements. Where Lacan
rightly insisted on the lack of symmetry, but anchored it, however symbolically, in men and women (men *have* the phallus, *Encore* argues, while
women *are* it),[45] Winnicott separates what he calls male and female elements from boys and girls. So doing, he demonstrates the usefulness of
the terms: it is practical still to talk about male and female, masculine
and feminine, despite the maelstroms through which the terms have
gone in the past quarter of a century. He also clearly demonstrates that
they are not symmetrical (which is why they can be dialectical, may
eventually reach towards conjunction – as Jung advocates).

Winnicott relies on work done with infants, and in particular on
Kleinian object-relation, in which the breast is the primary object. I quote
from the essay 'Creativity and its Origins', the argument being too intricate to sum up:

> The element that I am calling 'male' does traffic in terms of active relating or
> passive being related to, each being backed by instinct. It is in the develop-
> ment of this idea that we speak of instinct drive in the baby's relation to the
> breast and to feeding, and subsequently in relation to all the experiences
> involving the main erotogenic zones ... By contrast, the pure female ele-
> ment relates to the breast (or to the mother) in the sense of *the baby becoming
> the breast (or mother), in the sense that the object is the subject.* I can see no
> instinct drive in this.[46]

The 'relatedness of pure female element to "breast" ' paves the way for
the 'objective subject', 'that is, the idea of self', 'the sense of BEING'.[47] On
the other hand, 'the object-relating of the male element to the object pre-
supposes separatedness', a relation to the 'not-me', which requires 'complex mental mechanisms',[48] and is 'backed by instinct drive'.[49] In other
words, while 'impulse related to objects',[50] including oral eroticism, oral

sadism, anal stages, etc.,[51] is associated with the male element, 'the characteristic of the female element in the context of object-relating is identity, giving the child the basis for being.' Hence the crucial importance of 'maternal' (environmental?) provision. On whether it succeeds or fails to meet the earliest functioning of the female element depends the quality of 'the experience of being'. 'Now I want to say,' Winnicott concludes, ' "After being – doing and being done to. But first, being." '[52]

Male and female made (S)he them.

A Word about Order

For years I have been telling research students that you write your introduction last. I have been faithful to my own advice, but it has been a lot of trouble. For what I have found myself wanting to say about masculinity and femininity, the figures of the father and the mother, and creativity, where my thinking is now at, is not necessarily borne out by the essays that follow. Maybe that is where they were going, but often they did not know it. Written over the last five years or so, they came into being in all sorts of ways (for instance the chapters on the First World War sprang from work I had done on my family's history during that period). It was only as time went by that I began to see that these pieces of writing had something in common, that they were all concerned with sexual identity and creativity, that they all puzzled about male and female, returning again and again to the question of the female genesis: how she becomes, how she creates.

My thinking changed over the period. I became impatient, ill at ease with 1990s feminist theory. I became more and more interested in psychoanalytic thought, and not those forms that feminism has been most concerned with: I found food for thought in Jung and Winnicott and Klein rather than in Freud and Lacan. I found myself agreeing with Ricoeur rather than the adopted male gurus of feminism, Foucault or Deleuze or Derrida. I found I wanted to return to early loves (Symbolist poetry or D. H. Lawrence or Francis Ponge) without renouncing new ones (Angela Carter or Michèle Roberts). I did not want to use feminist theory to critique the male writers, or to extol or make sense of the women writers: I wanted to hear how each, the theory as well as the fiction, the analysts as well as the novelists, the men as well as the women, imagined masculinity and femininity. I felt all peculiar, between two stools, as it were: wanting to go beyond feminism, while still passionately interested in its questions. I know that this book is a thing on its way, that my thinking hasn't reached its goal, that other things, further changes, are coming: hence its conclusion.

What I have written above about the mother and the father as structuring our relation to femininity and masculinity is indeed borne out by the two main sections in this volume. But against all experience, all psychoanalytic knowledge, according to which the mother comes first, the father second, the female element (BEING) first, the second (DOING) later ... the first section here is about the father, the second about the mother. Things made sense that way according to both historical and personal chronologies. The chapters in the first section are about nineteenth-century and early twentieth-century writers/events, such as Balzac and the First World War. The essays on Balzac and the Papin sisters look at gender – how it can be constructed socially, historically and imaginatively. The essays on the Battle of the Sexes move on to the interrelation of male and female, masculine and feminine. Those in the second section are all on contemporary writers, though the chapter on metaphor plunges back into nineteenth-century poetry. I wrote the essays in the first section earlier than those in the second, though the First World War essays were recently rehandled. But as it is, the ways in which relations to the father and the mother figures are supposed to signify in terms of my claims isn't borne out by the form given to the book. I unapologetically point this out: there may be some meaning there in excess of what I fully perceive – an intriguing puzzle ...

Having things the wrong way round, however, is interesting for other reasons. For the essays here do not set out to demonstrate – as I might have done if, a number of years ago, my ideas about creativity and gender had been worked out – that it is through a combination of positive fostering by the mother and the father that, as Winnicott argues, a human being becomes creative. They are all about what happens *when things go wrong*. Which, in human affairs, and in literary creations over the past two centuries or so, they mostly do. The first section is called 'In Father's Lack'. There lie, under each story, missing or deficient fathers. The hard-pressed father of *A Daughter of Eve* abandons his daughters to the stringent ministrations of his wife. The Papin sisters had been abandoned by an appalling father, and they committed murder in an all-female, all mother-and-daughter, sister-and-sister situation. As for the First World War – Kipling spoke for the soldiers: 'If any ask you why we died / Tell them, because our father lied' ... The question that this grouping of the chapters makes me want to ask is, have we in the west, or at least in Western Europe, suffered from a crisis of fatherhood since – when? The French Revolution? The Romantic period, this revolution of the sons? Did what Hillis Miller called 'the disappearance of God' signify, express, a collapse of the fathers? Were we feminists misguided all along when we complained of the excesses of the patriarchy, when we should have been bemoaning its insufficiencies? In that sense it may not be so counterproductive to start with it, for it is the larger framework within which the individual dramas play themselves out.

I had thought, for symmetry's sake, of borrowing the marvellous title of Michèle Roberts's collection of short stories and calling the second section 'During Mother's Absence'. It would also have had a neat

Freudian/Lacanian ring: *fort/da*, gone/there. As observed by Freud, the mother, the spool in the little child's game, is absent, then present. The child attempts to control the mother's disappearances with his game. Mother's absence precipitates the child's entry into language, the need to control the pain, speak absence, *fort*, gone, and presence, *da*, there. But that was not, I came to see, what I had written about. Mothers were *not* symmetrical with fathers: I hadn't known that, but now I found out. For a start, there was not one mother in there, but a multitude of them. Mother was double as in Leonardo's painting of the Virgin and St Anne. Mother was good and bad. As in Melanie Klein's breast, good breast, bad breast. Mother was a series of projections. Mother is archetypal, is real. A dangerous bugbear, what condemns women to endless oppression, or the repressed force in women, yearning to be unleashed. Mother is also, as the essay on women and poetry discovers, a multitude. Not absent, no: a handful of trouble. Troublesome in her elusiveness, her power, her darkness and inadequacies, as is shown by poets' and prose writers' ever-reinvented metaphors of the sea, voyages over the sea to light-houses that turn out to be a bit of hard, prosaic rock ...

My previous collection of essays, *White Woman Speaks with Forked Tongue* was subtitled 'Criticism as Autobiography'.[53] It staked a claim on the inevitability as well as the value, of the personal voice, of personal experience, in criticism. The personal voice still speaks in this book, though in a more muted fashion. But either because I have become more aware of the complexities of such a voice, of the odds under the odds in even the most candid attempt to speak the self, or because I could not agree with myself, I have mostly eschewed the 'I' that previously I had laboured so hard to arrive at. In the more neutral modes that result, per-haps everyone is freer: including, I hope, the reader?

Notes

1 Judith Butler, *Gender Trouble* (London and New York: Routledge, 1990), pp. 148–9.
2 Marion Milner (alias Joanna Field), *A Life of One's Own* (London: Virago, 1986), p. 86.
3 Andrew Samuels, *The Political Psyche* (London: Routledge, 1993), pp. 130–1.
4 Butler, *Gender Trouble*, p. 128.
5 Ibid., p. 130.
6 Ibid., p. 131.
7 Ibid., p. 133.
8 Ibid., p. 135.
9 Ibid., p. 140.
10 Judith Butler, *Bodies That Matter* (London and New York: Routledge, 1993), p. 9.
11 Ibid., pp. 14–15.
12 Luce Irigaray, *Speculum of the Other Woman*, tr. G. C. Gill (Ithaca: Cornell Uni-versity Press, 1985), pp. 139–40.

13 Toni Morrison, *The Bluest Eyes* (London: Picador, 1990), p. 163.
14 E. Marks and I. de Courtivron, *New French Feminisms* (Brighton: Harvester, 1981), p. 137.
15 Rosi Braidotti, *Nomadic Subjects* (London: Routledge and New York: Columbia University Press, 1994), p. 164.
16 Donna Haraway, 'A Manifesto for Cyborgs: Science, Technology and Socialist Feminism in the 1980s', in Mary Eagleton (ed.), *Feminist Literary Theory: A Reader*, 2nd edn (Oxford: Blackwell, 1996), p. 399.
17 Linda Alcoff, 'Cultural Feminism versus Post-structuralism: The Identity Crisis in Feminist Theory', in Eagleton, *Feminist Literary Theory*, p. 381.
18 Braidotti, *Nomadic Subjects*, p. 164.
19 Haraway, 'A Manifesto for Cyborgs', p. 401.
20 In Marks and De Courtivron, *New French Feminisms*.
21 See Alice Walker, *In Search of Our Mothers' Gardens* (New York: Harcourt Brace Jovanovitch, 1983).
22 Audre Lorde, *Sister Outsider* (Trumansburg, N.Y.: Crossing Press, 1984), p. 22.
23 Antoinette Fouque, *Il y a deux sexes* (Paris: Gallimard, 1995), p. 35, my translation.
24 Elizabeth Badinter, *XY: De l'identité masculine* (Paris: Odile Jacob, 1992), pp. 85, 89, my translation.
25 C. G. Jung, *Symbols of Transformation: An Analysis of the Prelude to a Case of Schizophrenia* (London: Routledge and Kegan Paul, 1956), p. 125.
26 Ibid., p. 301.
27 In D. W. Winnicott, *Home is Where We Start From* (Harmondsworth: Penguin, 1986), pp. 191–2, 193.
28 Fouque, *Il y a deux sexes*, p. 25, my translation.
29 Ibid., p. 51.
30 Ibid., pp. 47–51.
31 Winnicott, *Home is Where We Start From*, p. 183.
32 Ibid., p. 193.
33 Ibid., pp. 186–7.
34 Ibid., pp. 187–8.
35 Camille Paglia, *Sexual Personae: Art and Decadence from Nefertiti to Emily Dickinson* (Harmondsworth: Penguin, 1991), p. 28.
36 Ibid., p. 16.
37 Ibid., pp. 38–9.
38 Ibid., pp. 17, 28, 36.
39 Keith Thomas, *Man and the Natural World: Changing Attitudes in England, 1500–1800* (London: Allen Lane, 1983).
40 See C. G. Jung, *Aspects of the Feminine* (London: Ark, 1982), pp. 95ff., 173; Christian Gaillard, *Jung* (Paris, PUF, 1995), pp. 79, 81.
41 Andrew Samuels, 'Beyond the Feminist Principle', in K. Barnaby and P. D'Acierno (eds), *C. G. Jung and the Humanities: Towards a Hermeneutics of Culture* (London: Routledge, 1990), p. 301.
42 See *Fémininmasculin: Le Sexe de l'art* (Paris: Éditions du Centre Pompidou and Gallimard/Electa, 1995).
43 In a fascinating essay 'Le *devenir-femme* de l'art', part of the introduction to the *Fémininmasculin* exhibition (ibid.), Bernard Marcadé interprets Brancusi's *Princess X* sculpture along lines that would seem to invalidate what I say here about it. He quotes Brancusi on *Princess X*:

    My statue, sir? ... It is 'Woman' ['la Femme'], the very synthesis of woman. It is Goethe's eternal feminine, reduced to its essence ... To extract this entity, to bring back this eternal type of ephemeral forms into the domain of the senses [dans le domaine du sensible], for five years I have simplified, planed down my work. And I think that, victorious at last, I have gone beyond matter. Besides, it would have been such a pity to spoil such a beautiful material [*matière*] by digging little holes for the eyes, the hair, the ears into it. (p. 31; my translation here and below)

Though Brancusi kept insisting to Signac, the president of the 1920 Salon des Independants, that his statue was *not* a phallus, it created a scandal and was removed when the minister visited the exhibition, and finally had to be withdrawn. Marcadé argues that *Princess X* embodies a certain conception of sculpture as an art of 'essence'. This goes back to Aristotle's description of matter as what desires form, to Michelangelo, Rodin – and Panofsky's description of Renaissance neoplatonism as ' "the suppression of the superfluous" ' (pp. 31–2). This conception makes woman into base matter, to be refined by means of sculpture. In the place of the little holes which would have spoilt the statue, but in effect in fear of *the* hole – of femininity, Brancusi, making a 'portrait' of Princess Marie Bonaparte (who will introduce Freud into France), erects the male organ like a Greek *phalloi*. '*Princess X* carries the priapic attributes of sculpture to the highest degree' (pp. 32–3). Marcadé contrasts *Princess X* both with Duchamp's *Fontaine*, made of an inverted '*pissotière*', ready-made, cloacal and exhibiting holes, and with Louise Bourgeois's *Fillette*, a hanging, vulnerable, worn penis shape, with balls that look like leg-stumps: for him, *Fillette* exhibits 'tenderness' towards the masculine sex, and the desire to self-protect against it.

I can't say that I see *Fillette* at all as Marcadé does: I see great damage and vulnerability and anger in it. But I do find myself perturbed by his interpretation of *Princess X*: did I, to provide an instance of a dynamic relation of masculine to feminine, pick an 'essentializing' erect phallus? Yet I would tend to agree with Marcadé's approval of Deleuze's *Mille Plateaux*: 'woman herself, as a biological and social entity, "needs to become woman, but in a becoming-woman of the whole of man" ' (p. 46; man, '*l'homme*', here I take means humanity).

Having looked, and again, and thought, I think that Marcadé's fascination with the phallus form of *Princess X* prevents him from seeing the Princess, and the tension between Princess and Phallus. Yes, maybe this is a sculpture that lassoos the female form, erects it – a pre-Lacanian object, as it were. *But* for an erect phallus it's bending the wrong way round, folding inwards upon itself ... which gives it grace, and meditativeness. The stem, which Marcadé sees as the neck, I see as a stylized bust. The balls, which he sees as breasts, I see as cleft and knees, or as a stylized, doubly pregnant form ... Whatever other meanings can be read into that shape, however subsuming it may consciously or unconsciously be, I keep seeing a dynamic tension of masculine and feminine forms in it ...

44 D. W. Winnicott, *Playing and Reality* (Harmondsworth: Penguin, 1971), p. 83.
45 Jacques Lacan, *Le Séminaire livre XX: Encore* (Paris: Seuil, 1975).
46 Winnicott, *Playing and Reality*, p. 93.
47 Ibid., p. 94.
48 Ibid.
49 Ibid., p. 96.
50 Ibid., p. 99.

51 Ibid., p. 97.
52 Ibid., p. 99.
53 Nicole Ward Jouve, *White Woman Speaks with Forked Tongue: Criticism as Auto-biography* (London and New York: Routledge, 1991).

IN FATHER'S LACK

Part I

Gendering the Female: Good/Bad Daughters

1

Balzac's *A Daughter of Eve* and the Apple of Knowledge

Natural Law and the Code are enemies, and we are the field on which they do battle.

A young bride in Balzac

... in the [Hegelian] scheme of recognition, there is no place for the other, for an equal other, for a whole and living woman.... Everything takes place as if, in a split second, man and being had propriated each other. And as if his relationship to woman was still at play as the possibility – though threatening – of the not-proper, not-clean, not mine; desire is inscribed as the desire to reappropriate for himself that which seems able to escape him.

Hélène Cixous, 'Sorties'

Women are different. Or so the 'Avant-propos' to the *The Human Comedy* asserts (1842). The model Balzac had found for his great work was zoology, the science which Buffon, Cuvier and Geoffroy Saint-Hilaire had recently developed. The different milieux in which man's action is deployed make as many men as there are varieties in nature. But society goes further than nature in its capacity for differentiation:

When Buffon depicted the lion, he sketched the lioness in a few sentences; but in Society woman is not always the female of the male. There can be two perfectly dissimilar beings inside a couple. The wife of a merchant is sometimes worthy to be that of a prince.... The Social State has hazards which Nature does not permit itself, for it is Nature plus Society. The description of the Social Species therefore had to be at least twice that of the Animal Species, if you considered but the two sexes.[1]

The need to give women the representation and importance which their difference required, and the feeling that the difference arose from their *marriageable status*, were there early in Balzac. His first major work is *The Physiology of Marriage*. He began it when he was twenty-three, in 1822,

and he completed and published it in 1829. He meant later to place it as
the coping-stone of the final architectural structure of *The Human
Comedy*. It was soon after completing the *Physiology* that, in the early
1830s, he embarked on the novels that were to become part of the *Scenes
from Private Life*.

Exploring women in society, Balzac felt he was doing something new,
'*The Thousand and One Nights* of the West' is what he calls *The Human
Comedy* in the introduction to *A Daughter of Eve* (1838). In the Arabian
tales there is no 'society', for woman only appears 'by accident and
always locked up'. 'Their "merveilleux" is wholly inspired by the seclu-
sion of women.' France, Balzac goes on to say, is the most socially,
'fecund' modern western country for a novelist because of the position of
the women in it. Autocratic power and a small privileged class oppress
and restrict Russia. Germany is full of confusion, the struggle of new
conventions against old ones. England, though it has vigorous 'modern
doctrines', is hampered by customs, bowed down under 'the empire of
duty'. Italy is not as free as France, and anyway the only possible Italian
novel has been written by Stendhal: *The Charterhouse of Parma*.[2]

It is significant that Balzac (here talking of 'freedom') should have
started with a 'physiology' of *marriage* – marriage, not love. Stendhal,
who, like Balzac, spent his life endlessly in love with women, wrote *De
l'amour* before he launched into fiction. Stendhal was frankly subversive.
In his quest for the absolute he had no time for the powers of the structures that be. His novels are never concerned with marriage as a happy
ending or a social reality with which the pursuit of the ideal should in
some way be conciliated. Stendhal is quite clear that love and marriage
do not mix, that the ideal and the real cannot be reconciled. Balzac was
not so sure; indeed, he passionately wished otherwise.[3] He had fallen in
love in 1835, when he was thirty-six, with a pen-admirer, a Polish lady
called Madame Hanska. She was married to an older man. He waited for
her all his life. Marriage to her became a millennial horizon, something
to be striven for. In the face of increasing disillusionment and waning
strength, he had to keep alive the possibility that marriage might work.
But even before his meeting with Eve Hanska, when he was writing the
Physiology, he had endorsed Rousseau's demand: marriage is nothing
without love. Novels like *A Daughter of Eve* sprang from the dream that
the two could be combined.

Balzac takes stock of the antagonism between morals and the law
where the fate of women in society is concerned. Even Bonaparte and
Portalis had noted it when they wrote the article 'divorce' of the *Civil
Code*, and Madame de Staël kept passionately denouncing it in novels
such as *Delphine* and *Corinne*. How can marriage, regarded as of public
utility, and demanding of women the sacrifice of their freedom and
ambition, be compatible with their happiness? Don't they, as human
beings, have a right to happiness? Corinne says she might as well kill
herself, since society, requiring that she sacrifice her faculties to the

accomplishment of duty, is willing her to kill herself morally. Balzac will echo her: one of his young brides exclaims that laws have been made by old men and austere philosophers and that society takes as its supreme law the sacrifice of woman to the family.[4] The *Scenes from Private Life* tirelessly denounce the failures and miseries of marriage such as it is. The 'amiable and honest' woman with whom several are concerned, the fruit of a rich and elaborate civilization, is shown to be delivered over to the temptation of adultery by her social prestige, beauty and idleness. She labours and sometimes breaks under shackles and a sense of violation. But unlike the Saint-Simonians and George Sand, with whom he was engaged in endless debate, Balzac neither wants to do away with marriage nor wants to reinforce the practice of divorce. His idea is slowly to correct and alter morals, collective mentalities.[5]

Girls see marriage as a promise of happiness. But, Balzac answers, 'marriage can be considered in political, civil, and moral terms, as a law, a contract, and an institution'; however, 'neither reproduction nor property nor children constitutes happiness.'[6] To make things worse, no one knows how to cultivate happiness. Yet this would help. To this end there must be a school for wives, but also a school for parents, and a school for husbands. Molière, to whose *School for Husbands* and *School for Wives* everyone is appealing in the period, including Balzac, is immensely relevant.[7]

Husbands were in much need of the tact which the *Physiology*, an *ars amoris* and an *ars erotica* rolled into one, tried to teach them. 'Never begin marriage with a rape': crude as this sounds, it was a necessary piece of advice if we are to believe George Sand and Marie Capelle.[8] There was no shortage of cavalier, brutal or cynical attitudes among bridegrooms, but even nice ones must have had something of a problem on their hands, given the ignorance, passivity, and sometimes terror of their brides. Upper-class young girls received no instruction, sexual or otherwise, which might fit them for their future roles. There was continuing reference in the period to the liberal ideas of Molière and Fénelon, Rousseau and Laclos, on the part of would-be reformers, ranging from the radical Saint-Simonians to 'bourgeois feminists' such as Madame de Genlis, Madame Guizot and Madame de Rémusat: they asked that girls be given a practical education, taught their rights as well as their duties.[9] Siding with the Saint-Simonians, Balzac boldly asks that they also be given some experience of men – but (by contrast with the Saint-Simonians) so that they will thereafter knowingly and virtuously accept the married state:

Do you want to know the truth? Open Rousseau, for there isn't one important question of public morality that he hasn't anticipated.... 'Among moral people, girls are promiscuous and wives virtuous'.... Perish the virtue of ten virgins, rather than the sanctity of morals, the crown of honour which a mother must wear![10]

Balzac as a youth had suffered from his mother's infidelity to his father. The early part of the *Physiology* suggests that for him the Fall is connected with woman's adultery. Interestingly, though, the novels do not bear out what the *Physiology* preaches. I cannot think of any occasion when the virtue of an upper-class young girl perishes (whereas it happens repeatedly in Stendhal, and it doesn't matter). But many of Balzac's wives and mothers gleefully wear the scarlet letter (and not a few of those who wear the crown of honour, like Adeline Hulot in *La Cousine Bette*, turn out to be bloody fools, at least as far as worldly existence is concerned).

Balzac was the historian of nineteenth-century society, not the writer of a utopia. Some of the fictions, however, adumbrate the possibility of a happier state of things, and offer meditations on how education could fit young girls for a successful married relationship.[11] *A Daughter of Eve* is doubly revealing in this context. It shows how dangerous an education in ignorance is, thus posing the question of what the right kind *of education* might be. It also offers itself as a school for husbands, prolonging the preoccupations of the *Physiology*. It is a novel of reprieve, in which the tragedy of adultery is avoided thanks to the tactful intervention of the husband. A lesson in fact, you might say.

The School for Husbands

A Daughter of Eve opens in a heaven-coloured 'boudoir', all blue and white, all elegance and luxury. The two women in it, who are confiding in each other, are in hell. They are sisters with heavenly names, both called Marie. The daughters of a magistrate, the Count de Granville, they have been brought up in the most despotic fashion by a bigot of a provincial bourgeois mother, to know next to nothing and marry the first man that offered. The elder sister, Marie-Angélique, is married to Félix de Vandenesse, a man committed to the fortunes of the Bourbons. The marriage took place in 1829, before their overthrow in 1830. It is now early 1835. The Granvilles have bought Vandenesse's title and position (higher than their own) in exchange for a large dowry. They have then used the second daughter, Marie-Eugénie, to compensate for the extra expenditure involved in the settlement of the elder. Parvenu banker Du Tillet, a supporter of the July Monarchy, glad to get a prize lamb from the upper classes, has recognized a large non-existent dowry to Marie-Eugénie in the marriage contract. Now both sisters are equally unhappy. Marie-Eugénie is treated like a slave by her husband. He bullies her sexually, keeps her under surveillance, exerts all sorts of petty tyrannies over her. He keeps her penniless but buys her splendid furniture, jewellery and carriages. He has made her into an unwilling, innocent and touching Mrs Merdle, a 'bosom' on which the husband's wealth is displayed, as in Dickens's *Little Dorrit*.

Marie-Angélique has been luckier. Félix de Vandenesse, world-weary and older than herself, has wisdom and tact. He is the hero of the 'school for husbands' side of the story. He has a loaded past, which has yet to be told within the framework of *The Human Comedy*: in *Le Lys dans la vallée*. In the introduction to *A Daughter of Eve* Balzac justifies having things the wrong way round by saying he is seeking a mosaic rather than a chronological effect. He is dealing with present, not past history: in the present you often hear of a man's past after you have met him in his mature state. Only what is genuinely over allows for chronological telling. The technique applies to the narration of most of his novels, including *A Daughter of Eve*, in which the stories of the sisters are told retrospectively, to explain their disconsolate state, a crisis point in their life, at the opening of the novel. The reader who is meant to read and *reread* the totality of *The Human Comedy* is free, however, to feed (or not) *Le Lys dans la vallée* into the character of Félix. If she does, she will know that he is one of the protagonists who is very close to Balzac's heart, and she may also know that Félix is close to Balzac autobiographically: his wretched childhood is modelled on Balzac's, his great love for Madame de Mortsauf, an older woman, on Balzac's love for Madame de Berny, his stormy affair with Lady Dudley on Balzac's passion for Countess Bolognini-Visconti, born Sarah Lowell. At any rate, all passion spent, Félix de Vandenesse has decided to be a model husband, and make his wife happy. He has initiated her with art and patience, he has formed her for society, completed her education, they have a child, he has indeed created an 'Eden' for her, a 'paradise' in the Faubourg Saint-Honoré where they live, rue du Rocher, street of the Rock.

Félix is a mixture of God and Adam. Apparently all-powerful and wise, he has failed to perceive the 'serpent' threatening his Eve, which is boredom, and with it the curiosity to know passion. A splendid, many-coloured serpent turns up in the person of Raoul Nathan, a Romantic poet, a jack of all trades also, a Bohemian, unkempt, dirty, flamboyant, a brilliant talker. Marie-Angélique meets him in the winter of 1833–4, when the first salons reopen after the upheavals of the July Revolution and the takeover of Louis-Philippe, the bourgeois king. Nathan has decided to go into politics through journalism, and is looking for an aristocratic, powerfully placed young woman to help him in his social ascent. Marie fits the bill: as pure and beautiful, she can be his Ideal, his Béatrix; as aristocratic and influential, she can help his career. What begins as an infatuation with love and poetry on Marie's part, and as a calculated mixture of ambition and flattered vanity on Raoul's, develops into an absorbing passion. Raoul has to deploy a prodigious activity, to hold his sundry enterprises afloat and to keep up with the relentless rituals of the rich so he can pay his court to Marie. This makes him keen. Marie discovers the Herculean labours and devotion he is putting at her feet and worships him for it. What she does not know is that Nathan has a mistress, actress Florine, for whom he writes plays and who gives him money to help in his ventures.

A crisis occurs. Nathan has had to sign *lettres de change*, to borrow money on short-term credit to keep his newspaper alive. The bills have become due and he cannot cover them. He does not know that the secret lender is Du Tillet, Marie-Eugénie's husband, who plans to discredit and ruin Nathan, a dangerous rival for the electoral college he is plotting to occupy with fellow bankers. At bay, threatened with dishonour and prison, Nathan attempts to asphyxiate himself. Marie-Angélique finds him, revives him. She promises to find the money for him, has thoughts of running away with him. With two days in which to find the 40,000 francs, she has come to her sister for help, but neither of them has any money. Du Tillet, eavesdropping, is suspicious.

Energized by her sister's despair, Marie-Eugénie finds an ingenious relay of lenders and endorsers of the *lettres de change* to save Raoul. But she also decides to tell Félix, fearing ruin and social ostracism for her sister. There was a famous example of such ruin, which the novel refers to. Marie d'Agoult, née Marie de Flavigny, a wife and mother, had eloped with the musician Liszt. She was all the more on Balzac's mind as at the time he was writing *A Daughter of Eve* he was also completing *Béatrix*, which is centred on a character very like Marie d'Agoult. The 'real-life' Marie had suffered from the way in which society had cast her off after her elopement, and from the state of financial insecurity she had brought upon herself.

Félix responds to Marie-Eugénie's revelation as a model husband. He blames himself. He sets about repairing the damage. He buys back the *lettres de change*. He teases his wife with the tale of Nathan's relationship with Florine, but kindly, and in such a way that she decides to own up, gives him Nathan's letters, which he burns; she might not forgive him later for having read them. He engineers a salvage operation of Marie's compromising letters to Nathan by meeting both Nathan and Florine at the masked ball of the opera, and revealing to Florine under disguise that Nathan is being unfaithful to her. She is furious. He gets her to find Marie's letters in Nathan's portfolio and exchanges them for the *lettres de change*. Confronted with all the marks of Nathan's duplicity and his intimacy with Florine, the countess experiences a revolution of feelings. Félix's diplomacy is vindicated. Nathan, who was already full of compromise, ends the novel politically compromised as well, a finished man. The count and countess riding in their carriage pass by Florine and Nathan on foot, scruffy and shabby-looking. The countess wonders how she could ever have loved such a man.

Thus Eve is saved from the serpent. The apple of adultery is gently removed from her hand just as she was about to take the fatal bite. The husband gains her a reprieve, ensuring a happy ending, keeping her in the earthly paradise of what she now comes to appreciate as a happy marriage. It is not a usual fictional situation in the nineteenth century. Indeed, I can think of no other novel, in France or in England, in which the *husband* is the saviour of his wife. Darcy saves Lydia Bennett by getting Wickham to marry her, in *Pride and Prejudice*; Louisa Gradgrind is saved from elopement with Harthouse by Sissy Jupes in *Hard Times*; Natasha, in *War and Peace*, from elopement with Anatol Kuragin, by Pierre, who at that time is not even her fiancé – Prince André is. *A Daughter of Eve* offers an unusual happy ending which is neither the prospect of an idyllic marriage (as at the end of all Austen novels) nor the fulfilment of desire, but the *avoidance* of adultery. The heroine realizes that happiness is here and now. Happiness is both negative (not doing it) and conservative. That it should be found inside the married state shows how important that was for Balzac as the place where the ideal and the real could be conciliated. He is aware that he is producing something close to a utopia, however. The introduction tries to cater for the possible disappointment of readers who might expect tragedy, the triumph of violent passions, as appropriate. This is a tale about youth, a merciful, tender tale, Balzac says. He certainly had a right to it, if you think how many of the *Scenes from Private Life* do have tragic endings.

In Félix, Balzac is providing a justification for the views of Bonald, whom he much admired. Bonald's ethics of the family derived from a political mysticism of power. In the circle of domestic life, he argued, the father, like the king in the state, embodied divine power: this may be why Félix is in the position of God as well as of Adam in the elaborate imagery of marriage as Eden, adultery as the Fall. Woman, for Bonald, appears as the minister of the power of the husband-and-father, the children as its subjects. Although bound up with legitimism and the Restoration, Bonald's views were gaining enhanced prestige in the July Monarchy, the bourgeoisie seeing in the family, as the *Memoirs of Two Young Brides* states, 'the only possible social unit'.[12] But you could also read the religious parable as a sign of the growing 'secularization of the sacred' which is taking place in the period.[13] This was brought forcibly home to me when, meditating on *A Daughter of Eve*, I came across the following verses in a hymn by John Newman:

> O living wisdom of our God
> when all was sin and shame
> a second Adam to the fight
> and to the rescue came.
>
> O wisest love! that flesh and blood
> which did in Adam fail
> should strive afresh against the foe
> should strive and should prevail.

If you put Félix in the place of Christ (the second Adam), this is most appropriate. Félix is also the first Adam. He has had tragic or erotic affairs; he is fallen in the flesh a first time. He says himself to Marie: 'Wouldn't we men be absurd, when we have been behaving foolishly for twenty years, to want you not to be imprudent once in your entire life?'

(p. 376). Falling, Félix has acquired a knowledge of *good and evil* (which makes him merciful). His fault is a happy fault. *Felix culpa*. That must also be why he is called Félix. As the first Adam, he has put his wife in paradise, has almost lost her to the serpent. As the second Adam, he saves her. The Old Testament and the New are rolled into one in the novel, which must be the reason why Marie is called Marie, not Eve. But salvation does not go very far. Man Félix cannot redeem the world, he can only protect his wife: 'I am indulgent; but Society is not, it avoids a woman who has caused a scandal ... but if I cannot reform the world it is at least within my power to protect you against yourself' (p. 376). Félix's power to do good, in moral and religious terms, has been reduced to the domestic sphere. Let us note in passing, for we are moving towards the question, that, for him to be given the chance, the woman must remain in the situation of a child, an innocent, one who does not know. Marie does not even know that Nathan has Florine.

To do good at all, Félix needs his wife – the more so as he cannot reform the world politically either. His class lost power in 1830. Having two couples in the story, placing Marie-Eugénie's fate at the hands of the banker Du Tillet next to that of Marie-Angélique and the aristocratic Vandenesse, Balzac is making a point about which class, and which brand of the monarchy, he would prefer to see as the rulers of France. He first thought of the novel in 1832, two years after the July Revolution. He makes the novel take place in 1833–5, when things were still in flux, as Nathan's journalistic and political ventures make clear (he does not quite know which party to back, which is the winning horse). Yet it was becoming clear that the Orléans dynasty and the moneyed bourgeoisie with it were consolidating their power. The bankers Du Tillet and Nucingen have got into the electoral college by the end of the novel. Félix, however, points out to Baroness Nucingen, to whom he promises favours in exchange for the *lettres de change* should he be returned to power, that political regimes are highly unstable in France. There was a hope of the return of the Bourbons even as late as 1838. Contrasting Vandenesse's enlightened, tolerant, adroit and fatherly performance as a husband who knows how to control his wife without wounding her pride or alienating her affections with Du Tillet's vulgar, slave-driving, reifying treatment of his, Balzac is saying, 'which ruler would you rather have?' The wife is placed in the position of the nation to be governed, and the reader invited to reflect on what makes for good government. It is in the interest of the political as well as the religious and moral lesson that the novel teaches that the wife remain *this* side of knowledge: passive. The position in which, according to Hélène Cixous, culture eternally places woman.[14] Taking stock of this, the reader is bound to wonder where this leaves Balzac's condemnation of girls' ignorance.

The School for Wives

Indeed, you could say that Marie's education has been devised to place her in the very position society requires her to occupy.

With his customary flair Balzac is wonderfully accurate in his account of the upbringing of these upper-class sisters. His tone is both compassionate and sarcastic; you might think he is overdoing it, but studies such as Isabelle Bricard's *Saintes ou pouliches* quite confirm what he describes.[15]

There were three possible courses for parents. They could place their daughters behind the railings of a convent school. New ones were being founded or reopened in Paris under the Restoration: the Sacré-Cœur, the 'Dames Anglaises' (where George Sand spent some time), L'Abbaye-aux-Bois, or Les Oiseaux. Girls could also be sent to one of the new lay schools, which Madame Campan had pioneered with the Légion d'Honneur under the patronage of the Emperor. Or they could be brought up at home. This was supposed to be the ideal thing: Fénelon among others had recommended it. Convent schools were imitating mothers in wanting to bring girls up on 'the knees of the church'. Mothers, especially since Rousseau, who did much to make motherhood fashionable and promote breastfeeding, were supposed to have the intuitive genius that would enable them to develop the specific 'feminine essence'[16] that was requisite. Women have 'more soul than man' (Monseigneur Dupanloup). According to the novelist Barbey d'Aurevilly, they have much less intellect – neither the 'creative faculty of invention' nor the 'synthesizing power of generalization'; they only have 'convulsive strength' (presumably meaning hysteria).[17] 'They lack the male faculties as radically as the Venus de Milo lacks the organism of Hercules.' Joseph de Maistre offers women a consolation prize:

> They have made neither the Iliad nor the Aeneid, nor Saint Peter nor the Medici Venus. . . . They have invented neither algebra nor telescopes . . . but they do something greater than any of this: it is on their knees that the most excellent thing in the world is formed: an honest man and an honest woman.[18]

How a mother who herself has been given very little instruction can accomplish the prodigy of so roundly educating her children is never explained. It comes with the milk: 'a mother alone knows or rather *feels* what her daughter needs, and any food that comes to the young girl's mind without going through the motherly channel is singularly suspect.'[19]

Like the real-life Marie d'Agoult, the two Maries have been educated at home by their mother. What in terms of the Rousseauist ideology has made that upbringing a parody is that their mother has no milk of human kindness. She is a bigot, a censor. The girls' curriculum has been a reduced version of what was taught in convent schools: 'grammar, the French language, history, geography, and the little arithmetic necessary for women' (p. 276).[20] History and geography for girls consisted in memorizing names, dates, chronology. It was similar to what was being taught in England, if we are to believe Jane Austen's comic *History*, which has one king die to be succeeded – surprise, surprise – by his son.[21] Literature and morals have been filtered by the Christmas *Leçons de littérature* and the inept *Choix de lettres édifiantes* by the Abbé de Montmignon, whom Balzac seems to have particularly detested.[22] Any other reading has been suppressed, even Fénelon's *Télémaque*, regarded as 'dangerous'. The entire drive of the education of the two Maries has been to make them as ignorant of men and sexual matters as possible. Their only walks have been in the garden; they have never been to the theatre, only to church. Their only company has been the bigots and elderly priests of their mother's circle. Their female tutors have been watched over by their mother's confessor (and they have conceived a strong distaste for religion). Drawing has been taught them by a 'spinster', and their notions of anatomy are such that they would have 'feminized' the 'Farnese Hercules himself'. There is a nice tautology there, when you reflect that women's lack of 'Hercules' organism' was for Barbey d'Aurevilly the sign of their imbecility, but that somehow it must be carefully hidden from them that such an organism exists. To make sure they do not know their own organism exists either, and nobody else knows, the sisters have had to sleep their entire life next to their mother's bedroom with the door left open. They have had to wear clothes that went down to their feet and up to their chins, even at the few balls they attended when they were of age. The only thing of equality that has been judged innocuous enough for them to learn has been music, the confessors having decided it was a 'Christian art'.[23] They have had an old male piano master, a German exile and musical genius, devoted, comical, one of life's true innocents. Under Schmucke's guidance they have become expert pianists, pouring their whole soul into music.

In *Albert Savarus*, accusing the 'University of France' of having quite ditched the problem of girls' education, Balzac suggests that the legislator in this case is between the devil and the deep blue sea: either you make girls knowledgeable, and they risk turning into Célimènes (the coquette of *Le Misanthrope*); or you repress their sensibilities, but you risk an explosion of the kind Molière portrayed in his Agnès in *L'École des femmes*.[24] Are we to suppose that music has made the two Maries dangerously susceptible, preparing the ground for Marie-Angélique's infatuation with a poet – or has it been the outlet which has stopped them from going mad? Balzac's position is unclear. He is lyrical about the music, the girls being 'Saint Cecilias'; he is also sentimental about the beauty of their being 'hidden flowers' brought up away from the eyes of the world in the 'thorny bushes' of a mother's vigilance. He twice concedes, in odd phrases, that it is 'the first duty' of a mother to preserve her daughter's innocence. Has he forgotten Rousseau's 'Perish the virtue of ten virgins. . .'? It is difficult to know whether he is being ironic, temporarily swayed by the rhetoric of innocence, or just pretending to assent to consensus opinion. That the text cannot make up its mind is interesting in itself: perhaps Balzac knows no better than the 'University of France' how to cut the Gordian knot.

It may be appropriate to talk, as Arlette Michel does, of a 'Balzacian feminism' in the sense that he repeatedly protests against repressiveness and bigotry in girls' education, and genuinely pleads for a humane and tender school for daughters and wives. But his attitude is more ambivalent than Michel is prepared to recognize. For, given the world as it is, hasn't Marie-Eugénie, for instance, had the best education possible to prepare her to be the wife of Du Tillet? You can try, as Balzac was doing, to reform mentalities through writing. But, until the Du Tillets of this world cease to have the power, how can you ensure that a Marie's best equipment for marriage won't be to know how to endure? The less developed a woman's faculties, the more repressed her spirits, the less pain she will have to bear. Perhaps the 'right' type of education is unthinkable until you have reformed the institutions themselves? Isabelle Bricard ends her book wondering that, with all the idiocy of the education girls were given, the century should have produced such sensible, charming, literate, and even happy women. It is true, however, that the most remarkable women were those who had a totally idiosyncratic upbringing, like Madame de Staël, who was given licence by an exceptional father, or George Sand, whose father was dead, and who was allowed to roam the library by an eighteenth-century-style grandmother. Balzac was forever arguing against George Sand, who did not believe in the institution of marriage such as it stood. His inability to produce effective suggestions for an education of girls for marriage, the fact that within the parameters he had chosen he could critique but not propose, shows that logic, at least, was on the side of the woman writer.[25]

Impossible Contradictions

You bring them up like saints, and sell them like fillies.

George Sand

What I have said Balzac is saying is by no means the whole story. A piece of fiction is a weave, made up of many strands, crossed and twisted. Or, to use his own simile, it is a mosaic, in which thousands of different pieces are juxtaposed. Only when you see the whole do you see the pattern. Extracting an intelligible narrative and a moral and political parable from it is rather like following lines or the variations of a colour in it. For them to have their meaning, you have to pay attention to what else there is.

It is an impossible task. Roland Barthes has shown how huge is the complexity of a Balzac text by producing some three hundred pages of analysis of a story thirty pages long, *Sarrasine* in his *S/Z*. *A Daughter of Eve* is 130 pages. To do anything like justice to it I would need several volumes. But I can at least suggest the direction which such an analysis would follow. The choice of a particular piece of language as the place of significance, and the decision to treat everything in it as significant, and potentially of equal weight, make it specific. It entails a distinctive treatment of ideas, lessons, political positions and so on. That Balzac should have chosen to deal with issues like marriage and the education of girls through novels, not treatises, after the *Physiology*, means that his purpose is different, more complete or less abstract. You maim his creation if you use it to extract ideological positions from it. There are positions, but they are inseparable from the network in which they are caught: if you pull, the whole fabric should come also.

Thus, having stated that the western woman, unlike the oriental one, is allowed to go out, Balzac the novelist fully accepts the consequences, even while he appears to half negate them. He does have 'scenes from *private* life', meant to contrast with 'scenes from *Parisian* (=*public*) life'. But the narrative pattern he has devised for *The Human Comedy* negates the distinction between public and private: he is a very anti-Victorian writer, an effective if not theoretical subverter of the domestic bourgeois ethos. *A Daughter of Eve* is the inside life of one (or two, or three) couple(s). But the fortunes of Marie, Félix, Nathan and Florine (not to mention Marie-Eugénie and Du Tillet) are mixed with the fortunes of the larger Parisian world, flow in and out of the *Scenes from Parisian Life*. When Balzac wrote the novel, he was elaborating the 'return of the characters' from one book to the next, which is the distinguishing feature of his collection, what binds it together and makes it into one society (the thing, he said, that was lacking in Scott). And so the future minister Rastignac (from *Le Père Goriot, La Maison Nucingen*...), the banker Nucingen (from 'What Love Costs Old Men' in *A Harlot's Progress*), Baroness Nucingen, Madame d'Espard (from *L'Interdiction*), Nathalie de Manerville (from *Le Contrat de mariage, Le Lys dans la vallée*), and many more, people the salons and devise the intrigues in which Marie and Raoul are caught. Indeed, Balzac emphasizes this in the introduction, where he actually produces Rastignac's pedigree and history as it can be culled from the other novels in which he figures, and he also explains who some of the other characters are. Furthermore, the year in which Balzac wrote *A Daughter of Eve* (1837; published 1838) is one of his most prolific periods. He had just finished *Béatrix*, and he was working on *Le Curé de village, Le Cabinet des antiques*, and the sequel to *Les Illusions perdues*, in which Nathan appears, several years younger, with Florine, and where his journalist friends Blondet and Lousteau also figure. Revising the proofs of *A Daughter of Eve*, he altered the names of some of the characters, like Blondet, who had taken shape in the intervening writing.

The effect of all the salon life, the political and journalistic intrigues, in *A Daughter of Eve*, is to half contradict the demand that the good aristocratic husband keep his wife within the boundaries of marriage. The wife is meant to be for the family only, a case of 'she for God in him'. She should not have lovers, let alone elope. Yet not only would there be no novel unless the wife at least threatened to take a lover (this signals she is different); but also by its format an aristocratic marriage requires that the wife should circulate socially, and should pretend by her costume and wit to be sexually available. This marks her out as different from a bourgeoise. Vandenesse's first task after his marriage is to educate an ill-formed young wife for society. That means wearing décolletés, looking alluring, flirting, having her own independent relationships. Thus she falls, unprotected, into the company of seemingly friendly upper-class bitches like Madame d'Espard and Nathalie de Manerville, who want to take their revenge against Félix and – another figure of the serpent – push Marie towards adulterous love. All these high-society women, in effect, have affairs, every one of them: Moïra de Saint-Héren (*La Femme de trente ans*), the Countess of Montcornet (*Les Paysans*), Mesdames d'Espard and de Manerville, Baroness Nucingen (with Rastignac). The rules of the eighteenth-century aristocratic marriage still prevail in this society: it is perfectly allowed for the wife to have affairs provided she keep up appearances; provided, above all, that she does not run away with her lover. Honest passion damns you in that world. One of the paradoxes Balzac is arraigning in the education of the two Maries is that they have been given no equipment to deal with this. That Marie should be genuinely naive, fresh in her feelings, given over to passion, exposes her to the risk of open elopement, therefore social damnation. Society is cruel, as Félix says. He could have added that it is also immoral. In that sense, a moral education ill fits you for it.

Indeed, taken seriously, the moral education incapacitates you. An earlier novel, about Marie's parents and their disastrous marriage, had spelt this out: *Une Double Famille*. The Count de Granville marries an angelic-looking provincial bourgeoise, Angélique Bontemps (hence the daughter Marie-Angélique's name). She is in the pockets of the 'Congregation' of repressive and ambitious priests, the Tartuffes of the nineteenth century, who poison her with excessive devotion, persuade her that religious virtue is incompatible with the demands her husband and society make upon her wifehood. She runs her house like a convent, refuses to go out décolletée to balls she regards as devilish (in this there were many authorities of the period with her, and even under the Second Empire the question of whether a young girl should waltz was hotly disputed; Madame Bovary's entranced waltz in the arms of the viscount caused a sensation). Angélique treats sex as if it were a 'duty', not a pleasure. She places a symbolic crucifix between her husband's bed and her own, whose ivory, the narrator said, is no colder than their life, and which bears the body of the 'crucified husband'. The husband gets a mistress, has a second family, then disaster strikes. It is made clear in the process that a husband needs a wife who will accept the values of society if he is to have a social existence himself.

In this system, wives are subject to a series of impossibilities (and it may be because they have to square the circle that they turn out to be so clever in the end). Brought up to believe everything they have been taught by convent schools or devout mothers till the day they are married, or till the day they hit the market (and then the shorter they are in it, the better their chances of a good marriage, since being unexposed and undamaged goods is of the essence of marriageability), from the day they are married they suddenly have to become the reverse. They are told by their mothers to be docile, and are soon expected by their husbands to be expert at love. They suddenly have to show all, or almost all – transparent veils under the Empire, deep décolletés under the Restoration and July Monarchy – this, after they have not even been allowed to undress when they were washing (they even had to wear a nightgown to have a bath) in their schoolgirl days. They have had to be submissive and show no understanding of anything a bit 'risqué' when they were maidens; now they're meant to be witty, independent, cutting even: it is a sign of class. Du Tillet reproaches his wife for her lack of impertinence – how bourgeois it is, he says – though he does not like it when she finally finds a tongue at his expense. The demand that girls, through the simple operation of a marriage contract and ceremony, should be transformed from one thing into its reverse is enough to drive anybody mad. One of Balzac's heroines, Honorine, actually runs away.

They are asked to be virtuous, on a religious/monarchical model. But they are also *not to believe* what religion says. Having been taught so much about renouncing the world and placing God above all things, they must now make their husband into an idol, a god, otherwise they are 'crucifying' him. Angélique Bontemps's bigotry, unlovely as it is, makes perfect sense. She's simply being consistent with what she's been brought up to believe.

A further impossibility is that, within the existing structure, a young woman must both apply a bourgeois morality (be faithful, devote herself to her children) *and* seek for an aristocratic type of fulfilment. Balzac rightly saw that aristocratic marriage, based on a 'chivalrous ideal, inscribed in history and meant to pass on a name and a race', was on the wane, and bourgeois marriage, meant 'to pass on property, and seeking sometimes to associate personal feelings with utility', was on the ascent.[26] Woman had fallen victim to the clash between the ancient 'Christian and chivalric ideal' and the new 'principles of reason and justice' advocated by the French Revolution, which it had, however, failed to extend to women.[27] There was no space in which to work out how women fitted in. As the values of bourgeois marriage were flourishing, yet in the upper circles the courtly ideal still floated, etiolated, almost ghostly. The only way left to a woman who wanted to conciliate the two was to pretend: to play, through clothes, wit, flirtation, with the possibilities of courtly love, that is, adultery – but not *do* it. The wife must be religious but not believe what religion tells her, be sexy but not sexual, appear available but not be so. This is all the more difficult as there is a *real* role, a political and social role, for aristocratic women in that society. The return of the characters shows this. We know perfectly well that Madame de Nucingen has made Rastignac's fortune through clever advice and use of her husband. Blondet has his entries into the salons that count, thanks to his affair with Madame de Montcornet: she's giving him his chance. Nathan is looking for a similar chance. What woman could resist the lure of actually counting for something, doing something? For, if the husband has access to social existence through the wife, the wife has access to a *real* social existence only by taking a lover.

That Balzac should choose to have Félix rescue Marie through a masquerade shows not only that the rescue half belongs to the world of fantasy, but also that in a sense the wife is being pulled back into the world of make-believe, the world of pretence, which is the only one she is allowed to inhabit. This pulls against the other lessons and happy parables that are being offered.

Circulations: Women, Letters, Money

Balzac is not contradicting himself. He is creating situations which are full of contradictions because they are so in life. I can read what I do because the text is giving it to me. How much or how clearly the author intends this to happen is another question. So it is with the contradiction between women's position as objects of exchange and their evident ability to do the exchanging.

Women pass on from fathers to husbands – from Granville to Vandenesse and Du Tillet. Elaborate marriage contracts are involved, the rationale of which is written both in French history and in the Code Napoléon. The two husbands have married into the Granville family, the one because he needed money and the other because he needed the social prestige; the Granvilles have given away their daughters for the converse reasons – 'The Bank has mended the breach made into the Judiciary by Nobility.' An equivalence is created between the fate of the young women and their dowries, all the more so as the one with a large dowry (Marie-Angélique) is the one who is treated kindly by her husband, and the one with a non-existent dowry is treated by hers as a 'slave'. Yet for the two Maries the financial end-result is identical: both husbands are rich; neither of the wives has a penny. Marie-Angélique can neither sell her diamonds (she will be found out) nor apply to brother, father or mother (though the latter remains a possibility). The only woman they find to help them out is Baroness Nucingen, herself an adulteress (Rastignac's mistress). She has a certain leeway because she closes her eyes to her banker husband's misdemeanours. She herself, however, is afraid of being given away by her husband's cashier: she is not that free.

Marie does not have the power to sign the *lettres de change*. Civil existence and effective literacy are denied her. Yet she can sign what gives others power over her. She does not get imprisoned, unlike Pamela by her noble boss Mr B., or Clarissa by her parents, then by Lovelace, or Emily by Montoni in Mrs Radcliffe's *The Mysteries of Udolpho*, or the girl with the golden eyes by her possessive lover in Balzac's story of that name. But her letters get imprisoned in her place. Baroness Nucingen puts Marie's acknowledgement of debt in a secret drawer. Nathan keeps Marie's love letters in a secret portfolio with a refined safety lock. When Félix knows all, his first task is to retrieve both the *lettres de change* and Marie's letter from the baroness. He then exchanges the *lettres* signed by Nathan for the love letters by playing upon Florine's jealousy. Retrieving the compromising trail of letters left by his wife, Félix is both freeing her from symbolic gaols (the secret drawers, the possibility of blackmail and exposure) *and* removing her from circulation. He signals that from now on she will remain in his possession.

What form of education would ensure that a woman, once she has passed from the father to the husband, will circulate no more? Again the thought comes to me that the passivity and timidity instilled into the sisters answers very well. Indeed, you could argue that making them literate at all is a mistake. In Molière's *The School for Wives* Agnès has been brought up to be as ignorant as can be by her tutor Arnolphe so he will not be cuckolded by her when he marries her. Arnolphe comes to regret bitterly that she has been taught to read and write at all when he finds out that Agnès can both read the love letters she receives from Horace, a young man who has seen her on her balcony, and reply to them.

You could also say that if Marie could neither read nor write she could neither fall in love with a poet (as Lady Caroline Lamb did with Byron) nor enter into correspondence with him. Here is yet another contradiction between the demand that an aristocratic lady be highly cultivated, and the demand that she be unresponsive to the consequences of literacy.

These consequences are double. Reading literature fosters feelings, but also the desire to apply those feelings, to act upon them, or to imitate them (as Madame Bovary does). But it also develops a dual consciousness, something akin to the knowledge of good *and* evil. Marie's access to double meaning is by way of poetry. She falls in love with poetry through a poet, as in Dante the courtly couple *par excellence*, Paolo and Francesca, have fallen in love by reading together about the love of Lancelot and Guinevere. Marie, who has been formed by music, is led to passion through the delights of imagination and metamorphosis. Courtly love and the poet's capacity to alter reality come to her both at once:

> The countess had been seized by ideas worthy of the times of knights, but quite modernized ... What a sweet thought! ... to be the secret creator of great fortune, to help a man of genius struggle with fate and tame it, to embroider his sash for the joust, to get arms for him, give him the amulet against evil spells and balm for his wounds! ... The least things in life now appeared charming to her.... *Toilette*, the magnificent poetry of feminine life, ... reappeared endowed with a magic she had not perceived before. It became for her what it is for all women, a constant manifestation of intimate thought, a language, a symbol. (pp. 327–8).

True, she fails to see through Nathan, who has seduced her with talk all white and blue, all angelic virtue and forget-me-nots, luring her with the thought she could be Rebecca to his Ivanhoe. But she knows she is courting danger; the narrator says that like all women she cannot resist the temptation to play with Bluebeard's bloody key. And if in the above passage the only poetry that she can make is that of *toilette* (she can *be*, not write, a poem), still her writing-box is also illuminated by love now, she can write letters – and for the first time in her life she responds to the magic of the salons around her.

As the novel goes on, with a contradictoriness which the reader must by now be accustomed to expect, she actually *becomes* the poet. 'Love was explaining Nature to the countess, as it had already explained Society to her' (p. 341). She becomes a visionary philosopher: 'Marie only lived for the life whose circles are intertwined like those of a sphere and at the centre of which lies the world' (p. 348).

I suggested earlier that the novel functioned according to the law of patriarchy, with the narrator as God/Adam, placing his main male character also in that position. Perhaps I was wrong. Lévi-Strauss defines women as the objects of exchange, what enables the symbolic, and culture as a collection of symbolic systems, to function.[28] On one level, Balzac's placement of Marie in relation to matrimonial rule and language/literacy verifies Lévi-Strauss. She *is* the object of exchange, the letter that circulates, not the one who does the exchanging. *And yet* she is also shown to be one who *can* know: she creates a language (*toilette*), rediscovers all by herself the world of symbols and the intertwined circles of the sphere. True, she does not actively become a poet, or a philosopher, or even a musician, though we are told that Mozart, Beethoven and others have 'developed in [the sisters] a thousand feelings that did not go beyond the chaste precincts of their veiled hearts but penetrated Creation where they flew on wide wings' (p. 280). It is clearly social constraints, not native incapacity, that makes feelings *and* mysticism the only realms of knowledge open to them: the vertical world is strangely open, it does not take them out of the precincts (*enceinte*), the closure of their hearts. Woman can only know the absolute from inside home or convent. But Balzac's Marie verifies what Catherine Clément describes as women's anomalous position in the eyes of anthropology. Marcel Mauss, she says, classes women with madmen, shamans and fairground acrobats as being double: on the side of the Rule, as wives and mothers; on the side of rules, *natural* periodicity, as something that disturbs the symbolic. Marie's doubleness is of a different kind. She is what has to be ruled (preserved from adultery) but also what has the power to generate the Rule: she has access to the symbolic. As a character, she defeats the patriarchal assumptions.

What makes all this so monumentally complicated is that the Rule keeps being altered by changing class assumptions. The nascent capitalistic ethos to which the coarser spirits in the novel subscribe wants Marie to circulate in a different way yet again. There is something about the processing of that exquisite idle product, the lady, that is seen to make her into an object of consumption for the lover, not the husband. After Nathan has first dazzled Marie, he goes out on a *souper fin* with bachelor cynics. Journalist Blondet spells things out for him:

> Blondet congratulated Nathan on having met a woman who was only guilty of bad drawings in red pencil, lean watercolour landscapes, slippers embroidered for her husband, sonatas executed with the chastest of intentions, who had been stitched for eighteen years to the maternal skirt, crystallized like sugar by religious practices, educated by Vandenesse and done to a turn by marriage to be savoured by love. (p. 308)

Projections and Subtexts

Surely, Balzac does not agree with Blondet?

Well . . . I go on saying Balzac, as if Balzac was one, not many, and as if the man and the author and the narrator were all rolled into one. Perhaps I need this one name to make it all cohere. For the contradictions that can be openly detected are compounded by those which the subtexts create.

Blondet may be a rake, but he has a point. Nathan has much more than a point. In many ways, Balzac has more in common with Nathan than with Vandenesse.

Socially, Raoul is closer to Balzac than Félix. Like Balzac he is an ambitious writer, hard up, hounded by creditors and bailiffs, a phenomenal worker, an outsider who wants to make it up to the upper classes and to use an upper-class woman to help him. Balzac had been helped by Madame de Berny, and it was another mistress, Madame de Castries, who had introduced him to the salons of the Fitz-Jameses and Madame Récamier – as Nathan is introduced by Blondet to Madame de Montcornet and Lady Dudley. Nathan, transformed from a Bohemian into a dandy, following Marie in the Bois de Boulogne, is like Balzac courting the Marquise de Castries. Nathan writes for the theatre; Balzac had just completed his play *L'École des ménages*. Nathan had left-wing opinions in his youth as Balzac did; he is veering towards 'juste milieu' as Balzac had to Carlism. Like Balzac he is a brilliant talker. Balzac the narrator says ironically that Raoul's speeches could go straight to his publishers, but that is presumably what his own did. Pointing out the similarities, the Balzacian critic Pierre Citron has called Nathan one of the 'affreux du miroir', one of the 'mirror horrors', Balzac projecting sometimes embellished, sometimes uglified, pictures of himself on to his characters. Nathan is also a compendium of contemporaries from the Bohemian milieu. His Jewishness and the assonance in the name Nath*an* recall Leon Cozl*an*, a writer and journalist. His physique, tall, powerful, almost gangling, bearded, long-haired, is that of Laurent Jan (note the assonance again), his unkempt, dirty looks before love has made him smart are those of Gustave Planche, a journalist friend of George Sand. His eventual support for whichever party is uppermost recalls Hugo's evolution from the Restoration to the July Monarchy. His boisterousness and success as a playwright are modelled on Alexandre Dumas, who had a liaison with an actress, Mademoiselle Ida, whom he eventually married, as Nathan does Florine. From his friend and fellow writer Théophile Gautier, Balzac borrows Nathan's waistcoat and extensive passages of writing. The two writers spent much time together in those years, influencing each other. Gautier corrected Balzac's scripts and made suggestions; Balzac quotes Gautier, or rather has Nathan ironically misquote a passage from *Mademoiselle de Maupin* about the 'blue flower' of the Ideal, after his love for Marie has come to nothing.

That Gautier, whom Balzac much admired, should be so pervasive, scattered throughout the text, and that Nathan should be drawn both from Balzac himself and from so many of his peers from the Bohemian milieu, changes the weighting of the novel. Certainly, Balzac reverses the roles. He, as narrator, chooses to make you, as reader, side with the husband rather than the Bohemian. But that, in the text, pulls against an undercurrent of sympathy for the lover. Nathan leads an exhausting life, sleeping four hours a night, writing, directing plays, editing his journal, supporting sundry enterprises, dealing in politics, *and* has to keep up with the social charade that allows him to see Marie. The contrast between the heroic exertions and financial acrobatics of the parvenu and the leisurely, despotic rituals of the rich is much to Nathan's advantage. There is also a moment when Nathan is genuinely in love with Marie, when the amount of labour Marie is costing him and the contagion of her own genuine passion are communicated to him. 'Besides,' Balzac explains, 'there is in any writer a feeling which is difficult to stifle, and which is the admiration for what is morally beautiful' (p. 341).

Yet another subtext informs Nathan's love. A seemingly unrelated and far-fetched epigraph to the Italian Countess Bolognini recalls happy days spent in Milan. The author cherishes them, he says, with 'truly Italian' constancy. Countess Bolognini was just a friend; her lover was Prince Porcia. The only visible link is that the countess's daughter was called Eugénie, and that initially Balzac had called his heroine Marie-Eugénie, not Marie-Angélique (he changed the names round); the countess will be a better mother to her Eugénie than the stern mother in Balzac's tale is to hers, the dedication says. Another, less visible, link is that Countess Bolognini and Prince Porcia were waiting for the death of the elderly husband of the countess, as Balzac and Madame Hanska were waiting for the death of Madame Hanska's husband before they could marry. The countess and her prince were luckier than Balzac and his Eve (Hanska), since they saw each other daily (Eve Hanska was in Poland). Thus, covertly, Balzac declares himself to be on the side of the lover. Thanks to Pierre Citron, we know who he was.

When in Milan, Balzac had also been made welcome by Countess Clara Maffei. It is said that upon meeting him she knelt at his feet, saying, 'I adore genius.' She was twenty-three, dark, small, slender, pretty, fond of music: Marie de Vandenesse is the exact replica of Clara Maffei. The situation of the two women, the real and the fictitious, is also similar. Clara was married, when very young, to an older, distinguished man, Cavaliere Maffei, who neglected her. She and Balzac met five years into that marriage; Marie has been married for five years when she meets Nathan. Like Nathan, to whom he gives his own age, Balzac had a mistress, Madame Hanska, whom he neglected while seeing Clara (as Nathan forgets Florine, who is touring *abroad*, at the height of his passion for Marie). Cavaliere Maffei got wind of the mutual infatuation, and wrote his wife a wise, affectionate letter. She should listen to him, he wrote, as if to *her own mother* (Félix likewise looks after Marie more like a protective mother than a traditional husband). Clara should beware of Monsieur de Balzac, who, though ugly (as Nathan is unkempt), has powerful charm, an extraordinary way with women, and the prestige of fame. He has the reputation of 'a libertine and an immoralist'. Clara is 'the love of Milan'. Were she to yield she would forfeit that love, be left a prey to 'grief and remorse'. Clara, it seems, heeded the letter – an effective piece of writing from the Cavaliere, which had removed his wife from circulation. Balzac returned to Paris. The 'truly Italian' constancy of memory he evokes, the proffered wish that his book could jump 'over the Alps', are not for Countess Bolognini but for Clara Maffei, or rather have been transferred from the one to the other. Writing *A Daughter of Eve*, Balzac was fictionalizing and disguising his own abortive love affair. Three years later he dedicated *La Fausse Maîtresse* (what a telling title!) to Clara.

Before he desired Clara, he desired Eve Hanska. Nathan desires Marie ... The narrator cannot always control his own desire for Marie. The wish for seduction at times runs away with the wish for protection. Only thus can some of the more bizarre contradictions be explained. Commenting on the cynical way in which rakes such as Blondet talk about Marie, speculate about her, the narrator says that women would think twice if they could hear men's talk. 'Fresh, gracious and modest creature that she was, how their jokes and buffoonery were undressing her and appraising her!' They're stripping her, he's indignant ... but he adds in the same sentence: 'but also what a triumph! The more veils she lost, the more beauties she revealed.' It is as if he wished her to be stripped. Her beauty is such, and so indestructible, that she'll be the more beautiful as she becomes the more exposed.

The Madonna and the Courtesan

> Bisexuality is not a fantasy of complete being, but the location within oneself of the presence of both sexes, evident and insistent in different ways according to the individual.
>
> *Hélène Cixous, 'Sorties'*

The narrative passes on, and with it the narratorial sympathies, from one character to another. Yet, as the title indicates, the centre is Marie. This is the story of a woman's temptation and her salvation from the Fall.

But that places her in a double situation. As the tempted, she is an active consciousness, she is fully human, she feels and acts: she does, after all, save Nathan from suicide and from bankruptcy. But, as Eve, to be saved from the serpent, that is, adultery, that is, knowledge of good and evil through love, she is passive. She is also the object of a struggle between husband and lover: she is the odds, the prize to be won. In short, she is, at one and the same time, someone who can and does know, and someone who is not allowed to know. The novel is indeed on a border, in the realm of the anomalous. Knowledge, for a woman, means both the opposite of ignorance and the opposite of innocence. Marie's education has aimed at making her innocent by making her ignorant. The novelist has – ambiguously – protested against this. Yet his narrative makes it clear that for Marie to help him achieve his dream of a good marriage (the reconciliation of woman's happiness with the sacrifice of her full human potential to society) she must remain ignorant: ignorant of the full depth of life. That is supposed to be innocence.

Marie must be seen as one who is ignorant of life, and the better for being ignorant. She is a child, who must learn to trust the husband Félix. She comes to know the extremes of heat and cold within the confines of her home, as once she had soared to creation on the wings of music, but within the *enceinte* of her chaste heart. Shame overtakes Marie when Félix reveals Nathan's affair with Florine: 'Fire was no redder than the cheeks of the countess.' When he asks her where her letters to Nathan are, and she realizes what this means, she suddenly feels cold. It is not passion as an adventure that makes her know extremes of feeling, this suggests, but the protected paradise of the rue du Rocher, the little rocky island where Félix has perched her. How narrow and *vertical* this makes woman's world! Yet, prior to this scene, Balzac has given her full stature as a heroine, he has entered her consciousness, made her encounter real life, struggle against the threat of death and ruin to the man she loves. He has invalidated his own thesis even before proving its validity.

This is not only because Balzac is so given over to his imaginary projections, so protean, that he records all that there is, including, again and again, the self-contradictory status of women in society, and the impossibility of solving that contradiction. It is also because of what has often been described as his own dual, or 'bisexual', nature. His own painfully repressed education at the hand of a cold mother equipped him with a ready sympathy for the fate of repressed girls. The heroine of his first novel, *Wann-Chlore*, is just such a girl, modelled on Balzac's sister Laurence – and she is called Eugénie . . .

But there is more to it than this. The introduction to *A Daughter of Eve* has a strange comparison in it. It describes the novelist as Scheherazade, condemned to telling a thousand and one stories (the almost infinite task of *The Human Comedy*). The public is the Sultan, always liable to have him executed if he ceases to please. The novelist has to pull himself back from the threshold of perdition. He is like Marie, whose secret text (the love letters, Balzac's own love for Clara Maffei?) has to be retrieved through a masquerade, a novel that can be exchanged for money (the *lettres de change*), that will sell and that in its turn will keep the audience in a state of suspense, will make them want to hear more, to read the next novel. The novelist is in the position of the woman as well as in the position of the man. He is writing something much more complicated than a patriarchal text, despite his title. He is both Félix and Marie. He is also Nathan, who needs Marie to save him. As the saviour, Marie is active, a tutelary figure, an end-point. If Nathan fails to make Marie his Béatrix, she has done better than that for him: she has almost been his Christ. (She has laid her reputation on the line to save him.) And perhaps Clara Maffei, as the true inspirer of the story, told by a writer who, unlike Nathan, was not a failure, has been Balzac's Béatrix.

It may be that Balzac was debating with George Sand and seeing her when he was writing this novel.[29] George Sand's own androgyny – if that's the right word – caused Balzac to perceive and accept that he himself, as writer, was both male and female, diving in and out of femininity. *A Daughter of Eve* at any rate acutely registers the fact that economic, social and political circumstances place men in feminine positions – if, by 'feminine', we mean passive and the object of exchange. Nathan, virile as he may be in so many ways and in contrast with Félix, who is as small, elegant and graceful as Nathan is tall, powerful and eloquent, is repeatedly 'feminized'. He is dependent upon patronage, a social outsider; he is kept to a certain extent by Florine, and Marie too has to find money for him; he signs *lettres de change* that circulate and put him in the power of lenders and bankers. Furthermore, he is Jewish, his father a bankrupt. Race as well as class are at work here. The bitchy Mesdames d'Espard and de Manerville complain of having to receive Nathan: it's all for the sake of the sweet revenge against Félix, but vengeance is dear.

Socially and financially vulnerable men, in Balzac, are often placed next to women. In *La Cousine Bette*, written a few years later, Balzac lodges his immigrant sculptor, the impoverished Polish Count Steinbock, in the same submerged, underprivileged quarter of Paris as the peasant spinster Bette and the illegitimate daughter/courtesan Valérie Marneffe. For a man to be dependent on the wealthy and institutionally powerful is almost tantamount to being a woman. Signing the *lettres de change* that can lead to his being expelled, the German music master Schmucke is being interchangeable not only with Nathan (who can go to gaol) but with Marie, who could be socially ostracized.

Schmucke is almost a possibility of *being* for her. For he is a true *innocent*, and his innocence is positive, not negative. He is drawn after an ideal model of the German man, all gentleness and naturalness, that several French writers of the period (Stendhal, Nerval) derived from their admiration for German Romanticism and German music. The figures of Bach and Hoffmann float around the eccentric chapel master. He has such purity, generosity and faith in his former pupils and present benefactresses that it doesn't seem to occur to him that by signing bills for such – to him – fantastic sums of money he is putting his life at risk. But he intimates that *if* he realized it he would do it with the same promptness. He is the real knight of the story. He is also someone whose gaiety and love of music elevate him above his dingy material circumstances: verticality is relevant to him too.

Marie's gradual involvement with Nathan literally acquaints her with dirt. When she gets the letter intimating he's committed suicide, she rushes out into the street in her nightdress, wrapped in a shawl, and gets a cab. Finding the squalid newspaper office and squalid stove at whose fumes Nathan is asphyxiating, she revives him, and drives him to a little hotel where the bailiffs will not find him. The compromising consequences of going to such a hotel with a man are obvious. She then sets about redeeming the *lettres de change* and this eventually takes her to Schmucke's rooms. They are incredibly, fantastically dirty. There is dust everywhere, shaving implements, leftover food and dirty crockery, and the whole thing is suffused with the yellow hue of pipe smoke. To get to the house, Marie only just manages to step over the mud in the street.

Mud is loaded in Balzac with metaphoric and metonymic implications. It signifies the poor, the downtrodden, the socially low. In a real way it *is* the mud of the streets of Paris: it was not until the Second Empire that the Prefect of Paris, Poubelle (who gave his name to dustbins), invented a systematic way of collecting refuse. Till then, mud, rubbish disgorged by houses, markets, shops, restaurants, mixed with the droppings of horses, made a walk through the often narrow streets impossible if you were not prepared thoroughly to dirty your clothes. Hence the enormous importance of arriving at a smart house with impeccable boots and trousers for a young man on the make, for it signified that he was sufficiently well-off to ride in a carriage or keep his own horse. Rastignac, the hero of *Old Goriot*, cringes when his spattered boots are shown up by dandy Maxime de Trailles's own dazzling boots and spotless trousers at the house of an elegant lady whose patronage he desires: the poor student that he is has had a lot of trouble getting the gear together, but he has not been able to afford a carriage. Ladies would not have dreamt of going on foot. Being seen walking in a dirty Paris street meant you were lost: you could only have been on an amorous appointment. Characters who are socially low in Balzac's Paris (like the trio Steinbock–Bette–Marneffe) live next to, and in, dirt.

You could almost argue that Nathan's dirty looks are left-wing, a declaration of sympathy for the lower classes. Bohemian artists liked to live on the margins of society; some of them wanted to be close to the People. Hugo meditated endlessly on the equation People = dirt, elevating dirt to a mythic status. *Les Misérables* contains an extraordinary exordium on the sewers of Paris, the 'intestine of Leviathan'. The refuse they carry could become manure, could become gold. As she stretches her hand towards the apple of knowledge, Marie descends from her rock into the muddy street, the dingy office, the louche hotel, Schmucke's filthy flat. She descends from her class to a lower one. So doing, she begins truly to learn something about life – becomes dimly aware of how, not the other half, but the other 90 per cent live. Pain and trouble energize her, develop her capacities:

> The countess ... spent the night inventing stratagems to get the forty thousand francs. In such crises, women are sublime. Driven by feeling, they arrive at designs that would surprise thieves, businessmen and usurers, the three classes of industrials. ... She went over the emotions [she had felt on saving Nathan] and felt herself more in love with the miseries than with the greatness. ... The countess had wished for emotions; they were welling up in her, awesome, but beloved. She was living more intensely through pain than through pleasure. (pp. 359–60)

Balzac in the period was writing a sequel to *Lost Illusions* called 'What Love Costs Old Men'. The old man in question is the banker Nucingen. He falls in love with a beautiful courtesan called Esther, who, under the masterly supervision of the convict Vautrin, pumps a million francs out of the banker. You could say that the countess has done as well as the courtesan. You say it even louder if you reflect that Nathan[30] has previously been kept afloat by Florine's generosity: she has sold her elegant furniture, the gift of wealthy lovers, to get the 50,000 francs he needed to start his journal, and she goes touring the provinces to earn him some more. Marie gets perilously close to being Nathan's whore, Nathan to being the pimp of the angel as well as the actress. Close: not there. Marie's love is 'sublime', 'charity' its basis. Schmucke is a 'Sainte Cécile' (bisexual too); Marie appeals to his disinterested love, which is religious, like his love of music. Marie does *not quite* touch the mud in the street.

The narrative has said earlier that Marie felt in her love the selflessness of the courtesan. The courtesan in Balzac is the double, but not the alienated double, of the good woman. How does it appear that Marie calls up Mary Magdalene? Well, there is Florine, to start with. At one point the narrator hints that, as Nathan has Florine to make love to, he does not press his suit quite so ardently as a less satisfied man might have done. Marie's virtue is partly saved by Florine. And, on a more metaphoric level, there is ... mud again, and its ability (as in Hugo) to turn into gold.

A cat inhabits Schmucke's apartment:

> The continuous use of a good old German pipe had suffused the ceiling, the wretched wallpaper scratched in a thousand places by the cat, with a blond hue that gave all things the appearance of Ceres' golden harvests. The cat, robed in magnificent dishevelled silk that would have made a concierge envious, was like the mistress of the house, free from care, grave under its beard. From the top of an excellent Vienna piano where it sat in judiciary splendour, it cast on the incoming countess the honeyed and cold look with which any woman struck by her beauty would have eyed her. It did not disturb itself, it simply waved the two silver bristles of its moustache and went on staring at Schmucke with its golden eyes. (p. 363)

The cat is female: it is Schmucke's companion, the mistress of the house, jealous of Schmucke's affection, queenly, it wears a splendid dress, it is a concierge, it regards the countess as a possible rival, and does whatever dusting takes place with its 'splendid tail'. It is also male, bearded and mustachioed, magisterial, the 'son' in the 'living trinity' composed of Schmucke, the cat and the pipe, a trinity in which the holy spirit, the pipe, suffuses everything with a golden haze, making it into a place of pagan and Christian splendour all at once: blond like Ceres' harvest, suffused with 'celestial rays' by Schmucke's smile, his 'sun'-like soul (pp. 364–5). Schmucke calls the cat 'Meinherr Mirr', Mirr, a name, he tells Marie, which he has borrowed from one of the fantastical tales of his great compatriot Hoffmann.[31] The whole scene makes you feel that Marie is being confronted by a world of magic, in which all dichotomies are transcended: all genders, all modes of being, the material and the spiritual, the materialistic, the surreal and the metaphoric, the pagan and the Christian. The power of transmutation which is there *can* make gold out of mud. 'This smoky bedroom, filled with litter, was a temple inhabited by two divinities': art and religion. But the countess remains on the threshold. Alice does not go through the looking-glass. There is not enough of the artist, or perhaps of the human being yet, in Marie for her to be able to *read* the reality that is being presented to her. She cannot interpret rubbish: in the 'heap of things' that are 'somewhere between manure and rags', Marie's eye is not 'exercised enough to find information about Schmucke's life': in the 'chestnut skins, apple peels, the shells of red eggs', the broken dishes 'crottés de *sauer-craut'*, 'muddied with sauerkraut'. Balzac is challenging his reader to go through the looking-glass, to dare to step into the mud. He is inviting his female reader to be a courtesan.

In the introduction to *A Daughter of Eve*, Balzac talks of the pains he takes to write, the nights of effort some paragraphs cost him. Through what seems an irrelevant and accidental choice, he quotes, as an instance of his most painstaking prose, a piece from 'What Love Costs Old Men'. It is the description of Esther's eyes – Esther the courtesan who pumps a million francs out of Nucingen. There are creatures in whose eyes the fascination of the deserts remains, for they are descended from races which have had a long intercourse with the vast spaces of deserts. Esther is such a creature. She is Jewish.[32] Her eyes are golden, like the eyes of another courtesan, the girl with the golden eyes.

The exotic courtesan is like gold, a currency that circulates. She is the locus of the dream of absolute pleasure, the dream of the oriental woman, almost, you could say, the gold standard of pleasure. She is 'an allegory of the "mystery" of bourgeois society', Marc Angenot states.[33] More and more as the century progresses, French literature will use the figure of the prostitute to create mystery, justify its fascination for refuse by making it exalting, use the prostitute as the 'synecdoche of modern society', the 'allegory of exchange value'. In Baudelaire, Zola and many others, the dichotomy whore/madonna will be elaborated. In Balzac, it is not a dichotomy. An earlier passage, describing Marie's gaze at Nathan, a gaze that is so unguarded that she risk compromising herself, says that it is 'violent and fixed', one of those gazes in which 'the will springs from the eyes, as luminous waves spring from the sun, and which hypnotists say penetrates the person at whom it is directed' (p. 362). Marie in love has the power and vulnerability of the courtesan. And in Balzac the courtesan is more than exploitable allegory. She can be golden in her own right. She can love. She never ceases to be human. In her passion she is self-forgetful and sublime. With all her vulgarity, jealous Florine is magnificent. The joke may be at the expense of Félix, ready to produce Florine's jealousy as a 'spectacle' for his wife.

And so, if we notice the parallels between the two visits, the visit to Schmucke and his cat, and the visit to the flat shared by Florine and Nathan, as untidy in its way as Schmucke's flat, if less dirty; and if we perceive the figure of Esther, the most sublime of courtesans, behind Florine and the cat – Esther whose eyes can fascinate because she is equal to anything, because she is descended from a race that has a millenary intercourse with the absolute – we have to ask where this leaves Marie's 'innocence'. In Schmucke's flat, she is poised on the verge of a world that is dirty but also heavenly, inhabited by true innocence, a religious artist.

She is on the verge of Hoffmann's fantastic world. When Félix has withdrawn her from the brink, is redeeming her letters from the soiled bedroom shared by Nathan and Florine, it is Florine, a vulgar and worldly yet passionate version of Esther, who remains in the world where transmutations can occur, where power is wielded. It is the world of ordinary material life, the narrative makes clear.

When Florine wants to rip open Nathan's secret portfolio with the letters of her rival in it, Florine first calls for a kitchen knife. 'C'est avec ça qu'on égorge les poulets' – 'That is what you slit the throats of chickens with,' she explains. 'Poulet', chicken, is also slang for a love letter. She then uses Nathan's razor to open the bag. A crude Freudian might say that Florine is the one who remains wielding the phallic tools, slitting open the 'female' bag. You could say, more to the point, I think, that if the voice of passion speaks plainly in her (she wants to cut her rival's throat), she is also the one who, through slang, remains mistress of metaphor. Knowledge, in its fullness, its ability to function on several levels at once, pertains to the fallen woman, who lives in dirt. Marie is left without true innocence (that remains with Schmucke) and without knowledge (that remains with Florine). It is difficult to know what to conclude: what to make of the haunting and ironic figure of the courtesan in a novel that has set out to prove that women would be well advised to remain perched on their paradise of a rock.

It is all the more difficult as Marie, the central protagonist, has been made to remain 'angélique', and as such could not *read* a text whose depth remains in excess of her. What does that make of a female reader such as myself who has endeavoured to decipher it? Woman's anomalous position in culture has been verified: her kinship is to other eccentric figures such as the Jewish poet and the immigrant Bohemian musician. What distinguishes her from these two, however, is that she is *split*. Knowledge and art are not taboo for them. Sex goes through Marie like a dividing line. Let us not forget that she is also *two*; there are two Maries, loving sisters so close to each other they are compared to Siamese twins at the beginning of the novel: marriage has parted them. Marie-Angélique, alias a daughter of Eve, must fall either on the side of innocence (be a Marie, a wife and mother) or on the side of knowledge (be Eve, or Florine). It is a mark of Balzac's bisexuality, the genuine ambivalence of the text, that he lets you see how phantomatic the dividing line is, how one sentence must contradict the other: how impossible the prevailing rule makes it to *think* that constructed chimera, woman.

Notes

Chapter epigraphs from Honoré de Balzac, *Mémoires de deux jeunes mariées*, in *La Comédie humaine* (Paris: Gallimard, 1966), vol. 1, p. 201; Hélène Cixous and Catherine Clément, *The Newly Born Woman*, tr. Betsy Wing (Manchester:

Manchester University Press, 1987) pp. 78 and 79. All translations from the French are mine.

1 Balzac, 'Avant-propos', in *La Comédie humaine*, vol. 1, pp. 4–5.
2 Introduction to *Une Fille d'Eve* (*A Daughter of Eve*), in the 1966 Bibliothèque de la Pléiade edition of Balzac's *Oeuvres complètes*, vol. 2, p. 263. References to this appear subsequently in parentheses in the text. I am much indebted to the excellent preface and notes by Roger Pierrot, especially for what concerns the 'subtexts' of the novel.
3 In this he is closer to the English novelists of the nineteenth century than to Stendhal: to Jane Austen or Mrs Gaskell, even to Charlotte Brontë or George Eliot.
4 Madame de Staël, *Corinne ou l'Italie* (Paris: Éditions des Femmes, 1979), and Balzac, *Mémoires de deux jeunes mariées*, p. 208.
5 The description of the upper-class young women is from Balzac, *La Physiologie du mariage*, in *Œuvres complètes*, vol. 1, pp. 694–5. On the debates of the period and generally speaking on the whole question, see Arlette Michel, *Le Mariage chez Honoré de Balzac: amour et féminisme* (Paris: Société d'Édition 'Les Belles Lettres', 1978).
6 Michel, *Le Mariage*, p. 66, and Balzac, *La Physiologie du mariage*, p. 646.
7 Molière was much discussed at the time. Théophile de Ferrière, in *Les Romans et le mariage* (Paris: H. Fournier Jeune), a novel published in 1837 (the year of *A Daughter of Eve*, indeed a novel which Balzac was answering in writing *A Daughter of Eve*), quotes both from *Les Femmes savantes* and *The School for Husbands* in his preface. Balzac himself directly referred to Molière's title in his play *The School for Married Couples* (1842).
8 See Isabelle Bricard, *Saintes ou pouliches: l'éducation des jeunes filles au XIXe siècle* (Paris: Albin Michel, 1985). Only 'liberated women' like George Sand and Clémence Badère, she says, dared speak of how they were 'brutalized' by their husbands; and she quotes Marie Capelle's account of her resistance to hers. Marie Capelle became Madame Lafarge, celebrated for having poisoned her husband with arsenic. Sentenced to life imprisonment, she wrote bolder memoirs than most of her women contemporaries. It is now thought that she was wrongfully accused and condemned (ibid., pp. 271–3).
9 Michel, *Le Mariage*, pp. 68–9.
10 Balzac, *La Physiologie du mariage*, pp. 661–3.
11 See *Modeste Mignon* and *Ursule Mirouët*.
12 Balzac, *Mémoires de deux jeunes mariées*, pp. 209, 279.
13 See Michel, *Le Mariage*, p. 197, and p. 188: 'Bonald connaît sous Juillet un regain d'actualité.'
14 Hélène Cixous, 'Sorties', in Cixous and Clément, *The Newly Born Woman*, pp. 84ff.
15 See the first three chapters of Bricard, *Saintes ou pouliches*.
16 Bricard's own term.
17 Jules Barbey d'Aurevilly, *Les Bas-bleus* (1st edn, 1877; Geneva: Slatkine, 1968), p. xxii.
18 Joseph de Maistre, *Lettres et opuscules inédits* (Paris, 1851), vol. 1, p. 148.
19 Dr Fonssagrives, *L'Education physique des jeunes filles* (Paris, 1869), p. 50.
20 Bricard's account of school curricula in France in the period could be a demonstration of Balzac's accuracy. See Bricard, *Saintes ou pouliches*, pp. 104–5, in particular.
21 The lot had to be learned by heart, even if your heart was not in it, which it could hardly be, if you were a girl and could inherit neither power nor title.

There is much irony in another Balzac novel, *Albert Savarus*, in which the clever but ignorant heroine, Rosalie de Watteville, is an expert at genealogy, one of the few things she has been allowed to learn.

22 The Abbé de Montmignon is inflicted upon other Balzac heroines, Rosalie (above) and Véronique Graslin in *Le Curé de village*.

23 Music was taught extensively at home and in schools. It was all piano. The convent of the 'Augustines Anglaises' had thirty and Saint-Denis had fifty in *one* room (Bricard, *Saintes ou pouliches*, p. 59)! It was thought, however, that music could have a dangerous erotic influence, as was said to have been demonstrated through experiments on animals. Music might hasten the 'oncoming of nubile desires' in girls. 'There is in melody something sympathetic which makes the heart melancholy and incites it to open up': a nice transference from the cunt to the heart! (*Dictionnaire des sciences médicales*; see Bricard, pp. 112–13.)

24 An 'explosion' is what happens to Rosalie de Watteville in *Albert Savarus*, in *La Comédie humaine*, vol. 1, p. 770.

25 George Sand in *Mauprat* (1837 – also the year of *A Daughter of Eve*), then in *Consuelo* and *La Comtesse de Rudolstadt* (1842 and 1844), argues that love alone, which makes man and woman into equals, will give back to marriage its sacred character. Only when this has come to pass will people be allowed to exclaim 'how beautiful humankind is!' – 'Que l'humanité est belle!' (See Michel, *Le Mariage*, p. 120).

26 Michel, *Le Mariage*, p. 195.

27 Balzac, *La Physiologie du mariage*, p. 69.

28 See Claude Lévi-Strauss, *Les Structures élémentaires de la parenté* (Paris and The Hague: Mouton, 1971), p. 73: 'The exchange of women has preserved its fundamental function. On the one hand, because women constitute the essence of property [*le bien par excellence*], but above all because women are not, to start with, the sign of social value, but a natural stimulant; and the stimulant of the only instinct the satisfaction of which can be put off ('différé, deferred'): the only one, consequently, through which, in the act of exchanging and perceiving reciprocity, a transformation can be effected from the stimulant to the sign, and thus defining the passage from nature to culture, blossom into an institution.'

29 On George Sand, see *Romantisme* pp. 13–14 (1976), special issue: *Mythes et représentations de la femme*.

30 The name Nathan in Hebrew means 'the one who gives'. Bizarrely, Nathan is the prophet who is sent to David to reproach him for his seduction of Bathsheba. My thanks to Marcelle Sanders for pointing this out to me.

31 The similar name 'Mürr' suggests *mürren*, to grumble, or *mürrisch*, surly or morose. The only readily available pun in German is *mir*, me (dative); so on the level of devious pun the cat may be Schmucke or Hoffmann, or of course Balzac. My thanks to Bob Jones for his help with this.

32 Esther is the (unknown) daughter of Gobseck, the Jewish usurer, one of the few truly wise men of *The Human Comedy*. Needless to say, it would be interesting to try for a 'Jewish' reading of *A Daughter of Eve*, with, as the title already suggests, its manifold biblical references.

33 See Marc Angenot, *Le Cru et le faisandé: sexe, discours et littérature à la Belle Epoque* (Montreal: Labor, 1986), pp. 189–91.

2
Maleness in the Act: The Case of the Papin Sisters

On the evening of 2 February 1933, in the quiet rural French town of Le Mans, a Monsieur Lancelin, a well-to-do retired solicitor, was annoyed. His wife and daughter, who were supposed to join him at a relative's for dinner, were late. He tried to phone home: no reply. He became worried, went to his house: the door was locked from the inside; nobody answered when he rang. Yet the maids at least must be home: a dim light shone in their attic window. M. Lancelin went to the police. A policeman climbed through the window at the back of the house. And the horror began. Madame Lancelin and her daughter, a young woman, lay across the landing. They had been murdered, were battered and slashed. Most horrible of all, their eyes had been torn from their sockets: so vile had been the fury of their assailant.

He must have been a mad burglar, a vicious and sadistic monster. And what about the maids, two young women who lived in the house, who had shown no sign of life, had failed to answer the door . . . ? They also . . . ? The policemen rushed upstairs to the attic bedroom. It was locked from the inside. They smashed the door open. The maids, the two sisters, Christine and Léa Papin, lay in each other's arms, in bed. They were clean, if dishevelled; they wore only pink dressing-gowns. Next to the bed was a hammer soiled with blood. They had killed their mistresses, they said.

In the second volume of her autobiography, Simone de Beavoir has produced a good account of the reaction of the French intelligentsia. The case immediately attracted a great deal of attention. The trial, which took place in September, was attended by forty Paris journalists, reporting for a fascinated readership:

The tragedy of the Papin sisters was immediately intelligible to us. In Rouen [where Simone de Beauvoir was teaching at the time] as in Le Mans, perhaps even among the mothers of my own pupils, there certainly were some of those women who subtract the price of a broken plate from their maids' wages, who put on white gloves to track down motes of dust that have been left on the furniture: in our eyes, they deserved death, a hundred times over. With their waved hair and white collars, how good Christine and Léa seemed, on the old photograph which the papers published! How could they have become the haggard furies which the snapshots taken after the drama offered to public indignation? What was responsible was the orphanage in which they had been put as children, the way they had been weaned, the whole hideous system devised by so-called good people and which produces madmen, murderers and monsters. The horror of society's grinding machine could only be exposed by a corresponding, exemplary horror. The two sisters had made themselves the instrument and martyrs of a dark justice. The papers told us that they loved each other, and we dreamt of their nights' caresses and hatred, in the desert of their attic.[1]

Simone de Beauvoir goes on to explain that she and Sartre ('we') had been bewildered by the defence's plea of paranoid delirium, and then convinced by it. It had meant that the murders were not a gesture of freedom, more one of blind terror. They were 'loath to believe this' and continued 'dimly to admire' the sisters. But when the psychiatrists for the prosecution declared them sane, they were 'indignant'; and so incensed by the complacency of the bourgeois members of the jury who sentenced the elder sister to death despite the fact that it was now evident that she was insane that they came to see society as worse than the sisters, 'tarnished' as their crime might have been by insanity. Since the victims were 'bourgeoises', the murderers had been made into 'scapegoats', so that 'so-called civilized society', which was no more enlightened than 'so-called primitive societies', could continue on its repressive path.

The passage is filled with a strange irony. Strange, because while the tone suggests that the writer is mocking the rigidity of young idealistic Parisian intellectuals such as Sartre and herself and some of their philosopher friends, nothing further is said to show that their wish that the sisters had killed lucidly – as existential heroes before the letter, as it were – was patronizing, or that other readings of the case might have been tenable. The mature Simone, who wrote this passage, seems unaltered in her hatred of petty-bourgeois employers and mother figures, or in her dislike of the 'grinding-machine' that produces murderers, then makes them into 'scapegoats'. What is noteworthy here, however, is that when you replace the passage inside the chorus of actions and representations that the case of the Papin sisters attracted in 1933, its sense of easy recognition strikes an unusual chord: the crimes were immediately 'intelligible'; the young Jean-Paul and the young Simone had no trouble detecting the 'mystifications'. But everybody else thought the case was deeply mysterious. Reason was struck blind by the sisters, as if their plucking out of their mistresses' eyes had metaphorically put out the eyes of the interpreters.

Take Jacques Lacan's essay, based on the findings of the psychiatrist
for the defence, Dr Logre, and published in 1933 in a Surrealist review:

> The two sisters, 28 and 21, have been for years in the household of these
> honourable bourgeois ... It has been said that they were model servants,
> that people envied the Lancelins for having them; they were mystery-ser-
> vants also, for if the masters seem to have been strangely lacking in human
> sympathy, nothing indicates that the servants' haughty indifference was
> simply a response to that lack; from one group to the other, 'nobody talked'.
> This silence, however, could not be empty, even if it was obscure in the eyes
> of the actors.
>
> One evening, 2 February, this darkness is materialized by a banal blow-
> ing of the fuses. It has been brought about by the clumsiness of the sisters,
> and the mistresses, who are not there, have already shown a quick temper
> on lesser occasions. What mood did the mother and daughter show when
> upon their return they discovered the slender disaster?[2]

Christine and Léa Papin had been about to do the ironing. The iron blew
the fuses through no fault of their own. Mme Lancelin had been
extremely annoyed when this had happened before. The iron had just
been mended. And at that point, Mme Lancelin and her daughter, who
had gone out shopping and were supposed to go straight from there to
their dinner, turned up unexpected at the house. Found it in darkness ...
And ...

And this is where the blinding, as well as the blindness, occurs. It is
twofold (of course: there are two sisters; everything has, as Lacan points
out in his article, a double dimension here). First, the motive: how can
something as *'mince'* (Lacan: thin) as a damaged iron or blown fuses provoke such a savage and disproportionate murder? Second, the idea of
metamorphosis: how can model servants turn into – as the sensational
review *Détective* put it – 'enraged ewes'?

Let us note – interestingly – that Simone de Beauvoir owns that she
and Sartre did find the second black or blind spot, the metamorphosis,
puzzling: 'what good girls they seemed ... how could they become the
haggard furies ... ?' But Simone, speaking for once very much for herself
– not saying 'we', as she does throughout most of the passage – has no
trouble with motive. She has only to think of the mothers of some of her
pupils, of her own anger at examples of domestic bourgeois tyranny, and
it makes the case 'immediately intelligible' to her. Unlike the communist
paper *L'Humanité*, she does not have to blacken the situation, imagine
that a system of slavery existed in the Lancelin household. I do find this
interesting: hers is a lone voice, and one that seems to arise from a gender experience – not just a female experience of domesticity, but identifying with the killers as daughters against the mothers. It is a point of entry
which the male commentators of the period seem to be lacking.

Two famous journalists reporting on the case, the Tharaud brothers,
on whose articles Lacan's paper was based, stressed the darkness at its
core:

No photograph can give an idea of the mystery that enters [into the court-room] with these two girls. Léa, the younger one, all in black, her hands inside the pockets of her coat, her eyes open, but you know not what they're seeing. Christine . . . remains motionless with a stiffness that seems corpse-like.

Her eyes are closed, and from 1 p.m., when the trial opens, to 3 a.m., when it closes, she will not open them once, not even to reply to the questions she is asked.[3]

One has her eyes open, but she does not see. The other has her eyes closed. The sisters physically embody the lack of rational vision from which the onlookers suffer. For, as one of the Tharaud brothers goes on to say, how do you reconcile the fact that everything that is said at the trial should evoke horror, but that, looking at the sisters, 'not once did I feel a horror corresponding to that act'? For them also, then, the darkness arises from the metamorphosis – but also from the lack of motive: how can such 'butchery' have taken place when the motive was 'nothing': *'un motif de rien'*, the episode of the iron?

Of course (you might say), women would understand the charge of domestic details better than men, and this is what Simone de Beauvoir is doing. So what? The real mystery, which is the mystery of madness – paranoid delirium, as Lacan calls it, and as even de Beauvoir accepts – remains intact, a matter for psychoanalytic explanation.

Yet the fascination of murder cases is that they do not stop at the crime itself, the perpetrators, the victims, the immediate surroundings. Every representation or explanation that is offered becomes part of it. Murders – partly because they touch chords we had rather not allow to vibrate in everyday circumstances, partly because they awake in us the desire for retributive violence (Lacan speaks of the gruesome literal appropriateness of the phrase 'an eye for an eye') – reveal things which nothing else reveals as clearly. The case of the Papin sisters is particularly significant in terms of gender.

It was the Surrealists Breton and Péret who, in a short, dramatic piece in their review *Le Surréalisme au Service de la Révolution*, launched the sisters as a literary phenomenon. Holding the notion of gender in mind, let us see how they tackle point two, metamorphosis: what mysterious alchemy changed model servants into 'enraged ewes'?

The Papin sisters were brought up in a convent in Le Mans. Then their mother placed them in a bourgeois home. For six years they bore observations, demands, insults, with the most perfect submissiveness. Fear, weariness, humiliations, were slowly begetting hatred inside them: hatred, the very sweet alcohol that secretly consoles, for it promises to add physical strength to violence one day. When the day came, Léa and Christine Papin repaid evil in its own coin, a hot iron coin. They literally massacred their mistresses, plucking out their eyes, crushing their heads. Then they carefully washed themselves and, freed, indifferent, went to bed. Lightning had fallen, the wood was burnt, the sun definitely put out.

They had come fully armed out of one of Maldoror's songs . . .[4]

Christine and Léa Papin (photograph owned by their mother)

Christine and Léa Papin after the crime
(police photographs)

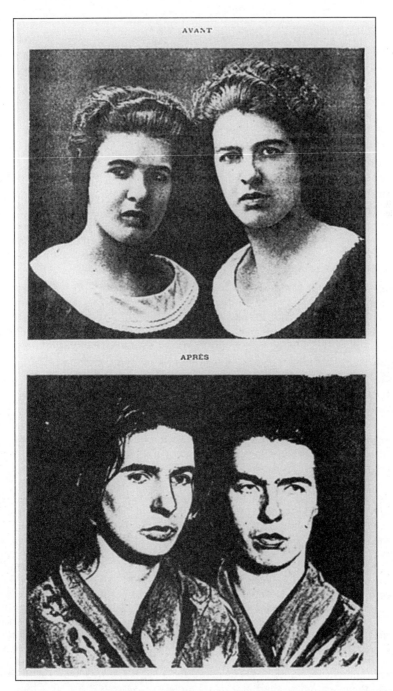

Photomontage: 'Avant' — 'Après' ('Before' — 'After'), from *Le Surréalisme au service de la révolution*, end 1933

Maldoror is the satanic rebel and eponymous hero of Lautréamont's poem *les Chants de Maldoror*, one of the Surrealists' favourite texts. The early, succinct details here register the female gender of the sisters: the convent education, the nun-like obedience, being in the mother's power. The final image is of Athena, emerging fully armed out of Zeus' head. Athena is a female goddess: femaleness seems to be consistent. Let us reflect, however, that the coming to power of Athena in the history of Athens signifies the waning of mother-right. Athena is born from a male god, without the intervention of any woman. Did the crime emancipate the girls from their mother, from all mothers? Furthermore, in this piece, Maldoror, a male hero-poet, conceives violence, as his creator, the male poet Lautréamont, conceived him. And in the photographic montage designed to accompany the article, the sisters 'before' look like proper young women. 'After', they do indeed look like young men. Indeed, the montage graphically exemplifies – and perhaps contrives – the metamorphosis. You cannot look at those two pairs of faces, at the captions 'before' and 'after', without thinking about the crime that separates them, that made the one into the other. In the context of the Surrealists' article, Christine in particular does rather look like . . . André Breton.

Does that mean that through the act of killing, women become men – that a nobler, a revolutionary, male and poetic self is thus born? Does this further imply that women as women cannot emancipate themselves, cannot kill? It certainly looks as if Breton and Péret, through this passage and through the montage, were recuperating what they saw as the poetic charge of the deed for themselves, young men such as themselves. They glorify the heroes, not heroines, who rebelled against the bourgeois order, got rid of the mothers. The transformation is effected through the image of hatred as a sweet alcohol, breeding violence and physical strength in the womb-like sisters. They are almost Pythonesses, the Delphic oracle through whose writhing body Apollo the liberating, vengeful male god can at last be born.

The protagonist of Sartre's short story 'Erostrate', written in the mid 1930s, has either been reading Breton and Péret, or is of a like mind:

> I have seen photographs of these two beautiful girls, the servants who killed and devastated their mistresses. I have seen their photographs 'before' and 'after'. 'Before', their faces swayed like tame flowers above their embroidered collars. They exhaled hygiene and a savoury honesty. A discreet pair of curling tongs had given their hair an identical wave. And, even more reassuring than their curled hair, their collars and their air of being at the photographer's, was their likeness as sisters, their so proper resemblance, that straightaway spoke of blood bonds and the natural roots of the family group. 'After', their faces shone like blazing fires. They had the bare necks of those about to be beheaded. Wrinkles everywhere, horrible wrinkles of fear and hatred, folds, holes in the flesh as if a beast with claws had gone round and round on their faces. And those eyes, always those large bottomless black eyes . . . Yet they did not look alike. Each bore in her own way the memory of their common crime.[5]

This is obviously a complicated passage, with several possible readings. It is fiction, spoken by an anarchist, out to commit an act of self-regarding terrorism. Erostrate is glorifying himself as criminal-to-be while and through glorifying the sisters. He is voicing his hatred to maidenly bourgeois propriety, but there is also a mixture of fascination and sadism there: he insists on the eyes, with the knowledge of what these women did to other women's eyes. He invents or adduces the decapitation motif: if anything, the sisters' necks are more bare in the 'before' than in the 'after' photograph; and it is as if he projected the hurt that the sisters inflicted on their victims on to the 'after' faces. I cannot see those holes and wrinkles he describes. Is the gloating, the fascination, meant to portray the mind of Erostrate? Only the mind of Erostrate? It seems evident to me that there are some recognizable Jean-Paul Sartre motifs here also: distaste for the ideology and the bourgeois order of the family. Distaste for neo-fascist theories, those that insist on blood bonds and sameness. The speaker's horror of the sisters' resemblance in the 'before' photograph conveys Sartre's individualism. The apparent gratuitousness of the deed introduces the Sartrean notion of freedom. Yet one thing is remarkable here. The gender of the sisters is visible only when they are being perceived as potential victims: when their *bien-pensant* look enables the speaker to voice his hatred of *bien-pensant* women – it is as if what had to be murdered was precisely this quality in the sisters, as if the 'after' women had killed the 'before' women. They are also perceived as female when their exposed necks, their belaboured faces, suggest decapitation or torture.

As killers, as sadists themselves, they are never seen.

It is, to say the least, worthy of note that male writers who are revolutionary in their lifestyle, discourses, poetic and fictional voices, are so conservative in their reading and writing of gender. Neither the specific class and familial reality of the maid in a domestic household, nor her sexual position, nor indeed the particular history and tragedy of the Papin sisters, bother them. Their deed becomes an empty vessel. Their bodies and the (hysterical?) inscriptions that can be read on their faces, that can be imagined on the eyeless bodies of the victims, become the bearer, the trace and the vacant container that enable the male poet or terrorist protagonist to make divine and murderous metaphor. The Breton and Péret text evokes familiar Surrealist tropes, deflagration and phosphorescence and sudden illumination ('lightning had fallen', 'their faces shone like blazing fires' in the Sartre), black suns ('the sun was definitely put out'), Bataille's *The Story of the Eye* with its displacements on to male genitals, its reference to Dali and to the eye as a 'cannibalistic titbit'. A 'phallic' tool ('the axe had fallen') replaces the servant's bare hands and use of any domestic implement that was to hand. The overall effect is very similar to what a conservative poet like Valéry might have achieved with his 'Pythie' whom the god Apollo possesses, through whose writing and wordless contortions Divine Language is born. It makes the sisters into the sufferers and recipients, not the actors, of their deeds. And in the process, it raises questions often raised elsewhere as to the use of women (in particular of lower-class women), and the imaginary use of women's bodies, by left-wing ideologies.

But perhaps one must turn to psychoanalysis for an open exploration of the mysteries of the case, the nothing motif, the metamorphosis of the sisters, the missing act? Certainly this was what Lacan thought; what many since have thought. Lacan's essay, written straight after the publication of his thesis on *De la Psychose paranoïaque dans ses rapports avec la personnalité*,[6] endorses the radical findings of the psychiatrist for the defence, and fleshes them out. It has been seen as seminal, the first formulation of the mirror stage.

For Lacan, there was one powerful sister, Christine, exerting her influence over the younger, more timid sister, Léa. Both sisters harboured a homosexual tendency directed at each other. The fact that sister loved sister shows that there was a strong element of narcissism in that love. Each sister loved the being most like herself, the being in the mirror. The 'sacrificial exigencies' of society were integrated as sadism. A love–hate relationship was at work, making the unattainable-because-tabooed sister into a persecuting figure, just as President Schreber, whom Freud analysed and found to be paranoid, had made God, the loved father figure, into a persecutor. A glass obstacle, the complaint of Narcissus, forever prevents the sufferers from this particular psychosis from being liberated from this love–hate relation to the persecuting figure. 'Between themselves the sisters were unable to take the distance that is needed to hurt one another. True Siamese souls, they form a world forever closed.'

Lacan suggests that the sisters killed their mistresses because they saw in them their own mirror image, 'the mirage of their own complaint. It is their own suffering that they project and hate in that other couple of women,' and they pluck out their eyes 'as the Bacchae castrated'. They kill their mistresses as they might kill each other and themselves. Too close, too 'Siamese' to take the right distance to hit at each other. And also female, therefore castrated, they are punishing other women for their own native mutilation.

A recent book by Francis Dupré, a Lacanian analyst, admiringly develops Lacan's analysis and adds to it a multiplicity of explanations. In particular, Dupré says, the verdict of schizophrenia, offered by the psychiatrist who examined Christine after her death sentence had been commuted to life imprisonment, must be added to that of paranoia. Dupré's book is called *La Solution du passage à l'acte: Le double crime des soeurs Papin*. The title itself suggests the answer: the deed, the murders, which contemporary commentators saw as the mystery, was itself the solution, the only solution, to the unbearable pressures created by a paranoid state that was verging on schizophrenia. That the deed should be the solution means in a sense that it cannot be spoken, it cannot be understood in words. Dupré argues that it is at the opposite end of the spec-

trum to Freud's Schreber, for whom, on the contrary, verbal systems prolif-
erated. With Christine and Léa, it is the deed that speaks. They themselves
have nothing to say, nothing about their deed. When, under lengthy questioning, they produced varying and self-contradictory reports, Léa very
much modelled herself on what she was told Christine had said. Their testi-
mony, you could say, defies reason. For instance, Léa claimed that she had
held one of Mme Lancelin's arms pinned down, her head back with
another hand, and battered her with a pitcher. The judge: 'You had three
hands then?' Léa: 'No, but I accomplished my foul deed just as I told you.'
Christine also produced some extraordinary answers, then refused to
speak. Muteness accompanies blindness. The act confirms Lacan: 'This
silence could not be empty, even if it was obscure in the eyes of the actors.'

Some of what Lacan says and most of what Dupré says comes across
as sympathetic, ingenious, convincing, or at least persuasive. I certainly
have no psychoanalytic expertise or counterexpertise to offer. If, however, I read their texts as texts, still with the idea of gender in mind, I am
struck by the concordance of what they say with the Surrealists or Sartre.
Lacan was, after all, writing for the Surrealist review *Le Minotaure*; he
was the Surrealists' friend. Perhaps, then, one should not be so surprised
at the recurrence of explanations that make the sisters into non-actors
(passive), non-speakers (silent), non-knowers (ignorant/innocent).

1 *Passive* They are compared to the Bacchae, who in a state of frenzy,
   possessed by the spirit of a male god (Dionysus), murder a male god
   (Dionysus). Not only is it the male in them that kills, but the enigma
   that bedevils them is that of female castration, a 'gaping wound'. It is
   their impotence, their frustration with their own inability to act out
   their desire for each other, that urges them.
2 *Silent* Duprés entire book is based on this: they cannot speak, they
   can only act.
3 *Ignorant/innocent* Lacan presents them as unaware of their own
   desire, as realizing it only after the murders, when Christine, in a state
   of despair and madness in jail, throws herself on to her sister, scream-
   ing, 'Léa, say yes.' There is strong evidence, however, to suggest that
   the sisters were lovers, and that Christine, a country girl, was not as
   'innocent' of the 'mystery of life' as Lacan says.

Not only, therefore, is there in the psychoanalytic accounts offered here
the same assumptions as one sees everywhere else – designed, it seems,
however unconsciously, to keep women in their place. Active/passive;
speaker/silent; knowing/ignorant; the binarisms that Derrida, Cixous
and Irigaray have pointed to as the hallmark of phallogocentrism, that
keep 'women' permanently in the inferior position, are at work. The discourse of psychoanalysis may well be as culturally relative and question-
able as every other one – all the more so as the explanations offered in
some instances contradict or disregard the known facts.

Dupré's sense that since an intuition of genius is at work here, the gaps or mistakes do not matter, and his desire to demonstrate the brilliance of Lacan's article despite the fact that his own findings show that he seriously misread things help to perpetuate stereotypes which, in the detail, he questions. Why does Lacan do nothing with the fact that he mentions in passing: that the young women had a brutal alcoholic father, who had raped or seduced an older sister, who had had a major impact on Christine's life? In the light of the work of the former psychoanalyst Alice Miller on the major repercussions of childhood abuse or trauma, and the abreactive quality of much mental illness, we may now wonder how central 'the enigma of female castration' was. The sheer mention of 'castration', suggesting impotence of some sort, when discussing a deed of shocking violence requiring exceptional physical strength, suggests that some unconscious motive is at work. Every man's account that has been examined so far seems to tend to one end: to guard against the unacceptable idea that women have killed. Either the act, or the sisters' gender, has to be suppressed. Why? Is it fear? Upset at the destruction of comfortable or nice ideas about women? Or not wanting to let them have access to a terrifying form of power?

I began with Monsieur Lancelin: Monsieur Lancelin being out of the house when the murders were committed, kept out by the door which the maids deliberately bolted before going to bed – out of kindness, perhaps, to spare him the awful spectacle, or because they felt he had nothing to do with any of it. That they should so markedly have signified that Monsieur was excluded makes it all the more ironic that so many men should have dealt with the case. It seems as if, for the sisters, the men of the powers that be – the police, the judiciary, the psychiatrists – were made genderless by their institutional quality. It is interesting that they were defended by a woman barrister, and that the more telling bits of evidence about their behaviour after their arrest came from female wardens. Also, the only piece of genuine research into the life and private history of the sisters was conducted by a woman, Paulette Houdyer, who wrote a novel about them called *Le Diable dans la peau*. Some of her findings contradict what Lacan, for one, suggests. Like Simone de Beauvoir, she has no sense that the case is unintelligible to the lay mind. Since the book is written as an imaginative biography, and is full of persuasive information, I shall describe it as if it were fact – on the understanding that in a case in which there were no witnesses, and about which the perpetrators always refused to say what they knew, everything is faction.

Christine and Léa Papin were the daughters of country people, from the vicinity of Le Mans. The father, Gustave Papin, worked at a sawmill and drank too much. The mother, Clémence, enjoyed the company of men. She was not the motherly type. She had to get married because the first daughter, Emilia, was on the way. When Christine, the second child, came along, she gave her to her sister-in-law, Gustave's elder sister

Isabelle, to bring up. When, seven years later, Léa, the third daughter, was born, she gave her to a great-uncle to bring up. Christine is reported to have been happy at her Aunt Isabelle's, and to have imbibed from her a distrust of men. Isabelle had had a small inheritance left to her by an elderly employer, whose maid she had been. She enjoyed her independence. She had seen her own mother destroyed by too many pregnancies. She disapproved of Clémence's activities: a woman was all right as long as she kept away from men.

Christine's happiness with her aunt came to a brutal end when she was seven. Her father, Gustave, had seduced Emilia, her elder sister, who was ten or eleven. Houdyer claims that Emilia was not Gustave's daughter, that she loved her father and was willing. Be that as it may, Clémence reacted with (understandable) fury, but also with (as Houdyer presents it) vindictiveness. She divorced Gustave: he never reappeared, fought in the First World War, then married someone else. He kept no contact with his daughters. Clémence put Emilia in a religious orphanage that was known for its harshness, the convent of Le Bon Pasteur in Le Mans. For good measure, she removed Christine from Isabelle's care (as Isabelle was Gustave's sister) and sent her also to Le Bon Pasteur. Baby Léa was entrusted to the great-uncle, and Clémence made a living as a maid, doing odd cleaning jobs.

The harshness of Le Bon Pasteur, where she spent eight years – between the ages of seven and fifteen, and where she learnt to be an excellent housekeeper and seamstress – was relieved for Christine by the protection and love of Emilia, whom she worshipped. At the end of the war, because she had lost all hope of getting her father back (according to Houdyer), Emilia became a nun. Clémence was furious: just when the girl could have started earning, could have been a help to her! Christine wanted to become a nun too. Clémence used her legal rights as a mother to forbid this and removed her from the convent, placing her as a maid. Christine was fifteen. From then on, she transferred all her love to her little sister Léa. Her aim in life became eventually to find a place where she could be with Léa, where Léa and she could be employed by the same people. She eventually found the Lancelin home, in which they had been employed for seven years when the tragedy occurred.

Still according to Houdyer – but this makes sense in terms of the other documents that have survived – Clémence loved Léa but not Christine. She tried to get the younger girl back in a variety of ways, and was to succeed much later, since Léa, after serving her ten-year sentence, went to live with her mother (Christine died of self-imposed malnutrition after a year in jail). But while at the Lancelins', Christine fought her mother for her sister's love, and won. Some time before the murders, when the Lancelins were away, the sisters went to see the town mayor, claiming that they were being persecuted, that their mother was the source of the persecution, and asking to have Léa emancipated from her mother's custody. The mayor thought they were disturbed, but nobody really took much notice of the episode. Mme Lancelin, however, had backed the sisters in their bid for emancipation. She had agreed to pay their wages directly to them, not to their mother. She sent Clémence packing if Clémence tried to see the girls. Clémence wrote strange letters, warning her daughters to beware of masters and priests, who take daughters away from mothers. As Dupré says, the Papin sisters were three, not two. The mother was the hidden third, also feeling persecuted. You might even claim they were four, if you think of Emilia in her convent, choosing the celestial Father, or husband. Certainly Christine and Léa showed no interest in men. They went to church; they saved money carefully. A medium had told Christine that in her next life she was to be her sister's husband. Their plan seems to have been to save enough to start a small business, then leave. And live together for ever.

It makes a lot of sense to see the disaster of the iron and the blown fuses in the context of the enormous passional domestic charge that had built up inside the Lancelin household. Mme Lancelin had come to occupy the position of the mother, the potential persecutor. Houdyer imagines that Christine and Léa were interrupted by their mistresses while they were making love. To the daughters of a man who had committed incest with their elder sister when she was a child, to women who believed that by keeping away from men they stood a chance to better themselves, to sisters who had found in each other's love all the compensation they needed for their disappeared father, their unloving and abandoning and dictatorial mother, their other lost sister, the words incest and homosexuality must have meant very little. They knew, though, that if they were caught in the act they stood to lose everything: their reputation as model servants, their chance of another job, each other ... their mother had intruded yet again, was about to separate them yet again ... 'I was black with anger,' Christine would say to one of her interrogators. It does not seem to me so difficult to understand why.

There is not the space here to comment fully on Houdyer's book, but it strikes me that while her documentation is impressive and her empathy makes her intuitive, some of her interpretations are open to doubt. Clémence the mother is presented in an unremittingly hostile light, when some of the details given make you feel sorry for her against the grain of the book. Was she more of a victim than a villain? And if she was so awful, why did Léa go back to live with her? More disturbingly, it is hard to swallow the idea that ten- or eleven-year-old Emilia was so happy to be seduced by her father. There is no evidence for this. One could read her entry into the convent as the refusal of men, and her sisters' equal refusal of men as the reaction of young women who have been thoroughly put off at an early stage. I mentioned Alice Miller above. In the light of the work that she and feminists have done in recent years on incest and child abuse, the bias of Freud's theories about the daughter's seduction and all that followed from this bias, surely a reading different from Houdyer's is possible.

I am struck, however, by the fact that when a woman writes about the case, it becomes intelligible, the act is written about as an act. Instead of 'female castration' you have *une histoire d'amour*, a love story.

This opens a can of worms, and I shall let the reader take a peep before I put the lid back on. Have I used the term 'gender' in the crassest possible way, arguing that when men write about the maids they see one thing; when women write they see another? Is it the case that each writer, man or woman, attempts to project the scenario that is most flattering, most agreeable, most self-aggrandizing to their own sex? Is there no truth, then – do men see women in a particular way, women see themselves in another, the two views being irreconcilable? Is it a question of power? Does sex determine a writer's gender position?

Evidently not: if it were so, perhaps Houdyer would not have been so forgiving to Gustave, so merciless to Clémence. Simone de Beauvoir would not have sympathized so readily with the murder of the mistresses. And a writer like Genet would not have written *The Maids* (1946).

Genet the homosexual, the thief, does not deny the sisters their act. Of course, since this play is by Genet, act here assumes the meaning of acting, actor, acting out, as well as of deed. But instead of the *'délire à deux'*, the twin delirium, that Lacan found, Genet focuses the entire play on the build-up to the murder. All is there to be seen, and all is theatre. What is blind and unrealized in the sisters according to Lacan is conscious and acted out in the Genet.

There are two sisters, Claire and Solange. Claire is the powerful one, as Christine Papin was. The two sisters both love and hate Madame. They play in turns at being Madame, and at being each other: Claire is Madame while Solange is Claire. The mirror, in other words, is not only present to their consciousness, they play at entering it and coming out of it, they constantly play at being other. It enables them masochistically to enjoy being humiliated as the maid and sadistically humiliating the maid as Madame. It also enables them not to be so, since it is make-believe. It enables them to act out their hatred in pretend rebellion and vengeance against Madame, and to plot the murder of Madame. The acting out is magic – it gives them distance from and control over their situation. Solange is never humiliated as Solange, but as Claire. Claire, pretending as Madame to humiliate her sister, is humiliating somebody called Claire. And vice versa.

Furthermore, the sisters not only know that they love each other, they are lovers. 'Their eye is clear,' Genet says, 'for they masturbate every night.' No plucked nor blinded eyes here, no after-the-event discovery. Whereas Lacan claimed that it was only after the murder that Christine Papin cried out to her sister, 'with the eyes of passion that at last is no longer blind: "Say yes, Léa, say yes" ', and whereas Lacan insists on female castration and blindness, on murders that are pure delirium, Bacchic possession, Genet creates lucidity, magic control, willpower. For in the end, as Madame has escaped from the sisters, as she has failed to drink the poisoned cup prepared for her by the sisters, Claire, dressed up as Madame, drinks it: thereby making both her sister and herself into the murderers they wanted to be. For Solange will claim to have poisoned her sister, and be guillotined for the murder. Claire and Solange choose to die impersonating whom they are not. They become murderers through a double suicide. In that sense Genet is not far from Lacan's claim that the killing of the mistresses by the Papin sisters is an attack against themselves. But he is a very long way from Lacan in every other way: in the sisters' recognition and acting out of their homosexual and incestuous desire, in their magic control over their fate.

You might say: it's all very well to claim that Genet makes the sisters lucid, and actors, where the Surrealists or Sartre or Lacan make them into Pythonesses, male heroes, or Bacchae. But Genet is completely reinventing the case – his maids do not kill Madame, they choose poison, they are clever, arguably sane, not a bit naturalistically presented; whereas all the others are representing or discussing the real crime, the real sisters. Genet can do what he pleases, and you may like it better. We can see you coming a mile off. You're about to argue that Genet, because of his own homosexuality – because of his real, and chosen, and enduring marginality – is better able to imagine femininity, to conceive of the maids as murderers and female, than these other writers who, whatever their motives, either virilized the sisters or saw them as prompted to castrate out of their unconscious horror at their own castration. Genet's play may be an agreeable alternative to you, but what does it have to do with reality?

More than meets the eye, I would answer. I would indeed hold that Genet, because of his gender position, was able to see things that none of the others could see. I would be tempted to add that it is precisely because there is so much theatre about his theatre that he puts his finger on truths the others were blind to.

His maids, for one, are, in terms of social and domestic power, infinitely more real than Lacan's or Breton's. Their talk is of sinks and spit and rubber gloves and putting on or dealing with Madame's clothes. It is of poverty versus wealth. It is of the strange female intimacy that the respective positions of maid and mistress generate – what was immediately clear to Simone de Beauvoir and to no one else. No slender disaster here, but an ongoing tragedy. His maids fail to kill Madame and are destroyed instead because in the real world maids do not kill their mistresses, and when the odd one does, it changes nothing in the system of mistress-ship or mastership: maids go on working and sleeping in cold attic bedrooms. The Papin sisters are recuperated as male revolutionary heroes by the Surrealists. The prosecution, presenting the Lancelin family's case, denies their humanity. Refusing the plea of insanity, the prosecution barrister said, 'they are not enraged dogs, they are snarling dogs.' Receptacles for a male god, or animals: women, never. And it seems to me that it is this denial of the Papin sisters' common humanity that Genet – among other things – dramatizes.

Genet insisted that the play was to be acted by men only: Madame, Claire and Solange must be played by male actors. Sartre saw this as Genet's dislike and refusal of the female sex:

> One might read this demand of Genet's as the expression of his pederastic taste for young boys; yet this is not the essential reason for it. The truth is that he wants from the start to *radicalize appearance*. No doubt an actress could play Solange: but the unreality will not be radical because she will not need to act being a woman. The softness of her flesh, the limp grace of her movements, the silvery sound of her voice will be *given*; they form the substance which she will fashion as she pleases to make it appear as Solange. Genet wants to make this female clay itself into an appearance, the result of a comedy. It is not Solange who must be a theatrical illusion, it is *Solange the woman*. To achieve this absolute artificiality, nature must first be eliminated: through the roughness of a breaking voice, the dry hardness of male muscles, the bluish sheen of a nascent beard, the degreased (streamlined), spiritualized female will appear as man's invention, as a pale, gnawing shadow – which cannot rise up to being on its own: the evanescent result of an extreme, temporary contention, the impossible dream men might have in a world deprived of women ... Everything must be so false it sets your teeth on edge. But as a result, woman, since she is false, acquires poetic density. Exfoliated from her matter, purified, femininity becomes a heraldic sign, a cipher. As long as it remained natural, the feminine blazon remained glued to woman. Spiritualized, it becomes a category of the imagination, an organizing schema of dreams: everything can be 'woman': a flower, a beast, an inkpot.[7]

This is seductive, and it contains some truth, although the unconscious misogyny is breathtaking: the female, all softness and limp flesh, is redeemed here only by being 'degreased', spiritualized – equal to an inkpot, mind you, neither the ink nor the pen – and made into a ... cipher. Passive, silent, ignorant, impotent, and now both a vessel and nothing. Oh deary deary deary me. How familiar. No wonder Simone de Beauvoir had a hard time.

I think that by stipulating male actors Genet is pointing to the fact that the men who write – or wrote – about the maids make – or made – them into men (rather as he insists that there must be a white audience for his play *The Blacks*). It is not that maleness or femaleness is this or that particular bundle of qualities, as Sartre claims, but that men have used the sisters as vehicles or receptacles, and Genet is subverting the show. Perhaps, as Philippe Lacoue-Labarthe suggests, 'masculinity imagines itself but poorly; it can only, at most, imagine itself by feminizing itself.' The Papin sisters' crime provided the Surrealists & Co. with something that nothing else provided – in particular an opportunity to feel good about the overthrow and destruction of the bourgeois mothers. Women had done it for them! Long live the Papin sisters! The matrix of the act, the empty socket, had been provided. All that was needed was to inhabit that space, put an eye in it.

There is a paradox at the core of the Surrealists', of Lacan's and even

of Sartre's representations. Here is an all-female crime: two women kill
two women. Here is a specifically female form of class hatred. It happens in the home, in a domestic set-up. 'Downstairs' erupts and floods
'upstairs' with the disorder it is supposed to contain. The kitchen –
where animals and vegetables are taken apart, made into appetizing
and tidy meals for the mistresses – dismembers the mistresses: kitchen
implements were used, incision as on to a rabbit made upon the
corpses' legs. Maids, *'bonnes à tout faire'*, exploited by their bourgeois
mistresses, but no more so than thousands of others, with no particular
degree of cruelty or ill-will on the part of the mistresses, turn on their
mistresses with an exceptional degree of violence. In provincial bourgeois households of that period in France a mother–daughter dimension
often pervaded the mistress–maid relationship. This was especially so in
the Lancelin household where Madame Lancelin had helped emancipate the sisters from their mother's power, had moved into the mother's
position, was even called at times 'Maman'. There was a double charge
to the relationship – mother/daughter, mistress/servant. It was coupled
with another doubleness – two mistresses, the mother and daughter;
two servants, two sisters, partly playing those roles, Christine being a
sort of mother to Léa. It was exacerbated by the daily rubbing against
one another, one lot of women washing the underwear and dirty plates,
ironing the clothes, making the beds and picking up the mess of another
lot – by the intimacies, the object-laden claustrophobia of a provincial
bourgeois home. It is hardly surprising that all this, given the sisters'
profoundly perturbed family history, should have brought hatred to a
pitch: being found 'bad', faulty, instead of *'bonnes'*, 'good', being
rejected, Cinderellas to the good daughter, was unbearable. 'Observations', critical remarks, *'Encore!'*, could not be borne. The blown fuse
blew the fuse. But as well as this specifically female set-up, men's
absences from the case are striking: no fathers anywhere, no lovers. All
the male roles have been redistributed among the women: Clémence
was possessive and authoritarian, claiming paternal rights to her daughters' earnings. Madame Lancelin moved into a legal, patriarchal position
as well as being master in her own house. Christine protected her sister
and wanted to be her sister's husband in some other life. I feel tempted
to say that the lack of a father figure of any kind is what made the situation ultimately murderous: in Kleinian terms, no penis on to which to
project and redirect the aggression against the bad breast. No one to
stand between the infant's desire to maul and shove bad things into the
mother's body, and that body. The sisters' attempt to get the *'maire'*, the
mayor whose title echoes the word *'mère'*, to emancipate them from
their mother argues an obscure desire to have a male, another source of
authority, stand in between themselves and the mother, cut across an
overcharged situation. The attempt failed, the mayor thought the sisters
were deranged (which of course they were): the call for help was not
heard. The absence of males from the scene may have been what made

the murder possible, perhaps inevitable. In that sense, the *act* was deeply *female*.

The paradox is that this being so, the male commentators saw a *male act*. Lacan sees castration: 'They kill as the Bacchae castrated.' But it is a king, a male, not a mother and daughter, that Euripides' Bacchae castrate ... Which suggests that Lacan, alongside Bataille and other Surrealists, sees the eye as phallic, a sign of potency: the plucking of the eyes is made at one with the plucking of balls. The Papin sisters are seen as violently protesting against female castration. I myself see this as a male anxiety about castration, a masculine angst projected in two ways: on to a fantasized phallic mother whose eyes need plucking out, so that male potency can be regained; on to the eye, seen purely as an agent of power, the sign of potency, both persecutor and what in oneself is most endangered, around which the threat of castration is at play. The wealth of images of aggressed, severed, pierced eyes in the Surrealists is evidence of this. So-called ocularcentrism or sexual vision has attracted many remarkable studies in recent years, and I refer my reader to their insights, especially where they concern the Surrealists. In his startling essay 'Oeil', a sort of companion piece of his 'Histoire de l'oeil', the Story of the Eye, which speaks contemptuously of 'les gens honnêtes', respectable citizens, as having 'les yeux châtrés', castrated eyes, Bataille evokes Buñuel and Dali's *Chien andalou* film, with its shot of a razor slitting through an eye. The eye is both what attacks, and what must be attacked. It has the horrible power of conscience, a godly, reproachful eye: as in Grandville's nineteenth-century plate, the eye can pursue the criminal even unto the sea, where changed into a fish it finally devours him (see illustrations).[8]

For Bataille as for Lacan the identification of the eye with male genitals describes their own preoccupation with potency and power, not the eye itself. It is their own fantasy. Eyes are eyes after all, and they do many things ... That Madame Lancelin should have made 'observations', which means both to observe as the eye does and to say something critical (pursuing the criminal into the recesses of the sea?) does not make her male. Her power is the power of the mistress, the mother, on a vulnerable child/menial. Who knows but that she, herself, as a child, had been subjected to 'observations' ... It is hatred of that power, that makes them 'nothing', that makes Christine and Léa attack. The eye that gets attacked is the mother's eye. Its being perceived as phallic is a projection – the projection of a wounded and anxious generation of men.

But in *The Maids*, although the three actors are men, there is no entry for men. The real sisters shadow Claire and Solange's performances, as a real black revolution is carried on in the wings while the blacks of the play by that name carry on their parodic rape and murder of a white girl by a black man for the benefit of a pretend white audience, or as the revolution rages and aborts while the women of the brothel-Balcony act out their clients' favourite fantasies. That Claire and Solange should fail to kill Madame and could only kill themselves, that they only achieve

From J.-J. Grandville's last drawings, 'Premier rêve – crime et expiation' ('First dream – Crime and expiation'), *Magazine pittoresque*, 1847. Referred to in Georges Bataille's 'Oeil' (1929) and reproduced in vol. I of *Oeuvres complètes* that contains 'Histoire de l'oeil' (The Story of the Eye)

symbolic and make-believe emancipation, is a comment on the fact that the Papin sisters failed to kill mastery: that the whole case is a theatre, a decoy, that enabled the powers that be to carry on in the wings. And yet – for in Genet there is always a swing of the pendulum; sometimes the revolution succeeds and sometimes it fails – the maids' symbolic triumph is a powerful, an exclusively female one: even though the case never ceases to be represented by men.

But there are no men in the cast of the play. Madame has a lover, Monsieur, but Monsieur never appears. Monsieur does not matter, Monsieur has nothing to do with the tragedy that unfolds entirely among women – just as there was no Monsieur Lancelin.

The sisters have not finished generating representations. There have been films, other plays ... there is a strange dynamic at work here that continues to vex interpreters. What emerges strikingly from the material considered here is the refusal of the act, the denial of the 'eye', the 'I' of the sisters by all commentators identifying with a 'male' position. I think this is through fear of the potency of the act, fear of potential female power. Certainly, such a case makes manifest the importance as well as the trickiness of the concept of gender. There can be no 'truth' that does not take it into account. 'My crime is great enough for me to speak the truth,' Christine said. The question of truth, it seems, is shot through with the question of gender. What is at stake in the interpretations seems almost more important than the interpretations themselves.

Through their account of the case, everyone expressed what it mattered to them to express. De Beauvoir showed that murder can be understood as a revolt against injustice. The Surrealists saw the deed as a Romantic rebellion against a bourgeois order that stank. Sartre saw it as fierce individualism, freedom from the glueyness not just of existence but of femininity. Lacan saw it as an attack against the self in the mirror, and hatred for female mutilation. Houdyer saw it as the extremity of passion; Genet as the individual's power to control his or her fate through symbolic words and deeds.

Whoever creates shadows brings forth a world. It seems to me that ultimately, for men and women alike, it is the nobility of the world called into being that matters. Genet's gift of tragic grandeur to his Solange and his Claire, however remote in point of fact they may be from the Papin sisters, makes him, for me, far superior to anyone else. His recognition that the sisters were somehow himself ennobled the man who was capable of such openness:

> Sacred or not, these maids are monsters, as we are ourselves also when we dream of being this or that. I cannot say what theatre is, I know what I won't allow it to be: the description of daily gestures seen from the outside. I go to the theatre so that I can see myself, on stage ... such as I could not – or would not dare – see myself or dream myself, and yet such as I know myself to be.[9]

'Pride is faith in the idea that God had, when he made us,' Karen Blixen wrote. 'The barbarian loves his own pride, and hates, or disbelieves in, the pride of others.'[10] Only the civilized being is able to love the pride of his or her adversaries, his or her servants or bosses, his or her lover. Startlingly, of all the men who wrote about the Papin sisters, only Genet the outcast, Genet the thief, was civilized.

Notes

1 Simone de Beauvoir, *La Force de l'âge* (Paris: Gallimard, 1960), pp. 136–7. All translations in this chapter are mine.
2 'Motifs du Crime paranoïaque', *Le Minotaure*, no. 3–4 (1933).
3 Jérôme and Jean Tharaud, in *Paris-Soir*, 30 Sept. 1933.
4 *Le Surréalisme au Service de la Révolution*, no. 6 (1933), p. 28.
5 In J.-P. Sartre, *Le Mur* (Paris: Gallimard, 1947).
6 Published by Éditions Lefrançois, Paris, 1933.

7 J.-P. Sartre, *Saint Genet, comédien et martyr* (Paris: Gallimard, 1952), pp. 361–2.
8 Georges Bataille, 'Oeil' and 'Histoire de l'oeil', in *Oeuvres complètes*, vol. 1 (Paris: Gallimard, 1970), pp. 187–9 and p. 45. On sexuality and vision see Rosalind E. Krauss, *The Originality of the Avant-Garde and Other Modernist Myths* (Cambridge, Mass.: MIT Press, 1984) and *The Optical Unconscious* (Cambridge, Mass.: MIT Press, 1993); Jacqueline Rose, *Sexuality in the Field of Vision* (London and New York: Verso, 1986); Hal Foster, *Compulsive Beauty* (Cambridge, Mass.: MIT Press, 1993); David Michael Levin (ed.), *Modernity and the Hegemony of Vision* (Berkeley: University of California Press, 1993); Martin Jay, *Downcast Eyes: The Denigration of Vision in Twentieth Century French Thought* (Berkeley: University of California Press, 1994).
9 J. Genet, *Les Bonnes* and 'Comment jouer les bonnes', *Oeuvres complètes*, vol. 4 (Paris: Gallimard, 1968), p. 269.
10 Isak Dinesen, *Out of Africa* (New York: Vintage, 1985), p. 271.

Part II

Masculine/Feminine: The Battle of the Sexes and the First World War

3
The Missing Men and the Women's Sentence

The missing men   Barbara Tuchman, describing the 'bloody punishment' which the First French Army in Lorraine received as early as August 1914:

> *Offensive à outrance* found its limit too soon against the heavy artillery, barbed wire and entrenched machine guns of the defense. In prescribing the tactics of assault, French Field regulations had calculated that in a dash of 20 seconds the infantry line would cover 50 meters before the enemy infantry would have time to shoulder guns, take aim, and fire. All these 'gymnastics so painfully practised at maneuvers', as a French soldier said bitterly afterwards, proved grim folly on the field. With machine guns the enemy needed only 8 seconds to fire, not 20.[1]

The result: men mown in rows as by scythes. Staggered arcs of corpses littering the fields.

The missing men   During the course of the First World War, one-quarter to one-third of the male population of Brittany between the ages of sixteen and sixty was killed.

   Keegan, the celebrated author of the *The Face of Battle*, tells how, in the Battle of the Somme, in the first hour, 20,000 men died on the English side alone. Half a million men died in that battle, counting the German and the English sides.

The missing men   From my grandfather's First World War notebooks, 29 October 1916:

> Brayon, my 'infirmier major', returning home from leave has seen at Saint Just military station a soldier raging at being sent back to the front. He had

been freed and returned from Germany for being grievously wounded. He
was protesting against being sent back, showing to the entire station that he
no longer had penis or balls. The captain who'd come to shut him up, on
seeing him went away without daring to say anything, seeming to think
that he was right.

A chapter from Gilbert and Gubar's *No Man's Land 2*, which examines
the literary battle of the sexes around the First World War, suggests that
what my grandfather saw was the experience of the many:

> From T. S. Eliot's mysteriously sterile Fisher King and Ernest Hemingway's
> sadly emasculated Jake Barnes to Ford Madox Ford's symbolically sacrificed
> O None Morgan and Lawrence's paralyzed Clifford Chatterly ... the
> gloomily bruised modernist antiheroes churned out by the war suffer
> specifically from *sexual* wounds, as if, having travelled literally or figura-
> tively through no man's land, all have become not just no-men, nobodies,
> but *not* men, *un*men.[2]

The missing men   From Charles Carrington, a veteran: 'On this side of
our wire everything is familiar and every man is a friend, over there
beyond the wire is the unknown, the uncanny.'[3]
   From Ford: 'goblin pigs ... emerging from shell-holes, from rifts in the
torn earth, from old trenches.'[4]
   From T. S. Eliot's *The Waste Land*:

Who are those hooded hordes swarming
Over endless plains, stumbling in cracked earth
Ringed by the flat horizon only[5]

Sassoon, in 'Counter-Attack':

Mute in the clamour of shells he watched them burst
Spouting dark earth and wire and gusts from hell,
While posturing giants dissolved in drifts of smoke.
He crouched and flinched, dizzy with galloping fear,
Sick for escape, – loathing the strangled horror
And butchered, frantic gestures of the dead.[6]

The missing men   Many went mad, of course. What had been regarded in
Charcot's days at the Salpêtrière and by Freud and Breuer as *the* female
malady, hysteria (connected by a long line of medical interpreters, from
Hippocrates and Galen onwards, with *hyster*, the uterus, the womb),
now, in the later years of the Great War and in the years following it,
became a *male* malady: there were more male sufferers than women, and
they had gone through the war. Ironically, if that be the word, the very
enforced powerlessness which had contributed to the men's breakdown
was of the essence of some of the treatments they received. In *Hysterical
Disorders of Warfare*, Dr Lewis Yealland describes how in his clinic at

Queen's Square, London, in 1917, he dealt with a soldier who had gone mute. Elaine Showalter recounts:

> The soldier was fastened down in a chair, his mouth was propped open with a tongue depressor, and strong electric currents were applied to his pharynx, causing him to start backwards so that the wires pulled out the battery. At this point Yealland explicitly reminded his patient of the obligations of his masculinity: 'Remember, you must behave as the hero I expect of you ... a man who has gone through so many battles should have better control of himself.'[7]

Septimus Warren Smith, the returned poet-soldier in Woolf's *Mrs Dalloway*, similarly advised by general practitioner Holmes that 'health is largely a matter in our own control' and he should try 'bromides, porridge, the music hall, hobbies and cricket' (while nerve specialist Bradshaw threatens to have him committed), jumps out of the window.

Colette's Chéri has survived the war better than most. Being in the trenches, month in, month out, year in, year out, required above all patience, the ability to endure idleness: brought up as Chéri was in a milieu of leisurely courtesans, himself the gigolo of the ageing courtesan Léa, he has known how to do nothing. He has not gone mad, unlike so many of the soldiers whose fates are evoked in Pat Barker's novel *Regeneration*, despite the trauma of having had his friend Pierquin struck dead and thrown upon him by a chance explosion. Yet like Septimus Warren Smith, Chéri kills himself after returning from the war. Haunted by the realization that the Léa and the pre-war world he loved, and the Chéri he was, are now dead, he chooses the 'manly' exit: he shoots himself.[8]

The missing men   'Saturated'. That's the word that witnesses use to describe the battlefields where you see nothing but earth, the men being dug deep inside the trenches. 'Saturated'. The word that comes to be used for an earth that's so full of men's corpses that it can't absorb any more flesh. Akhmatova's poem 'July 1914' – pre-war – is appallingly prophetic:

> If the land thirsted, it was not in vain,
> nor were the prayers wasted;
> for a warm red rain soaks
> the trampled fields.[9]

To Rupert Brooke's words of November–December 1914, 'If I should die, think only this of me: / That there's some corner of a foreign field / That is forever England', there answers Owen, 11 September 1918 – the first draft of 'Smile, Smile, Smile': 'This Nation, one by one, has fled to France / And none lay elsewhere now, save under France.'[10]

The women's sentence   How to survive when the men are missing. How to keep things going, the fields, the factories, the buses, themselves, the children, when the men are gone. How to survive the sons', husbands', brothers', sweethearts' deaths. Millions of unmarried, unpaired women throughout Europe. How to endure the mourning, one's own breakdown. Out of such experience, Vera Brittain wrote her *Testament of Youth*.

My own great-aunt Zeth, rather like Vera though of a more modest home in Marseilles, learnt to overcome her fear of men while working as a nurse throughout the war. In 1918 she fell in love with an air-pilot who had been disfigured. They became engaged. Her – one-legged – father insisted she break up the engagement out of duty to the family, and because 'the children might be born disfigured'. She gave him up. When she died, we found a small biscuit tin with one love letter and one poem in pencil. She asked to be buried in her nurse's uniform. The uniform could not be found until too late . . .

The women's sentence How to go back home after all the excitement of work, of the public place. How to readapt to ancient roles, patriarchal family structures, how to deny what you have learned, how you have grown, for four years. As the woman in the pub scene in Eliot's *A Game of Chess* says, 'Now Albert's coming back, make yourself a bit smart.'[11] How to cope with the returning soldiers. Their neurasthenia. Their suicides. The wrecked landscape of the front, the perhaps unprecedented segregation of the sexes and disparity between the experiences of men and women for close on five years, struck terrible blows at the relationships of the married survivors, and of future couples: there could never have been a time before when such huge numbers of men and women had lived apart, doing such different things, for so long. Vera Brittain spoke of 'a barrier of indescribable experience' between men and women, possibly becoming 'a permanent impediment to understanding'.[12] In his 1918 letters home, my grandfather keeps wondering, after a leave, which is the 'true' life, so alien are the front and 'l'intérieur' that each in turns appears to be a dream.

Aldington wrote to his wife H.D.: 'There are still two more years at least for you to face without me . . . I shall be 28 then, a little bitter, disappointed, my work perhaps ruined, my mind infinitely agitated, myself useless for making money. Dooley, Dooley, I'm not worth the waiting for.'[13]

I used to have a vision of the twenties as one of severe misogyny. Every modernist writer or poet (Even Sassoon, Owen, Rosenberg – but I mainly thought of Eliot, Pound, Ford, Lawrence) seems to say something hateful or contemptuous about women and femininity. There is matrimonial vitriol in Picasso's period paintings, white phallic female statues in De Chirico's deserted townscapes. The French Surrealists formed an all-male movement, relegating women to exclusive wife-and-mistress roles or making iconic wax emblems of them to hang on the ceiling or lay beneath lobsters on the feast table of the Marquis de Sade. Hatred, contempt: then erasure. It's taken a lot of recent digging to discover that there were a lot of women Surrealists, just as it has taken second-wave feminism to rediscover the plethora of formidable women, and women writers, from West to Holtby and H.D., in England in the 1920s. When Woolf, in *A Room of One's Own*, goes in search of the missing women in the British Museum library, and discovers male *anger*, she was encountering the spirit of the decade face to face.

Two ventures altered my perception. In the process of writing a novella about an affair of the German Crown Prince in the 1920s, and imagining what it must have felt like – being the Kronprinz, having his father the Kaiser lose the crown without himself having ruled despite his own strong views, having been forced to obey orders to continue the holocaust at Verdun despite his early understanding that the bleeding by numbers bled nearly as many German as French soldiers – I gained strange sympathies. Strange, because as a little child in the Second World War, and through reading unbelievably patriotic children's literature from the First World War, I had acquired tenacious nationalistic prejudices, so that it was quite an eye opener to see things from the other side, knowing how Germany was to turn out, what brewed out of that defeat of empire. Strange, because I experienced from the inside of a character what male impotency must feel like. A couple of years later, I found and began to work around family papers from the First World War. They'd been kept by my grandfather, were his diaries, notebooks, bundles of letters he'd kept. He was totally unheroic, a doctor, a pacifist, not from principle but from temperament: an only son, doted on by his parents, headstrong and individualistic – but also open and inquisitive. He hated the war from the first. On 6 November 1914, enjoying a respite, he writes to his cousin Albert, not in the war (he was a Jesuit):

> Ah my good Albert the motherland is a fine thing when one is in Marseilles close to a good fire and a well-made map on which every day one places little flags. But when you see for what motives and with what casualness they take your life to risk it in the bloody game of war, then it's another business!

He doesn't mind being regarded as 'bizarre', or risking his life to go into the trenches to dress wounds or nurse a fever. What he hates is 'being a slave'. 'I suffer atrociously from being a cog in an abhorred piece of machinery. What is heroic about acting under compulsion?'

> What has this immense conflict of commercial interests to do with me? And let them not talk to us about Alsace-Lorraine. It isn't worth the skin of one of our soldiers. . . . Fine talk, 'the country's higher interest' and all those fine phrases. Don't let yourself be taken in. Try to escape from this terrible slavery.

My grandfather was lucky. He was only wounded once, and lightly. But the main sad story that the notebooks told was of such pain and alterations in both himself and my grandmother that, as the wear and tear of five years took its toll, one could begin to imagine how such a great love as theirs could have died as thoroughly as it did in the post-war years. A journal entry of 1930 quotes Colette's *Ces Plaisirs* about all loves coming to their 'aboutissement', and there being nothing left to theirs. As a child and adolescent, I was brought up by great-aunts on the legend of my grandparents' great love. I witnessed it as anger, bitter resentment, vindictiveness.

Jungian analysts Maria Torok, Nicolas Abraham and Viviane Jullien-Palletier have worked on the transmission of what they call 'zones mor-tifères' from generation to generation, up to the third and fourth. It became clear to me that love between the sexes was, as Vera Brittain says, one of the worst long-term casualties of the Great War, and that the 'mortiferous zones' are still with us: that in that sense I was as much implicated in the fate of the men as in that of the women.

This is not to suggest that the battle of the sexes hadn't raged before. Keats's 'La Belle Dame Sans Merci', Vigny's threat in his 'Samson', wounded as he was by his lover Marie Dorval's affair with George Sand, that from now on 'les deux sexes iront chacun de leur côté,' plus all the evidence adduced by studies like *No Man's Land*, amply show that the problem in itself was not new. There are many excellent studies of fin-de-siècle sexual angst, from Praz's *The Romantic Agony* to Djikstra's *Idols of Perversity* and Stott's *The Victorian Femme Fatale*. What was new it seems to me was that, in Europe at least, there never had been a generation of men so thoroughly slaughtered and unmanned before, and that the women found themselves in their turn unwomaned by the missing men. I no longer take the 1920s misogynist pronouncements at face value. The mystery, it seems to me, is why, 'half the seed of Europe' having been (to use Owen's image) butchered by fathers who, unlike Abraham, would not substitute a ram for their sons, in male imaginations this becomes repeatedly transformed into female devoration? Yet there was not a single female politician or general to give an order to march to battle?

> If any question why we died
> Tell them, because our fathers lied

says Kipling's 'Common Form'.[14] Pat Barker's *Regeneration* lends a very similar train of thought to her Rivers, a character strongly based on the real, deeply humane psychiatrist who treated traumatized men at Craiglockardt, among them Owen and Sassoon. At church, after the con-gregation has sung Hymn no. 373, the nation's most popular hymn since the Somme (God moves in a mysterious way / His wonders to perform), Rivers looks at the stained glass scenes above the altar: a crucifixion, and Abraham's sacrifice:

> Obvious choices for the east window: the two bloody bargains on which a
> civilization claims to be based. *The* bargain, Rivers thought, looking at

Abraham and Isaac. The one on which all patriarchal societies are founded. If you, who are young and strong, will obey me, who am old and weak, even to the extent of being prepared to sacrifice your life, then in the course of time you will peacefully inherit, and be able to exact the same obedience from your sons. Only we're breaking the bargain, Rivers thought. All over northern France, at this very moment, in trenches and in dugouts and flooded shell-holes, the inheritors were dying, not one by one, while old men, and women of all ages, gathered together and sang hymns.[15]

Pat Barker is very canny in attributing to Rivers such an insightful capacity to lay the blame at the patriarchy's door. Or accurate: what else was my grandfather writing to cousin Albert about, complaining of being sacrificed to the commercial interests of nations, and bemoaning the 'légèreté', the casualness, with which the generals threw men's lives into battle? Yet such voices are infrequent. I am struck by contrast with the abundance of images that *feminize* the slaughter. Ezra Pound shared in the vision of lying powers, of a lying ideology:

Died some, pro patria, non 'dulce' non 'et decor' . . .
walked eye-deep in hell
believing in old men's lies, then unbelieving
came home, home to a lie,

Yet a *female* image rises up in his 'Hugh Selwyn Mauberley' as the great culprit:

There died a myriad
And of the best, among them,
For an old bitch gone in the teeth,
For a botched civilization,[16]

Why 'an old bitch'? Because the trope of the prostitute which the second half of the nineteenth century had elaborated comes readily to hand? How come the landscape of death in Isaac Rosenberg's 'Dead Man's Dump' turns into some gigantic, inescapable, destructive/destroyed mother's body?

Maniac Earth! howling and flying, your bowel
Seared by the jagged fire, the iron love,
The impetuous storm of savage love.
. . . .
What dead are born when you kiss each soundless soul
With lightning and thunder from your mined heart . . .[17]

Who are these 'Daughters of War' who in another Rosenberg poem 'Beckon each soul aghast from its crimson corpse'?[18] Who the women who, in Lawrence's 'Eloi, Eloi Lama Sabachtani', 'Feed on our wounds like bread, receive our blood / Like glittering seed upon them for fulfilment'?[19] Such images carry into the 1920s and 1930s. Sexual violence and devoration are everywhere. So normative does the war of the sexes seem in that period that it gets taken as read. Thus a witty 1993 review of Anaïs Nin's *Journals* describes Henry Miller as a falcon swooping 'suddenly into a tight and deadly accuracy' in his account of Nin's practice. Miller writes of Nin: 'The hatches are down, the sky shut out. Everything – nature, human beings, events, relationships – is brought below to be dissected and digested. It is a devouring process in which the ego becomes a stupendous red maw.'[20]

The review produces its own answer. It creates a shaded and sympathetic account of Miller's sexual confusions and projections in relation to Nin. 'Have I been brutal enough for you?' Miller asks of the previous day's cavorting in the bath. It shows Miller elaborating a wispy aesthetics of the 'feminine' to reconcile his own doubts as to Nin's writing, her demand that he do something about promoting it, and his need to express sexual gratitude and use what power he has to retain a hold on her. Above all, the review produces an answer in that it does not notice how gender-clichéd are the metaphors that are being elaborated by both Miller and itself: Miller as deadly, swooping falcon – hence perhaps uniquely able to escape the 'stupendous red maw' of Nin's *vagina dentata* diary.

But perhaps such metaphors are forever. Dangerous female Chthonian stuff, 'Nature red in tooth and claw' – the tropes travel from Darwin and Tennyson to Camille Paglia. Are they as old as Western civilization, post-Plato, as Irigaray suggests in her reading of the metaphor of the Cave, the subsumed mother's body? The 'silent substratum of the social order' is 'the mother's body, she argues in an interview. 'The whole of our western culture is based upon the murder of the mother.'[21] That murder lies under the murder of father by sons which Freud imagines as foundational in *Totem and Taboo* – under the murder of sons by fathers which the Abraham story adumbrates and which Barker's Rivers sees as the cornerstone of the patriarchal order. Men, Irigaray further argues,

> project the infernal (in the Greek sense) element of their desire for the mother on to us. The anxiety they feel in relation to women is also a kind of blindness on their part about relations with their mothers. . . . Once the man-god-father kills the mother so as to take power, he is assailed by ghosts and anxieties. He will always feel a panic fear of she who is a substitute for what he has killed. And the things they threaten us with! We are going to swallow them up, devour them, castrate them . . .[22]

Does this run throughout Western civilization, as Irigaray states? Has habit made those images of the devouring mother archetypal, are they there to be drawn on every time disaster strikes? My own guess would be that the tenor and drift of such images is historical, that each period elaborates them in different ways, and that for the mother's body to be made so lethal it takes a huge combination of things – things that happened quite precisely and terrifyingly around and through and after the First World War. But the images *were* around. The previous century, at any rate, had elaborated them. How then, with such a tradition behind, all around one, how to resist the slippage from pitted earth and bloodied trench and grave and bodily wound to red maw to womb? From power, absolute and deadly, highly mechanized and haphazard, hierarchical and impersonal and petty all at once, to the once absolute power of the archaic mother? Where else to project one's anger at being wounded, but on the nurser of the wound? For in actuality, the division of parts that the war enforced (the women safely at home, the men enduring all sorts of dangers and abominations – the women often patriotic at little cost to themselves, like Jessie Pope in her awful poem 'Will You My Laddie?' in which she taunts her young male contemporaries to be heroic and reap the rewards, whereas the men had to pay the lethal and messy cost of such patriotism) led to acute resentment. In 'Glory of Women' Sassoon (unjustly but who knows in what childish history, in what fear and anger such resentment was rooted) suggests that it was all somehow the women's fault and they should be punished for it:

> You love us when we're heroes, home on leave,
> Or wounded in a mentionable place.
> You worship decorations; you believe
> That chivalry redeems the war's disgrace.
> You make us shells. . . .[23]

One shivers at the feel of the anger that gets injected in the sexual relation that makes e. e. cummings mix in his 'etceteras': his 'sweet old etcetera / aunt lucy' told 'you just / what everybody was fighting / for'; his 'mother hoped that' he 'would die etcetera / bravely of course'. Meanwhile he, lying in 'the deep mud', dreams of 'Your smile / eyes knees and of your Etcetera'.[24]

Rare are those who do not project their anger at the landscape of destruction around them. One such is Richard Aldington. 'In the Trenches', because it is filled with compassion for mother earth, because it links the soldiers' wounded souls with the wounding of the landscape rather than accuses the landscape of the wounding as Rosenberg does, makes it clear that the projections need not be antagonistic, that the mother figure that is being hallucinated need not be hostile, but is made so elsewhere by deep-seated anger or guilt: it is not weariness or fear that destroy the soldiers,

> Each wound on the breast of earth,
> Of Demeter, our Mother,
> Wound us also,
> Sever and rend the fine fabric
> Of the wings of our frail souls,

Scatter into dust the bright wings
Of Psyche![25]

But then, if one *is* filled with a sense of powerlessness, with anger, how
to vent one's despair at one's impotency, but by punishing the bearers of
the womb? How to resist the fear of hysteria now threatening the males, if
you are male, but by redirecting it towards the *hysteros* – the 'Mother' as
hysteria was called in the Renaissance – the womb? Thus D. H. Lawrence,
at the end of an essay that began with a beautiful search for the reality of
peace, to be found in inner stillness, waxes angry. His prose flickering
here and there then fanned into wild destructive flames by the frustration
within, he transfers the violence of precisely the warfare he wanted to
oppose to the relation between the sexes: true peace will be found in the
battle of the sexes, by male predatoriness being released against female
(and not on the battlefield) – 'Not of the conjunction with the hart is [the
doe] consummated, but of the exquisite laceration of fear as the leopard
springs upon her loins, and his claws strike in, and he dips his mouth in
her. This is the white-hot pitch of her helpless desire.'[26]

And thus the scene becomes filled with murderous images of women,
with images of women *wanting* to be murdered. It may be because the
murder of the mother, and guilt for that mother, lies at the root of
western civilization, as Irigaray argues, although the sons sometimes, as
Aldington does, side with the mother, feel destroyed by what hurts her –
recognize their own femininity? Or it may be that the twentieth century,
caught in the huge and widespread traumas from the warfare, elaborates
particularly violent, unprecedented versions of the murder of the mother
– which psychoanalysts such as Irigaray then read backwards.

The 1920s (and 1930s) see the establishment of psychoanalysis centre-
stage. One of the most earnestly researched and anxiously debated areas
is that of female sexuality. My own immersion in 1970s and 1980s feminist debates about psychoanalysis had made me very much privilege
Freud's own essays from that period, 'Some Psychical Consequences of
the Anatomical Distinction Between the Sexes' of 1925[27] and 'Female Sexuality' of 1931.[28] The first, which returns to the question of female sexuality after a gap of over twenty years (Freud's major earlier venture had
been around the 'Dora' case, a case of female hysteria (1900)), maps out
female sexuality in relation to that of the male and elaborates the celebrated concept of 'penis envy'. The little girl is described as falling 'a victim to envy for the penis' upon having made the 'momentous discovery'
of a brother's or playmate's 'superior counterpart of their own small and
inconspicuous organ'. The 1931 essay returns to the question, shading
and altering some of the earlier concepts; and among other things proposes that little girls experience a longer 'pre-Oedipal period' than little
boys – largely uncharted: hence the famous phrase about the 'dark
continent of femininity'.

Freud's essays, together with some of Lacan's seminars in the 1960s and 1970s, especially *Encore*, seemed to form the bulk of the definitions of femininity with which women analysts and theoreticians in France and Italy (beginning with Irigaray in *Speculum of the Other Woman*), then the Anglo-Saxon world, took issue: indeed, a volume of Lacan translations was put together by Juliet Mitchell and Jacqueline Rose under the title *Female Sexuality*. I am not here concerned with Lacan, despite the importance of his interpretations or reformulations of Freud, but with Freud, with psychoanalysis in the years following the First World War, and with the elaboration of devouring or murderous images of women I have been discussing.

Although I had, in passing, read Karen Horney and Melanie Klein, and even Juliet Mitchell, whose early and highly literate *Psychoanalysis and Feminism* provides a multiple approach, I had remained very much locked inside the mainstream feminist debates, according to which everything, or almost everything, revolved round Freud and Lacan (with Klein increasingly thrown in). It is only the accident of recent readings that has altered my sense of things.

It was not only in the 1960s and afterwards that what Janine Chasseguet-Smirgel and others call 'phallic sexual monism', that is, Freud's (and Lacan's) contention that the only sexual organ is the penis/phallus, was hotly and convincingly contested by members of the Freudian school; it was being contested in the 1920s and 1930s – and, it seems to me, disproved – by the work of women analysts such as Horney and above all Klein. It was being complemented and shifted by Lou Andreas Salome's theory of bisexuality. It was also being very powerfully shaded by Ernest Jones. And, last but not least, it was being challenged by a quite different notion in Jung, according to which each sex has an inner, as well as outer, relation to the other (men to a female anima, women to a male animus). It is there that Lawrence's contention that 'men and women need each other', that we 'seek all the time to come into true human relationship with other human beings', that 'it has to happen, this relationship, almost unconsciously', that indeed it cannot happen 'deliberately', might find verification.[29] The same anxieties, compensatory manoeuvres, and explorations play themselves out in the psychoanalysis of the period, as they do in literature and in the arts. And they also arise from the crisis in masculinity, the crisis in the relationship between the sexes, brought about by the war. It isn't that psychoanalysis is somehow the theory that explains the literature and the arts in the 1920s any more than it does in the 1970s or 1980s or indeed 1990s, but that both psychoanalysis and the arts are grappling with the same pressures, the same realities: with the missing, the traumas, the projections, and the ensuing difficulties the sexes have in relating to each other. The discourses both produce and are coloured by the anxieties and projections of the discourse-makers, the form-givers. Chicken and egg, all round.

My own recent discovery of the resistance to sexual monism of the

1920s analytic debate changed my perception of the period. What De Groot and Deutsch and Freud and Horney and Klein and Jones are talking about, besides female sexuality, is male sexuality. An underground battle is being waged in which each sex portrays the other or its own in ways which are generous, defensive or vindictive. Talking about female sexuality, the sexes are talking about male sexuality, projected as fear, power, etc., and they are talking about the relation between the sexes.

Janine Chasseguet-Smirgel points out that the women are often as (or more) misogynist as the men, and that between them Jeanne Lampl-de Groot, Helen Deutsch and Marie Bonaparte have, for complex reasons, no compunction about 'mutilating' women, 'castrating' them 'of their activity (or their pleasure), their orgasm, their clitoris'. Klein and Jones, on the other hand, each posit awareness of the womb (the mother's, and for the little girl, her own) as a sexual organ in both sexes. For Jones, both sexes have a positive Oedipus, and the ultimate fear in both is aphanisis, the abolition of sexuality, not the fear of castration. Klein stresses how primary, how active, the mother's part is in the infant's development. The relation to the breast as primary object is seen as foundational: that to the penis, which is complex and follows on from the relation to the mother, comes later.

Recalling the concourse of circumstances that led Freud to form a profoundly gloomy view of life in the 1920s (the impact of the war, his beloved daughter's death, which other commentators have, justifiably or not, linked with the writing of *Beyond the Pleasure Principle*, and then, in the early 1930s the throat cancer), Janine Chasseguet-Smirgel sees the theory of phallic sexual monism as coloured by – a reaction to – a period of great sadness and doubt. It is not, she suggests, a description of children's knowledge of sexuality, but an ideology, a defensive theory (which if prevalent in the psyche can lead to an 'éclatement du Moi' and a 'perverse organization'). It is a dangerous one, Chasseguet-Smirgel suggests, because the devaluing of the womb and the mother can in turn lead to the 'eradication of the father and the father's universe'. We all need a relation to both the father and the mother. Paradoxically, denigration of the one can lead to devaluation of the other.

Phallic sexual monism, as elaborated by Freud, stems from an awareness of the human infant's long immaturity. Unlike other animals, human infants are totally dependent on the mother till at least eighteen months. Confronted with the primal scene, the mating of the father and the mother, the child (male is here implied) is confronted with the reality of the mother's womb, his own inability to penetrate her because of his own weak organ, and his father's ability to do so. What confronts him is both sexual difference and generational difference. There ensues a painful narcissistic wound, which phallic sexual monism as a theory aims to erase: if the child totally ignores the existence of the womb, he has nothing to envy the father for. He can preserve the phantasy that he could satisfy the mother just as well as the father does. In his desire to be free from the all-powerful archaic mother, who has such power over him because of his prematuration, and of the Oedipal mother whom he is unable to satisfy, the child projects power on to the father, and the father's penis. Freud's theory of the phallus as the only sexual organ magnifies this projection for consolatory purposes.[30]

The First World War in its atrocities and absurdities produced a savage repetition of this pattern, on a huge scale. No wonder that it was so easily metaphorized by writers and artists alike. No women were to be seen on the entire length of the front, in a parodic and bitter culmination of the Victorian public–private, extreme divide of the sexes. Caught in a private and public generation gap (subjected to the orders of the Fathers, the generals and the politicians), sometimes charged with cowardice by the women (in real life and in propaganda) if you did not risk all for a cause that rapidly seemed absurd, launched again and again against an enemy dug in the ground and blasting you with missiles, is it any wonder that there should have risen the ghost of a nightmare primal scene in which you were ever-impotent to make any inroads on the terrain occupied by the father? The Oedipal mother was forever unattainable, at times urging you on to your own annihilation, your own aphanisis through mutilation. The archaic mother was overwhelming. Millions of young men were reinfantilized, grown-up men made to be totally dependent on preposterous, deadly, orders, from the *offensive à outrance* that relied upon fire taking twenty seconds to mow the men, instead of the eight that it really took, to the grotesque assaults of Verdun and La Somme, no lesson learnt despite millions of dead and two years of evidence. It is said that some English regiments marched to fire bleating, the only way they could protest about being ordered forward as lambs to the slaughter. How then be indignant about Lawrence's gendered exaltation of the individualistic Tiger, his contempt for 'the nauseous herd', the 'hideous myrmidons of sheep'[31] which, unlike Blake, he sees as full of 'jeering malice', not 'clothed' in 'delight'. He's trying to guard himself against the fate of the men at the Somme. In defensive ideology, in dread at the inescapable machinery and propaganda of the war, he reverts to the archaic, the infantile. The sheep are 'all *will* and belly and prolific womb'. Sheep are here feminized as the ultimate insult. And biology is further flouted, for ewes are not prolific: they tend to have one lamb only, once a year, in the spring. How angry and frightened must you be to care so little about reality.

Thus also Norman Mailer on Henry Miller:

> For he captured something in the sexuality of men as it had never been seen before, precisely that it was man's sense of awe before woman, his dread of her position one step closer to eternity (for in that step were her powers) which made men detest women, revile them ... Men look to destroy every quality in a woman which will give her the powers of a male, for she is in their eyes already armed with the power that brought them forth, and that is a power beyond measure.[32]

Millett's comment on this is that Mailer's 'powerful intellectual comprehension' is exceeded only by his 'attachment to the malaise'.[33] I think that Mailer's comprehension here is not intellectual, but subliminal, and might be accurate indeed as a diagnostic were it not so hopelessly ahistorical.

The forms of feminization of men that had taken place in the course of the First World War were not in actuality of the kind described by Miller and Mailer, which were projections. They had more to do with what Pat Barker deftly makes her Rivers perceive. Listening to the traumatized or anguished officers under his care, Rivers notes that they have had to develop caring, paternal/maternal, indeed *domestic* relations to their men, worrying about 'socks, boots, blisters, food, hot drinks', developing the 'perpetually harried expression' he'd also seen 'on the faces of women who were bringing up large families on very low incomes'. Furthermore, the war, instead of turning out into 'the Great Adventure', has '*mobilized*' men 'into holes in the ground so constricted they could hardly move'.[34] The breakdowns, the fact that the path to the cure lay in accepting that 'horror and fear were inevitable responses to the trauma of war and were better acknowledged than suppressed, that feelings of tenderness for other men were natural and right, that tears were an acceptable part of grieving', went right against 'the whole tenor' of men's upbringing in the period. It was tantamount to being 'sissies, weaklings, failures'. But Rivers, the real Rivers, if he indeed thought as Barker makes him think, was exceptional. Angry projections were much more the currency. As Séverine Auffret has shown, post-war Europe for the first time in twenty-four centuries produces versions of the Oresteia, all written by men playwrights, in which the mother is bitterly hated by the daughter, as a way of expressing the son's particularly high level of hatred for the mother.[35]

Thus one important question, as – a man (Jonathan Culler, who astutely juxtaposes Miller and Millett)[36] – puts it, is: how does a woman read male authors who voice such hatred or fear? My answer – what this essay is struggling to do – is that it is only by understanding how and why, while aggressed by men (enemy armies, generals, politicians, neurologists), the soldier-poets at war and the returning men should have construed women as the cause, made women the emissary goats, that I can be free from such constructions. Freed: for otherwise I might in turn have been made so angry by the deprecation or misogyny that they might throw me off-balance (as I feel sometimes happens with Kate Millett). If I allowed resentment to sway me in turn I would miss out on, become alienated from, writers who mean a great deal to me. I would seek for refuge in an idealized all-women, maternal world, and be impeded in my capacity to search for a relation to both the paternal and the maternal which Janine Chasseguet-Smirgel argues, persuasively for me, we need in order to achieve maturation as human beings. Chaotic, infantile and wrong-headed though Lawrence for instance often is, he is after something which means a great deal to me. I also think that his constant harping on 'we need one another', his grail quest for a possible, life-giving, balanced relation between the sexes is serious, important, moving. So is Woolf's quest for a place for the feminine, some reconciliation of masculine and feminine through her dream of androgyny. For alongside the projections, striving against them, one thing does strike me about a number of writers in the period. And that is, with what good will, what imaginative efforts, each sex writes from the other's vantage point. Each sex attempts to recreate its own sexuality, to mend the wounds inflicted, by means of and through an imagination of the other's.

Why else would Joyce use Molly Bloom as he does, except to speak that 'yes' to desire and jouissance and life that his men, caught as they are in negatives, cannot utter?

Why else would Lawrence repeatedly write desire through female characters? The women are questing. The women are, in some strange way, still whole. They are divining rods. The real McCoy. The grail-seeking men are almost as ill as the Fisher King. Wounded, eccentric, skirting the edges of ridicule and femininity, the characters of Lawrence: Birkin, Aaron, Summers, Lily, the captain from 'The Captain's Doll' ... Oh they're opinionated, bloody-minded, obstinate creatures, seeking to balance out with other men through uneasy gladiatorials or the differentials of class or style, keeping embers alive in the taut pit of their innards, be those inside skull or belly. But the women, the lost girls, the virgins, the ladies, Daphne from 'The Ladybird', Constance from *Lady Chatterley's Lover* – there is spring in their sex, the inspiration of archaic, restorative forces in their restlessness. It is their desire for manhood that might resurrect, or reinvent, it. It seems to me that in his deepest fictional seeking, Lawrence is quite different from what he preaches. The active ones, the more credible Percivals, are the women.

Notes

1 Barbara Tuchman, *The Guns of August* (New York: Macmillan, 1967), pp. 231–2.
2 S. Gilbert and S. Gubar, *No Man's Land: The Place of the Woman Writer in the Twentieth Century*, vol. 2: *Sexchanges* (New Haven and London: Yale University Press, 1989), p. 260.
3 Ibid., p. 267.
4 Ibid., pp. 267–8.
5 T. S. Eliot, *The Waste Land and Other Poems* (London: Faber, 1972), p. 38.
6 Siegfried Sassoon, 'Counter-Attack', in John Silkin (ed.), *The Penguin Book of First World War Poetry* (Harmondsworth: Penguin, 1979), p. 130. For a sense of the prodigious, long-lasting impact of the First World War, see Paul Fussell, *The Great War and Modern Memory* (Oxford: Oxford University Press, 1977).
7 Elaine Showalter, *The Female Malady: Women, Madness and English Culture, 1830–1980* (London: Virago, 1987), p. 177.

8 Virginia Woolf, *Mrs Dalloway* (Harmondsworth: Penguin, 1964); Colette, *Chéri and The Last of Chéri* (1920 and 1926), tr. Roger Senhouse (Harmondsworth: Penguin, 1954); Pat Barker, *Regeneration* (Harmondsworth: Penguin, 1992).

9 In Silkin, *Penguin Book of First World War Poetry*, pp. 264–5.

10 Rupert Brooke, 'The Soldier', from *1914, Poetical Works* (London: Faber, 1946); and see Wilfred Owen, *The Complete Poems and Fragments*, ed. John Stallworthy (London: Chatto and Windus, 1983).

11 Eliot, *The Waste Land and Other Poems*, p. 28.

12 Vera Brittain, *Testament of Youth* (London: Virago, 1979), p. 143. For a fine study of women in the First World War, see Sharon Ouditt, *Fighting Forces, Writing Women* (London: Routledge, 1993).

13 Quoted by C. J. Fox in *Times Literary Supplement*, 19 Mar. 1993, p. 6.

14 In Silkin, *Penguin Book of First World War Poetry*, p. 136.

15 Barker, *Regeneration*, p. 149.

16 Ezra Pound, 'Hugh Selwyn Mauberley (Life and Contacts)', in *Personae: The Collected Shorter Poems of Ezra Pound* (New York: New Direction, 1950), pp. 190–1.

17 In Silkin, *Penguin Book of First World War Poetry*, p. 212.

18 In ibid., p. 213.

19 D. H. Lawrence, *Complete Poems*, ed. Vivian de Sola Pinto and Warren Roberts (2 vols, London: Heinemann, 1964), pp. 741–3.

20 Claudia Roth Pierpont, 'Sex, Lies and Thirty-Five Thousand Pages', *New Yorker*, 1 Mar. 1993, p. 80.

21 Luce Irigaray, *The Irigaray Reader*, ed. Margaret Whitford (Oxford: Blackwell, 1991), p. 47.

22 Ibid., p. 49.

23 In Silkin, *Penguin Book of First World War Poetry*, p. 132.

24 In ibid., p. 140.

25 In ibid., p. 142.

26 D. H. Lawrence, 'The Reality of Peace', in *Phoenix: The Posthumous Papers of D. H. Lawrence*, ed. and introd. Edward McDonald (London: Heinemann, 1936), p. 692.

27 In Sigmund Freud, *Standard Edition of the Complete Psychological Works of Sigmund Freud*, gen. ed. James Strachey (24 vols, London: Hogarth Press, 1953–74), vol. 19.

28 In ibid., vol. 21.

29 D. H. Lawrence, 'We Need One Another', in *Phoenix*, pp. 188–91.

30 Janine Chasseguet-Smirgel, *La Sexualité féminine: Recherches psychanalytiques nouvelles* (Paris: Payot, 1964), pp. 23, 30–1, 61–2.

31 D. H. Lawrence, 'The Reality of Peace', pp. 685, 684.

32 Norman Mailer, *The Prisoner of Sex* (Boston: Little, Brown, 1971), p. 116, quoted by Jonathan Culler, see note 36 below.

33 Kate Millett, *Sexual Politics* (New York: Doubleday, 1970), p. 39.

34 Barker, *Regeneration*, p. 107.

35 Ibid., p. 48; Séverine Auffret, *Nous, Clytemnestre: du tragique et des masques* (Paris: Des Femmes, 1984), pp. 39–46, 182–9.

36 Jonathan Culler, 'Reading As a Woman', in R. Warhol and D. Herndl (eds), *Feminisms* (New Brunswick: Rutgers, 1991), pp. 512–13.

4
D. H. Lawrence: Womb Envy or A Womb of his Own?

At Higher Tregerthen, in Cornwall, in 1916, at the height of the First World War, two literary couples – D. H. Lawrence and Frieda, Jack Middleton Murry and Katherine Mansfield – spent time living close to each other. Lawrence had advocated his dream of a 'community' – had sought a supplement to his relation with Frieda in a relation with both the Murrys. Katherine's 'aloofness' discouraged the double relationship, so Lawrence sought Jack out. Jack shrank from the invitation, couched, according to him, in terms of 'blood-brotherhood', and not openly sexual. The dream of a blood-brotherhood between men is explored by Lawrence through the relation between Gerald and Birkin, the central male protagonists of *Women in Love*, written in that same year 1916. In the chapter 'Gladiatorial', the nude wrestling between the two men brings them close in a way that was never achieved between Lawrence and Murry. But the hope for an unbreakable bond between the two men fails in the novel too.

In actuality, Katherine Mansfield had been disgusted by the – physically violent – rows between Lawrence and Frieda, the 'morning after' reconciliations. A letter to Ottoline Morrell describes her having felt ' "like Alice between the Cook and the Duchess" ' as pans ' "hurtled through the air" ': ' "Lawrence has definitely chosen to sin against himself and Frieda is triumphant. It is horrible." '[1] The Murrys had gone away. When *Women in Love*, that in its depiction of the relation between Gerald and Gudrun seemed to offer a pretty lethal critique of the relation between Jack and herself, had been published later in the year, Katherine had been further angered. She encouraged Ottoline Morrell, lethally dealt with in the novel as Hermione, to sever ties with Lawrence.[2] Yet with typical Katherine ambivalence, she also recognized, in later years, her deep kinship with Lawrence.

She was not the only woman friend to have a far-reaching relationship with Lawrence. Elaine Feinstein's *Lawrence and the Women* goes some way towards describing the rich patterns of Lawrence's friendships with women, which often generated such a sense of kinship.[3] This was also experienced by Hilda Aldington, the poet H.D. H.D. also saw Lawrence during the Great War, felt, like Katherine Mansfield, that a bond was there: how real that bond was she discovered in afteryears through her relation to Freud whom she visited in Vienna in 1933. She later described the visit in her *Tribute to Freud*.[4]

H.D. first met an unbearded Lawrence at the outbreak of the war, in August 1914. She went on to have an alternately fascinated and exasperated relationship with him – disliking *Women in Love* and *Lady Chatterley's Lover*, annoyed by Lawrence's rejection of Freud. Yet in her 1933 encounter with Freud, Lawrence returns; is all over the place for her. The Professor's 'charming', 'wrinkled smile' reminds her of Lawrence's.[5] In a dream the early, 'unbearded' Lawrence looks like her father – or brother. Anniversaries converge. D.H. and H.D. become twins: 'For one day in the year, H.D. and D. H. Lawrence were twins. But I had not actually realized this until after his death. He was born September 11, 1885: I was born September 10, 1886.'[6] Above all, the two of them become wound up in a haunting memory/dream/fantasy of H.D.'s. It is of a huge green caterpillar killed with salt on a tobacco plant – of a moth she as a child tried to rescue and that choked in its box. The giant moth, which in another variation crawled on to an Indian skull in her father's study, becomes associated with a print on the Professor's wall, *Buried Alive*, and with Lawrence's last book, which a friend brought to her after Lawrence's death: *The Man Who Died*. The friend has said, ' "Lawrence wrote this for you" ':[7] she is the priestess Isis in the story. It makes H.D. think 'Lawrence was imprisoned in his tomb ... We are all buried alive.' Freud, through whom and thanks to whom all this circulates, becomes drawn into that image of a living death: for the Jewish professor was being threatened in anti-Semitic 1933 Vienna: threatened with being buried alive in a city gone mad. H.D. thinks of 'the crucified Worm' as she leafs over the Viennese newspapers, reading the atrocity stories, struck by the huge swastikas in Freud's street. She recalls Lawrence's phoenix symbol (will the man who died rise again after all?) and thinks of the Professor 'as an owl, hawk or sphinx-moth'.[8] In death, the Lawrence who told her about a haunted house in Cornwall returns as her true complement: 'Lawrence came back with *The Man Who Died*. Whether or not he meant me as the priestess of Isis in that book does not alter the fact that his last book reconciled me to him. Isis is incomplete without Osiris, Judy is meaningless without Punch.'[9]

Katherine's kinship with Lawrence had more violent elements in it than H.D.'s. She acknowledged it in her 1918 *Journal* after she had been terrified by her own fit of temper ('You look *all dark*,' Jack says to her, and she perceives herself as having turned '*green*', 'a deep earthy colour'). She wrote, no doubt thinking of the rows she had witnessed a couple of years before at Tregerthen, perhaps reflecting on her then disgust: ' "These fits are Lawrence and Frieda over again. I am more like L. than anybody. We are *unthinkably* alike, in fact." '[10]

On 27 March 1919, Lawrence writes to Katherine. He claims he has been told by Frieda that Katherine was cross with him, that he *'repulsed'* her. This does not seem to trouble him. He has no doubts about his relationship with her: 'you I am sure of – I was ever since Cornwall.' He has, he writes, dreamed 'such a vivid little dream' of her the previous night, that is concerned with her illness. In his dream she was clear from the consumption but still could not walk up a hill (was *he* also dreaming of his own illness, identifying with her on that count too?):

> So you went out with me as I was going. It was night, and very starry. We looked at the stars, and they were different. All the constellations were different, and I, who was looking for Orion, to show you, because he is rising now; was very puzzled by these thick, close brilliant new constellations. Then suddenly we saw one planet, so beautiful, a large, fearful, strong star, that we were both pierced by it, possessed, for a second. Then I said, 'That's Jupiter' – but I felt that it wasn't Jupiter – at least not the everyday Jupiter.
>
> Ask Jung or Freud about it? – Never! – It was a star that blazed for a second on one's soul.[11]

What a beautiful dream. What a statement of kinship – and what a beautiful letter for a woman to receive. Lawrence's female correspondents, and Mansfield in particular, are often treated, if not to such a vivid recognition – such a tribute – at least to direct statements of ideas, feelings, luminous sharp impressions – the feel of the morning air, the exact seasonal colouring of the grass, the pattern of molehills in a field. They are also addressed with an extraordinary truthfulness, that comes across as a recognition of who they are: thus Amy Lowell gets told off for doing Japanese poems, making things up 'from the outside'; 'Do write from your *real* self, Amy' (23 March 1917).[12]

Write from your *real* self. Be yourself, *Fantasia of the Unconscious* (1923) commands: 'The final aim is not *to know*, but *to be*.'[13] Despite his own will to know, Freud was not of a different persuasion. His discovery of the power of the libido, of unconscious drives, of the death principle – his phrase 'where id was, there ego shall be', his notion that the conscious self can be healed through integration of the unconscious, are not far from what Lawrence is exploring at the time. Jung in the same period is also close to Lawrence in some of his thinking. His 1918 essay, 'On the Unconscious', stresses the need to come to terms with and learn to love the 'animal' in us. Earlier religions, he argues, which were in touch with the animal element, with impulses, allowed the very laws and forms which tamed and broke the animal element to spring from those very impulses, from the animal itself. Christianity has repressed the pagan animal, substituted a sacrificial lamb for the Mithraic sacrificial bull. It has dissociated the animal from consciousness. When the animal now erupts, it is without rule or capacity for mastery. Such an irruption 'always ends in a catastrophe, in self-destruction'. That is why, Jung adds, clearly referring to the then ongoing war in Europe, 'no other church but the Christian church is so stained with cruelly spilt innocent blood, that is why the world has never known wars as bloody as those which have opposed Christian nations among themselves.' If each of us had a better relation to the animal in us, he or she would then grant quite a different value to life.[14] What else is Lawrence arguing in his own confused anger with 'sheep', in his nostalgia for the tiger or leopard, in his essay on 'The Reality of Peace'? What else is he exploring in his 'Snake' poem, or through the stallion St Mawr? All these end-of-war, immediate post-war texts seem retrospectively so prophetic of what was to come, Nazism in particular ... 'Buried alive'. Were the voices that knew buried alive?

There is little doubt that Lawrence, writing about the psyche, about sexuality, is on the same territory as contemporary psychoanalysis: his letters, his vocabulary, his need to write *Fantasia of the Unconscious* and *Psychoanalysis and the Unconscious* in the post-war years testify to his own awareness of this. It also seems clear that he had only a schematic and passing knowledge of psychoanalysis. *Sons and Lovers* (1912) may have been received by Ivy Low as 'a book about the Oedipus complex' and described by Lawrence himself to Edward Garnett as such – it was ' "the tragedy of thousands of young men in England" ' (19 November 1912):[15] the fact remains that Lawrence had not read Freud, and any Freudian influence came at the revision stage (1913) via Frieda from Otto Gross. In later years, Lawrence did read some Freud and some Jung. His letters keep referring to such readings. One such letter to Katherine Mansfield after a dip into Jung comments: 'This Mother-incest idea can become an obsession. But it seems to me there is much truth in it: that at certain periods the man has a desire and a tendency to return unto woman, make her his goal and end' (5 December 1918).[16]

Lawrence saw, corresponded or discussed with people – Dr David Eder, a translator of Freud's *The Interpretation of Dreams*, Dr Ernest Jones, Barbara Lowe – who had first-hand knowledge or experience of Freud and psychoanalysis.[17] But he also felt antagonistic, suspicious: 'Ask Jung or Freud? Never!' He is afraid of what he sees as vivisectionist in the scientific claims of psychoanalysis. In *Psychoanalysis and the Unconscious* Freud is presented as a ' "straw man" ' who brought to light ' "unspeakable horror[s]" '. But he is also praised as some ' "supreme explorer" ' who had stepped ' "out of the conscious into the unconscious, out of the everywhere into the nowhere" '.[18]

Like Freud, who after the war writes *Beyond the Pleasure Principle*, like Jung, who in 1918 meditates on the terrible danger of repressed violence in all of us, Lawrence struggles with the violence of the First World War. *Women in Love* was begun on 24 April 1916 – the day of the Dublin Easter

Rising – as Delaney, the author of an astute study on Lawrence and the First World War, points out.[19] Its writing coincided with some of the bloodiest battles of the war, with Verdun. Lawrence's humiliating struggle against conscription, his stay at the Bodmin barracks, just preceded the battle of the Somme, the most disastrous day in British military history.[20] A first scheme of the novel *The Sisters* had been written in 1913. But *Women in Love* takes its particular colouring and agenda from the war: 'I should wish the time to remain unfixed,' the foreword says, 'so that the bitterness of the war may be taken for granted in the characters.' The bitterness is not just in the characters, unless what they sense is to be read as projections, which does not seem to be intended. What is amazing is that the war, through similes and metaphors, imbues everyday social situations. Thus at Breadalby, Hermione's grand mansion, despite the good food and dream-like sense of an enclosed, 'delightful, precious past, trees and deer and silence', Ursula feels an unease that is couched in surprising metaphors:

> But in spirit she was unhappy. The talk went on like a rattle of small artillery, always slightly sententious, with a sententiousness that was only emphasized by the continual crackling of criticism, the continual spatter of verbal jest, designed to give a tone of flippancy to a stream of conversation that was all critical and general, a canal of conversation rather than a stream.[21]

From an early draft of Wilfred Owen's 'Anthem for Doomed Youth':

> —Only the stuttering rifles' rattled words
> Can patter out your hasty orisons.[22]

The one writer, Lawrence (through Ursula's consciousness), hears war sounds in ordinary talk, safely at home in idyllic rural England; the other, Owen, hears talk (anger, religious stutter, 'wailing shells') in the sounds of war, at the front. What is surprising is not that each should feel such anger (muffled as irritation in Ursula), such a sense of falsity – but that for Lawrence the feelings should be repeatedly directed at what seem to be the wrong targets.

Perhaps this was because of a sense of multiple impotency. Lawrence was not conscripted, not because he was against war as such – he was no conscientious objector, he hated pacifists such as Bertrand Russell – but because of ill-health. He was against this particular war, was profoundly at odds with the patriotism all around him. He was looked at askance on account of his union with a German woman, he hated France, Russia and Belgium much more than he did Germany. He also thought (strangely, like my grandfather) that compulsion was the last straw, that for a human being to maintain 'the integrity of one's being' was the primary duty. There were not many in England who shared in his particular vision, apart from the women (like Catherine Carswell)[23] to whom he wrote such things, and he was powerless to do anything about any of his contradictory feelings, except write essays such as 'The Reality of Peace', riven (as I have suggested about the sheep 'all will and belly and prolific womb') by such a contradictory vocabulary. And so everything is driven inwards: 'Peace and war lie in the heart, in the *desire*, of the people . . . Germany, nations – are external material facts. The reality of peace, the reality of war, lies in the hearts of the people: you, me, all the rest,' he writes on 25 November 1916 to Lady Cynthia Asquith.[24]

And so it all went inwards: 'At present my real world is the world of my inner soul, which reflects on the novel I write. The outer world is there to be endured, it is not real – nor is the outer life,' he wrote to Ottoline Morrell.[25] And it all got transformed into a battle of the sexes. People worship Ares and Aphrodite: 'both gods of destruction and burning down', they are full of 'the lust for hate and war, chiefly hate of 'each other', he adds in the letter to Cynthia Asquith. He further writes 'let us *make* something else out of our own hearts. – Germany, peace terms etc. don't matter. It is a question of the living heart – that only.'[26] *Women in Love* is full of this: of how 'the will' is powered by the lust for war, the lust for destruction, and how it kills the 'living heart. The *Wille zur Macht*, the mechanical will, shows itself in Gerald's subduing of the mare, of the workers in the mine, in his fight between 'his will and the resistant Matter of the earth'[27] and eventually in Gudrun's corrosive, sensation-based will, that drives her to destroy Gerald her mate: ironically, Lawrence provides her with the very question that puzzled Freud – 'Was will das Weib?' – 'What does woman want?' In this particular case, Lawrence answers: when will powers her, she wants her man dead.

> What was it, after all that woman wanted? . . . Was it sheer blind force of passion that would satisfy her now? Not this, but the subtle thrills of extreme sensation in reduction. It was an unbroken will reacting against her unbroken will in a myriad subtle thrills of reduction and breaking down, carried out in the darkness of her . . . [There was] only repetition possible, or the going apart of the protagonists, or the subjugating of the one will to the other, or death.[28]

First Gerald almost strangles Gudrun. Her will is too strong for him. He walks away towards the wilderness of snow. Later he is found dead on the surface of the ice.

Bewilderment overtakes me at this juncture. First I've found myself wondering whether defeated Gerald could be read as Germany (Gerald has, by Birkin's own admission, the *Wille zur Macht* – through his taming of the miners he represents mechanized power – he is blond and handsome, the proper Aryan, dying on the ice like some Wagnerian hero) and Gudrun, France (she is, after all, fascinated by Decadence, the Bohemian world of artists)? Birkin would be England, who might have made an alliance with Germany but it didn't work ... Then decided that this was too silly for words: why would the winning country be feminized, against all codes? Silly as this might be, it says something about the almost surreal transferences from the war world to the shires which Lawrence's internalization and genderization of the conflict creates.

The next thought that came up was that following some of the war images in *Women in Love* had led me to score an own goal. I began to look into Lawrence with the idea of countering the argument I had previously arrived at, that is, that male writers project negative images of women on to the war as a way of dealing with their anxieties, their sense of impotency, their anger. I had been led to think that alongside such projections there is also an attempt, in Lawrence in particular, to recreate the fabric of relations between the sexes by imagining reality from the vantage point of female characters, and that this goes hand in hand with real empathy with women friends such as Katherine Mansfield. But a brief look at Gudrun seems to reveal her as a cross between a praying mantis and a painting by Miro – atomized sensations ... Perhaps Katherine Mansfield was taking her own revenge for recognizing elements of herself in Gudrun when she urged Ottoline Morrell to break all relations with Lawrence. Maybe *she* didn't want to lose him altogether by breaking off relations herself. Getting Ottoline to do it was keeping her cake (Lawrence) and eating it (let him be punished by having sorely misrepresented, indeed slandered, women friends cast him away).

I feel that reading *Women in Love* as a *roman à clé* works no better than reading it as a historical allegory. There is plenty of malice, of bias, at times of misogyny in Lawrence's writing. But he did write novels, novellas, plenty of short stories, in which elements of Frieda (I was going to write, the spirit of Frieda because that's what it feels like, not details, but a spirit) are modulated into many different shapes. And, of course, elements of *himself*. It seems to me that there probably is as much of Lawrence himself and his relationship to Frieda in the Gerald–Gudrun couple as in the Birkin–Ursula one (Lawrence and Frieda were after all the ones who had the terrible rows), and as much or more invention, modulation. It is in a way an experimental novel. One situation, one set of people, one animal gets set up in one chapter after another, and becomes the occasion for one of the couples or the other to live out their fascination, anger, hatred, lust ...

In *The Rainbow* Ursula was more like Gudrun, had elements of the wild virgin about her, was treated by the narrator more like a rival sibling than as a loved female character. Kate Millett claims that Lawrence

> had made the same difficult climb through the horrors of slum school teaching to the university, and his narrative of Ursula's suffering along the way is an odd mixture of sympathy – when he lapses into autobiography and identification with the character – mingled with acrid resentment, at the thought of one of her sex achieving this much. The splendid old maternal women posed no threat ... Ursula as the new woman clearly does.[29]

Millett has a point, though she overstates it – I would speak of fear, of ambivalence, of rivalry, not of 'acrid resentment' – here a projection of sibling Kate on to rival brother Lawrence? In the two couples in *Women in Love* Lawrence explores rivalry, the struggle for dominance, through continuous *relating* – it is as if the couples seek for some way of balancing through struggle: Ursula has an inner substance, a generous self-sufficiency which enables her to fight back tolerantly without feeling endangered by the aggression or desire for dominance that Birkin keeps projecting at her. In the chapter 'Mino', Birkin talks of the tom-cat's 'superior wisdom' to the 'belle sauvage' cat it is courting. Ursula gets cross with his 'assertion of male superiority'. It is 'bullying' she says – it is just like Gerald Crich's *Wille zur Macht*. Birkin agrees the *Wille zur Macht* is 'base and petty'. But what he is talking about is 'the [Mino's] desire to bring this female cat into a pure stable equilibrium', as Adam kept Eve in paradise, 'like a star in its orbit'. This is, you might think, an improvement on the doe finding fulfilment when the leopard plants its claws into her flanks, in 'The Reality of Peace'. But Ursula is not cowed:

'Yes – yes' cried Ursula, pointing her finger at him. 'There you are – a star in its orbit! a satellite – a satellite of Mars – that's what she is to be! There – there – you've given yourself away! you've said it – you've dished your-self!'
He stood smiling in frustration and amusement and irritation and admi-ration and love. She was so quick, and so lambent, like discernible fire, and so vindictive, and so rich in her dangerous flamy sensitiveness.[30]

The Ursula of *Women in Love* gathers to herself some of the elements that are in the earlier generation women in *The Rainbow*, though not in Ursula herself. Kate Millett, again overstating her case, but again quite incisively, reads *The Rainbow* as 'celebrating the power of the womb'. Lawrence is an 'authentic case of the disorder' of 'womb envy', which Karen Horney is supposed to have maliciously invented to counter Freud. 'So entirely does the womb dominate the book that it becomes a symbol, in the arch of Lincoln cathedral, or in the moon ... The womb is so portentous and enviable an organ that the men in the book make some effort to participate in the marvel ...'[31] But Ursula, in that novel, so little participates in this happier womb-powered world that she 'cas-trates' Anton 'by a series of extremely tenuous and hazy bouts of magic. Her vehicle of destruction is moonlight, for Lawrence is addicted to the notion of the moon as a female symbol ...'[32]

Millett goes on to claim that the masculine attempt to play lord and master is 'the very stuff of Lawrence's later work'.[33] She doesn't seem to have noticed that those of Lawrence's male characters who find a way of living are precisely those who repeatedly fail to become lords and mas-ters. They are repeatedly balanced out by the female characters, and this is their salvation. (It also works the other way round, as in 'The Captain's

Doll': only men who do not allow themselves to be made into dolls, and women who accept not to make them into dolls, save the integrity of their being.)

Whatever else, Ursula in *Women in Love* does feel for the moon. The urge to destroy is Birkin's, and as in the 'Breadalby' passage the war produces the novel's vocabulary for this urge. Birkin, in 'l'intérieur', is possessed by the war lust to destroy: as if by contagion, or to demonstrate what 'The Reality of Peace' and Lawrence's letters argue, that is, that wars are made in human hearts. Birkin attempts to smash the moon, throwing large stones at its reflection, its 'white-burning centre', in a pond. It is as if he were trying to export his own destructiveness, to inflict upon a peaceful English moon-lit pond the damage of heavy shelling, to make it into 'a battlefield of broken lights and shadows'.[34] As in Richard Aldington's poem 'In the Trenches', quoted in Chapter 3, 'each rush and crash / Of mortar and shell' wound 'the breast of earth, / Of Demeter, our Mother' – and the men's 'frail' psyche. It is amazing how similar to the confusion of war the scene becomes as Birkin stones

> till there was nothing but a rocking of hollow noise, and a pond surged up, no moon any more, only a few broken flakes tangled and glittering broadcast in the darkness, without aim or meaning, a darkened confusion, like the black and white kaleidoscope tossed at random. The hollow night was rocking and crashing with noise, and from the sluice came sharp, regular flashes of sound. Flakes of light appeared here and there, glittering tormented among the shadows, far off, in strange places; among the dripping shadow of the willow on the island. Birkin stood and listened and was satisfied.
> Ursula was dazed, her mind was all gone.[35]

Birkin is exporting his own inner disintegration – engineering an outside reflection of his own inner violence. This is close to schizophrenia. Rereading the passage as I was writing it down, I've been reminded of the journey through hell that Bessie Head's schizophrenic protagonist, Elizabeth, undergoes in *A Question of Power*. It is not the First World War, but the horrors of colonialism, apartheid and post-colonial Africa that Elizabeth is being invaded by: it's as if she were Birkin's pond under attack:

> Suddenly, a terrible thunderbolt struck her heart. She could feel wave after wave of its power spread over her body ... As the last wave died down, she simply shot up into the air.... [Sello, one of Elizabeth's 'invaders', tells her] he had been the Osiris who had been shattered into a thousand fragments by the thunderbolt of Medusa.[36]

Sure, every situation (period, history, place, individual) is different and, sure, in gender terms there is some difference: Lawrence's 'alter ego' character, Birkin, does the stoning. Head's alter ego, Elizabeth, is the one who is struck. Birkin attacks something he perceives as female, 'the

inviolable moon', that keeps 'drawing itself together with strange, violent pangs'.[37] Elizabeth is attacked by two male figures, Sello and Dan.
But then, Elizabeth *is* aware (such lucidity is astounding) that it is also
because *she* contains destructiveness inside herself that she can thus be
invaded: 'It only needed someone to bring the hot lava to the surface for
her to find that a process of degradation, scorn and wild, blind cruelty
had its equivalent of wild, savage vengeance in her.'[38]

In *Women in Love*, it is by the great good luck of Ursula being
around and being who she is, being strong in her femininity and as a
person, that Birkin's destructiveness is contained. Ursula has been
watching, feeling as if she were being attacked by Birkin's attack on
the moon (so it isn't true to claim, as Millett does, that the association
between strong women characters and the moon disappears in
Lawrence's later work). But she hasn't fallen to bits. She lets him know
what he has been doing:

> 'You won't throw stones at it any more, will you?'
> 'How long have you been there?'
> 'All the time. You won't throw any more stones, will you?'
> 'I wanted to see if it could be quite gone off the pond,' he said.
> 'Yes, it was horrible, really. Why should you hate the moon? It hasn't
> done you any harm, has it?'
> 'Was it hate?' he said.
> And they were silent for a few minutes.[39]

If Kate Millett is right, and Lawrence does associate moon and womb,
what does this scene imply?

Breast. Womb. Phallus. The vulgarized concepts of psychoanalysis,
and either our supposed 'liberation' in matters sexual – or our *volonté de
savoir*, our will to know, as Foucault calls it – have made us target-happy
about using such words. Lawrence used them. He is so bold, so breath-
takingly direct about using them. Katherine Mansfield taunted him with
what she felt to be ridiculous in his vocabulary search for male dominance, threatening to call the cottage Lawrence shared with Frieda 'the
Phallus'. At the end of the chapter 'Moony', Gudrun reminds Ursula
how insufferable Birkin's solemnness and intensity are: 'He cries you
down ... and by mere force of violence ... living with him would be ...
too wearying, too exhausting ... He would want to control you
entirely.... And then, the real clumsiness of his mind, is his lack of self-
criticism.'[40]

But then, this comes precisely after Ursula has been able to hold her
own in the face of Birkin's attack. And Gudrun is described by the narrator (if there is such a person) as 'fearing' and 'despising' men, though
admiring their activities 'overmuch'. If so much is rolled into speaking
for, and mocking, 'the Phallus', what is rolled into the female organs?

I have written 'organs'. The distinction between breast and womb
strikes me as important.

While Paul's relation to his mother, in *Sons and Lovers*, does stand in the way of his relation to other women, while readers of Lawrence, and Lawrence himself, kept harping back to the Oedipus story – the 'Mother-incest idea ... that at certain periods the man has a desire and a tendency to return into the woman', as Lawrence's letter of 5 December 1918 to Katherine Mansfield states – it seems to me that Lawrence evolved from breast to womb in the course of the war years in a way that showed maturing, integration of elements of his personality.

Melanie Klein's work has shown the primacy of the breast as a first object to which a relation exists for the infant. Some of Lawrence's poems celebrate the woman's breast – the return to the mother's body – as the only relation that can provide comfort in a chaotic, war-driven world. In the 'Song of A Man Who Is Loved' the breasts are almost an umbilical cord:

> Between her breasts is my home, between her breasts.
> Three sides set on me chaos and bounce, but the fourth side rests
> Sure on a haven of peace, between the mounds of her breasts.
> . . . .
> And the chaos that bounces and rattles like shrapnel, at least
> Has for me a door into peace, warm dawn in the east
> Where her bosom softens towards me, and the turmoil has ceased.[41]

But the man who sings the 'Song of Man Who Is Not Loved' is terrified by the space that surrounds him:

> I hold myself up, and feel a big wind blowing
> Me like a gadfly into the dusk ...
> . . . .
> How shall I flatter myself that I can do
> Anything in such immensity? ...[42]

Yet, perhaps precisely because of the depth of his early intimacy with his mother, Lawrence did not only have nostalgia for union; he had a remarkable capacity to seek for fulfilment in and through *relationships*. In his difficulties in separating from his mother, he had struggled with boundaries. Now, in 1916, as Delaney perceptively points out, the combination of the Murrys leaving Tregerthen and the sense of 'paranoid exacerbation' which made him 'fearful and "sick of mankind" ' leads Lawrence to want something different from woman (who in this particular instance must have a lot to do with Frieda): no longer to provide her breasts as a refuge against the 'chaos and shrapnel' of the world, but to help him 'build up higher the walls of his ego'. A poem actually called 'Manifesto' makes a bid for separation:

> She has not realised yet, that fearful thing, that I am the other
> She thinks we are all of one piece.
> It is painfully untrue.[43]

'Since everything must rely on its opposite for definition, the differences
between men and women must be kept sharp lest both be left suspended
in the void of nonbeing', Delaney explains.[44] Though in 'Manifesto' the
'differences' have their weird and angry side. The male is aligned with
the predator, the female with the prey. Not the leopard, as in 'The Reality of Peace', but the 'blazing tiger', that in a paradisal hereafter 'will
spring upon the deer, undimmed'.

Lawrence, Cowan argues, was much closer to the relational/structure
model of personality (as represented by, among others, W. A. D. Fairbairn, Winnicott and Heinz Kohut), which holds that ' "human nature is
completely realized only in relationship, interaction, participation with
others" ', than to the drive/structure model of Freud, Heinz Hartmann
and Lacan. But, 'for all his effort to articulate the "trembling balance" ',
Lawrence was carrying too heavy a baggage from childhood to achieve
it. Cowan sensitively describes this baggage – the over-great dependency
on the mother, the lack of a father who could either stand between his
mother and himself or provide an idealizable figure, hence the need, in
later life, to seek nurturing and supportive male figures, strong male figures too (from Jack Murry in real life to Rawdon Lilly in *Aaron's Rod* to
Ramon Carrasco in *The Plumed Serpent* to Kangaroo. Lawrence's 'wounds
to the soul' 'had to do with nurturance, in the formation of his archaic
nuclear self, not with triangular sexual competition in the "family
romance" ':

> That is why Lawrence's fictional themes, with few exceptions, do not center
> on oedipal guilt but on male autonomy . . . The ambivalence of the son who
> struggled for independence from the strong mother, whom he loved but
> whose overwhelming possessive love served only her own need for suste-
> nance more than his need for normal psychological growth . . . is echoed in
> the ambivalence toward women and struggles for male autonomy on the
> part of protagonists like Rupert Birkin or Aaron Sisson.[45]

This is another, empathetic way to say what Janine Chasseguet-
Smirgel argues about 'phallic sexual monism'. The vulnerable little boy
fantasizes about precisely what he feels he lacks so he can protect himself
against the mother's power: in Lawrence's case, the father had addition-
ally been lacking. Yet what strikes me in all this is almost the reverse of
what Cowan argues: that is, how capable of relations to women, actual
and fictional, Lawrence is. How much his own quest for being, for singleness as he calls it after 1916, travels through the strength and singleness
of women. It is shot through with aggression, with contradictions, with
bouts of hatred – his treatment of characters like Hermione and at times,
Gudrun – the recurring phantasy of the male as tiger or leopard over-
coming the female deer – though none of his actual male characters *ever*
does that. Lawrence's males endlessly talk tough: but they act gentle.
Destruction only happens when a female character 'wants' it – ho ho ho

– in the unique case of 'The Woman Who Rode Away', the woman who finds fulfilment through religious self-sacrifice to an Indian sun god, and it is done as ritual fantasy. I can only speculate, as countless have done before me, that the strength of Lawrence's actual *relationship* with his mother, and the strength of his later relationship with a woman of Frieda's calibre, made this possible. This is what makes him into the sort of man who could write the 'star' letter to Katherine Mansfield.

It was the artist in him that made him so empathetic, Cowan argues. He quotes Frieda's beautiful little piece about Lawrence finding a gentian: ' "I remember feeling as if he had a strange communion with it, as if the gentian yielded up its blueness, its very essence, to him." ' Cowan comments: 'And this empathy carries him to unexpected dimensions of quickness, pregnant with the potential for further transformation and change.'[46]

'Pregnant'. What an interesting word. A lapse? A hint? Faced up with it I remember that Kate Millet had found in Lawrence the 'disorder' of womb envy. Is Cowan falling into the disorder too, wanting to arrogate for Lawrence the power of female creativity? Or is he putting his finger on Lawrence's strength? Is such creativity, as I have hinted, a progress – from the need to take refuge in the breast at a time when the world of men has gone war-mad, to the desire to escape, to differentiate from and counter, the power of the breast, to an integration by a male artist of the feminine dimension in himself, of his (imaginary) womb?

In her essay 'The Bodily Encounter with the Mother', discussing 'what is known in analytic therapies as orality, infinite thirst, the desire to be gratified by [the mother]', Luce Irigaray proposes that it is because the mother's body is censored, because language is conceived as something that is superimposed 'upon the archaic world of the flesh', as something which 'makes a hole in the bellies of women and in the site of their identity', that the Oedipus myth has been given such prominence. The essential separation is from the uterus, 'our first home'. 'The unavoidable and irreparable wound is the cutting of the umbilical cord.' The castration threat is simply a reiteration of something that has already happened;

> when the child makes demands of the breast, isn't it demanding to receive all? The all that it received in its mother's belly: life, the home in which it lived, the home of its body, food, air, warmth, movement etc. For want of being situated in its time, its space and their exile, that is all displaced on to oral avidity.[47]

Certain men and women, Irigaray goes on, reinforcing the point made by Janine Chasseguet-Smirgel, defensively project power on to the mother, phallic or otherwise, 'on to the abyss of a silent and threatening belly. Threatening because silent?' 'The womb, unthought in its place of the first sojourn in which we become bodies, is fantasized by many men to be a devouring mouth, a cloaca or anal or urethral outfall, a phallic threat, at best reproductive.'[48]

I find Lawrence to be doing precisely the reverse of this. The womb is indeed ever present in fictions like *The Rainbow*, and its arch remains the image of the 'home' where balance might be found: even the 'singleness' of which 'Manifesto' dreams is expressed through the image of the rainbow:

> we shall love, we shall hate
> but it will be like music, sheer utterance,
> issuing straight out of the unknown,
> the lightning and the rainbow appearing as unbidden, unchecked, like ambassadors.

Lawrence's writing carries such memories of the bliss of being related to another body, through the umbilical cord, and thus of existing through connection with the 'I am not':

> I am that I am, and no more than that: but so much
> I am, nor will be bounced out of it. So at last I touch
> All that I am-not in softness, sweet softness, for she is such.[49]

Above all, because of his own, imaginatively accepted, femininity (which includes, but is in excess of, his own acceptance of what drives him, and his male characters, to be fascinated by and want to love other men), there is in Lawrence, unlike in Freud, no recoil from the pre-Oedipal, the archaic – on the contrary, there is an ongoing search for it. Whereas Freud, in 'On Female Sexuality', confesses himself nonplussed by 'the dark continent of femininity' – projects it outwards, on to women – Lawrence seeks for it inwards:

> [In] the dark continent of myself, I have a whole stormy chaos of 'feelings' ... some of them roar like lions, some twist like snakes, some bleat like snow-white lambs, some warble like linnets, some are absolutely dumb, but swift as silvery fishes, some are oysters that open only on occasion.[50]

It is through women's voices – here, through Lou, in *St Mawr* – that in the post-war years the search for life is pursued: 'think, mother, if we could get our lives straight from the source, as the animals do, and still be ourselves' ... 'Why can't men get their life straight, like St Mawr [the stallion], and then think? Why can't they think quick, mother: quick as a woman ... ?'[51] And yes, Lawrence would like the men to think better than the women: 'only farther than we do', Lou adds ... And she is questioning her mother: as if the mother could (from the depths of her womb?) produce the living men that would be the answer. Lawrence is the best answer anyone's got in that period, it seems to me: a man capable of a *jouissance* 'beyond the phallus' as Lacan might put it, even though his own quest for the phallus never got him where he wanted. 'Might not this *jouissance* which one experiences and knows nothing of, be that which puts us on the path of ex-istence? And why not interpret one face of the Other, the God face, as supported by feminine *jouissance*?' (Lacan).[52] You do not have to be a woman to be capable of it, whatever Lacan might say: all you need is a relation to the womb. From what a depth of acceptance or recall of the womb, of the dark continent of himself – Jung might have said, of the 'anima' in him – was Lawrence, with all his wounds and anger, able to produce these questing women characters, still rich with life, with 'quickness', with desire – to rise to the blueness of a gentian? Did he not, with Frieda,[53] enjoy access to what Kristeva calls 'Woman's Time'?

> We had lost all ordinary sense of time and place. Those flowers that came new to Lawrence, the fireflies at night and the glow-worms, the first beech leaves spreading on the trees like a delicate veil overhead, and our feet buried in last year's brown beech leaves, these were our time and our events. (Frieda Lawrence, 1935)

Was it not this capacity for fulfilment that enabled Lawrence to write to Katherine Mansfield of that one moment when she in his soul was at one with him: 'Then suddenly we saw one planet, so beautiful, a large, fearful, strong star, that we were both pierced by it, possessed, for a second'?

Notes

1 Paul Delaney, *D. H. Lawrence's Nightmare: The Writer and His Circle in the Years of the Great War* (Brighton: Harvester, 1979), p. 230.
2 Ibid., pp. 224–31, 275–6.
3 Elaine Feinstein, *Lawrence and the Women: The Intimate Life of D. H. Lawrence* (London: HarperCollins, 1993).
4 H. D., *Tribute to Freud* (Manchester: Carcanet, 1985).
5 Ibid., p. 128.
6 Ibid., p. 141.
7 Ibid., p. 134.
8 Ibid., p. 135.
9 Ibid., pp. 149–50.
10 Quoted Delaney, *D. H. Lawrence's Nightmare*, p. 231.
11 D. H. Lawrence, *The Letters of D. H. Lawrence*, ed. James T. Boulton (Cambridge: Cambridge University Press, 1984), vol. 3, p. 343. All quotations below also from vol. 3.
12 Ibid., p. 105.
13 D. H. Lawrence, *Fantasia of the Unconscious and Psychoanalysis and the Unconscious*, Phoenix edn (London: Heinemann, 1961), p. 64.
14 C. G. Jung, 'De l'Inconscient' (1918), French tr. from the German by Alix Gaillard-Dermigny, *Cahiers Jungiens de Psychanalyse* 84 (Autumn 1995), pp. 43–64, at pp. 58–9.
15 Quoted James C. Cowan, *D. H. Lawrence and the Trembling Balance* (University Park: Pennsylvania State University Press, 1990), p. 258.

16 Lawrence, *Letters*, p. 301.
17 See ibid.; also Daniel J. Schneider, *D. H. Lawrence: The Artist as Psychologist*, and Frederick J. Hoffman, 'Lawrence's Quarrel with Freud', in *Freudianism and the Literary Mind* both cited in Cowan, *D. H. Lawrence*.
18 Cowan, *D. H. Lawrence*, pp. 259, 270.
19 Delaney, *D. H. Lawrence's Nightmare*, p. 226.
20 Ibid., p. 239.
21 D. H. Lawrence, *Women in Love*, with an introd. and notes by Charles L. Ross (Harmondsworth: Penguin, 1982), p. 139.
22 In John Silkin (ed.), *The Penguin Book of First World War Poetry* (Harmondsworth: Penguin, 1979).
23 Delaney, *D. H. Lawrence's Nightmare*, p. 238.
24 Lawrence, *Letters*, p. 39.
25 Delaney, *D. H. Lawrence's Nightmare*, p. 228.
26 Lawrence, *Letters*, p. 39.
27 Lawrence, *Women in Love*, pp. 213, 300.
28 Ibid., p. 549.
29 Kate Millett, *Sexual Politics* (London: Rupert Hart-Davis, 1971), p. 260.
30 Lawrence, *Women in Love*, p. 213.
31 Millett, *Sexual Politics*, pp. 258–9.
32 Ibid., p. 262.
33 Ibid., p. 259.
34 Lawrence, *Women in Love*, p. 323.
35 Ibid., p. 324.
36 Bessie Head, *A Question of Power* (London: Heinemann, 1974), p. 39.
37 Lawrence, *Women in Love*, p. 323.
38 Head, *A Question of Power*, p. 98.
39 Lawrence, *Women in Love*, p. 325.
40 Ibid., p. 341.
41 D. H. Lawrence, *Complete Poems*, ed. Vivian de Sola Pinto and Warren Roberts (2 vols, London: Heinemann, 1964), vol. 1, p. 249.
42 Ibid., p. 223.
43 D. H. Lawrence, 'Manifesto', in *Complete Poems*, vol. 1, p. 266.
44 Delaney, *D. H. Lawrence's Nightmare*, pp. 286–7.
45 Cowan, *D. H. Lawrence*, pp. 264–6.
46 Ibid., p. 268.
47 Luce Irigaray, *The Irigaray Reader*, ed. Margaret Whitford (Oxford: Blackwell, 1991), pp. 40–1.
48 Ibid., p. 41.
49 D. H. Lawrence, 'Manifesto' and 'Song of the Man Who Is Loved', in *Complete Poems*, vol. 1, pp. 268, 249.
50 D. H. Lawrence, 'The Novel and the Feelings' (1925), quoted Cowan, *D. H. Lawrence*, p. 260.
51 D. H. Lawrence *St Mawr*, in *The Short Novels*, vol. 2, Phoenix edn (London: Heinemann, 1956), pp. 57, 56.
52 In Juliet Mitchell and Jacqueline Rose, *Jacques Lacan and the École Freudienne: Female Sexuality* (London: Macmillan, 1990), p. 147.
53 Following quote from Rosie Jackson, *Frieda Lawrence: Including 'Not I, But the Wind'* (London: Pandora, 1994), p. 119.

5

Virginia Woolf: Penis Envy and the Man's Sentence

In section 9 of 'The Window', in *To the Lighthouse*,[1] Lily, about to speak to Mr Bankes, catches him gazing in a rapture of love at Mrs Ramsay. What Lily had been about to say

> paled beside this 'rapture', this silent stare, for which she felt intense grati-
> tude; for nothing so solaced her, eased her of the perplexity of life, and
> miraculously raised its burdens, as this sublime power, this heavenly gift,
> and one would no more disturb it, while it lasted, than break up the shaft of
> sunlight lying level across the floor. (p. 48)

In her turn Lily gazes herself at Mrs Ramsay, remembering her own moment of rapture as she had once sat on the floor with her arms round Mrs Ramsay's knees, desiring the 'art to press through' into the treasure 'chambers of the woman who was, physically, touching her'. Lily longs for, it seems to me, the same at-oneness which Lawrence enjoyed with Katherine Mansfield in his dream of the bright star. Lawrence was content that it should have blazed 'for a second on one's soul'. Lily wants a more complete communion. It is not expressed through images of light, but through images of fluid – does not take place in the outdoors night, but (strangely) in chambers like those of the 'tombs of the kings':

> What device for becoming, like waters poured into one jar, inextricably the
> same, one with the object one adored? Could the body achieve it, or the
> mind, subtly mingling in the intricate passages of the brain? or the heart?
> Could loving, as people called it, make her and Mrs Ramsay one? (pp. 50–1)

What Lily is after is woman-specific – has to do with the pre-Oedipal, with union with the mother: much that is profound has been written about this (Clare Hanson, Françoise Defromont, Makiko Minow-Pinkney,

Elizabeth Abel, Rachel Bowlby . . .). It has to do with lesbian desire, a desire directed towards the mother. Lily wishes for the (phallic?) 'art to press through', but ends up longing for fusion. The way Lily's desire appears in *To the Lighthouse* is reminiscent of that one moment of 'illumination' in *Mrs Dalloway*, oft-quoted: Clarissa remembers Sally Seton, and the flash of memory strikes her like 'a match burning in a crocus; an inner meaning almost expressed'. Yet what does happen in *To the Lighthouse* in the passage I have quoted retains a relation to heterosexuality. Lily has witnessed Mr Bankes's look of love for Mrs Ramsay. Reality, the adult world, further intervenes, interrupting Lily's longing. Mr Bankes becomes interested in her picture. He has 'seen' it:

> This man had shared with her something profoundly intimate. And thanking Mr Ramsay for it and Mrs Ramsay for it and the hour and the place, crediting the world with a power which she had not suspected, that one could walk away down that long gallery not alone any more but arm in arm with somebody – the strangest feeling in the world and the most exhilarating – she nicked the catch of her paint-box to, more firmly than was necessary, and the nick seemed to surround in a circle for ever the paint-box, the lawn, Mr Bankes, and that wild villain, Cam, dashing past. (p. 53)

The section shuttles between three moments of union: Mr Bankes's blissful contemplation of Mrs Ramsay; Lily's imagined 'intimacy' with Mrs Ramsay; and her shared intimacy with Mr Bankes. They will be thought of as 'little daily miracles' by Lily many years on, towards the end of the novel. The same image as had been used in *Mrs Dalloway* recurs: 'illuminations, matches struck unexpectedly in the dark' (p. 150). The image is more man-made, more fragile than Lawrence's 'strong' bright star, and the moments or quests, unlike Lawrence's, not sexual: Mr Bankes's adoration for Mrs Ramsay is platonic, his shared moment with Lily is one of companionship, not passion. Only Lily's memory of sitting with her arms round Mrs Ramsay's knees has longing in it, one that strangely mingles the need to *penetrate* into 'chambers' (be they of the womb, or brain) with the desire to fuse with Mrs Ramsay *inside* those chambers, as if they could contain them both. It is like a combination of phallic desire and a desire for oceanic union in a fantasized womb-space, that is both the beloved's and larger than the beloved's. Yet it is as though Woolf had the same register of images as Lawrence's, in that heterosexual relating is expressed, as in Lawrence's letter to Katherine Mansfield, through the image of a star – though not a welcome one. Lily's flashing memory of Paul Rayley is like a 'star slid[ing] in the sky, a reddish light' burning 'in her mind', dangerous, rising with a 'roar' and 'crackle', making the sea run 'red and gold', and bringing with it, for Lily, the urge to 'throw herself off the cliff and be drowned looking for a pearl brooch on the beach', as well as 'fear and disgust' at its predatoriness (and at Mrs Ramsay's) (p. 163).

By contrast, the moments of union or illumination in 'The Window' are gentle. Triangular: both Mr Bankes and Lily experience them in relation to Mrs Ramsay before an intimacy of understanding occurs between them. Triangular: like the 'odd-shaped triangular shadow over the step' that, almost at the end of the novel, appears as the memory or ghost of Mrs Ramsay, 'alter[ing] the composition little' (p. 185), making Lily's dream possible – Lily who wants to both respond to the ordinariness of experience and yet be able to feel, 'It's a miracle, it's an ecstasy' (p. 186). And they – the moments of union – also occur *inside* the space, the circle, provided by the existing heterosexual – parental – couple: 'And, thanking Mr Ramsay for it and Mrs Ramsay for it and the hour and the place', Lily, as she over-firmly nicks the catch of her paint-box, feels as if 'the nick seemed to surround in a circle for ever the paint-box, the lawn, Mr Bankes, and that wild villain, Cam, dashing past.' The union in the (archaic, pre-Oedipal, Minoan–Mycenaean, to use Freud's archaeological metaphor about the pre-Oedipal) Egyptian tomb of kings, its 'chambers', never takes place. But moments of union occur, by contagion or in relation to, the strange-wombed Mrs Ramsay (for why should she feel herself to be, when most herself, a 'wedge-shaped core of darkness' (p. 60)? Why the *tomb* feature of the 'chambers'? Because Mrs Ramsay is destined to die? Because the figures of death and the mother keep merging at a deep level? Because death and darkness are in all of us?). Moments of union occur in the pre-war days presided over by, Mr and . Mrs Ramsay. Man and wife. The world they make between them contains their children and guests, circles their moments of relating, of illumination. The child Cam, 'dashing past', seems to have been generated by the momentary coupling of Lily and Mr Bankes, itself held inside the larger parental couple of Mr and Mrs Ramsay.

In the war section of To the Lighthouse, 'Time Passes', it feels as if Virginia Woolf had picked up on all the war poets' images of the wounded earth as *mother*. She weaves into one tight fabric the decay of the mother-house, the mother's death (Prue in childbirth as well as Mrs Ramsay) and the devastation of war. The mother's death signals the end of communion – of relating. Meaning and mirroring bleed out of nature as through a vast miscarriage. The 'thud of something falling' seems to drop into the 'stillness', as a shell explodes, killing Andrew Ramsay, among others in France. For those who, on the English shore, go to 'pace the beach' and look at the sea, there is 'the silent apparition of an ashen-coloured ship for instance, come, gone; *there was a purplish stain upon the bland surface of the sea as if something had boiled and bled, invisibly, beneath'* (pp. 124–5; my italics).

As mourning Lily returns to the house with the mourning Ramsays in the third part of the novel, after the war, the 'circle' that the Ramsays had made possible in the first part is broken. Nothing gells. Lily's painting has lost meaning. Only the strenuous work of memory and mourning enables her to eventually create her 'mirror' – to have her 'vision'. At the start, preyed upon by Mr Ramsay's own mourning – his demandingness, his blackmailing his own children with his despair, his search for someone who will do for him what Mrs Ramsay used to do – she is paralysed: 'But with Mr Ramsay bearing down on her, she could do nothing. Every time he approached – he was walking up and down the terrace – ruin approached, chaos approached. She could not paint' (p. 139).

The female artist's – Lily's – predicament is central to the novel. Through the figure of the mother, the novel is also female-centred. Clare Hanson is right to point out that Woolf is closer to Melanie Klein than to Freud in her presentation of the mother as primary and active.[2] James perceives his mother as 'the self-contained source of life and creativity', pouring 'erect into the air a rain of energy, a column of spray'. But his father is sterile, his rival for Mrs Ramsay's ministrations, plunging 'into this delicious fecundity ... like a beak of brass, barren and bare. He wanted sympathy ...' (p. 38).

It is female Cam, 'that wild villain', who on the boat with her father and brother on the way to the lighthouse, recaptures something of the oceanic capacity, the capacity for communion and joy, for finding mirroring and meaning in nature, which Lily and Mrs Ramsay both experienced in the pre-war section, and which the war and the mother's death seemed to have destroyed: on contact with the sea 'streaming through her fingers, a spray of seaweed vanishing behind them', Cam feels her father's anger, James's obstinacy and her own anguish stream away:

> From her hand, ice cold, held deep in the sea, there spurted a fountain of joy at the change, at the escape, at the adventure (that she should be alive, that she should be there). And the drops falling from this sudden and unthinking fountain of joy fell here and there on the dark, the slumbrous shapes in her mind ... (p. 174)

And yet, with all its woman-centredness, the book seeks for balance between the sexes. It carefully distributes text between male and female characters, imaginatively enters both male and female consciousness. In the third section in particular, the text shuttles between Lily and Mr Ramsay, Lily and the Ramsays on their way to the lighthouse – between, on the one hand, contemplation/memory/creation and memory/action. The novel pays generous attention to specifically male-centred perspectives. James is given even more space than Cam. The growing up of the two children, their relation to sex, continuously balances male and female needs, as in the episode of the boar's skull which Mrs Ramsay both covers/mediates for her daughter and preserves intact for her son. The son needs to know that the symbolic male organs are still there, though hidden by Mrs Ramsay's shawl. The daughter needs to be protected from the fear of the 'horrid thing, branching at her all over the room', lulled to sleep by the rhythmic evocation of 'beautiful mountains' 'with valleys and flowers and bells ringing and birds singing' (p. 106).

More text is devoted to James than to Cam though, and in particular to James's savage bouts of anger against his father, which have led many to talk about the Oedipus complex. Yet it is not Mr Ramsay's patriarchal interventions that jar, but his own inadequacies as a father. His own dependency on his wife, his own need to be mothered make him his children's rival rather than their father (and once his wife is dead, make him demand that the world, including his own children, should mother him). When James wants it to be fine tomorrow so he can go to the lighthouse, Mr Ramsay does not speak what Lacan calls the 'Non [Nom] du Père', does not utter the Father's 'No' that would enable the son to separate from his mother. He petulantly and self-centeredly asserts that 'it won't be fine', not out of care that his son should come to terms with the reality principle but out of his own need to state things as he sees them, without regard for others' feelings. Moreover, what he states so categorically is not a verifiable truth, it is a prediction about the weather: accurate, as it turns out. But still a prediction, still a statement in the future mode. He does not say, 'You cannot go to the lighthouse,' nor 'It is not convenient that we should go tomorrow to the lighthouse but we will go some other day'; he uses the weather to gloomily deflate his son's joy. Not a grand stance for a guardian of the law. Not a very patriarchal stance. If anything, it is not the Oedipal conflict that is the source of James's angst; it is rather that Mr Ramsay is not enough of a father.

It seems to me that there is great imaginativeness (no doubt based on a considerable amount of observation and memory) in Woolf's ability to portray such a specific (and typical?) father–son tussle. There is also great generosity. For, willy-nilly, somehow, with all his inadequacies, Mr Ramsay ends up being a 'good enough' father (to use Winnicott's celebrated qualificative). As their boat approaches the lighthouse, almost at the end of the novel, Mr Ramsay does give James what James had wanted all along: he gives him approval: ' "Well done!" James had steered them like a born sailor.' Cam thinks (maternally?), 'There!', 'You've got it at last' (p. 189). And this approval comes at the point when James has been able to detach enough from his resentment against his father to be able to accept that his father's aggressiveness could be regarded as impersonal. He has the image of a huge wheel crushing a foot – and the image of a harpy swooping down from nowhere. His urge to strike 'his father to the heart' goes:

> now, as he grew older, and sat staring at his father in impotent rage, it was not him, that old man reading, whom he wanted to kill, but it was the thing that descended on him – without his knowing it perhaps: that fierce sudden black-winged harpy, with its talons and its beak all cold and hard, that struck and struck at you . . . (p. 170)

James knows that it will be 'that', that thing, the harpy, that he will fight as tyranny, as despotism, for the rest of his days, wherever he finds it, and not the old man who is his real father, 'very sad, reading his book'. But isn't he also becoming aware of his own projections? Is the harpy Mr Ramsay attacking his son, or is James's fury against Mr Ramsay projected on to the father, who is then fantasized as the attacker? For Mr Ramsay is generally unaware that his interventions are felt as attacks. He is needy, but not nasty . . .

In *To the Lighthouse* as in *Mrs Dalloway*, Woolf bravely battles with relations between couples, the search for balance between male and female, the attempt to both understand and imagine masculinity as well as femininity – no doubt, with the hope which also seems to me to be there in Lawrence, that by both imagining and reimagining, something of what has been maimed by the war might begin to heal. Both Lawrence, and Woolf in *Mrs Dalloway*, work to free manhood from Kiplingesque demands. 'If': if you are brave, unflinching, unfeeling . . . 'you will be a man my son,' Kipling's celebrated poem prescribes, making manhood an impossibly idealistic prize to attain. The scandalously wasteful and industrial warfare of the First World War forced many like Lawrence and Woolf to ask, does the courage the military life requires make a man, or unmake him? Lawrence showed that the repression of feelings, the forcing men to go against their gut instincts, was perverting, in stories such as 'The Prussian Officer', or 'The Thorn in the Flesh'. 'The Thorn in the Flesh' focuses on Bachmann, a young German soldier. His manhood is found wanting according to military codes. He cannot stand heights, is forced by the sergeant to go up a climbing-ladder, goes sick, pees himself in an agony of shame and is screamed at by the enraged sergeant, whom he hits. He has to flee, and hide – but then his true manhood is *not* found wanting in his encounter with the maidservant Emilie: 'And he was restored and completed, close to her. That little, twitching, momentary clasp of acknowledgement that she gave him in her satisfaction, roused his pride unconquerable.'[3]

'Coward' is the accusation of the patriarchal, unimaginative doctors when Septimus Warren Smith in *Mrs Dalloway* jumps to his death, driven mad initially by the repression of feelings that surviving the horrors at the front has forced upon him, then further driven to the edge by the threat of interment. In the alignment and identification and textual to-ing and fro-ing and touching of Septimus and Clarissa, Woolf, like Lawrence, reopens the question of courage, political or otherwise, the question of power, the question of gender difference. What is the value, she asks, of a society that calls repression and denial, manliness? Couldn't the alliances, and the matings, be between men and women of related, but unoppressive sensibilities, like Septimus and Rezia, Clarissa and Peter Walsh, rather than between the bullies and the bullied? *To the Lighthouse* rewrites the terms of power and creativity, distributes them in a different way between men and women. It seeks out ways in which women might create, and men, like James and his father, might find a solution to their antagonisms, go beyond personalities to the impersonality of oppression, and fight that. In their twin focus on male and female, Woolf's two novels of the mid-twenties deliberately seek to imagine a heterosexual world.

Orlando is written in 1928, only one year after *To the Lighthouse*. *A Room of One's Own* (1929) just a year later. They both foreground androgyny.

Has anything happened to make Woolf despair of a more balanced relation between the sexes? Or is the Lily Briscoe inside Virginia Woolf too weary of trying to hold forth what only extreme effort makes possible in too dark a world? 'Yes, she thought, laying down her brush in extreme fatigue, I have had my vision' (p. 192). In the early thirties, Lawrence, equally weary no doubt, will move towards the shrunken world of *Lady Chatterley's Lover . . .*

The world of the first part of *To the Lighthouse*, in which it *is* possible for Lily to know moments of communion inside the circle made by the Mr Ramsay–Mrs Ramsay couple (and one of those moments with Mr Bankes, a man) is a pre-war world, idealized perhaps, though it has its darkness, its power struggles, its class, generational and gender clashes. It is a world in which lyricism and a certain kind of chivalry are still strong (in Mr Bankes's *'amour courtois'* for Mrs Ramsay, but even Charles Tansley responds to Mrs Ramsay; Mr Ramsay is a Walter Scott fan). Mrs Ramsay reads poetry, recites it to herself:

> And all the lives we ever lived
> And all the lives to be
> Are full of trees and changing leaves.[4]

Whether fantasy, or reality, it is a world which for Woolf the war has changed and irredeemably, whatever the momentary reparation of the final part.

In *A Room of One's Own*, listening to the background murmur of the men's after-dinner talk, the writer fails to catch the 'humming noise' that would have been there before the war. It would, she feels, have gone something like Tennyson:

> There has fallen a splendid tear
>   From the passion-flower at the gate.
> She is coming, my dove, my dear;
>   She is coming, my life, my fate

What the women might have hummed was Christina Rossetti:

> My heart is like a singing bird
>   Whose nest is in a water'd shoot;
> My heart is like a rainbow shell
>   That paddles in a halcyon sea;

My heart is gladder than all these
    Because my love is come to me.[5]

The narrator makes an unfavourable contrast between living poets who
'express a feeling that is actually being made and torn out of us at the
moment' and the Victorian poets who could 'excite ... one to such aban-
donment, such rapture ... so that one responds easily, familiarly'. Why,
she asks,

Why has Alfred ceased to sing
    She is coming, my dove, my dear?
Why has Christina ceased to respond
My heart is gladder than all these
    Because my love is come to me?

Shall we lay the blame on the war? when the guns fired in August 1914, did
the faces of men and women show so plain in each other's eyes that
romance was killed? Certainly it was a shock (to women in particular with
their illusions about education and so on) to see the faces of our rulers in the
light of the shell-fire. So ugly they looked – German, English, French – so
stupid. But lay the blame where one will, on whom one will, the illusion
that inspired Tennyson and Christina Rossetti to sing so passionately about
the coming of their loves is far rarer now than then.[6]

I find it touching, as well as sad, that Woolf, a contemporary of my
grandfather's, should be reacting to the war so very much like him, and
that she should also have found that love between the sexes was one of
the great casualties of the war. But what is strange is how she goes on
from there. Alison Light, in her most interesting study *Forever England:
Femininity, Literature and Conservatism Between the Wars*, sees something
revealing about this very passage. Having come upon the thought that
perhaps war, destroying the illusions the sexes had about each other,
might have 'put truth in its place', Woolf leaves truth suspended: 'For
truth ...' She cannot carry on. Cannot know what truth is, how public
and private, subjective and official, match or are mismatched. This inde-
terminacy is symptomatic of, and part of the making of, modernity, Alison Light argues. 'Woolf is of her time in citing the war as marking the
moment from which it no longer seemed possible to divorce the dramas
of the interior life from the mainstream of history.'[7]

Alison Light goes on to say that 'it is not coincidental' that the rest of
A Room of One's Own should be concerned with 'what a feminine relationship to knowledge and the past might be'.[8] Woolf's 'anger at exclusion' is fed by her comparisons of (privileged) male and
(underprivileged) female colleges at an imaginary Oxbridge – by her
readings of male-authored texts full of anger against women in the
British Museum library. Unlike Alison Light, I do find a contradiction
there – a bizarre gap. I don't see why bemoaning that the war should
have destroyed love between the sexes should lead to considerations of

women's traditionally impeded relation to learning. Not that I wish to fault Woolf on the grounds of logic (she *is* at Oxbridge and one thought leads to another, and in any case women's relation to learning is what she has been asked to talk about). But the contradiction speaks of something else than what is being said. For if the past tells a history of male privilege, of male denigration of women, of men denying women access to knowledge and creativity – if, in short, men and women in the past have had a lousy time of each other – how come Tennyson and Rossetti could sing so lovingly? How come Woolf feels such nostalgia for the time when such singing was possible, how can she miss the loving 'murmur' that was in the background of pre-war conversations unless it was there? Or is it only the would-be female scholars and creators, the Judith Shakespeares, the third-generation Ursulas from the *Rainbow*, the educated New Women, potential rivals to the men – the Lily Briscoes who are told by the Charles Tansleys of this world 'women can't paint, can't write,' who are, and have always been, excluded from the reciprocities of love? But then, how could Alfred sing, how could Christina Rossetti '*respond*'? And how could Lily, but a year before, despite Mr Ramsay's demandingness and her own mourning, still complete her painting?

Or is the 'murmur' a romantic, a poetic illusion? A fantasized memory? Is the pre-war world of *To the Lighthouse*, harmonized and centred as it is by the lighthouse – the mother of light – Mrs Ramsay – who loves poetry – a fantasy? Difficult to credit, given the realism of that fictional world – the lack of money, the precise domesticity, the frictions, the power struggles, the mourning in that novel. But, having endured four years 'dominated' (in Leonard Woolf's words), 'not only by the war, but also by Virginia's illness',[9] as time passes, as the twenties move to an anguishing close, as that pre-war world becomes more remote, is it becoming impossible, for Virginia Woolf, to remember what a more luminous reality might be? It has disappeared in the lurid light of shelling: all that can now be seen are the ugly faces of 'our rulers', the powerful patriarchal faces, male privilege, women's underprivilege. Now that she is a more established writer, a successful literary Lily Briscoe as it were, is envy all that is left for Woolf to feel for men?

Penis envy?

For it is a little alarming to work out how Woolf's argumentation as she proceeds through *A Room of One's Own* matches the pattern described in Freud's almost contemporary, 'Some Psychical Consequences of the Anatomical Distinction Between the Sexes' (1925). Or are both texts *symptoms* of the same thing?

Post-war Bloomsbury discovered Freud, along with, as the poet Bryher claimed, 'all literary London'.[10] Elizabeth Abel, in her *Virginia Woolf and the Fictions of Psychoanalysis*, observes that the literary slant Bloomsbury put on psychoanalysis went a long way to realizing Freud's ideal of a movement divorced from psychiatry.[11] The Memoir Club, which began

its meetings in March 1920, gathered again the members of the Bloomsbury group, scattered during the war. Papers were read that were close
to, or downright in, analytic territory. Of its members, Virginia's own
brother Adrian Stephen trained as a psychoanalyst. His wife Karin was
also a convert to Freudian theory. James and Alix Strachey, who moved
to Vienna to be analysed by Freud in 1920, were by 1923 members of the
London Psycho-analytic Society, founded by Ernest Jones in 1913. Strachey was to undertake the translation of the Standard Edition of Freud's
work, the first volume of which was the third publication of the Hogarth
Press, delightedly recorded in Leonard Woolf's autobiography, *Downhill
All The Way*.[12] Alix Strachey became friends with Melanie Klein: both
were in analysis with Karl Abraham in 1924–5 in Berlin. The relationship
between Bloomsbury and psychoanalysis were multiple, and enduring:
Leonard and Virginia Woolf paid a visit to the exiled Freud in Hamp-
stead in 1939.[13]

But it also seems clear that, while Virginia Woolf was initially fascinated by Freudian ideas – by, for instance, Lytton Strachey's account of
the Oedipus complex and of 'incest between parent and child when they
are both unconscious of it'[14] – and while her explorations of sexual difference might be, as Rachel Bowlby has argued, 'uncannily close to
Freud's',[15] she was also very reticent about psychoanalysis, and claimed
only superficial knowledge of it – from hearsay. She only read Freud,
and the late Freud at that, very late, prior to meeting him in 1939. Maybe,
as Abel suggests, she was anxious about a rival discourse that posed as a
science, an 'authoritative discourse on "the dark places of psychology"
to which she also staked a claim'.[16] No doubt as to the strength of that
claim, no doubt as to Woolf's originality: the mother's Kleinian power in
To the Lighthouse, the particularity of the Oedipal relation between Mr
Ramsay and James, discussed above, are eloquent examples. So when I
mention Freud's essay on 'Anatomical Distinction Between the Sexes'
(1925) with reference to *A Room of One's Own* (1929), I am not in the least
suggesting that Woolf had Freud in mind. But that her denunciation of
sexual discrimination uncannily fits what Freud had described as penis
envy. And that, by comparison with her generous imaginativeness
towards male characters in her earlier 1920s works, this seems a step
backwards.

For, lo and behold! Having wined and dined exquisitely at an
Oxbridge male college, Woolf's narrator in *A Room of One's Own* eats
prunes and custard and partakes of a jug of tepid water at a women's
college. Back in her hostess Mary Seton's room, conversation flags.

> The human frame being what it is, heart, body and brain all mixed together,
> and not contained in separate compartments as they will no doubt be in
> another million years, a good dinner is of great importance to good talk.
> One cannot think well, love well, sleep well, if one has not dined well.
> (p. 20)

Mary Seton explains in what poverty-stricken circumstances, after what struggles, the women's colleges were founded. 'So obviously we cannot have wine and partridges and servants carrying the dishes on their heads, she said. We cannot have sofas and separate rooms' (p. 22).

Little girls, Freud says, are 'destined to make' a 'momentous discovery':

> They notice the penis of a brother or playmate, strikingly visible and of large proportions, at once recognize it as the superior counterpart of their own small and inconspicuous organ, and from that time forward fall a victim to envy for the penis.
> [The] little girl ... makes her judgment and decision in a flash. She has seen it and knows that she is without it and wants to have it.[17]

Woolf has certainly seen 'in a flash' that exquisite fare and after-dinner port and good conversation are 'superior' to 'inconspicuous' or downright dreary prunes and custard and water and lagging conversation. What does she then do? What Freud describes the little girl as doing. Having become aware of 'the wound to her narcissism', 'she develops, like a scar, a sense of inferiority.' She realizes that 'that sexual character is a universal one' and 'begins to share the contempt felt by men for a sex which is the lesser in so important a respect'. She then turns on her mother – resents her – begins to hate her – for having 'sent her into the world so insufficiently equipped'.[18]

> At the thought of all those women working year after year and finding it hard to get two thousand pounds together ... we burst out in scorn at the reprehensible poverty of our sex. What had our mothers been doing then that they had no wealth to leave us? Powdering their noses? Looking in at shop windows? Flaunting in the sun at Monte Carlo? (p. 22)

> I thought ... of the admirable smoke and drink and the deep arm-chairs and the pleasant carpets; of the urbanity, the geniality, the dignity which are the offspring of luxury and privacy and space. Certainly our mothers had not provided us with anything comparable to all this ... (p. 25)

But there is worse. What goes with a resentful state of mind – what Freud sees as part and parcel of femininity – is indeed deeply ingrained. Even the women who might have been born with a big one, a 'gift for poetry' – Shakespeare's hypothetical sister, Judith Shakespeare, born as gifted as he was – would have found that 'all the conditions of her life, all her own *instincts*, were hostile to the state of mind which is needed to set free whatever is in the brain' (p. 52). Lacking 'a room of her own', a quiet room, financial independence, lacking encouragement, fostering, confronted by the 'obscure masculine complex', the insistence that '*he* shall be superior' (p. 56), Shakespeare's sister – hampered by 'the desire to protest, to preach, to proclaim an injury, to pay off scores' – would never have been able to produce that 'free flowing' and 'unimpeded' poetry, that 'incandescence' that shines as Shakespeare's mind (p. 58). Thus were women writers over the ages found universally wanting as a sex, thus did they fall, Charlotte Brontë or George Eliot who, armed with the men's sentence, 'committed atrocities that beggar description'. Only Jane Austen, perhaps, had enough independence ... Jealousy, Freud points out, though 'not limited to one sex', 'plays a far larger part in the mental life of women than of men and that is because it is enormously reinforced from the direction of displaced penis-envy'.[19]

There are two immediate retorts to what I seem to be suggesting by juxtaposing Freud and Woolf here, that is, that *A Room of One's Own* might be dismissed as penis envy, or be regarded as symptomatic of it. The first is that Woolf is describing the historically accurate *class* dimension of gender. She is talking about cultural attitudes arising from socio-economic realities. She is talking about finance, laws that debarred women from owning wealth, from holding professional positions, from having access to education: the very things Freud is blind and deaf to. Who can tell whether it is not male (= gendered) class privileges, with the thought patterns that have been developed as a result of those privileges over time, which are being read as sexual givens, a 'strikingly visible' organ, 'of large proportions'? Who can tell whether it is not unconsciously to defend those privileges that a thinker like Freud would interpret as *penis* envy what is the desire to enjoy the same privileges, along with the realization that the order of things makes such enjoyment impossible, or puts categorical obstacles in its path: 'Can't paint, can't write'? Those phrases had changed meaning over time, of course: how gender codes have mutated through the ages, how subtle those historical shifts are, Woolf had explored in much greater detail in *Orlando*, presenting a much more shaded picture than the rather monolithic one of *A Room of One's Own*. But even *A Room of One's Own* can be used to question Freud just as much as I was using Freud to question Woolf.

For she does question. Not Freud himself: she has not read him. But the 'professors' who over centuries have spouted forth about the 'mental, moral and physical inferiority of women' (p. 33). Anger was at the root of these pronouncements, she feels. But 'anger disguised and complex, not anger simple and open' (p. 34). She can tell the 'professors' are angry because they do not write 'dispassionately' (p. 35). 'She develops, like a scar, a sense of inferiority,' Professor Freud had said: is this dispassionate language? Can a naturally constituted and undamaged human being experience their sex as a scar? 'Life for both sexes' being, Woolf reflects, so 'arduous', calling for such 'gigantic courage and strength', isn't it tempting to cradle one's self-confidence 'by thinking that other people are inferior to oneself', 'by feeling that one has some innate superiority – it may be wealth, or rank, a straight nose, or the portrait of a grandfather by Romney' – or one's sex (p. 36)? 'Women have served all these centuries as looking-glasses possessing the magic and delicious power of reflecting the figure of man as twice its natural size' (p. 37). Does the little girl's 'small and inconspicuous organ' serve to magnify the little boy's 'superior counterpart', 'strikingly visible and of large proportions',[20] or does Freud need this reflected superiority and all the imaginary privileges that go with it ('only men can paint, can write') to soften what is too painful in life, the political realities of the war and post-war period, his own cancer, his exploration of the death instinct, as Janine Chasseguet-Smirgel suggests? Is Woolf suffering from penis envy, or is the Professor's notion of penis envy a projected dream of superiority? Who sees whom, and what does each sex do with the mirror-image of the other?

There is however one passage in *A Room of One's Own* in which Woolf does tip into fantasy. It is the passage in which she reflects on how women, who 'think back through [their] mothers', have no tradition behind them, and cannot go to the great men writers for help. Man's mind has a 'weight, pace and stride' (p. 76) too unlike woman's, and the sentence current at the beginning of the nineteenth century 'ran something like this perhaps'. She then quotes/forges:

> The grandeur of their works was an argument with them, not to stop short, but to proceed. They could have no higher excitement or satisfaction than in the exercise of their art and endless generation of truth and beauty. Success prompts to exertion; and habit facilitates success. (p. 77)

I never could make sense of this sentence, except as an overgeneralized, mildly pompous Johnsonian statement vaguely to do with the Romans and with artistic achievement, till it occurred to me that it was a parodic and tongue-in-cheek description of male sexuality. For 'the grandeur of their works' read organs 'of large proportions'. Read 'excitement', 'satisfaction', 'exertion' and 'success' in erotic eighteenth-century parlance, 'generation' as real begetting, 'habit' as growing confidence, and developing a taste for it: it then becomes self-evident that the sentence has to do with males, and is not applicable to females . . .

But does it follow that as a *form*, as a sentence, it is unusable by females? Doesn't a clever (conscious, or unconscious?) sleight-of-hand here confuse the content with the form? Winifred Holtby was sceptical of the pictures of a 'feminine' and a 'masculine' novel Woolf goes on to draw after this passage:

> She speaks of the special creativeness of women. Yet looking round upon the world of human beings as we know it, we are hard put to it to say what is the natural shape of men or women, so old, so all-enveloping are the moulds fitted by history and custom over their personalities. We do not know how much of sensitiveness, intuition, protectiveness, docility and tenderness may not be naturally 'male', how much curiosity, aggression, audacity and combativeness may not be 'female'.[21]

But to return to the sentence which supposedly can only be used by

men – which then turns into a judicial sentence excluding women writers. Woolf quotes Thackeray and Dickens as having 'based' their prose
upon it. But did they? I think of the opening of *Bleak House* ... Of De
Quincey, whose prose, Baudelaire said, 'est naturellement spirale', naturally takes a spiral shape ... Of Woolf's own male contemporaries: what
had Lawrence or indeed Joyce taken from 'the man's sentence'? What
Woolf really wants is space for the kind of writing that she herself is
doing, and for what she perceives as realistically possible for contemporary English women writers. Above all, she wants space for what she
finds in Mary Carmichael, space for a woman to write 'Chloe liked
Olivia' – what it had taken the elaborate historical transsexual and transvestite disguises of *Orlando* for Woolf herself to explore. Is the subsuming of the woman's body in the arrogant 'man's sentence' that she
devises a way of protesting against the cultural norm of heterosexuality?

Yet it remains that in that underground protest Woolf imagines a situation in which by virtue of their sex men have an enormous, an oppressive advantage over women. The 'man's sentence', sexual as it is, is
usable by any male writer. It excludes all female writers.

We are indeed back to a more subtle, and this time more real, form of
penis envy. One that cannot be justified as resentment of economic and
social privilege: the 'man's sentence', 'strikingly visible and of large proportions', stands there in women's path, an eternal reminder of what
they do not have.

Analyst Maria Torok has written suggestively about 'The Meaning of
"Penis-Envy" in Women'.[22] Unlike Freud, she does not produce an
account of what happens to the little girl; she discusses what analysts
hear when they analyse women. Penis envy is heard in all female
analysands, she says, sometimes as episodic, at other times as central.
The feeling that what *I* haven't got, others have – feelings of lack, with
the fantasy that others have what I lack – jealousy, envy, despair, etc. –
are common to both sexes: but *only women attribute this lack to the nature of
their sex*. It is because of this 'devalorization' by women of their own sex
that Freud came to believe in women's actual biological inferiority.[23]

But, Maria Torok points out, woman's desire to 'have a penis'
'denounces itself as a subterfuge precisely because it is felt as envy'. It is
of the nature of primary drives that they can be satisfied. A desire is primary: an envy, never. Under envy there lies a real desire, buried because
forbidden. Both Jones and Melanie Klein, she points out, have unearthed
it, and neither considers penis envy as irreducible. Once analysis has
improved the primary relation, the relation to the breast, envy in general,
and penis envy in particular, dissolve.[24]

In penis envy, she goes on to argue, it is not the penis itself that is at
stake, be it as an objective biological or even as a sociocultural thing.
'Penis-envy is always envy of an idealized penis.'[25] On to the penis are projected all the qualities women want: infinite power, safety, freedom from

anguish and guilt ... The self-confident 'man's sentence', a statement of success and the right to success ... What the little girl idealizes, and hates her mother for not giving her is a fantasized object by means of which she conceals her own anger at having had her genitality repressed by her mother, at her own anality having had to fall under her mother's control, and expresses the desire to reassure the mother in order to retain her love. Since it's a penis she covets, the little girl does not have to attack the mother. Her one way to recover the acts, the powers taken from her by the anal Mother would have been to identify with her. Penis envy testifies to the lack of any such identification.[26]

Isn't it revealing that when she writes about the book needing 'somehow to be adapted to the body', Woolf doesn't talk about female desire, 'jouissance' and 'écriture féminine', but about the book needing to be 'shorter', adapted to interruption. Diminutives and negatives: is this all that the female body is about? Is repression talking here? Is it in order to protect the mother from her own aggressiveness that the narrator in *A Room of One's Own*, though she thinks at first that 'our mothers' had gravely mismanaged their affairs, leaving the daughters so little in the way of culture, ends up insisting that 'we relate to tradition through our mothers if we are women'?

But ...

> if Chloe likes Olivia and Mary Carmichael knows how to express it she will light a torch in that vast chamber where nobody has yet been. It is all half lights and profound shadows like those serpentine caves where one goes with a candle peering up and down, not knowing where one is stepping.[27]

The image is strangely reminiscent of Lily's longing for Mrs Ramsay – her vision of underground caves or Egyptian funeral chambers, containing the 'tombs of kings' ... Is all-female desire the only way into the repressed organ, then? Is 'a room of one's own' really about a 'womb of one's own', only to be glimpsed when women are alone, where 'half-said words' can form themselves 'no more palpably than the shadows of moths on the ceiling', freed from the 'capricious and coloured light of the other sex'? 'What art was there, known to love or cunning, by which one *pressed through* into those secret chambers?' Lily asked herself, pressing her arms round Mrs Ramsay's knees.[28] Does Woolf now fantasize that this 'art' pertains to men, equipped with a line to the man's sentence? I find myself speculating: in between *To the Lighthouse* and *A Room of One's Own* Woolf had had an affair with Vita Sackville-West. Had she, in the heartache of a real relationship, discovered how impossible true fusion is, how impenetrable another human being's secret recesses are, rather than found fulfilment? Was she now fantasizing that if she had been a man, if she had 'had one' she might have been able to 'press through'?

Moths ... Mother. Mother-tomb. Mother-king. Was fecund Mrs Ramsay too powerful then, an archaic Demeter accruing to herself both the power of ancient goddesses and the power that the 'sterile' father lacked and needed to feed upon? Was she a Phallic Mother, her power in her 'spurting' fecundity, but her womb, despite her many children, the vaults of the dead? Was Woolf the author-narrator mixing the experience of her own mother's death into her creation of Mrs Ramsay, so that Mrs Ramsay holds death deep inside her while seemingly so vibrantly alive, and Lily has an intimation of this? Is Lily's own repressed genitality making her imagine the womb as the tomb of kings? Though the whole novel is bathed in marvellous rhythmic fluidity, there is very little room in it for the womb. *While Mrs Ramsay preserves the boar's skull for James, she gives no intimation to Cam of her own genitality. She gives her fantasy instead: a dream of mountains and valleys with singing birds. She offers an imaginary return to the womb as refuge against threatening male genitals.* Nor is there any account of why Cam should feel so threatened by the boar. Louise DeSalvo persuasively argues that the boar's head, in a much rehandled passage, stood as a metaphor for the 'pigs' half-brothers who had sexually molested young Virginia.[29] If she is right, then it isn't necessarily the mother who has, as Maria Torok suggests, repressed the little girl's sexuality: it has been driven underground by family abuse.

Or should the death of Mrs Ramsay be read, as I have suggested earlier, as symbolizing the death of the pre-war world? 'Demeter, our Mother', as Richard Aldington writes, is wounded to death, and our 'psyches' with her . . .

Or did she (the 'Angel in the house') have to be killed so that the death that was in her should take *her*, or so that her over-great power should be removed, and some of the others could survive, Lily to create, and Mr Ramsay – the lacking, the 'missing' father – to become however haltingly and passingly 'good enough'? Mrs Ramsay, all marriage plots and harmonizing pressures, was a threat to Lily: Lily needed her dead. But why can't the Lilys inherit the 'fecundity' of the Mrs Ramsays? Does it go to the Cams, who are content to be in life, not to create? Cam has been protected enough by Mrs Ramsay's fantasy to retain her capacity for joy. But why don't the Cams of this world have a future in Virginia Woolf's fiction? For the ability to delight in life – to find illumination in a gentian, or a crocus, or trailing your hand in the sea from a moving boat, or to be a 'wild villain' 'dashing past' – isn't this what life is about?

I find myself thinking I have been more generous to Lawrence than to Woolf. Why did I accept so readily that Lawrence should have a relation to the womb, while I have so struggled with Woolf's relation to the penis? For of course – if Lawrence was awake to his anima, Woolf was to her animus. Witness her analytic powers, her ability to produce shapes – 'arcades' and 'domes' as she calls them, into and out of all that fluidity: not just Lily's circles, triangles, lines, but the marvellous structure of each novel. The 'spurting fountain' which Cam experiences as joy, which is Mrs Ramsay's fecundity, is also Woolf's creativity. It has, in this sense, as creativity, no more to do with penis envy than Lawrence's capacity for joyful empathy has to do with womb envy. It is her very real phallic dimension: in that sense it is right to talk about androgyny, or about bisexuality. As it would be about Lawrence's. But those terms are also inadequate given the complexity of what both writers do. Talking of a relation to the *other* might be more appropriate.

Throughout these chapters, drawing on both literature and psychoanalysis, using each to reflect on and comment on the other, I have looked at how the battle of the sexes, or each sex's effort to establish a relation to the other or position itself in relation to the other, was affected by, symptomatic of and a reaction to the First World War. The dips I have taken into both Lawrence and Woolf, however brief, have shown how specific each writer is, how much each vision is rooted in a complex psychosexual and familial, as well as sociopolitical, history. Though I have summarily evoked the pattern of events that surrounded the conception and writing of *Women in Love*, I have refrained from attempting to place precise biographical or historical events side by side with the fiction or poetry I have been discussing. I have chosen instead to interrogate moments in the writing, and in particular metaphors – to let them resonate, echo, answer and confirm or clash with each other, around the themes of both creation and destruction. I have paid attention to what archetypal images of the mother and imagined father figures suggest about crises in relating, not studied what happens to couples or to family relations in the post-war period. The aim was to listen, in particular to the voices of the unconscious: listen to what each sex had to say about its relation to the other.

As the war proceeded and in the years that immediately followed, it seems to me that both men and women writers attempted to recreate the fabric of a relation between the sexes, to make up for, to *repair* some of the deaths and maimings, both physical and emotional, suffered by the men, the emotional damage inflicted upon the women, and the crises of identity which the huge shake-up in gender roles had also produced. I have only looked at a little of Lawrence, a little of Woolf ... My hope is that enough that is suggestive or even persuasive has been said to make a case. I could have adduced Colette: her Chéri, pre-war and post-war, is her strongest, her most successful male character. The 1920s somehow enable her to imagine masculinity, to write across gender, just as they seem to enable Lawrence and Woolf. There is a powerful animal dimension in Chéri, as there is in Lawrence's imaginings of masculinity in the period, in *St Mawr* or *The Fox*. Writing *La Paix chez les bêtes* in the middle of the war at the time Lawrence was writing 'The Reality of Peace' and Jung reflecting on our loss of a relation to the animal in us, Colette had turned to the animal world as the one living world left untouched by the war, the one place in us perhaps that might be retrievable. Sadly, as the twenties draw to a close, it is as if each sex's attempt to recreate itself through its relation to the other becomes muted, shrinks, loses heart ...

I had a parallel in mind when I first drafted these chapters five years ago. I was thinking of the contemporary Battle of the Sexes, as evidenced by Susan Faludin's *Backlash*.[30] Here was a return of the very thing Woolf had been confronted with in the British Museum library: anger ... Since then, much has been written, Harold Bloom has accused 'feminists' of ruining the greatness of literature, but the battle has somewhat abated. It remains that relations between men and women have been shaken by feminism along with a host of other things. It remains that acceptance of the other, the ability to have a relation to the other, especially the sexual other, is particularly difficult today. There is a crisis in masculinity, much soul-searching as to what it means, being a woman, being a man. It is so much easier to feel angry or aggrieved, to blame the other sex for what's gone wrong, than to face up to oneself – and to reality.

Why, I then asked myself, have I as a feminist interested in psycho-analysis in the 1970s and 1980s been so absorbed by debates about female sexuality which carved out the lion's share to Freud, and those of Freud's interpreters that hold to phallic sexual monism (though they don't call it that), Lacan most prominently? With a little digging it becomes clear that as early as the 1920s denials of the womb as a sexual organ had been debated and disproved. And that the 1960s (viz Janine Chasseguet-Smirgel and her book *La Sexualité féminine*) had been rich in complex and shaded debates. Is it the case that one can only see the 'enemy' one wants to see? One's own shadow? Did some of us feminists enjoy pitting our wits against the denying, the denigrating fathers (not knowing how wounded they might be), setting Freud and Lacan on pedestals so we could attack them and – and what? Prove our own phallic credentials by doing so? Looking at the complexities and struggles of a bisexual dimension in artists such as Lawrence and Woolf makes it so clear, to me at least, what clumsy tools terms such as womb envy, or penis envy, or the Oedipus complex, are. They are useful – they give one something to navigate by. But only the specifics of texts, a detailed enquiry into what each image means, can produce something like a sense of inner reality. And that inner reality is expressive of the large, the historical realities.

I do feel it is important to go beyond the catchwords to textual realities. It isn't just that more understanding can come out of empathetic than out of confrontational readings. It is that when Woolf, with *A Room of One's Own*, became more confrontational – began to see the 'man's sentence' as what barred her way to creativity as a woman, she was on her way to *Three Guineas*, the sense that women have nothing to do with men. She was on her way to the lack of communication, the submerged violence that pervades *Between The Acts*. Was she being *symptomatic* – responding, giving expression to a worsening relation between the sexes, the rising despair of the 1930s, riddled with a violence no individual could do anything about except record – or was she contributing to it?

Notes

1 Virginia Woolf, *To the Lighthouse* (London: Grafton, 1977).
2 Clare Hanson, *Virginia Woolf* (London: Macmillan, 1994), pp. 74–8.
3 D. H. Lawrence, 'The Thorn in the Flesh', in *The Complete Short Stories*, vol. 1, Phoenix edn (London: Heinemann, 1955), p. 130.
4 Virginia Woolf, *To the Lighthouse*, p. 109.
5 Virginia Woolf, *A Room of One's Own* (Harmondsworth: Penguin, 1945), p. 14.
6 Ibid., pp. 16–17.
7 Alison Light, *Forever England: Femininity, Literature and Conservatism Between the Wars* (London and New York: Routledge, 1991), pp. 3–4.
8 Ibid., p. 4.
9 Leonard Woolf, *Beginning Again: An Autobiography of the Years 1911–1918* (London: Hogarth Press, 1964), p. 147.
10 Elaine Showalter, *The Female Malady: Women, Madness and English Culture, 1830–1980* (London: Virago, 1987), p. 189.
11 Elizabeth Abel, *Virginia Woolf and the Fictions of Psychoanalysis* (Chicago: University of Chicago Press, 1989), p. 132.
12 Leonard Woolf, *Downhill All the Way: An Autobiography of the Years 1919–1939* (London: Hogarth Press, 1967), p. 64.
13 Ibid., pp. 163–6.
14 Virginia Woolf, *The Diary of Virginia Woolf*, vol. 1: *1915–1919*, ed. Anne Olivier Bell and Andrew McNeillie (London: Hogarth Press, 1977), entry of 21 Jan. 1918, p. 110.
15 Rachel Bowlby, *Virginia Woolf: Feminist Destinations* (Oxford: Blackwell, 1988), p. 65.
16 Abel, *Virginia Woolf*, p. 14.
17 Sigmund Freud, 'Some Psychological Consequences of the Anatomical Distinction between the Sexes' (1925), in *Standard Edition of the Complete Psychological Works of Sigmund Freud*, gen. ed. James Strachey (London: Hogarth Press, 1953–74), vol. 19, p. 252.
18 Ibid., pp. 253, 254.
19 Ibid., p. 254.
20 Ibid., p. 252.
21 Winifred Holtby, *Virginia Woolf* (London: Wishart, 1932).
22 Maria Torok, 'La Signification de "l'envie du pénis" chez la femme', in Janine Chasseguet-Smirgel, *La Sexualité féminine* (Paris: Payot, 1964), pp. 181–219.
23 Ibid., pp. 181–2.
24 Ibid., pp. 182–3.
25 Ibid., pp. 184, 186.
26 Ibid., pp. 187–9, 190.
27 Woolf, *A Room of One's Own*, p. 84.
28 Woolf, *To the Lighthouse*, p. 50; my italics.
29 Louise DeSalvo, *Virginia Woolf: The Impact of Childhood Sexual Abuse on her Life and Works* (London: Women's Press, 1991), pp. 177–9.
30. Susan Faludin, *Backlash: The Undeclared War Against Women* (London: Chatto and Windus, 1992).

TROUBLESOME MOTHERS

Part III

The Female Creator

6

'Mother is a Figure of Speech ...': Angela Carter

> Mother is a figure of speech and has retired to a cave beyond consciousness ...
>
> Angela Carter, *The Passion of New Eve*

'Silly old Bataille,' Angela Carter said.

In her most devastatingly angelic, little-girl's voice.

1978. We were at one of Emma Tennant's *Bananas* launching parties. This particular *Bananas* issue had included 'The Immaculate Conception', one of the stories from *Le Spectre du gris*, which I had published with Éditions des Femmes. Later Virago would bring it out, Englished, as *Shades of Grey*.

She liked 'The Immaculate Conception', Angela Carter had said. She was generous to other women writers. Well, some. Why she was generous to me I wondered in later years, given her scathing dislike of the victim syndrome. Elizabeth Smart should have written *By Grand Central Station I Tore Off His Balls*, not *Sat Down and Wept*: that's what she exasperatedly suggested to Lorna Sage.[1] My story was about a woman who gets destroyed. Why hadn't Angela Carter hated it? Perhaps she enjoyed the tone, which was tough. Or the mock-Surrealist title. Or the destruction job, which was thorough.

She was writing a book on de Sade, she said. I gulped. As a young, foreign graduate student in Cambridge in the 1960s I had researched a thesis on the Satanic, Gothic and Byronic hero. The librarian had vetted me as a security risk (a French girl eerily homing in on the Frenchest of French stuff), then granted me access to the Divine Marquis: but I had to read him in a special quarter of the university library. There sat I, week after week, in splendid isolation, in the penumbra of a palatial room, a quarantined bitch from abroad, the local scholarly population safe from rabies. I romped through the Apollinaire edition and old prints with wobbly first and last lines and s's that looked like f's, feeling for all the world like a freak spy who has wandered into a genteel script, or the *au pair* suspected of wanting to make off with the family silver when she only means to give it a good polish. I remember enjoying *Justine* and *Juliette* (they made me feel daring and free), and relishing the elegant eighteenth-century disquisitions of *La Philosophie dans le boudoir*.

Making access so difficult, academia was treating me as my father had. As an adolescent I had stayed in on Sundays under cover of swotting, found the key to the forbidden books cupboard, and worked my furtive and excited way through *Les Liaisons dangereuses*. Sex was under lock and key. It went with the eighteenth century, a bloody, revolutionary age that wrote exquisitely precise understatements in limpid prose. Most forbidden of all, de Sade was the ultimate. The white goose that I was filled notebooks with extracts: about the savagery of nature, about wolves never eating one another. I now remember that in 'The Company of Wolves', Little Red Riding Hood's hunger matches the wolf's. Clever Angela. My own beast was an alien. But I did jot down the bit about women's appetites being greater than men's. I liked that. *The 120 Days of Sodom*, however, speedily made me reach saturation point. I quit over its systematic tediousness. That finished de Sade off for me, and wasn't I glad it had when I saw Pasolini's *Salò*. With the arguable exception of Foucault's *Pendulum*, I don't think a book has ever so bored me.

Time passed. Things happened. Simone de Beauvoir's *Faut-il brûler Sade?* annoyed me in its sanity. I was perplexed by Roland Barthes's *Sade, Fourier, Loyola*. The indecency of equating the sadistic pornographer, the religious founder and the utopian socialist! System builders all three might be. The structuralist decision to consider 'nothing but' affronted me. And now here was this angelic-sounding Englishwoman, wading into it all as if nobody had been there before. Cool as a cucumber. I felt robbed. Who'd just waded into *my* bloody chamber? Dangerous stuff, I said. Reality may overtake fantasy. Look at de Sade. Look at Bataille, what he did with – to – Laure . . .

'Silly old Bataille', she said.

To mistake fantasy for reality, she meant.

Lucky you, my good woman, I thought, who can so thoroughly distinguish between them.

I couldn't. Nor could I read her books. Understand anything about them, that is. In a strange way, the story of my relationship with her work is a story of misunderstandings and misreadings. The stuff was so close, I couldn't but relate to it. I was so different from her, I couldn't but be shocked, offended. It rubbed me up the wrong way. Just as well. I have noticed in nature films that tigers lovingly smooth and wet the felled leopard's hide with their tongues prior to tearing it with their fangs. Makes it easier to swallow. I write as a lone French leopard, still trying to find its way through the forest. I write out of close on twenty years of misreadings. The only appropriate tribute, because it is precise. No soul-to-soul for Angela Carter. Explanation, exegesis or – worse – canonization would lubricate the tiger's hide. She meant to stick in our gullets.

'Silly old Bataille,' she said.
    'Silly old Nicole,' I heard.

A History of Misreadings

Love was the first Carter novel I read. I found it baffling, and on balance I disliked it. The heroine – if that's the word – did seem too unfazed by the nasty things being done to her. She didn't even seem to mind being done in. The whole thing was cool – too cool in its Baroque and seedy precision; too socially accurate, with its black-nailed lank bovver-boys and decaying Beardsleyish decor, for the degentrified neo-*Story of O* I remember as *Love*. Maybe it's not at all like that and I've retrospectively made it up.

Then out came *The Sadeian Woman*. I wanted to hate it. I was in parts nonplussed, in others half persuaded. There was a strong point there. Threw me back to those days in the wainscoted room of the Cambridge University Library – why had *I* been there, if not for something very like what *The Sadeian Woman* was saying? *I* hadn't known how to explore it, let alone express it. One passage, however, tipped the balance against the book for me. Eugénie, the heroine from *La Philosophie dans le boudoir*, is being initiated, let loose, allowed to have her fantasies, by libertines. She has her mother raped by the libertines, impregnated with the pox, then sewn up. I had forgotten that bit. Carter talks about de Sade's creativity in thus allowing a daughter to be indulged in her most aggressive drives against the censoring mother. Liberating. At this the mother that I then was, the mother of an often angry fourteen-year-old daughter, felt affronted. Again that fucking business of fantasy and reality, I thought. All very well for that bitch to indulge herself. Unencumbered by a daughter of her own, she completely identifies with the daughter's point of view. What would she feel if she were at the receiving end – if she were the mother? Not quite so agreeable, is it?

I was determined to have another go. I knew that the intellectually snooty Éditions du Seuil had bought *The Passion of New Eve*. I found a copy on York station, Pan Books, with a black-booted, fishnet-stockinged blonde on the cover, complete with whip. Surprising what packaging does. You approach that book in a very different spirit now that it has a tasteful, intriguing, arty Virago Modern Classics cover: with such hallmarks of feminist gentility, who can help but have their critical antennae bristling? Mine weren't. I bad-temperedly toyed between displaying and concealing my s/m blonde from the frosty lady in tweeds who sat across from me at the BR table. It wasn't like having *chosen* to read porn. More like being caught with my hand in the till when I was putting money in, and all for the sake of bloody feminism. No doubt prospective glee at readers' discomfort played its part in getting Angela Carter to approve such a cover – or did she relish the drop on to the ledger of Inferior Culture? There is a question of class lurking about somewhere – the middle-class girl (Melanie or Little Red Riding Hood) leaving respectability behind, bonding into an exotic, sexy working class. The virgin and the gypsy. Sometimes porn is to erotica as lower class is to upper class. Be it circus, brothel or music hall, Carter always chose the lower class.

I wanted to shout at the lady in tweeds: 'This is LITERATURE, not porn, you know' – then I remembered how years before, when I was teaching Italian literature, elderly Miss Easthwaite, who always wore a knitted bonnet and mittens, having trotted away with Moravia's *La Noia* in her canvas bag, trotted back the following week and asked, in her sweetest voice, 'I beg your pardon. But isn't it PORNOGRAPHY?' Throughout *La Noia* an ageing painter makes love over every bit of ground that offers itself to an adolescent girl whose belly spasms at the moment of orgasm are so exquisite he can't leave off getting his tummy button glued to hers. He eventually dies on the steep staircase of his studio at a maximally spasmodic moment. I had ordered umpteen copies of the book for my class on the strength of Moravia's name, and was loath to be found out casting wickedness upon the waters at the expense of Hull Adult Education. 'No no, Miss Easthwaite,' I said, cheerfully, 'it is EROTICISM.' 'Oh, I see,' she said, 'but excuse me. Could you explain to me what is the difference?'

Weekend *Guardian*, January 1994. Pages of magazine devoted to Joan Collins. Married four times, the journalist explains: to a sadist, a neurotic, a junky and a cad, in that order. She posed in thigh-high black boots for *Marie-Claire*. Page of main section given over to Camille Paglia's diary. She suffers from TV deprivation in Europe (not enough exposure) and also posed in black leather and studs for some other magazine. This is star-gazing of the most baffling kind, I reflect. Formations of Fantasy. Madonna & Co. Is it enough to be a glamorous toughie, or the mistress of the game, to join the New Left platform? If so, Juliette has won. Carter was a prophet, as always. Indeed, even Justine has ceased to be a victim today. She cuts off the assaulting male's penis with a kitchen knife. No more sitting down and weeping. The Bobbitt case makes it to the front page all round the western world. When, in the early 1980s, I wrote my study on the Yorkshire Ripper case, I felt that I was boldly venturing into awesome territory where angels feared to tread, and very few women had trodden. Now the serial killer, including the female serial killer, is almost as common as sliced bread. Nobody bats an eyelid. Angels wear boots. The lambs have turned into wolves. The early nineties certainly put my trouble with the cover of *The Passion of New Eve* in historical perspective. If this book survives long enough for anyone to come by this essay in ten years' time, who knows where we will be? For in the meantime, neo-Nazi movements grow . . .

Anyway – there was I, almost twenty years ago, on the train, with *The Passion of New Eve*. The – bloodlessness? – with which a ghastly series of Doomsday horrors were being narrated fazed me. The ultimate in nihilistic cynicism, I thought. Revenge on the decadent male with whose unpalatable persona one remains saddled till the bleak end. Having his tail surgically removed barely improves Evelyn. Now he's become mythical Eve, the best you can say for her is that s/he is at the receiving end of pain, where he inflicted it. But whether the pain is hers or someone else's, s/he does keep a near-psychopathic inability to feel it. Empathy my eye. Unreality is the name of the game. Bloodless was the right word. No blood flowed from any wounding instruments – not the bungling abortionist's needle when Evelyn's girlfriend Leilah gets messed up, nor the emasculating knife that descends upon Evelyn. Zero's Manson-like orgy of destruction, when his gang swoops on Tristessa's mansion, left me feeling 'Oh, well . . . having a romp?' Feelings – love, nostalgia – so much hot air. Puppets all. Sawdust and celluloid. But there was no denying the clear, cold grace of the writing.

Then two things happened. An American student in one of my classes, reading aloud an extract (Mother about to perform surgery on Evelyn), and reading it in an easy-going, unfazed, deadpan way, got the whole class (myself included) in hysterics of laughter:

> Oh, the dreadful symbolism of that knife! To be castrated with a phallic symbol! (But what else, says Mother, could do the trick?)[2]

All right: I had missed the point. Then my fifteen-year-old son, seeing the whip and fishnet stockings on the cover, made off with the book. At thirteen he had pinched my *New French Feminisms* and passed it round the gym locker room at his comprehensive: boys looking for the spicy bits must have received quite an education. My son found *The Passion of New Eve* terribly clever. It defeated every pornographic expectation from its male readers, he thought. Goes to show how sophisticated these youngsters can be, damn them. He went on to read every Carter novel and story he could lay his hands on. I followed suit. Reported his reaction to Angela Carter the next time we met, thinking she would be pleased. 'But of course,' she said. Damn her. Was I the only daft one? But I had by that time become a sort of convert.

I didn't dare own how thoroughly *I* had misread her. But I've always been struck since then by the ease with which young people 'get it'. Get her. Something about the spirit of the time, her being ahead, in tune, getting the whiff of things to come. Which she did. Playfulness. Speed. Everything up – not for grabs, but for suspension, deflation, metamorphosis.

I hadn't much liked *The Infernal Desire Machines*, nor *Fireworks*. *The Bloody Chamber* was the first Carter book I actually enjoyed. Perhaps it was the territory – Perrault, the Grimm Brothers, folk, Gothic. Always loved the stuff. And for the first time I picked up the extraordinary, deft array of literary and cultural references, the rewriting and weaving in of other writers. Fireworks indeed. In the first, the Bluebeard story that gives its name to the collection, I recognized a canny reader of Colette. It shimmered with skilfully modified bits from the *Claudine* novels, from *My Apprenticeships*, *My Mother's House* – and put to impertinent use a wonderfully intimate knowledge of the art and life of fin-de-siècle French Decadence. 'The Tiger's Bride' pleased me. Not just because of the way it reverses 'The Bloody Chamber', the story of poor young girl married to rich, lordly, hairy older stranger. Though she's cast in an archetypal patriarchal script, sold to pay her father's gambling debts, made to strip down to 'white meat' by the pandering valet, the bride is not afraid of the Tiger. He's a Tiger, not a Marquis, as in 'The Bloody Chamber'. She holds 'the key to the peaceable kingdom in which his appetite need not be my extinction',[3] not the key to bloody murder. When the Tiger fails to smell fear on her, he purrs. The walls of his castle crumble. A happy as well as a witty Fall of the House of Usher – ushers, panderers, familial prostitution, valet, gone. The Tiger was as much the prisoner of the pornographic spell as the girl. Her fearlessness frees them both. As he begins to lick her white skin, it falls away, and there appears in its place shining fur. 'Nascent patina.' It made me think of the wet fur of a new-born colt. Of the glowing dark fur of sea lions as they hoist themselves out of the water, shaking themselves. When they've dried themselves on the rocks, their fur is thick, the colour of golden sand. Their ecstasy is equal whether they're diving and shooting through the waves, rolling about, jumping, or blissfully spread on a rock, belly up, so that the air can cool their fin-pit. 'My ear-rings thawed and I was shaking water out of my beautiful fur.'

Yes, that's it, I thought. That is the state. The active state of pleasure in which you become stripped not just of old clothes, habits, but of the old skin. There is a lot of territory to cross to get to that state, and it seemed to me that this was what Angela Carter had done: gone through the pornographic spectrum in order to come out at the other end. Unnervingly and irreverently explored the alienating figures of Romance, the rebellious Heathcliff-type hero (Jewel in *Heroes and Villains*), then the Wild Older Man (de Sade, Bluebeard, Mr Rochester, Colette's first husband, Willy) and disposed of them. Out with demon lover and patriarch. In with gentle boys, piano tuners, students wheeling their bicycles into vampiric castles and being jolly nice about it. And if Mr Wild Older Man still strolls in, he's been mellowed by a cocktail of alcohol, Joycean literacy, Scott Fitzgerald desperation, and a certain trouble with potency: he's Irish, alias the Ross O'Flaherty of *Wise Children*, and he imparts prodigious skills of metaphor to his young, un-coy mistress.

Fear had to be conquered. Nothing sacred. Fear it is that makes predators of our wolves and tigers. 'If Little Red Riding Hood had laughed at the wolf and passed on, the wolf could never have eaten her,' said Colette.[4] 'The tiger will never lie down with the lamb; he acknowledges no pact that is not reciprocal. The lamb must learn to run with the tigers' (*The Bloody Chamber*, p. 84). Girl's fearlessness delivers man from his beastliness.

Or am I being sentimental? Pulling Angela Carter in a direction she wouldn't acknowledge. *She'd* never write about a *real* sea lion, now, would she? So busy transforming every little thing into artifice. 'Feux d'artifice' is the French for fireworks. She won't even allow earth to be earthy – or rather, to symbolize what is genuine, and can, through symbolization, become a means to power. In *Wise Children*, the casketful of authentic Stratford-upon-Avon earth that Shakespearian actor Melchior Hazard takes to Hollywood, to sprinkle on the American cast of *A Midsummer's Night Dream*, is meant to imaginatively reclaim, colonize, American soil. Sacred relics upon which you build the new churches, the films. But what happens? When Melchior's illegitimate children look for the casket, it turns out that the cat's been using it as a shit-box all the long train voyage from New York to LA. And beyond. So what do the girls do? They replace it with a bit of local loam, as in the story of Big Dan's ashes that have been lost by the little girl to whom they had been entrusted when the men made a beeline for the pub, and the little girl refills the jar with ashes from the grate, and the men returning from the pub have a good cry and say: What a small thing we are, and all that's left of us is a handful of ashes and a few burnt eggshells. Hey presto! as Carter would say. Nobody the wiser.

I am of the earth-loving persuasion. Though I was bred in a provincial city flat in the South of France, I love the country, trees, rocks, sea. Carter is city through and through. No time for twilights, identifying birds or plants by name. I – though your genuine exile, living in a country other than the one I was born in, or perhaps because of that – have put down roots in a variety of places. Over sea, one ocean. They tug at me, bewilder me. Carter, moored in the one place, London, was an imaginative wanderer, a lover of the picaresque. The high road is her way. Only in her last novel do characters claim roots: Brixton. It's taken me half a century to shed my Romanticism, and I still love myths, symbols, religions, silence, solitude. Angela Carter was, as she said herself, in the demystifying business. Her books swarm with characters, brim with unhampered, unromantic promiscuity. You say 'soul' to me, and I like it. You say 'soul' to her, and she throws up. Invite her characters to a party, and they perk up. Take me to a wood, and I revive.

I write all this because recognizing her for what she is as precisely as I can, and identifying the reasons for my distance from her, is my way of not absorbing her, refusing to kill her off. I had rather be wrong, or unsubtle, than play an academic game of theorization and explanation that would enable the tiger that she was to be tamed, shorn of its claws. The most violent and shocking things – hard-core porn, serial murder – have in recent years become fashionable, under pretext of the innocuousness of fantasy, the right to public knowledge, or the supposed seriousness of looking into our fascination with crime. But the very jadedness which so much exposure and play provoke almost makes psychotics of us all. We no longer feel, we play, as if the 'real' violence media circuses invite us to play with thereby ceased to *be* violence, and did nobody any harm. The charge in Carter, the gunpowder that's in every one of her rockets, is her subversion of the images, the processes of alienation themselves. She won't cease to play – not because she won't feel, but because she wants to reveal the power at work in the game shows. She pulls the plug. Meets fire with fire – or rather, the sacralized with wit.

It is, it now strikes me, a gross mistake to read the antics of the day's idols as Carter's prophecies come to pass. The Joan Collinses and Camille Paglias, red in lipstick and nail polish, only seem to be the flesh-and-blood fulfilment of what *The Sadeian Woman* praised in Juliette. They do have in common with Carter's Lady Purple, Daisy Duck or Tristessa that they serve to embody media fantasies. But Carter's puppets and divas are man-made. Her writing, its antics and self-deflating rhetoric, exposes, unpicks the fabrication process: never promotes the illusion. It shows the divas to be the ideological products of light and celluloid, issued from the mirror chambers of a narcissistic, *male* imaginary. New Eve in the mirror is ex-Evelyn's dream girl. His dream diva, Tristessa, is a man in drag. My adolescent son was right. *The Passion of New Eve* is almost as carefully geared to a male readership as Genet's *The Blacks* is to a white audience. In *Wise Children* Saskia, the carnivorous Delia Smith of a TV show, in her highbrow, successful-career-woman version of domesticity, is the very picture of predatory alienation. If the powers that be love you, that means they are using you. Ask who produces and who consumes, whose interest you serve. Angela Carter was that thing she said Sade failed to be: a moral pornographer. She refused to promote any vested power, patriarchal or other. She wouldn't let herself be bought, play anybody's game, be taken in. It would be a disaster if her present vogue turned into fashionableness. Which is why my own distance, and one-time dislike, are so useful.

At the 'Shape and Tone' at a York lowbrow gym: 'Did you see that piece about Joan Collins in the *Express*?' 'Well, if I had her money ... She's got a special teacher that makes her work out two bloody hours every morning.' 'If she had to pack up for three every morning ...' 'We would all have her figure, girls, if we had her money. Wouldn't we now?' 'Course we would.' All about Mammon. In *Wise Children*, Dora finds out that Mammon is what Hollywood amounts to. Yet the fascination is so acute, the flirting with its glamour so compulsive.

But there is more.

The story that most delighted me when I first read *The Bloody Chamber* was 'Puss-in-Boots'. The romping Cavalier's voice – Rabelaisian in its relish, its physicality – eighteenth-century interloping Figaro with its gift of the gab and *roué* pirouettes: the original tale demystified in terms of class and period, yet the childish pleasure at animal antics found anew. I thought there was a great future in that voice, the sheer *jouissance* (there goes a big word) of the verbal inventiveness. In the ensuing years, it seemed to me, food and sex and class and materiality became combined with a phenomenal gift of the gab in ways that made me think of Joyce, Dickens. . . . Suddenly Carnival was there. Queen Carnival. Belching, farting, drinking, dyeing, flying, dancing, fucking, in the train of Puss-in-Boots there came Fevvers, from *Nights at the Circus*, then Dora and Nora among the multitudinous twins of *Wise Children*. The Bloody Chamber had been crossed. The initiation rites, menstruation and all, gone through. The beasts, the tigers and the wolves had been encountered, mated with. Body was there. Dare I say – feelings? It wasn't deconstruction any more. If it was still postmodernism (if the word hadn't been around, someone would have had to invent it for Angela Carter) it had a considerable amount of gut.

Dare I go further? Let postmodernists shout 'Off with her head!' Reading *Wise Children*, I had to admit that I empathized with the *values* of the twin sisters. Do credit to a good Christian, of the 'By their fruits ye shall know them' variety. Much too much sex of the exclusively non-marital kind for an institutional Christian, yes, but let him who is without sin . . . Dora and Nora, now, remain uncorrupted by Mammon, impervious to snobbery or fame; restore husbands to their distraught spouses, renouncing in the process a girl's best friend, a diamond as large as the Ritz. They take in the old, the orphaned, the abandoned and the handicapped, be they stepmums or cats; have hearts as big as houses, an endlessly innocent capacity for delight . . . 'Except ye . . . become as little children. . . .' Warmed the cockles of my heart, it did.

Another misreading? Am I still wanting life, and people, and your GENUINE article, earth? Never learn, will I?

She and I, like chalk and cheese.

Chalk is the genuine thing. Comes from cliffs.

But you can eat cheese.

When I sent Angela Carter my book on Colette, she sent back a Christmas card with fat puddings on it. Inside it said: 'Read it at one gulp. Mmmm.'

Fantasy and Separation

What has all this to do with the mother?
    She's been the story under the story. I knew it years ago, when I was
repelled by Carter's endorsement of the sexual punishment meted out to
Eugénie's mother in *La Philosophie dans le boudoir*. Felt that it was purely
the daughter's point of view.
    What about the mother? I want to ask again.

There is a link between my difficulties about fantasy and my insistence
on the mother. People who are able to distinguish clearly between reality
and fantasy, psychoanalysis tells us, are people who are grown up. They
have separated off from the mother. They are differentiated. Individuated. Mature.
    This is so according to Freudian patterns: maturation occurs when the
Oedipus complex has been successfully overcome. It is also so according
to Jungian patterns. Jung pleads for a separation between the image of
the mother, sung and celebrated in all times and languages, and the
'human being called mother whom chance made the bearer of that experience'.[5] When we have arrived at a knowledge of this, we no longer
bring the enormous weight of meaning, of 'heaven and hell', to bear
upon those 'weak and fallible beings' who were given us as mothers.
You could say that it is because she is truly detached from the mother,
because she can distinguish between the real and the imaginary mother,
that Angela Carter has no compunction about attacking the *archetype*:
Mother has nothing to do with mother.
    'Poor old Bataille.' Poor old Nicole, who did not know the boundaries
between fantasy and reality. But Angela Carter kept everything separated. She was the *moral* pornographer, using Pornography to make her
reader think, instead of indulge, or want to imitate. She kept herself,
her life, anyone remotely resembling her family, lovers or friends, out
of her books. None of her novels is autobiographical, not in any visible
way. She was individuated. Even fantasy, in her hands, is not allowed to
be a lure, an indulgence. For there are types of fantasy which give form
to our secret dreads, our censored wish to violence: like Mary Shelley's
Frankenstein. If such fantasy is subversive, it is only because it dares what
the decencies of realism forbid. Yet it upholds the decencies. The unreal
guarantees the real. *Unheimlich*, the uncanny – literally the un-homely –
maintains home, the *heimlich*. And fantasy (as in horror) can be self-
indulgence. Safe fear, which serves to make danger or destructiveness,
inside or outside us, unreal. The fantasized solution mothers us. It pro-
tects us from having to seek active solutions in the real world. But in the
work of Angela Carter, fantasy is always at one remove. The reader
neither enjoys Evelyn's wickedness nor gets a kick out of Mother's castrating knife. There is no narrative safety, no cosy resolution, be it bliss

or apocalypse. The very appeal of pornography, of fantasy, of dream, is being deconstructed. Exposed as so much machinery. Well individuated indeed. The very coolness with which Angela Carter looks on at the horrors done to Eugénie's mother, and sees them as fantasy, is a sign of her detachment. Her advanced state of maturity.

This convinces my brain, but not my gut. Writing is not only what is intended, what is proffered. The very fact of returning again and again to a particular theme, or trope, is significant. Would anyone spend so long in the houses of pornography unless they were fascinated by them? Would the mother be so severely under attack unless there was deep anger against her somewhere? In Carter's work the patriarch is repeatedly shown to be shallow, his power mechanical or not so great after all. But the fiercest rebellion is against the mother, what she stands for. At least up to the last two novels.

The Fiction of Maternity

At the end of *Portrait of the Artist as a Young Man*, Joyce's Stephen Dedalus leaves Ireland to go into exile. He quite self-consciously leaves the mother behind. She's winded, jaded, 'forever mending' Stephen's 'second-hand clothes'. The mother is a lot of things: Mother Country, Irish nationalism, myths of origins and identity, biology, realism. She also stems from the character's 'real' mother. At the beginning of *Portrait*, the child Stephen associates the mother's goodnight kiss with the wet mud into which he has been, that day, thrown by bullies at school. The word 'kiss' is made to connote moistness, nausea.

There's a story called 'Clay' in *Dubliners*. Sweet, elderly, spinsterly, naive, know-your-place Marie visits her nephew and family for Christmas. The children play: blindfold her, lead her to touch, and guess at, a cold wet substance that remains unnamed except in the title. Clay – or shit? The nephew is angry, and tells the children off. Then waxes sentimental at an old song: tears prevent him from finding the corkscrew.

Marie ... Mother ... Mud, clay, earth ... No casketful of Irish earth in Joyce's luggage (and no cat either, one presumes). The mother's had it, she's jaded. All she can do is tamper with a worn-out past. From the mother Stephen turns to the father: 'Old father, old artificer, stand me now and ever in good stead.' Last words of *Portrait*.

When written-from-exile *Ulysses* picks up on Dublin, the mother is dead. Guilt haunts Stephen. He wanders in search of an adoptive, an artificial father. Bloom is a very unpatriarchal father figure. Called Bloom, for a start. Peaceable, uncompetitive. Content to watch the 'limp father of thousands' float in the bathwater like a languid flower, he combines the 'old artificer's' gift of playful language with an infant's corporeality. Very oral and anal, Mr Bloom. Consciousness lies comfortably amid digestive processes. He enjoys kidneys, shitting, the descent of wine down his gullet, the rise of desire ... Lusting, wanking ... Perhaps rooted in Molly Bloom's gracious willingness to wallow all day in bed, brimming with juices. Never mind her afternoon visitor, Blazes Boylan. Wearing the horns is a small price to pay for the knowledge that Ghea, Great Earth Mother, is there, prone, non-stop, free-associating, 'Yes' incarnate. Bloom it is, however, who enables Stephen to find father and home rolled into one.

In a disquisition, Stephen, meditating on Hamlet, says:

> Fatherhood, in the sense of conscious begetting, is unknown to man. It is a
> mystical estate, an apostolic succession, from only begetter to only begotten.
> On that mystery and not on the madonna which the cunning Italian intellect
> flung to the mob of Europe the church is founded and founded irremovably
> because founded, like the world, macro- and microcosm, upon the void....
> *Amor matris* ... may be the only true thing in life. Paternity may be a legal
> fiction.[6]

Paternity is a fiction. A creative fiction. It is the fiction that enables fiction to be regenerated, endlessly to self-generate. With the fiction of paternity does freedom come. It makes everything possible: multiple bastardry, adopting and inventing fathers, freeing the individual talent from tradition, from the anxiety of influence. Thanks to that fiction you can take off, leave them all behind: the ideologies, Irish folk, nationalism, the Celtic twilight, the Catholic Church, being a macho man, the romances of the last Romantics. Yeats's wild swans. You're freed from reverence. You can twist and shake and mix and warp language, wrench up sound from thing, let sound take the lead. Kiss connotes mud. You can let puns and rhetoric do the wake, Finn-again.

Isn't the boy who buries the articulated swan in Angela Carter's *The Magic Toyshop* called Finn? The novel's patriarch, Uncle Philip, has used a huge puppet of a swan to pretend-rape Melanie, in a staged replay of the myth of Leda and the Swan. Only a puppet, neither animal nor god, Carter answers Yeats's 'Leda and the Swan'. Rape of mortal woman has nothing to do with political violence. The trope is a patriarchal power trip. Uncle Philip's swan has neither knowledge nor power. He is all cardboard, and creaking machinery. Only Melanie's fear makes him overwhelming. Joycean Finn is her ally in this demotion of the myth. And her lover. There's a long way from that to seventy-five-year-old Dora finally making it with wandering, self-exiling, conjuring red-haired centenarian 'Joycean' Uncle Peregrine in *Wise Children*. But again Joyce surfaces there. If at the last, by means of Dora, Carter wanted to consummate her lifelong passion for Nuncle Joyce on Daddy Shakespeare's bed, she would have been a fool to deny herself. As it is, they go at it so vigorously that they almost bring down the chandelier on the whole theatrical show downstairs.

There is a paradox. Father figures and patriarchal power (if I dare to use the word) are attacked, deconstructed, shown to be hollow or vulnerable in Angela Carter, whether as de Sade or Uncle Philip or Bluebeard or Melchior. But in her choice of artifice, her relentless demolitions of myths, stereotypes, images, then carnivalization of the whole show, Carter is Joyce's illegitimate, self-doubling niece. She severs the cords between words and things, words and beliefs, images and power. In so far as archetypally, as image or as language, the mother stands for bodily writing, oneness with 'reality', lack of differentiation, Carter could be said to have chosen the way of the father, not the mother. I find it significant that she should have written one of her rare autobiographical pieces on 'Sugar Daddy', not on her mother. It is a beautiful and loving piece. The brief evocations of the mother are ominous: 'he always thought he could buy us off with treats and so he could and that is why my brother and I don't sulk, much. Whereas [my mother] – '7 'If I am short-tempered, volatile as he is, there is enough of my mother's troubled soul in me to render his very transparency, his psychic good health, endlessly mysterious. He is my father and I love him as Cordelia did, "according to my natural bond".' She does object, she quickly adds, to the notion of a 'natural bond', but whether it is cultural or not, that bond is strong, 'And I do think my father gives me far more joy than Cordelia ever got from Lear.'8

Her books attack archetypal and traditional images of the mother. Biology or motherly love my eye. Down, indeed, with all bonds in flesh. Virginia Woolf had written of the need for the woman who will be an artist to kill the Angel in the House. Carter goes one better: to the end of the daughter's anger. She advocates the savage punishment meted out by de Sade to Eugénie's mother. Mothers or grandmothers, in her fiction, are speedily and neatly disposed of (thus wolf eats grandmother). Or they contradict all motherly representations: the girl's mother in *The Bloody Chamber* is a tiger-shooting, horse-riding, pistol-wielding heroine who takes over from damsel-saving Western cowboys and the brothers of the Perrault tale, bumping off Baddie Bluebeard in the nick of time. As for Mother in *The Passion of New Eve*, though outwardly she conforms to the Matriarchal Goddess pattern of the Mary Daly or pre-Minoan variety (she's black, archaic-looking and sports tiers of breasts), though she behaves like a Freudian little boy's worst fantasy, she's also a cosmetic surgeon and mad futurist dictator. *Nights at the Circus* Fevvers is brought up by a brothelful of adoptive mothers, with matter-of-fact cockney Lizzie as faithful attendant and fairy godmother. Even the vestigial physiological mother of Nora and Dora in *Wise Children*, 'Pretty Kitty', the seduced foundling who dies in childbirth, turns out at the end to have (possibly) been a fiction invented by 'Grandma' Chance to mask her own production of the twins, at fifty. No other writer I can think of has so repeatedly and passionately jousted against what feminists call 'biological essentialism'. If Simone de Beauvoir and countless others are right, and it is woman's biology, her being the 'sex that gives life', which 'destines' her for second place, then Carter's systematic and endlessly inventive attacks on images of motherhood, her divorcing 'biology' from mothering, are so many blows for women's freedom. In her last two books, Lizzie and the Hazard girls, none of them biological mothers, do some excellent mothering: you could add that Carter has recreated the part of motherhood that could be salvaged. 'Mother is as mother does,' Nora remarks: Grandma Chance, whether she was their biological mother or not, has made the girls feel safe as houses.

In *The Passion of New Eve* Angela Carter hunted the archetype down to extinction. Having vainly travelled through underground conduits in a parody of mythical journeys to the Underworld, Eve finds that 'Mother is a figure of speech, and has retired to a cave beyond consciousness.'[9] You cannot ever access mother's body. What you *can* invent is mothering. In come Lizzie, Grandma *Chance*, Dora and Nora: the septuagenarian twins beat today's quinquagenarian technological reproduction mothers at the anti-ageism game, becoming as they do the new twins' father and mother. Both.

Feminine Mr Bloom was, after all, father and mother combined.

Why did I say, then, that Carter chooses Joyce's way of the father? She may choose artifice, but she goes one better than Joyce, beyond the fiction of paternity: she promotes the fiction of maternity. Denying the mythical Earth-Mother, whom Joyce called Ghea–Tellus, making mother's body absent, a figure of speech, and the narrative a process of endless invention, she frees Molly Bloom. No need for Molly to stay in bed, to be the 'real' body whose presence guarantees the show, assures the boys, the fictional daddy and son, Stephen and Bloom, that homecoming is possible. If the Child is father of the Man, Dora asks in *Wise Children*, who, then, is mother of the woman? Well, in Carter's 'The Bloody Chamber' she comes charging in and delivers you from the Sadeian aristocratic husband. As Lizzie in *Nights at the Circus*, she has a magic clock in her handbag, and also delivers you from the fantasies of an evil aristocratic libertine. As outsize Fevvers, the ultimate male fantasy, large as Ghea–Tellus and self-proclaimed *intacta*, she is a trapezist, she can fly: she is a confidence trickster. Carter substitutes backstage for back into the archetype. She finds ropes and pulleys, props, make-up, dye, sequins, where others saw gods, virgin mothers, stars, angels.

And so – what am I going on about? Not the way of the father – beyond both father and mother. Subverting both, combining both, demoting both. All that's left is the act. The performance: conjuring or doing.

All about freedom. A form of feminist existentialism.

Daring to imagine and endorse the daughter's anger against the mother, her wish to sadistically punish her, delivers the possibility of a new, cheerful, active, duty-free form of mothering. In *Wise Children* it comes as

Naturism, the non-nuclear family, and fun all round. Skirting as close to incest as you might wish: getting laid by your father's twin brother, as Dora does by Uncle Peregrine (who, moreover, has always been thought to be her dad), is not a bad way of flouting the taboo. Bataille, who claimed that Eroticism could be found only through defying taboos, might have approved.

I argued above that it was Angela Carter's imaginative courage in traversing the pornographic scene that delivered the sexual delight of *The Bloody Chamber*, and the later novels. She couldn't have done it without having precisely that ability to separate fantasy from reality which – I also argued above – is made possible by separation from the mother. No need to cling, to feel endangered by what comes to you, from outside you. Lamb can lie down with wolf. Mother's body can be lost – indeed, sent down the drain: no need to go looking for it, to make caves into its substitutes. Mother can be absent: child will play. Mature adult can be as parodic with words and forms as she pleases. Reinvent mothering if need be.

'Old father, old artificer, stand me now and ever in good stead.'

I hear a weird echo of the last sentence of Joyce's *Portrait* in the last sentence of Carter's *Passion*:

'Ocean, ocean, mother of mysteries, bear me to the place of birth.'[10]

Does it mean that the mother, *in extremis*, is allowed back in? Or that, as ocean (traditionally male, as against feminine sea), she is just what you travel on – not the place, but a guide to the place, where birth can happen?

Writing and the Mother

'Can the mother write?' Tillie Olsen and Adrienne Rich asked in the 1970s. Does woman, 'alienated from [her] real body and [her] real spirit by the institution – not the fact – of motherhood',[11] need violently to detach from motherhood? If she wants to create, must she be 'Kali, Medea, the sow that devours her farrow'?[12] Does she need to become pure mind or, on the contrary, to reclaim her body from all institutions? Have women, by being reduced to their mothering function, been alienated from their own bodies, their desire, their pleasure, and should they strive to find them? 'Our skin is alive with signals; our lives and deaths are inseparable from the release or blockage of our thinking bodies.'[13]

Is motherhood the root cause of the trouble? Women, Nancy Chodorow argues, 'tend to remain bound up in preoedipal issues in relation to their own mothers'. Mothering 'involves a double identification for women, both as mother *and* as child'. This makes women find motherhood a satisfying way of expressing 'their mothering capacities'.[14] The girl – the daughter – has the tricky role of needing both to identify with her mother in order to become a mother herself, and to become 'sufficiently differentiated to grow up and experience herself as a separate individual'.[15] As for the mother, once a mother, how does she perform the balancing act? Finding a way out of alienation seems just possible for the daughter: is it impossible for the mother? Does this mean that mothering ought to be separated off from motherhood?

Debates have raged over the last twenty years. Some women writers – Olsen, Toni Morrison in *Beloved*, Christa Wolf in *Cassandra*, Michèle Roberts in *Daughters of the House, During Mother's Absence, Flesh and Blood* – explore motherhood from the inside. Others identify it as the enemy. Carter is in that camp. She never writes from the vantage point of the mother. Always that of the daughter. In Woolf's *To the Lighthouse*, the adoptive daughter, Lily Briscoe, has to refuse both mothering and motherhood in order to create in painting. Yet her attachment to, love for, grief at the disappearance of Mrs Ramsay made her relation to the mother part and parcel of the creative act. Androgyny, perhaps? But Carter rebuts, demotes and negates the mother:

> If the daughter is a mocking memory to the mother – 'As I am, so you once were' – then the mother is a horrid warning to her daughter. 'As I am, so you will be.' Mother seeks to ensure the continuance of her own repression.[16]

> The goddess is dead.
> And, with the imaginary construct of the goddess, dies the notion of eternity, whose place on earth was the womb.[17]

Carter does not only kill the Angel in the House, she goes for the genitals of the creative archetype. Where Jung said that each of us has to come to terms with the Mother in us, Carter answers: 'nothing but a figure of speech'. Wind and piffle. In the face of the theorists – Jacqueline Rose, for instance[18] – she denounces the misleading romance in assimilating the maternal body with the unrepressed. She exposes the 'relation between the theoretical occulting of femininity by maternity and the engulfment of the daughter by the mother'.[19]

But what if, instead of being emancipatory, the downgrading and refusal of motherhood was the ultimate in phallocracy, the perpetuation of women's subjection? What if the counterview – to be found in some so-called French feminisms – was right? According to that view, the pre-Oedipal – the early symbiosis with the mother, undifferentiation from her body, said to be a longer stage for the little girl – is a source of power, not impairment. Women's celebrated longer immersion in the pre-Oedipal, which Freud saw as archaic, as unknown to 'us' as 'the pre-Minoan civilization before the civilization of Greece',[20] is their strength. Or can be. It means, in early Cixous, that the mother's body is imaginatively available, a source of writing. Fantasy here, interestingly, is not the realm of words as detached from reality but the suppressed, the unconscious:

Let's look not at syntax but at fantasy, at the unconscious: all the feminine texts I've read are very close to the voice, very close to the flesh of language, much more so than masculine texts. . . . There's *tactility* in the feminine text, there's touch, and this touch passes through the ear. Writing in the feminine is passing on what is cut out by the Symbolic, the voice of the mother, passing on what is most archaic.[21]

Julia Kristeva's concept of the semiotic – as the irruption of drives that have to do with the archaic body, closeness with the mother's body, desire for incest with the mother – has been much discussed and much used, and goes in the same direction as Cixous. Neither Kristeva nor Cixous argues that there ever could be language that would be all semiotic, or feminine: the archaic would be only babble. Any language is an interplay between the symbolic and the semiotic, even if (like the language of science, or the law) it seems to leave no room for the semiotic. But poetic, revolutionary or 'feminine' writing makes for a high incidence of unconscious impulses. It unleashes the repressed. It allows the semiotic to erupt rather than keeping it at bay.

In her early work Irigaray also argues that what gets repeatedly censored in women is the mother's body. Women can profitably search for 'the imaginary and the symbolic of intrauterine life and of the first bodily encounter with the mother':[22] through eroticism, through writing. They can thus be redeemed from the 'darkness', the 'madness' in which they have been abandoned. For these French writers, different as they may be, mother is most definitely *not* a 'figure of speech'. She is not to be left to the 'cave beyond consciousness'. Indeed, to refuse to explore the 'dark continent of the dark continent' (as Irigaray calls it) – that is, the mother–daughter relationship – is to perpetuate an ancient repression, refuse one's own womanhood. Is this what Carter does, at least up to *Nights at the Circus*? Does she, in her rejection of the mother, produce another form of suppression?

My feeling is that she does. That she needed to do it, because she had such accounts to settle with the mother. (Things do change in *Nights at the Circus* and *Wise Children* – largely, I would venture, because of the experience of motherhood. But I will not draw that in: Carter kept her life too carefully away from her writing for me to want to trespass. 'Look! Don't touch!' Fevvers signals. If Carter rejected the 'femininity' of touch in favour of the eye, of display, of the confidence trick, I should take her at – face value? 'There is nothing like confidence' is the last phrase, Fevvers's, in *Nights at the Circus*.) My feeling also is that both *The Passion of New Eve* and *The Sadeian Woman* lend themselves so readily to being read as counter tracts to French theory of the 1970s – Lacan, Cixous in particular[23] – that it is almost certain she knew exactly what she was doing. I once introduced Angela Carter to Hélène Cixous in London – they were doing a *mano a mano* like rival bullfighters – and Carter professed terror at the encounter. I now wonder whether her terror had something to do with coming face to face with what she had attacked.

Yet reflecting on seventies' and eighties' debates on *écriture féminine*, having felt initially certain that none of it could be found in Carter, I now wonder ...

Up to and excepting *Wise Children*, Carter's language is all wild sex and mind, with nothing in between. Breasts? Good Lord no. Guts – they creep in, in the later period. You couldn't have all that Rabelaisian stuff without, could you? No heart, but nominally. Nor womb, except surgically: technology and artifice. It occurs to me now that Joyce who goes for the thingness of names, the materiality of language, who lets words mutate and beget of their own accord, allows in much more of the mother's body than Carter (and that is why he can be Cixous's nuncle as well as Carter's – they are after very different parts of him). Not that Carter doesn't have a wonderful ear. She can alliterate as well as the next person. But one word does not lead to another. One word can move without the other. Plot is continuously being invented. It does not proceed out of an internal necessity. Images do not grow out of their own momentum. Symbols (caves or colours) are not allowed to signify, except ironically, like the brand of the key on the bride's forehead at the end of 'The Bloody Chamber'. The Bloody Chamber itself is full of machinery: not the Red Deeps. Textuality is not allowed the initiative. Wit – mind – is in charge.

In all these senses, Carter does not write 'feminine' texts. No 'tactility', as Cixous puts it; no voice of the mother, no 'innermost touch'. No 'giving': 'Look, but don't touch!' (Fevvers). 'You can look if you pay': what Carter says Colette's texts are saying. No 'endlessness'.[24] No ' "other meaning" always in the process of weaving itself, of embracing itself with words, but also of getting rid of words in order not to become fixed, congealed in them'.[25] Quite the reverse. Carter has a gift for the cryptic, the lapidary, the frozen. 'He had made himself the shrine of his own desires, had made of himself the only woman he could have loved!' (Eve about Tristessa).[26]

Yet to my surprise, as I think more about it, in other ways she does. Cixous also describes a feminine text as 'wandering', full of excess, unpredictable, disturbing. This fits the bill. Irigaray advises the woman writer to accept being inside and doing mimicry, but as masquerade. This more than fits the bill: it seems to be a blueprint for what Carter does. As does Kristeva's plea for plurality, her endorsement of carnivalesque modes as *Polylogue* ...

Are they the modes of the daughter? Could they be those of the mother?

The Mother's Desire

The revolutionary gesture, for Irigaray, would not be to vent one's anger against the mother, nor to make her gallop to the rescue, wielding a (phallic?) pistol, but to allow the mother to be sexed: 'if mothers could be women, there would be a whole mode of a relationship of desiring speech between daughter and mother, son and mother.'[27]

Desire between daughter and mother, son and mother. I can't think of any examples in Carter's novels, though there's plenty of desire. Younger woman and older man, daughter and surrogate father, yes. Cousin and cousin, yes. Man–woman and woman–man, yes. All from the vantage point of the daughter. Mother's desire: no. In *Wise Children*, Saskia, an older woman who has an affair with her nephew, is much frowned upon. A baddie through and through. Not much sympathy, either, for Lady Margarine's infatuation for her brat of a son. Grandma is, *in extremis*, discovered to have had it off with Father Melchior, and desired to marry Uncle Peregrine. Dora is perfectly reconciled to Lady A, now Centenarian Wheelchair, having taken a tumble with Peregrine. But these sexed mothers are in the wings. The narrative never goes over to them. No daughter ever desires a mother, let alone a return to the archaic body. No mother is seen as desiring. Though at the very last, the trope appears. Shortly before her death, Carter made a TV film about the Christian story. It's Western iconography was presented as God's family album. God had taken the snapshots. The story ended cruelly with Michelangelo's *Pietà*, her beloved son's corpse in her arms. Was History, Carter's voice asked, fuelled by the Father's jealousy of the love between mother and son? 'O Ii-sis ... und Osiiris' ... We were getting close to the myth ...

And yet, to be fair, I see, rereading *The Sadeian Woman*, that de Sade is criticized specifically for lacking the courage to admit that the maternal function could be 'corrupted into the experience of sexual pleasure and so be set free'.[28] Eugénie may dare to attack her mother: she remains a prisoner of the father's authority. Yet in her own fiction – except *in extremis*, as I said, when Grandma Chance is discovered on page 223 of *Wise Children*[29] to be both mother *and* sexed – Carter never explores that freedom she blamed de Sade for not allowing. But perhaps having done it *in extremis* is enough? It makes me sad to reflect that in her presentation of the dead son in the mother's arms, in Michelangelo's *Pietà*, Carter was displacing what she knew was coming: the death of the mother herself. And the son's *Pietà*.

Playing

I think that myths are great stories. Inexhaustible sources. If they are lies, it is only in so far as they are stories, or as we freeze them into gendered meanings.

The more cultures we look at, the more infinite the permutations of the mother. And the father.

The idea that I live in a postmodern world does nothing for me. I do not believe that technology is women's great ally, as Carter has claimed, or that artificial reproduction is going to liberate me (helpful as contraception is). Freedom will come from getting to a state of balance between inner and outer. Self and shadow. Me and world.

I see our relation to the mother as our attempt to navigate between our need for closeness and our need for independence. The father is consciousness, and what structures the need. The mother is our tussle with reality, the reason why we endlessly attempt to make sense of the world. Desire for the mother fuels us. The father compels us, and enables us, to let go. The mother is earth, water. Materiality, feeling. The father is air, fire. Thought, inspiration, light. The mother is what enables me to think, my relation with the earth. The father, with the sky. I don't care twopence about binaries. Or hierarchies. One doesn't move without the other. There is no model of creation that humans have invented, artistic or otherwise, which is not in some way bisexual. Even 'gender trouble' feminists most opposed to maternal thinking keep talking about the *matrix* of a position. One may object to the institutional use to which our doubleness, and sexual complementariness, are put. To motherhood being the means to the subjection of women. It doesn't mean that the baby should be thrown out with the bathwater. If there is creation, the mother is there somewhere. If I wish to exterminate her, tear her to pieces, it's because she's there. If I am here, it's because she's been there.

There is such a thing as the unconscious. There is an unconscious in any creative text. I haven't gone looking for it much in Carter, except as a tussle with the mother that changes with time and experience, but there is much that could be said about the unconscious in her texts.

Where does this leave me?

I have spent years, through dreams, analysis of dreams, wide-ranging reading and looking at paintings, through relationships, through writing: looking for the mother. It's been a great surprise to me that I should need to go on such a quest. I always thought I had more problems with the father. But it wasn't so. It's been an even greater surprise to discover, and begin to accept, that I wasn't going to find her. Not because she was a figure of speech. Not because she has retreated to a cave beyond consciousness. We can go to the caves beyond consciousness. Where id was, there ego can be. But the quest for mother seems to lead me to acceptance of her absence. I do not know whether this is what they call separation. By chance, I come across this, from Michèle Roberts, whom I would have thought would be at the antipodes of Angela Carter, in *The Wild Girl*: 'So this ... was the Mother, of whom I had so complaisantly sung before I knew her properly.... She was an absence – with no division between night and day.... I crawled ... believing this to be the moment of my death.'[30] How bizarre, I thought, hearing an echo of the end of *The Passion of New Eve*, that the wish to destroy the fiction of maternity, and the wish to find the mother, should end at the same point! But is it the same point? And is it an ending?

Reflecting on the course I have travelled, writing out what has been in my mind for so long – some of it, at any rate, since I have travelled alongside Angela Carter for so many years – I find this:

It is no accident that the books of hers that I have been able to love should be the late ones. They are the books in which Carter begins to negotiate a different relation to the mother. One of accident – Grandma *Chance*. Of metonymy: the old crone by the seaside Eve finds at the end of her passion is just there, singing, the forerunner of other strange figures to come in later books. It is also a relation of acceptance.

In *Wise Children* Dora recognizes the limits of what she does. The narrator is no longer taking on the world, and subverting it. Dora quotes Jane Austen: 'Let other pens dwell on guilt and misery.' She acknowledges the limits of carnival. The war was 'no carnival, not the hostilities. No carnival'.[31] As the First World War killed Mrs Ramsay the mother, in the 'Time Passes' section of *To the Lighthouse*, so does the Second World War kill Grandma Chance, as time is swiftly passed over. The Time of Shakespeare's *The Winter's Tale* hovers here also: but it is their decision to clear Grandma Chance's room of its possessions, and paint it white for a nursery, that propels the old sisters back into life, just as it is the two old cleaning women, Mrs Bates and Mrs McNabb, in Woolf, who begin to revive the house.

No doubt knowledge of Carter's ensuing death makes me sentimentalize this book, but let that be – I'll stand by that. I sense that Carter, feeling the end coming, jumped with both feet over tragedy, and landed in Shakespeare's late plays. Infra dig, backstage, and on the wrong side of the blankets, of course. There are joyful, as ever subversive, resolutions: resurrections, long-lost daughters and sons finally recognized by long-lost or denying fathers or recognizing undetected mothers. Dora does register, though, that it is other people's tragedies that make our comedies.

Jungians (and Winnicottians?) say that out of maturation, the internalization of mother and father in us, the child can at last be born. And play. How strange, I think, that Carter, having spent her writing career so resolutely subverting fathers and mothers, should end it with the birth, and adoption, of wise children by playful parents ... Jung talks of the *divine child*. Carter answers: wise, not divine; and plural. Carnivalesque to the last.

But here I touch her.

And want to play.

Notes

Only works actually quoted are included in the notes. Among criticism that has made me think, I wish to mention Elaine Jordan's essay in Linda Anderson (ed.), *Plotting Change* (London: Edward Arnold, 1990); Lorna Sage's essay in *Women in the House of Fiction* (London: Macmillan, 1992); and Geraldine Meaney's bits and pieces in *(Un)like Subjects: Women, Theory, Fiction* (London: Routledge, 1993).

1 Lorna Sage, 'The Death of the Author', *Granta* (1992) pp. 235–54, at p. 247.
2 Angela Carter, *The Passion of New Eve* (1977; London: Virago, 1982), p. 70.
3 Angela Carter, *The Bloody Chamber* (1979; Harmondsworth: Penguin, 1981), p. 88.
4 Colette, *Journal à rebours*, in *Oeuvres complètes* (Paris: Flammarion, 1948–50), vol. 12, p. 50.
5 Quoted in Elie J. Humbert, *C. G. Jung* (Paris: Éditions Universitaires, 1983), p. 59.
6 James Joyce, *Ulysses* (Harmondsworth: Penguin, 1971), p. 207.
7 Angela Carter, 'Sugar Daddy', in U. Owen (ed.), *Fathers by Daughters* (London: Virago, 1983), p. 22.
8 Ibid., p. 30
9 *The Passion of New Eve*, p. 184.
10 Ibid., p. 191
11 Adrienne Rich, *Of Woman Born: Motherhood as Experience and Institution* (London: Virago, 1977), pp. 38–9.
12 Ibid., p. 32.
13 Ibid., p. 284.
14 Nancy Chodorow, *The Reproduction of Mothering: Psychoanalysis and the Sociology of Gender* (Berkeley: University of California Press, 1978), pp. 204–5.
15 Ibid., p. 177.
16 Angela Carter, *The Sadeian Woman* (London: Virago, 1979), p. 124.
17 Ibid., p. 110.
18 Jacqueline Rose, *Sexuality in the Field of Vision* (London: Verso, 1986), p. 36.
19 Jane Gallop, *Feminism and Psychoanalysis: The Daughter's Seduction* (London: Macmillan, 1982), p. 114.
20 Sigmund Freud, 'Female Sexuality' (1931), in *On Sexuality*, Penguin Freud Library, vol. 7 (Harmondsworth: Penguin, 1977).
21 Hélène Cixous, 'Castration or Decapitation?' *Signs*, no. 7 (Fall 1981), pp. 41–55.
22 Luce Irigaray, *The Irigaray Reader*, ed. M. Whitford (Oxford: Blackwell, 1991), p. 39.
23 Sally Keenan, 'From Myth to Memory: The Revisionary Writing of Angela Carter, Maxine Hong Kingston and Toni Morrison', Ph.D. thesis, University of Essex, 1992.
24 Cixous, 'Castration' or 'Decapitation'.
25 Luce Irigaray, *This Sex Which Is Not One* (Ithaca: Cornell University Press, 1985), p. 29.
26 *The Passion of New Eve*, pp. 128–9.
27 Irigaray, *The Irigaray Reader*, p. 52.
28 *The Sadeian Woman*, p. 128.
29 Angela Carter, *Wise Children* (London: Vintage, 1992).
30 Michèle Roberts, *The Wild Girl* (London: Methuen, 1984), no. 1, pp. 115–16.
31 *Wise Children*, p. 163.

7
'No One's Mother': Can the Mother Write Poetry?

> For me, poetry was where I lived as no-one's mother, where I existed as myself.
>
> A. Rich, *Of Woman Born*

Let me suppose that the paradise of poetry is gendered. And Greek. I find two myths: one male, the other female.

The male myth Homer stands on its Olympus. Singing *The Iliad*. Of human deeds strong and simple as the passions they stem from. Words that speak the heart. Hit like blows. Invite our marvelling eyes to plunge into the wine-dark sea. Song effective as deeds. Human beings who are one. From Homer on, it's all the way downwards for those who, like Marx, dream the Homer dream: down through tragedy, through Christianity, eventually down to Hegel's 'wretched consciousness'. The shadow falls: between feelings and consciousness, desire and act, words and deeds. Doubt and guilt cloud the scene. The hallmarks of Western Modernity.

The female myth It's an early myth. Its traces are almost gone. In the human re-membering we call history, it surfaces here and there, becomes erased, resurfaces. It's much around in our century, charged with resentment, angry at erasure. We relate to tradition through our mothers if we're female, Virginia Woolf claims. Resentfully: why – she also asks – why did our mothers so mismanage our affairs? She is talking about finance; but does she imply, 'Why weren't they poets'? 'Why did they leave us such a patchy tradition, barely a tradition really'? In that myth of the mother-who-would-be-a-poet-and-thinks-she-had-every-right-to-be, Sappho is the dream. Sappho who wrote for her daughter Cleis:

There is no place for grief, [Cleis]
in a house which serves the Muse;
our own is no exception.[1]

In Sappho's house, through service to the Muse, to which everyone is
entitled, everyone is also entitled: to joy, to love, to making poetry. The
mother sings to her daughter.

Is there a women's fall in the West, a fall from the mother's house, the
house that served the Muse, and knew no grief? A fall so complete that
the very memory that such a house existed became destroyed, along with
most of Sappho's poems? A separation so savage that (Emily Dickinson is
eloquent on this) only the memory of the separation remains?

Parting is all we know of Heaven
And all we need of Hell.[2]

Is it because this loss has disempowered 'the second sex' that Simone
de Beauvoir claims that 'humanity' has gone over not to the sex that
gives life, but to the sex that kills? Gone, that is, to Homer's *Iliad* war-
riors, and their descendants. Not to Sappho's. Isn't it out of nostalgia for
the lost mother-poet figure that many women poets this century have
fantasized about Greece, gone to live on Greek islands (Renée Vivien,
H.D. ....)? Why else the fascination for mother goddesses, Demeter – or
Colette's Sido: for the poetic prose writers have been searching too.
    Men fall from oneness with themselves. Women, from oneness with
the Mother.
    The banned, the denied, the patchy, the suppressed, the suffocated
Mother makes an uncanny return. *Unheimlich*, to use Freud's word. The
Erynnies, the avengers of blood-right, driven underground by Athena,
tamed to become the benevolent guardians of the home in the new city,
return, summoned by Night their mother, as in Hélène Cixous's play *La
Ville parjure, ou le retour des Erynies*.[3] The Mother becomes she whose
haunting presence estranges women from themselves. In Simone de
Beauvoir, the Mother estranges women from humanity. For Adrienne
Rich, poetry can only be written by the part of the self that is no mother.
Evoking her difficulties as a young mother, her struggle with words, she
explains: 'For me, poetry was where I lived as no-one's mother, where I
existed as myself.'[4] Mme Ponteillier, in Kate Chopin's *The Awakening*,
had already said, 'I would give my life for my children, I would not give
myself.'[5] But there was no tug-of-war for Sappho, was there?
    Can the Mother *no longer* write poetry then?
    Never again?
    Must a woman poet kill the mother in herself, at least while she is
writing? Do women write out of different selves? (Do men? Proust certainly thought there was nothing in common between the man who lives

and the man who writes. He did not say that the man who writes has to kill the man who lives. Though he eventually did, closeted in his cork-lined room writing *A la recherche du temps perdu*. But that was not so as to kill part of himself. That was to *find* himself. To become one.)

But the woman poet – must she cut off part of herself – must she renounce motherhood if she wants to become a great poet?

Sappho did not have to choose. Descend the course of ages. Who are the women poets? Isn't Camille Paglia right when she claims that creativity is male, that 'Man, the sexual conceptualizer and projector, has ruled art because art is his Apollonian response towards and away from woman,' and that females only create when their male side wins over?[6] Androgynes. 'Male' women. Athenas, fierce unmothered virgins, smouldering under constraints. Wild and deadly Artemises. The Emilys, Brontë and Dickinson. True, there are the passionate lovers, Louise Labbé, Marguerite de Navarre, Elizabeth Barrett Browning, H.D. But look at Plath: is it accident that she is a young mother, alone to deal with the children, when she succeeds at last in what she's always made into an art, dying?

Is motherhood, being bodily 'occupied' by the other, is mothering, caring for others, compatible with lyric flight, freedom? Can you for that matter imagine Dante changing nappies, Milton getting up in the middle of the night to bottle-feed, Rochester helping with the maths homework, Byron knitting booties, Valéry making soup, T. S. Eliot on a Monday morning searching for the gym kit under the bed?

Am I mixing things up? Gender with sexual difference? Mixing economics, practicalities, societal roles, with sense of self? I am certainly mixing gender and class: sure, as Elizabeth Badinter has shown,[7] motherhood has changed enormously over the ages, and sure, an aristocratic woman would have had everything that could be required to make writing possible: the literacy, the congenial cultural milieu, the servants to do the housework, the leisure time – which the peasant woman would not. Being able to be a poet should have been a question of class. But there would have been other constraints for the aristocratic or well-to-do woman despite all her privileges: upbringing, expectations, role models, duties, all that Wollstonecraft & Co. deplored ... how many of them became poets, *and* mothers? As for the current run of literate females ... In *Silences*, Tillie Olsen described the sheer physical and emotional absorption, the hard work, of mothering, whose demands over the ages have debarred so many women from writing. She puts together a (slender) list of mothers who have been writers also: but how many of those, poets? In motherhood, Olsen urges, it is neither the capacity nor the need to create that is lacking, but

> the need cannot come first. It can have at best only part self, part time ... Motherhood means being instantly interruptible, responsive, responsible. Children need one *now* (and remember, in our society, the family must often

try to be the center for love and health the outside world is not). The very facts that these are needs of love, not duty, that one feels them as one's self; *that there is no one else to be responsible for these needs*, gives them primacy. It is distraction, not meditation, that becomes habitual; interruption, not continuity; spasmodic, not constant, toil. Work interrupted, deferred, postponed makes blockage – at best, lesser accomplishment. Unused capacities atrophy, cease to be.[8]

Even today, unless a new race of superwomen has sprung up, an income equivalent to Woolf's £500 a year (however earned, but leaving leisure time) and a room of one's own, with a good nanny and supportive companionship thrown in, remain the basic ingredients for any mother to be a poet. Even so, what of the interruptions, the illnesses, the sleepless nights? Somehow I feel that the steadiness of prose is more compatible with motherhood: I think of Mrs Gaskell and her four daughters, of immensely productive George Sand and her two children (she *was* a phenomenon). What mother could afford to roam the roads of exile, composing *The Divine Comedy*, or the five years' total, ascetic immersion in music that enabled Rimsky-Korsakoff to develop as a composer? The work is a needy infant. The Muse is a demanding mistress. She loves celibates. Commands that her devotees choose which offspring they best love: of the body, or of the mind? There only are twenty-four hours to each day. Can you give your all to both?

And what of the incompatibility between the caring, the considerateness, the nurturing that mothering demands, and tends to develop in its practitioners, and the cruelty that creation requires? Can a human being serenely suckle their young and write Lady Macbeth's speech about braining their babe rather than not murder Duncan? Watch over a sick child while composing the 'Ode on the West Wind'? Georges Bataille wrote of the bond between literature and evil.[9] Camille Paglia harps on how goodness never produced good art. Angela Carter, that free spirit, edited the book of *Wayward Girls and Wicked Women*. Isn't it Plath's *savagery* that moves us? But 'Be nice,' the voices of 'Godfathers' urge Carol Ann Duffy's invisible poet-listener. You will get 'immortality at cost-effective price' if you remember that it is not 'the business of poetry / To stop the rot or rock the boat / or change anything': 'have a care/to keep emotion down to Gas Mark 2.'[10] The underlying message that emerges from the anger the poem exudes is that it is precisely through doing the reverse of what the 'Godfathers' advise that the ('Gas Mark 2': hence, I feel, female) listener-poet has a chance to write good poetry: by *not* being nice. By rocking the boat, not the cradle. Isn't it even more imperative for the woman poet than for the woman novelist to kill the Angel in the House? Can you be a poet and not draw upon your darkest, your most destructive self – since you must draw upon your deepest, your whole self – that which dares wrestle with sexuality and death? Troubled, I tested friends with these questions:

Can you be a mother and want to be a bad one? And not want to be
  'good enough'?
Can you be a poet, and be good?
Does Mother imply good, and Poet, bad? (Romantic, daemonic . . .)
Can you think of great poets that were 'good' men – or women?

Adrienne Rich returns, an insistent echo:

> I do know that for years I believed I should never have been anyone's
> mother, that because I felt my own needs acutely and often expressed them
> violently, I was Kali, Medea, the sow that devours her farrow, the unwom-
> anly woman in flight from womanhood, a Nietzschean monster.[11]

I got some interesting answers and a lot of jokes. 'Mallarmé asked the
identical male question,' a (male) French friend said. ' "Can you be a
Father, and be a poet?" Are the demands of good fathering compatible
with the demands of poetry?' Another (also male) named a woman poet
who'd said that if her marriage broke down she would leave her children
with her husband because she couldn't cope with both demands (creating, mothering) and creating was the more important for her. Another
(ironic – female) said, to be a good poet you've got to suffer a lot; mothers are supposed to suffer a lot; therefore mothers are eminently destined
to be poets. A necessary but not a sufficient condition, another replied.
Then I got the jokes about, there was (as Lacan points out), a 'père-verse'
(perverse), but not a 'mère-verse': or could we invent one?
    But it got me thinking. What did I mean when I said, poet? When I
said, 'mother'? Had I created false questions by naming 'mother' and
'poet' as if they were identities? Was I working with the notion that each
thing we are, or might be, is part and parcel of the whole, that (as
Husserl would have it) the yellow of the lemon is continuous with,
expressive of, its tartness and juiciness? 'Motherhood, in the sense of an
intense personal relationship with a particular child, or children, is *one
part* of female process; it is not an identity for all time,' Rich points out.[12]
Might it not be the case that the tug-of-war between motherhood and
poetry was at its most intense when the children were small, most
dependent? That the way Western societies organize mothering (virtu-
ally no support for the mother, in the UK hardly any crèches or nurs-
eries) had created material and emotional incompatibilities between the
two occupations? That the problem was, whatever might be claimed
about myths, wholly historical and cultural? There have been, over the
ages in Europe, countless Judith Shakespeares and Elizabeth Smarts –
countless women with remarkable gifts with language, whose genius
was swallowed up by material impossibilities, childcare first among
them. Times are changing: the era of technological reproduction may be
coming . . .
    But in that Brave New World, who would do the mothering?

Can you for years strive for, as Rich again says, 'the qualities that are supposed to be "innate" in us: patience, self-sacrifice, the willingness to repeat endlessly the small, routine chores of socializing a human being'[13] *and* write *The Flowers of Evil*?

So then, what do I mean by Poetry?
Lyricism. The lyre.
The impulse to sing. And dance. Move to rhythm. Make music with words. Patterns with words. Numbers. To alternate one and two; and three. And five and six and eight and ten and twelve. The even, and the odd.

To celebrate, vent, state, soothe, rock, explore, express, in words that sing and dance. Surrender and concentration, at once. As in the story of the young man who had to learn both to admire the beauties of the surrounding world and not to spill the two drops of oil that were in the spoon he was holding.

The Aeolian Harp. The tree in whose leaves and boughs the wind makes sound. The Drunken Boat, abandoned to the elements, yet still one, still afloat, suffering and riding the sea-swell.

As in the Catholic Church there are three series of mysteries in the telling of the rosary, joy, pain and glory, so there are three realms of poetry. (1) Innocence: one of its Blakean names is 'Infant Joy'. Soul that 'clap[s] its hands and sing[s]' (Yeats's 'Sailing to Byzantium'), children in the foliage, 'hidden excitedly, containing laughter', as in T. S. Eliot's 'Burnt Norton', in *The Four Quartets*. (2) Experience, with all its shades of knowledge, and of pain: its epics and tragedies and its lyrics. (3) And Glory: Pindaric odes, celebrating the victor at Olympus. Horation odes, Renaissance odes, and closer to us, Whitman and Claudel and St John Perse. Hopkins and H.D. at one quiet end of the spectrum, Pound at the noisiest.

Poetry I also see as transformation. As metaphor, that is voyage, change. From the most lapidary (Dickinson) to the most ample (Wordsworth's *The Prelude, or Growth of the Poet's Mind*). Poetry is metamorphosis. Binding by means of symbol. Discovering the hidden face of reality. Transforming pain into pleasure by means of cadence. Transmutation of frustrated desire, of ever-renewed longing, into song. Losing Syrinx, whom he's pursued and lusted for and who, at her prayer to the river-god, has been changed into a reed to escape him, Pan picks a reed and makes music.

Are women debarred from any of these, except through power of tradition, rule or circumstance? I don't think so. You could imagine Phaedra, frustrated in her love for Hippolytus, lover of horses, making music out of horsehair: isn't that what the bow of violins is strung with? Or Echo, instead of pining to death for love, hewing down the sycamore at whose foot Narcissus bends over his watery image, and making a violin out of its wood. Eurydice, killing the snake that ravishes her to Hades,

and making strings for her lyre out of its guts to call to her beloved
Orpheus ... Why don't we have any of these myths? We do have Renaissance French poet Louise Labbé, wishing herself the ivy that winds
round her lover's body. Do women have to cling? (And to the lost *Mother*
under the guise of a lover?)

Perhaps the difficulty is only there when I think of the poet rather
than of poetry. The writing of poetry. The obduracy and imaginary hold
is in the gender roles, not the *act*.

Indeed, the poets that have been floating in my mind as I have been
trying to say what poetry was for me have been the canonical ones, the
high priests and the castaways, the Orphic ones, the damned and
the exiles, from Dante to the Romantics and the French Symbolists.
Or the Establishment figures. Or groups of devotees, the Pléiade French
Renaissance poets, the Surrealists, the Black Mountain poets (have there
ever been *schools* of women poets?). Detach the persona from the act,
poetry from traditional images of the poet, and the impossibility ceases.

The Mother, certainly, fits none of the above. Unless she is in an alternative world: Sappho in Lesbos.

Where does the Mother fit in then?

As an object of desire. The object of desire. What the poet's language
attempts to recapture.

The Mother is a sort of universal Syrinx, forever lost, and by everyone,
forever sought by means of the poem. Sought by women, as well as men.
Kristeva lists men writers only in her famous passage on the semiotic,
but couldn't what she says also apply to women poets? I quote at length
because it is such a compact and evocative statement. The 'semiotic
activity, which introduces wandering or fuzziness into language and, *a
fortiori*, into poetic language', Kristeva explains, is 'a mark of the work-
ings of the drives (appropriation/rejection, orality/anality, love/hate,
life/death)' and 'stems from the archaisms of the semiotic body', which
is that of the infant, preceding the entry into the symbolic, into language:

> Language as symbolic function constitutes itself at the cost of repressing
> instinctual drive and continuous relation to the mother. On the contrary, the
> unsettled and questionable subject of poetic language (for whom the word
> is never uniquely sign) maintains itself at the cost of reactivating this
> repressed instinctual maternal element. If it is true that the prohibition of
> incest constitutes, at the same time, language as communicative code and
> women as exchange objects in order for society to be established, poetic lan-
> guage would be for its questionable subject-in-process the equivalent of
> incest: it is within the economy of signification itself that the questionable
> subject-in-process appropriates to itself this archaic, instinctual, and mater-
> nal territory; thus it simultaneously prevents the world from becoming
> mere sign and the mother from becoming an object like any other – forbid-
> den. This passage into and through the forbidden, which constitutes the
> sign and is correlative to the prohibition of incest, is often explicit as such

(Sade: 'Unless he becomes his mother's lover from the day she has brought him into the world, let him not bother to write, for we shall not read him' – *Idée sur les romans*).[14]

I prefaced this by saying it could apply to women writers as well – but could it? Kristeva goes on to add the names of Artaud, Joyce and Céline to that of Sade. No woman *is* mentioned. I am struck on reflection by her very Lévi-Straussian sentence about the prohibition of incest (a contract established between male subjects) both establishing language as communicative code and women as exchange objects. This has long been debated in feminism, and I myself have discussed it elsewhere.[15] But what this illuminates is why the myths I have mentioned (Narcissus, Orpheus, Syrinx) don't have their counterparts: we do live in a culture in which the poetic subject, the subject-in-process, is imagined as male. No wonder then Paglia's gut reaction: I say gut reaction, because she does not seem to be aware of what she is really saying, of her denial (of femininity? motherhood?). As *Sexual Personae* powerfully imagines them, it is in so far as they are androgynous, as there is maleness in them, that both Brontë and Dickinson can be poets. The same unconscious assumption applies to Bataille's essay on Emily Brontë.[16] He imagines her as positioned in relation to the death that is in the reproductive act itself *as if she were a male subject-in-process*.

But female subjects-in-process also desire the mother. Is it then in so far as they unconsciously position themselves as male subjects, as both using women as an object of exchange in using language as communication, and preventing the word from being only sign, and the mother from being forbidden through introducing semiotic disruption into language (word-play, word mutations, archaic sounds, rhythms, repetitions . . .), that women can write poetry? And if then women have to as it were play an unconscious male part in order to write poetry, then what hope in hell can the mother have to write poetry? It follows that when a woman writes, it never can be the mother in her who writes.

Q.E.D.

But a sad Q.E.D.

Can we do better out of another French writer, Hélène Cixous, interested in what she calls 'feminine' writing? Though elsewhere she does argue that it is found in men as in women, here she relates it to women writers, and links it specifically with the mother. Feminine writing, 'Castration or Decapitation' suggests, is

very close to the voice, very close to the flesh of language . . . perhaps because there's something in [the women writers being discussed] that's freely given, perhaps because they don't rush into meaning, but are straightaway at the threshold of feeling . . . Writing in the feminine is passing on what is cut out by the Symbolic, the voice of the mother, passing on what is most archaic. The most archaic force that touches a body is one that enters by the ear and reaches the most intimate point.[17]

This is more hopeful in relation to the mother. What strikes me is the phrase 'passing on what is cut out by the Symbolic'. What passes on goes through the ear and reaches 'the most intimate point'. For this is about the daughter not having had to separate from the mother's body – oneness with the mother, which is exactly what I started from, using Sappho's fragment as a mythic image of a women's paradise of poetry. I am struck by the fact that the myths of poetry I have evoked – Orpheus and Eurydice, Pan and Syrinx – are all about losing the beloved's body and making poetry out of that loss. Is it the case then that the woman poet, if she wants to remain 'womanly' rather than 'androgynous' or 'male', can somehow hang on in and through words to the mother's body without having to go through the cruel loss that the male poet has to deal with? This would tally with a lot of contemporary stuff about women having less need to detach from the mother than men. Is this why Louise Labbé expresses her longing and love through the image of the ivy *clinging* to the trunk of the tree?

Yet, in Kristeva as in Cixous, the focus is on the daughter who writes. Not the mother . . .

Still no answer to my question: can the mother write poetry?

And it matters. Why else would a 1995 combination of workshops and symposium in Cardiff have called itself 'the mothers of invention', stating in its prospectus, 'The dignity of mothering is often undermined by a cultural ethos that intimates that the acts of creation and procreation are *incompatible*. The Mothers of Invention challenges the assumption that motherhood somehow interferes with rather than enhances creativity.' And it resourcefully threw down the gauntlet.[18]

Which returns me to Sappho. Extraordinary Sappho. Able to write as both daughter and mother. To write of continuity and separation. Of tradition and individuation. Of binding and of fire. Of loss and searching. Able to love both mother and daughter, and recognize that they are distinct from her, unreachable. According to an ancient biography, both her mother and her daughter were called Cleis:

> my mother [used to say that]
> in her youth it was thought to be
> very fine to bind up your hair

> with a dark purple [headband] – yes,
> extremely fine indeed, although
> for a girl whose hair is golden

> like a torch flame [better] to wreathe
> in it garlands of fresh flowers;
> recently [I saw] a headband,

> brightly coloured, from Sardis . . .

But for you, Cleis, I do not have
a brightly coloured headband nor
do I know where I may find one . . .[19]

And what of the Mother?
I have been writing as if she were one. But as I try to reflect what the
Mother is, both inside and outside me, she multiplies. A veritable cast of
characters, in which the unconscious, the dream-like, insists on mixing
with reality. And the 'real' women, who are mothers – don't they write
out of those Mothers!

(1) First there is Darkness. Night. The mystery I come from. Which
seizes me when, faced with images of what the Hubble telescope has
photographed of galaxies in formation, I seem to be seeking for my own
origins as I wonder at the origins of the world – the power that 'rolls
through all things'. I became formed in my mother's womb: it is that
womb, not the tiny snaky tadpole that, clever little chap, one among millions, found its way to my mother's egg in its white surge of spawn, that
is for me the place of wonder.
But – having had children of my own – I know the eerie reality of
those labour pains which one of Plath's *Three Women* experiences as an
overwhelming sea:

Far off, far off, I feel the first wave tug
Its cargo of agony toward me, inescapable, tidal,
And I, a shell, echoing on this white beach
Face the voices that overwhelm, the terrible element.[20]

(2) Mother number 2. She is what I have used Cixous earlier to suggest:
the source of food – the source of care – the source of language, the first
speaker – the first voice I hear. I drink from her with all the force of my
bare gums. She is what Melanie Klein has called the Breast. Good. Bad. I
project my first love, my first hate, on to her. She is my first mirror. If she
is cold, indifferent, lacking, I shall carry coldness, indifference, lack,
inside me all the days of my life. Unless other people come to help me . . .
And the 'real' mother? The lacking, the needy, the bewildered flesh-
and-blood mother, herself possessed by her own dream of the Mother?
Plath again:

Here is my son
. . . .
He is turning to me like a little, blind, bright plant.
One cry. It is the hook I hang on.
And I am a river of milk.
I am a warm hill.[21]

Whose desolation, whose rage at the hugeness of need – the mother's,
the baby's? – speaks in 'I Want, I Want'?

Open-mouthed, the baby god
Immense, bald, though baby-headed,
Cried out for the mother's dug.[22]

(3) Then there's the Mother Kristeva invokes, the Mother from whom
the Oedipal child must learn to separate, the Mother who is the object of
desire – who surfaces as semiotic incest in poetic language. But does the
desire have to be expressed as the semiotic? Can it not form itself into a
clear newborn image, a bold little language explorer, searching for a
new, a fantasy mother?

The Language Issue

I place my hope on the water
in this little boat
of the language, the way a body might put
an infant

in a basket of intertwined
iris leaves
its underside proofed
with bitumen and pitch,

then set the whole thing down amidst
the sedge
and bulrushes by the edge
of a river

only to have it borne hither and thither,
not knowing where it might end up;
in the lap, perhaps,
of some Pharaoh's daughter.[23]

(4) Archetypal then, the Mother? Ready to surface everywhere, whenever I speak, paint, draw – but above all whenever I allow images to take
over?

The Mother is my strength. Through her I bond with the earth, the
sea. She is the underworld also, the spaces before memory. She is the life
in things, the life in words. She frees me from intellect, from the distance
of sight:

My mind felt white and bloodless. I was trying to write an academic piece
on Katherine Mansfield in the few hours a day I had free from domestic
chores ... and then, suddenly, I found that as soon as I tried to find words
for the black shine of black trees in the rain, say, or the noise of heels knock-
ing on a pavement at night, I could respond quite sharply to everything. . . .
It was like coming back to life.[24]

The Mother is archaic: is powerful. She allows me to be naked. She strokes and eases me. The sweet water of her creeks receives me. Her caves and shades give me shelter. In her recesses I hibernate. She feeds me honey, berries. Like Antaeus, I am reborn whenever I touch her. With Feinstein's speaker, I accept myself:

Patience

In water nothing is mean. The fugitive
enters the river, she is washed free;
her thoughts unravel like weeds of
green silk: she moves downstream
as easily as any cold-water creature

can swim between furred stones, brown
fronds, boots and tins the river holds equally.
The trees hiss overhead. She feels their shadows.
She imagines herself clean as a fish,
evasive, solitary, dumb. Her prayer:
to make peace with her own monstrous nature.[25]

The Mother makes the sun and the seasons return, the moon and tides swell. My bond to her is my dream of fusion: of omnipotence. I call her Ghea. I find her in my body: easily. She makes metaphor easy. From 'White Asparagus' by Sujata Bhatt:

Who speaks of the strong currents
streaming through the legs, the breasts
of a pregnant woman [. . .]?
. . . .
Who speaks of the green coconut uterus
the muscles sliding, a deeper undertow
and the green coconut milk that seals
her well, yet flows so she is wet
from his softest touch?[26]

And from Grace Nichols:

In My Name

Heavy with child

belly
an arc
of black moon

I squat over
dry plantain leaves

and command the earth
to receive you

in my name
in my blood [...]

my tainted

perfect child
my bastard fruit
my seedling
my sea grape
my strange mulatto
my little bloodling

Let the snake slipping in deep grass
be dumb before you.[27]

Yes, I know: I blanket so much by simply seeking for the distant rumble of some archetypal voice in poems so charged with other dimensions: the (raped or seduced?) (slave?) mother in her solitude and deprivation in Nichols's poem turning anger, mixed blood, powerlessness, bastardy, around through the power of her love: in whose name is this done, the name of love, the naming power of language, the mother daring to name outside patriarchal naming? Does the snake cease to be symbolic, the sign of the (sexual, Christian) fall, the sign also of a powerful value system, to re-become a dumb beast, a real snake that can no more tempt Eve than bite Eurydice, or threaten the child? In the Sujata Bhatt poem, here speaks that wonder of wonders whom Kristeva and others seek like salvation: the *desiring* mother. No, I will not invoke the blunt concepts of race and colour, or the hardly less blunt ones of culture or ethnicity to distinguish these poems from others in which I try to hear mothers' voices. It would be glib, and probably untrue, to contrast the easier, earthier relation to coconut or plantain leaves or moon of these two poems with the anguish in Plath, the hospital context of Elaine Feinstein's 'Calliope in the Labour Ward' in which women, 'as little squeamish as / men in the great war', 'grunting in gas and air' 'give birth / bleak as a goddess'.[28] It's not a matter of the happier, more sensuous and loving non-Western women poets versus their more technology- or depression-ruled Western counterparts. Bhatt and Nichols write in English and in England, for one thing. I'm not trying, as the phrase goes, to do justice to the poems, so full of specifics and complexities. I'm listening for something. Ghea. Her echoes.

Ghea is life. Is death. The twin and opposite mother figures in Michèle Roberts's 'After my Grandmother's Death': mother, grandmother, spinners, weavers. In and out of death, of life:

my mother's womb spun me a fine cocoon
spun me round and out, death tugged
my umbilical cord, she grinned
and tied me into her weaving

the moon who eats babies on winter nights
has her dark face, and rubbery hands
but grandmother rescued me
and held me close, she shone
steady for me, then I felt so blessed

then death strode out
trawling, trawling
and grandmother was mackerel to her silver net

the womb is the house of death
and each woman
spins in death's web; as I inch
back to the light
death pays out the bright thread[29]

(5) Enter the Madonna, pensive and patient. The wise virgin, with oil in her lamp. Come the Angel, wind and wings, she is ready: 'I am the servant of the Lord.' She is the sign that the lowly will be exalted, and the powerful brought down. That the world's values will be overturned. I figure her as a very young girl. Now she has her child. She holds him gently. Unpossessively: she knows he is not for her.

She crushes the dragon's head. She is spotless. She can keep me from sin. She knows no sex, but is infinitely available: to me. She is thousands of Western images: haloed in gold, painted in bright colours, the colours of dream. She is mercy incarnate: on the western side of cathedrals, her rose contains the fire of judgement. But oh how easily she slides into her more ambiguous predecessors, the protective, the fertility-making goddesses of the crossroads, the hidden springs, the secret places. Forms of Ghea linger.

But look at the Pietà. Absolute suffering, the worst: yet accepted. The fainting Pietà, the fainting St Theresa: how easily they become eroticized. Female Masochism, Kristeva's 'Stabat Mater' would remind me: 'Feminine perversion [père-version] ... promotes feminine masochism to the rank of structure stabilizer ... ; by assuring the mother that she may thus enter into an order that is above that of human will it gives her her reward of pleasure.'[30]

Darts pierce the mother's heart: as if the heart were the womb's deepest recess. Sex only known, only allowed, through pain. Ecstasy through self-extinction: Plath all over again, is it?

But what of the young Mary, the mother with child? Who writes her?

(6) 'And what about', Suniti Namjoshi who heard a first version of this chapter asked, 'what about the Amazon mother? The Lion Mother, Stevie Smith's lion aunt? The Unlicensed Mother? The Two-Headed Mother? The Servant Mother? The Knight-Mother, in shining armour?'

(7) Oh yes. And then there is the Bad Mother. The castrating Mother, the Destroyer. Her name is Kali. Her name is Medea. She wants me dead. She gives me poison to drink, a bitter pink draught that is all dregs and that I call the Mother of Vinegar. Hysterically I suffocate, and this is called the Suffocation of the Mother. Or else she is fragile, and her brittleness threatens me. From 'Mother' by Nagase Kiyoko:

> I am always aware of my mother
> ominous, threatening
> . . . .
> She prevents all freedom of movement
> if I move she quickly breaks,
> and the splinters stab me.[31]

From 'Mother' by Nancy Morejon:

> Her eyes mirrored no clear-edged branch
> but countless garrottes.[32]

The bad Mother persecutes me. She sabotages everything I do. She wants my youth. She wants my cunt, now that nobody wants hers. She wants to subdue me, make me into her thing. She punishes me: I hide from her. If I want to live, I'll have to kill her.

(8) And then there is real mother. A human being, who had her mother too, and that mother her mother. To whom things were passed down. Qualities and faults. Gifts and traumas. The fallible human being on whom we project the archetypes of the unconscious, Jung argues:

> Up till now everybody has been convinced that the idea 'my father', 'my mother', etc. is nothing but a faithful reflection of the real parent, corresponding in every detail to the original ... [A] supposition of identity by no means brings that identity about. This is where the fallacy of the ... 'veiled one' comes in.... X's idea of [her mother] is a complex quantity for which the real [mother] is only in part responsible, an indefinitely larger share falling to the [daughter]. So true is this that every time [she] criticizes or praises [her mother, she] is unconsciously hitting back at [her]self.[33]

I have substituted 'she' for 'he', 'mother' for 'father' and 'daughter' for 'son' in this passage: it still makes a lot of sense. Those we imagine to be our fathers and mothers are complex projections of anima and animus. It is important, according to Jung, to dig them out of the webs in which they are caught, or else tragic results may ensue: 'They are quite literally the father and mother of all the disastrous entanglements of fate ... Together they form a divine pair ... Those who do not see them are in their hands, just as a typhus epidemic flourishes best when its source is undiscovered.'[34]

The Mother is the figure of the emotional investment I make in people, in things. Look after me, love me, care for me, approve of me, protect me, work things out for me. Admire me, desire me. Save me from fear, of life, of death, of the future, of myself. I cling to the Mother-Father, institutions, the police, pension schemes, hospitals, the dream socialist state. I want to be able to say to the Mother, 'I hate you,' hurl stones at shop windows, and she won't bash me on the head, she'll answer, 'I love you.'

From 'Mother' by Cheryl Moskowitz:

> You gave me these lips
> Mother
> and I wanted to use them
> to say it was your fault –
>   so that nothing I could do would hurt.
> . . . .
> I wanted to blame you with my mouth
> so you could use yours
>
> to kiss away the tears.[35]

The Mother is she whose fault it endlessly is that things go wrong. It's her fault I am lonely frustrated plain unsuccessful unknown unloved. If only she took me in her arms and loved me better everything would be all right. But she won't, the bitch. Right then. I'll batter and punish her till she gives me what I want. She still won't? OK. I'll hurt myself and make myself into pure pain and *that* will be her punishment. Plath, 'Ariel':

> And now I
> Foam to wheat, a glitter of seas.
> The child's cry
>
> Melts in the wall.
> And I
> Am the arrow,
>
> The dew that flies[36]

Oi, oi. I have been bad. I haven't done the right thing. I'll be good, Mother, I swear: then you'll make everything right. Anne Halley's speaker is the 'bearded mother' who has discovered 'twelve hairs on [her] / formerly smooth, virgin round chin'. In mock terror at having turned into one of Neumann's monstrosities of the primordial archetype through neglect of all the Mother-Goddess pieties (vegetarian, ritualistic and witch-like), she comically begs the 'Great Moon Mother' like a guilty little girl:

> It must be the red meat I've been eating.
> That I abandoned
> the sweet sisterhood of weavers
> · · · · · · · · · · · · · · · · ·
> I neglected likewise
> the prescribed ritual baths, came at the wrong
> moon and other times, refused.
> · · · · · · · · · · · · · · · · ·
> didn't look in the oven for days
> but swept away the cobweb
> and my true friend, the spider, unregarded.

The speaker ends with a prayer, 'by the hairs of my chinny-chin-chin', that 'we' may not 'be punished too cruelly', 'made into myth', 'turned into stone' – by mother-Medusa.[37]

One reason why the Mother is such a big chunk for women is that the primary human being who bears us, the figure that embodies mother-hood and generally does the mothering, is also the figure we, potentially at least, are as women meant to become. 'Mothering ... involves a double identification for women, both as mother *and* as child,' Nancy Chodorow points out. 'The whole preoedipal relationship has been inter-nalized and perpetuated in a more ongoing way for women than for men.'[38] This is a source of greater inner contradictions: 'The *wants and needs* which lead women to become mothers put them in situations where their mothering *capacities* can be expressed. At the same time, women remain in conflict with their internal mother' (I would add, *and* with the archetypal figures of the Mothers) 'and often their real mother as well.'[39] '*Wants and needs*': Chodorow italicizes. It is those same wants and needs, especially the need for power, often denied women in the patriarchal system, that drives women to seek the realm of the maternal as especially privileged, Kristeva maintains in 'Stabat Mater'.

When I mother my own children, I am pulled apart by the Mothers. The ideal ones, Ghea the fusional the sensuous the all-powerful, Mary the virginal the kind the both humble and powerful. The real one, in 'my' mother and in myself, easily exhausted, short-tempered, resentful of demands: how easily she becomes Medea, or the martyred Pietà, as in Anne Stevenson's 'Generations'.

Generations

Know this mother by her three smiles.
One grey one drawn over her mouth by frail hooks.
One hurt smile under each eye.

Know this mother by the frames she makes.
By the silence in which she suffers each child to scratch out the aquatints in
her mind.

Know this mother by the way she says
'darling' with her teeth clenched.
By the fabulous lies she cooks.[40]

And behind these mothers there's the Ideal Mother, whom I want to be
because I do want to love: and I want her approval. But I am a real
mother. The Ideal Mother in my head punishes me. It's the real mother's
fault. I'll punish her: my mother, myself.
    And so it goes.

And which of these mothers writes poetry?
    Don't they all? Haven't I just shown it?
    Women write: not the Mother, but mothers, plural: about mothers,
about motherhood, about mothering. About themselves. Like Diogenes
demonstrating to the Sophists that movement existed by getting up and
crossing the room, women poets stage the conflicts of the Mothers, in
mothers. A great many answers to Rich's question 'Can the mother
write?' have been found in the last twenty years, through mothers writing poems.
    The question, 'can the Mother write Poetry?' thus begins to dissolve. It
was a false question. It came from making identities of 'Mother' and of
'Poetry': not acts and experiences in a continuous process of change and
reinvention. It came from being invested by archetypes, projections.
Answers came of themselves once I began to search within myself for
what the Mother was, and found mothers. Once I began to listen to real
mothers writing real poems.
    The seventies, with Rich, questioned Motherhood as an institution.
The eighties worked at separating motherhood from mothering. I want
to argue for further types of separation, for distinguishing the archetypes
and projections from the real mother, and the real self. In *Mothers Who
Leave*, Rosie Jackson attacks the mythology of the perfect Mother. She
agrees with Dorothy Dinnerstein's view that *'the problem is that woman
has been constantly apprehended as a fantasy Mother and not as a separated
being in her own right.'*[41] Jackson argues that our nostalgia for the imagined body of the Mother is a search for a wholeness which our secular
culture does not allow:

the desire to merge with something beyond the personalised separated self,
to move into a non-linguistic, oceanic state, need be neither unconscious nor
regressive. It is the bliss of union consciously sought as the height of mature
mystical experience.
    Fantasies of the Mother take on such power and numinosity precisely
because we are locked in a materialistic and secular society, where desire for
another realm has nowhere else to locate itself.[42]

There is truth in that statement. And mothers do write poems. But I would bet that the question of the Mother and Poetry will not go away. For three reasons: (1) Every time a child is born, there is a need, a long-lasting need: who will fulfil that need? Realities haven't changed much since Tillie Olsen wrote: economic and social and political realities. (2) The Mothers will continue to do battle inside us, and more especially in mothers-who-write, until humanity has become very much wiser. (3) Ethics and Poetry don't necessarily match. If human beings become wiser or more fulfilled the world will be a great deal better but individuals might well not produce better poetry as a result. The worst mother may be the best poet . . .

Notes

1 Sappho, Fragment 76, in *Poems and Fragments*, tr. Josephine Balmer (London: Brilliance, 1984), p. 75.
2 Emily Dickinson, 'My Life Closed Twice Before its Close', in *The Complete Poems of Emily Dickinson*, ed. Thomas H. Johnson (Boston: Little, Brown, 1960), vol. 2, p. 703.
3 Hélène Cixous, *La Ville parjure, ou le retour des Erynies* (Paris: Théâtre du Soleil, 1994).
4 Adrienne Rich, *Of Woman Born* (London: Virago, 1977), p. 31.
5 Kate Chopin, *The Awakening* (London: Women's Press, 1978), p. 80.
6 Camille Paglia, *Sexual Personae: Art and Decadence from Nefertiti to Emily Dickinson* (Harmondsworth: Penguin, 1991), p. 31.
7 Elizabeth Badinter, *L'Amour en plus: Histoire de l'amour maternel (XIIe–XXe siècle)* (Paris: Odile Jacob, 1992).
8 Tillie Olsen, *Silences* (London: Virago, 1980), p. 33.
9 Georges Bataille, *Literature and Evil*, tr. Alastair Hamilton (London: Marion Boyars, 1985), pp. 15–31.
10 In *Purple and Green: Poems by 33 Women Poets* (London: Rivelin Grapheme Press, 1985), p. 22.
11 Rich, *Of Woman Born*, p. 32.
12 Ibid., p. 37.
13 Ibid.
14 Julia Kristeva, *Desire and Language* (Oxford: Blackwell, 1980), p. 136.
15 See Nicole Ward Jouve, *White Woman Speaks with Forked Tongue: Criticism as Autobiography* (London and New York: Routledge, 1991), chs 4 and 5.
16 In Bataille, *Literature and Evil*.
17 Hélène Cixous, 'Castration or Decapitation?', *Signs*, no. 7 (Fall 1981).
18 'The Mothers of Invention', The Point, Cardiff, Wales, 28 Aug.–3 Sept. 1995, workshops and symposium.
19 Sappho, *Poems and Fragments*, p. 74.
20 In Sylvia Plath, *Collected Poems*, ed. Ted Hughes (London and Boston: Faber, 1981), p. 179.
21 Ibid., p. 183.
22 Ibid., p. 106.
23 Nuala Ní Dhomhnaill, *Pharaoh's Daughter*, tr. from the Irish by Paul Muldoon (Oldcastle, Ireland: Gallery Press, 1990).

24 Elaine Feinstein, in Jeni Couzyn (ed.), *The Bloodaxe Book of Contemporary Women Poets: Eleven British Writers* (Newcastle: Bloodaxe, 1985), p. 115.
25 Elaine Feinstein, 'Patience', in her *Some Unease and Angels* (Hutchinson, 1977).
26 Sujata Bhatt, 'White Asparagus', in her *Brunizem* (Manchester: Carcanet, 1988).
27 Grace Nichols, *i is a long memoried woman* (London: Karnack House, 1983).
28 In Couzyn, *The Bloodaxe Book of Contemporary Women Poets*, p. 117.
29 In Michèle Roberts, *Touch Papers* (London: Allison and Busby, 1982).
30 Julia Kristeva, 'Stabat Mater', in Toril Moi (ed.), *The Kristeva Reader* (Oxford: Blackwell, 1986), p. 183.
31 Nagase Kiyoko, 'Mother', tr. from the Japanese by Kenneth Rexroth and Ikuko Atsumi, in Illona Linthwaite (ed.), *Ain't I a Woman! Poems by Black and White Women* (London: Virago, 1987), p. 96.
32 Nancy Morejon, 'Mother', tr. from the Spanish by Kathleen Weaver, in Linthwaite, *Ain't I a woman!*, p. 97.
33 Carl Jung, *Aion: Researches into the Phenomenology of the Self* (London: Routledge, 1959), p. 18.
34 Ibid., p. 21.
35 In *Purple and Green*, p. 115.
36 In Plath, *Collected Poems*, pp. 239–40.
37 Anne Halley, 'Prayer to the Mother', in *The Bearded Mother* (Amherst: University of Massachusetts Press, 1979), pp. 4–6.
38 Nancy Chodorow, *The Reproduction of Mothering* (Berkeley: University of California Press, 1978), p. 204.
39 Ibid., p. 205.
40 Anne Stevenson, 'Generations', in her *Travelling Behind Glass* (Oxford University Press, 1977).
41 Rosie Jackson, *Mothers Who Leave* (London: Pandora, 1994), p. 283.
42 Ibid., p. 285.

Part IV

Creation, Gender and the Imaginary

A Boat by the Sea in the Caribbean, photograph by Cathy Ward

8

Metaphors and Narrative: Of Tongues, Shells, Boats, Oranges ... and the Sea

Epictetes is a Stoic philosopher. Epictetes is a slave. One day his master says, 'I have guests tonight. Cook for us the best things that there are.' When the guests are seated, Epictetes brings in the courses. Casseroled lambs' tongues, grilled ox-tongues, roast swans' tongues ... The irate master calls Epictetes. 'What have you done, you insolent wretch? I ask you for the best things, and you serve us nothing but tongues!' 'Ah, Master,' Epictetes replies. 'Does not the tongue sing the victor at the Olympics? Does it not, in the public place, persuade the people to follow a wise course? Does not the tongue speak the truth about the universe, about human life and the gods?' 'True,' said the Master and laughed, and so did the guests. 'But then,' the Master added, 'tomorrow night you will serve us another meal, and to our same guests. Let it be of the worst things that there are.'

The following evening, after much speculation and wagers, the guests see the dishes brought in. Marinated tongues, grilled, fried, spiced tongues ... The master calls Epictetes. 'Use that nimble tongue of yours to save your head,' he rants. 'You have tried my patience too far. You have humiliated me in front of all my guests. You will die for this.' 'Master, you should have known what you were asking for,' Epictetes mildly replied. You said, 'the worst things'. Isn't it with the tongue that we corrupt and spoil the life of our nearest and dearest? That we get our enemies put to death, poison human relations and the body politic, betray trust and the truth, curse the gods and send armies, or whole peoples to their destruction? Is there anything worse than the tongue?' The master nodded. He had heard.

Best and worst. The most matter-of-fact of the apostles, James, was much in agreement:

My brethren, be not many doctors, knowing that we shall receive the
greater condemnation.
... If any man offend not in word, the same is a perfect man, and able
also to bridle the whole body....
... Behold ... the ships, which though they be so great, and are driven by
fierce winds, yet are they turned about with a very small helm whitherso-
ever the governor listeth.
Even so the tongue is a little member, and boasteth great things. Behold,
how great a matter a little fire kindleth! ...
For every kind of beasts, and of birds, and of serpents, and of things in
the sea, is tamed, and hath been tamed of mankind:
But the tongue can no man tame; ...
Out of the same mouth proceedeth blessing and cursing. My brethren,
these things ought not so to be.
Doth a fountain send forth at the same place sweet water and bitter?
Can the fig tree, my brethren, bear olive berries? either a vine, figs? so can
no fountain both yield soft water and fresh. (James 3:1–12)

But the tongue does. Human speech is paradoxical, as humans are. 'The
depository of truth, and an imbecile earth-worm', Pascal will say of
'man' sixteen hundred years later. 'The glory and refuse of the universe.'
   We are, as James puts it, 'many doctors'. It is vital to the welfare of
the commonwealth that we handle our little helms as wisely as we
can. The commonwealth is the better or the worse for it. Literature,
which is the tongue at its most complete, because at its most varied, at
its most embodied, is or should be the tongue at its best, even when it
articulates the worst. It is its paradox, and its alchemy, that it can give
beauty to evil, rhythm to despair, as well as sing the true and the beautiful. 'To purify the dialect of the tribe.' That was what T. S. Eliot, after the
French poet Mallarmé, thought was the poet's task. I like the alchemical
metaphor that underlies the phrase. But I would want to talk of the
tongue as diverse, rather than pure, especially in today's context. Many
and one, as well as best and worst. I would want to insist on the creative-
ness of multiplicity. On the creative need for diversity.
   Imagine the world of the Thousand and One Nights, instead of a
world in which embattled and oppressed fundamentalisms are left face
to face with the libertarian Babel of postmodernism, which is where *The
Satanic Verses* left Salman Rushdie. In the Baghdad of Calif Haroun-el-
Rachid, an offending storyteller might well have been sentenced to
death. But he would have been given a chance to save his head by telling
another tale. It would have had to have been a jolly good one. But the
wagging of his tongue could have earned his reprieve. It might be
utopian to dream of such a world, a world in which there would be the
many, and the one. But dreams can be creative: a dream not understood
is a message left unread.

Speech. Tongue. Language. In French, the same word, 'langue', means
tongue and language. As in, 'the mother tongue'.

As 'langue', language posits itself as of the body. The organ that, in conjunction with teeth and palate and saliva, eats and articulates words. Feeding tongues to the Master and his guests, Epictetes makes them eat their words, as well as reflect on the tongue, on their capacity to make words: what is 'best', what is 'worst', what is the difference? By contrast James in his Epistle spreads a metaphorical net: the tongue is the helm of a boat, a horse on whom we can put a bit, a fountain producing poison or sweet water. The strength of the examples or metaphors that Epictetes and James serve up, literally for dishes or as means towards understanding, comes from their being of the body, or close to it: tongue is made to eat tongue, the bit that curbs is placed on the horse's tongue, the fountain produces water as the mouth spittle. Interestingly, the body here is not gendered. It could be that of a man or a woman.

Metaphor is a trope, or a figure of speech. According to Aristotle's *Poetics*, metaphor is the transference of the usual name of a thing to another thing by virtue of their likeness. The tongue can be called a helm because both are very little yet steer large things, a boat or a human being. You need a sentence for a metaphor: one word is not enough. That sentence, or series of sentences, is very important, for it enables what is an illogicality, an impertinence (saying that the tongue is a helm, which is nonsense) to become pertinent. The logical space changes.

Through poetic effects, which have to do with sound, with rhythm, reality becomes transfigured. As sentence adds to sentence, as metaphors multiply and mutate, as the plurality of language, with its unconscious effects, its use of symbols, sensuous, emotional and aesthetic values, which pertain to metaphor, combine with mimetic values, which pertain to narrative, to create the world of the text, which makes the world a world habitable by humans. Thus the French philosopher Paul Ricoeur argues in a body of work that I find open and congenial. We find ourselves, Ricoeur says, following Heidegger, thrown into the world. We make it habitable through the fables that we make, by projecting our own possibilities on to the world. As readers, we can only come to understand ourselves through 'the great detour of the signs of humanity deposited in the works of our culture. What would we know of love and hatred, of ethical feelings and generally speaking of all that we call the "soi", if it had not been carried into language and articulated by literature?'[1] To understand is 'to understand oneself in front of the text'. Refusing to impose on the text our own finite capacities, we expose ourselves to the text, and receive from it a vaster proposition for living, more appropriate to the proposition of the world. As one had to let go of logic to accept that a tongue is a helm, so as a reader we accept losing ourselves in the text so as to find ourselves.[2]

What I like about this is the implied dialogue between self-in-the-making and text, the way plurality is recognized, but not incompatible with the construction of self as a subject. And what is said about distance and losing, which seems to me central both to the process of writing and the process of reading. Yet the attractive universality of writing and reading in this account conceals a host of problems.

'There is no understanding of the self that is not mediated by signs, symbols and texts,' Ricoeur argues. Thanks to writing, discourse becomes triply independent: of the speaker's intention, of the first readership, of the circumstances of production. It becomes a 'devenir-texte', a 'becoming-text', read as part of the process of becoming.

How does the mediation occur? Is it so indifferent, who does the reading, who does the writing? And who does the talking?

Writing is making a proposition about the world, which makes the world habitable, something I can feel at home in. Reading is encountering propositions about the world, and, through the mediation of the text, of its signs and symbols, impelled by its narrative, constructing myself as a subject. As a reader I lose myself in the text, so that I can find myself. I encounter the becoming-text and in the process, I myself become. Many, and one.

Implying as he does that, as epistemological and experiential practices, reading and writing are universal, Ricoeur has a point. Maya Angelou recounts how, a twelve-year-old girl from the South of the United States, she had lost speech as a result of being raped by her stepfather. She found her way back to language through reading Dickens's *A Tale of Two Cities*. 'It was the best of times, it was the worst of times . . .' A black female adolescent is led back to subjecthood and speech by the text of a white Victorian Englishman about the French Revolution. You can be an Indian female and love Conrad's *Heart of Darkness*, which is all about men, and colonialism. You can be a European male and love Brazilian Clarice Lispector, or the medieval Japanese Lady Murasaki. As readers we are many. We understand almost everything. Things we could never be or know.

But as readers also we read for the one. We read for those important moments when literature gives us words for what we are: the words for what we did not know we were. And what we are also entails class, rich and poor, as Mrs Ramsay would say. It entails racial and ethnic and cultural and sexual identifications. The same is true of writers. The writer is also situated. And in particular, if the writer is female, her relation to the creative act may be different. Partly because the world is full of great literature written by men, to which a man can easily find a filiation. As women, Virginia Woolf suggested, we relate to tradition through our mothers: if so, filiation for a woman is by no means so evident. Furthermore, throughout the ages, at least in the Western tradition such as I know it, woman, and the female body, have been used as a mediation, an elaborate set of images or figures of speech, a metaphor in short, whereby the 'being-at-home' of texts could be established. I quote from Gayatri Spivak, in an essay called 'Displacement and the Discourse of Woman', which engages with Derrida's essay 'Becoming Woman', which itself engages with Nietzsche's reflexions on woman as the metaphor for truth: on woman as hymen, as paradox, as the veil. Spivak is quoting Hegel:

> Since it is in thought that I am first at home [*bei mir*], I do not penetrate [*durchbohren*] an object until I understand it; it then ceases to stand over against me and I have taken from it its ownness [*das Eigene*] that it had for itself against me. Just as Adam says to Eve: 'Thou art flesh of my flesh and bone of my bone', so mind says: 'This is mind of my mind' and the alienness [*Fremheit* as opposed to *das Eigene*; alterity as opposed to ownness] disappears.[3]

The last twenty-five years have seen extensive and most impressive debates on the woman question, which Simone de Beauvoir had relaunched with *The Second Sex*. What is woman? Is she second, Other, enigma, truth, Madonna, whore or both, biologically or culturally destined, a subcategory of the universal category Man, a series of sexual deviations from the masculine norm, a heterosexual and prescriptive marker? Does she exist? Should we say, women, since there are such differences of race, of religion, of class, of culture, of sexual identity, of wealth? Should we not use the word at all?

Woman's tongue. How does she create in a culture in which, if we follow the Hegel as quoted by Spivak, the figure of speech that represents thought's ability to make the world one's own is Adam's possession of Eve? A culture which ever since Plato and Aristotle, as Hélène Cixous has argued, always places the terms that connote woman as inferior to terms that connote man? Woman is content, matter, flesh, void, object. Man is form, spirit, mind, god.

Speak as she might, Valéry's 'La Pythie' cannot find her own voice: 'Qui me parle, à ma place même?'[4] In spittle and in foam, chewing her own tongue and hair, writhing in the fit of possession by the god, the Pythoness is spoken by another. She gives herself the lie. She is the source neither of the blasphemies that she utters nor of the lightning truths that she vents. Valéry is embodying the poetic process. He is also giving form to what we all, as speakers possessed by the drives in language, may at some time or other go through. Lacan did use the end of 'La Pythie' to represent the fantasy that through the discourse of science it is nature that we actually hear. He is oblivious of the violent feminization of nature which quoting from Valéry here implies: the 'Honneur des Hommes, Saint Langage' – the 'white' voice which issues from the Pythoness's tortured and possessed body, and speaks with *her* tongue – knows as it sounds that it is nobody's voice, but the voice of the 'antres et des bois', of the caves and woods.[5]

But who pays the price for such an achievement? This may be language at its most pantheistic, reaching towards impersonality, embodying the world. The fact remains that both in the Valéry and in Lacan's quotation it is through investment of an 'impure' female body that the voice which is the 'Honour of Men' – poetry or science – comes into existence. The metaphor does not only act as resemblance: it appropriates and subsumes the female body. The Pythoness is the unknowing vessel and channel through which the god, who is male, speaks. 'Who speaks, in my own place?' the Pythoness asks. Can woman speak? Is her silence constitutive of speech? Hélène Cixous, in the 1970s, urged women to write, to explore the 'dark continent' of femininity which, she said, is 'neither dark nor unexplorable':

> Je m'empare de cette langue à moi qui est aussi ma mère et celle de toutes mes filles.
> Et avec elle j'ouvre la bouche des yeux.
> Alors tout ce qui voit parle et chaque parole allume un autre monde de sens.

> Et quoique solidement arrimée dans ma bouche . . . encore que tu ne puisses changer de lieu, pourtant tu changes de place . . .[6]

> (I get hold of this tongue/language of mine which is also my mother and all my daughters.
> And with it I open the mouth of the eyes.
> Then everything that sees speaks and every word lights up another world of meaning.

> And though solidly moored to my mouth . . . though you cannot change location yet you change place . . .)

Tongue, mother tongue. Tongue, and the mother. We generate ourselves through speech. The speaking muscle in our bodies is permanently immersed in liquid, like the foetus in the womb. We all come from the inland sea of the womb. We all go through the evolution of the species from the tiny speck of conception through life in liquid through entry into the world of earth and air and fire. What was, in the 1970s and 1980s, called 'écriture féminine', writing the (female) body, was not, as it was ironically represented, writing in blood and milk instead of with 'the piffle' or 'prick', as the Earl of Rochester and Henry Miller claimed they did, but an attempt to moor the act of writing in a female body that had been, through the ages, presented as the container or channel, never the source, of creation. In the Cixous passage, the speaker-writer is *both* tongue and mouth, rower and boat and river. Ink, let us remember, used to come from octopuses, swimming in the depths of the sea.

In a psychoanalytic, textual rereading of Plato's celebrated metaphor of the cavern, Luce Irigaray, in *Speculum of the Other Woman*,[7] points out that what is left out of Plato's account is the body of the mother. The prisoners are chained inside a cave, turned to the back of the cave. A fire placed behind them projects images there as on a screen. Those images are the shadows that we mistake for reality. We need a Socratic philosopher who, acting as midwife (and Socrates was the son of a midwife), would force us to come out through narrow passages into the light of day, the real world, where there are reflections, in water or shadows. Eventually, the former prisoner would be freed from appearances, and gaze upon the Sun, the Idea, or Truth.

It does not take much of a Freudian reading, though it took Irigaray to decipher it, to see that the cavern is like a womb. Irigaray shows that the Intelligible here is reached through eliding the role of the mother's body as also engenderer. The primal scene, the sexual coupling of father and mother, is avoided. There is no relation between sun and cave. Disembodiment is the condition of Intelligibility. Truth is the absence of any reflection – the sun itself. In order to reach it the maternal body, which is conceived as pure materiality, which functions only as screen, or water that reflects, has to be left behind.

> Homme libre, toujours tu chériras la mer!
> La mer est ton miroir; tu contemples ton âme
> Dans le déroulement infini de sa lame,
> Et ton esprit n'est pas un gouffre moins amer.[8]

Baudelaire's poem 'L'Homme et la mer' begins as a hymn to freedom. Did he not write that two or three marine miles are enough to give man the idea of infinity? Yet rapidly all that the sea does here is reflect. It becomes a mirror, of the abyss in man. By the end it has become an enemy brother, as hungry for death as man. Through the inevitable pun, as old as the French language, 'la mer', the sea, echoes 'la mère', the mother. 'Amer', bitter, is also 'a-mer', motherless. An unmothering, a cruel sea.

The sea, so often central to Baudelaire's poems, he never merges with. He fights it, he rides it. Sea-like, music gets hold of the boat-poet. It leaves him in 'calme plat, grand miroir / De mon désespoir!' Like Baudelaire, French Symbolist poet Rimbaud speaks his relation to the sea through a boat. His 'Bateau ivre' his 'drunken boat', though he has wildly gone to sea, scattering helm and grappling hooks, and tasted the green water, sweeter than to children the flesh of tart apples, though he longs for the sea – 'oh que j'aille à la mer' – can no more sink, become lost in the sea, lose his separateness than can Baudelaire's ships. The speaker of Valéry's 'Le Cimetière marin', perhaps the most celebrated poem about the sea in the French language, is equally separate, though in apparent control. He stands in his 'ownness' above the Mediterranean in a hill graveyard. The metaphors proliferate: the sea is so still it seems solid, a roof on which white sails, dove-like, are pecking. An emblem of eternity, threatening stasis, it makes the poet into what Valéry said the thinker was: a Lazarus, a man dying, and trying to return from death. The sea also gathers in its net of sparks every mythic mirage. The sea is

delirious like a Pythoness, spotted like a panther. It is a chlamis in which
the sun bores thousands of holes, a hydra that bites its own tail . . . Myths
of the Terrible Mother flash in and out of the verse:

> Oui! grande mer de délires douée,
> Peau de panthère et chlamyde trouée
> De mille et mille idoles du soleil,
> Hydre absolue, ivre de ta chair bleue,
> Qui te remords l'étincelante queue
> Dans un tumulte au silence pareil,

> Le vent se lève! Il faut tenter de vivre![9]

The sea is female. The wind male. The poet tears himself away from
the contemplation that threatened death thanks to the wind that ruptures
the (hymen-like) surface of the sea, that sends pages of spray flying on to
the rocks.

I am not trying to knock those poems. I love Baudelaire, and Rimbaud. I know 'Le Cimetière marin' by heart and have lived with it for
years with a mixture of fascination and exasperation. I'm not the
metaphor police. I know that as human beings we make metaphor out of
everything we are, and that life has made us. We let go of logical sense (a
tongue is not a helm) in order to find meaning at the other end, through
similitude and fable. *Meta*: beyond, after. Travel and transport are at
work in metaphor, as well as being and non-being. Male poets have,
throughout the ages, made a glorious job of singing reality. I would not
be without their song. But some of the propositions that they make don't
leave me room. I need the other sides, as it were, the many repressed
sides. Among these, for a more complete, a multiple world, one in which
Fremheit is not sublated, in which there is contradiction and complemen-
tarity, a world in which there could be 'an abundance of the other', as
Hélène Cixous puts it, I need the woman creator. And she is not so easy
to imagine, because of the ways in which woman has been metaphorized
as sea as Pythoness as screen as cave as mirror. 'Qui me parle, à ma place
même?' 'Who speaks me, in my own place?': in place of myself?

Can we engender ourselves, as creators, without making another
human being, of a different sex or colour or culture, subservient to us?
Perhaps a utopian question, but one which has large political implications.

White Mythology: the *Usure* of the Sea Mother

In 'White Mythology' Derrida attacks what he calls the *usure* of
metaphor. *Usure* means both the wearing out and the profit, the surplus

value made through usury. There is, Derrida recounts, an Anatole France dialogue in which the characters reflect on how a coin, put to the grindstone, might have the effigy on it effaced, then be sold at an inestimable value. This is what the metaphysicians have done. They started with material, sensuous images, connected them analogically with concepts, then let the concept become abstract, even though it implicitly carried the image that had been bound with it. Thus 'breath' has disappeared from 'spirit', 'sun' from 'God' or 'Idea'. Any expression of an abstract idea, the dialogue concludes, ' "can only be by analogy. By an odd fate, the very metaphysicians who think they escape the world of appearances are constrained to live perpetually in allegory. A sorry lot of poets, they dim the colours of the ancient fables, and are themselves but gatherers of fables. They produce white mythology." ' 'Metaphysics', Derrida comments: 'the white mythology which reassembles and reflects the culture of the West: the white man takes his own mythology, Indo-European mythology, his own *logos*, that is, the *mythos* of his idiom, for the universal form of what he must still wish to call Reason.'[10] Metaphysics proceeds by *usure* indeed: the original fable, analogy, covered in white ink, the metaphor worn out, but enabling Western man to make profit out of it – set up classifications, systematize forms of power, privilege his own version of things as 'Truth', as 'Logos', as against for instance Oriental, more image-making forms of thought. Derrida quotes Hegel as making the whole system explicit, especially in his concept of *Aufhebung*, of *relève*, meaning both (for Derrida) taking over and raising (a word) from a sensory to a spiritual meaning.[11] The central metaphor is that of the sun, metaphorically presented (as in Plato's *Republic*) as the 'invisible source of light', 'sowing' its 'seeds'. The sun *as eventually Truth, as eventually Being*, becomes charged with a male, a patriarchal dimension, becomes connected with the eye, death, the 'proper name',[12] which then becomes elided, eroded yet profit-making. Thus oppositions like 'nature/spirit, nature/history, sensual/intelligible are formed 'under the master category of dialectical idealism'.[13]

I would like to turn this, not to ideas of 'whiteness', the construction of Western metaphysics, as Derrida does, but to how gender works in the metaphors of language and the sea which I have been playing with. For the profit by usury which Derrida says flows from the use of metaphor by metaphysics is loaded in gender terms: if the sun be indeed the central metaphor, it is privileged as male over, for instance, the earth as female. French feminisms, Cixous in particular, eloquently pointed this out in her celebrated 'Sorties' essay.[14] It is clear that Irigaray, in what she says about Plato's cave and the way it both elides and refers to, the womb, and about the Sun as the Intelligible (sower, father, Truth), is unpicking the same 'master categories' as Derrida, though she proceeds in a different perspective. The conclusion however would be similar: it is particularly difficult for women to create, and imagine the creative process, because of the way the imaginary has become bound up with the cultural, the socioeconomic – mother, or woman, have been caught as container, recipient, matter, etc., through endless and endlessly reinvented 'worn' and idealized metaphors, and this happens to correspond with the way in which women have been repressed or suppressed over time, in which women have been told 'Can't paint, can't write', as Charles Tansley in Woolf's *To the Lighthouse* tells painter Lily Briscoe. The mythology is not just white: it is patriarchal. It has become so normative that the question of sex has become bound up with the question of creation. No need to expand: thousands of women have written about this, and second-wave feminism has been particularly eloquent on the topic. What however strikes me when I look at how the figures of the mother and the father, and the creative process itself, are imagined, is that what Irigaray and Derrida describe is not as rigid as they make it, and that it is the last two centuries perhaps more than others which have intensified the sense of alienation between the sexes, making the creative act more gender-biased than at other periods.

This is, I realize, a historically wobbly statement, and I am not sure where the cut-off point should be – perhaps as early as the seventeenth century, or even the Renaissance? But returning to Dante after many years, with these images of creation on my mind, I am struck by how playful, and paradoxical, and on the side of the mother his description of poetic language is. He had to choose the mother tongue for his *Divine Comedy*, he said: the mother tongue is 'on the side' of the fourteen Italian dialects. He needs to pursue *his own* tongue so as to invent it, as one would ride through a forest in pursuit of a panther 'whose scent reaches every corner, but which will never allow itself to be seen'.[15] The poetic tongue flees through the forest, a female prey to a male rider, you might say: but she is beloved, she is to be snared in a net, not destroyed, and she is the poet's *own*, not somebody else's... But she is also the 'vulgar' tongue (nothing to do with Mallarmé's or Eliot's 'purity'). She is archaic (like Kristeva's 'semiotic'?). She is like an enveloping medium, the language by which the baby has been fed – and it is a woman who has taught it: 'I call vulgar tongue that with which little children are made familiar by those who surround them, when first they begin to form diverse sounds; or to put it more briefly, by vulgar tongue I mean that which we speak without any rule, imitating our nurse' (Dante).[16]

And so, perhaps, metaphors of creation do not have to subsume one gendered entity under another? Do *mer* and *mère* only rhyme with *amer* when the poet carries a particular bitter history within himself (or herself)?

What I want to say is that metaphors of creation do not *have to* carry the gender privilege, or gender charge, that the metaphor of the sun is seen by Derrida to carry. Inspired and enlightening as I find Derrida's manoeuvres, I agree with Ricoeur's critique in the name of 'la métaphore vive' – of live metaphor. It is not because the metaphoric process has been used by metaphysics to its profit that metaphor must be worn, *usée*, must lose its dynamism: every time it is reactivated, every time it becomes image-making, and the sensuousness of the sensory term is made vivid, it is reborn;[17] and where does this most happen if not in poetic language? Derrida places the metaphor of the *demeure*, the dwelling-place, the house, alongside the metaphor of the sun: and yes, you could say that every time a habitation, cave or other, appears, as in Plato, then the womb is not far. And that when Ricoeur says that literature is about making the world habitable, he is transferring to literature a dwelling, a protective, a mothering image: hoodwinked, Derrida might say, by 'white mythology'. But that is to leave aside the experiential dimension of metaphor, its being born from the paradox of living. That is to ignore that fusion in the womb is a primary experience for both sexes, and that the degree of protection by the mother, or the first environment, and the satisfaction of primary needs are essential to the development of creativity, whether we are male or female – dependence on the *environment* is the lot of all human beings:

> We find that individuals live creatively and feel that life is worth living or else that they cannot live creatively and are doubtful about the value of living. This variable in human beings is directly related to the quantity and quality of environmental provision at the beginning or in the early phases of each baby's living experience.
> . . . here at this point where creativity either comes into being or does not come into being (or alternatively is lost) the theoretician must take the environment into account, and no statement that concerns the individual as an isolate can touch this central problem of the source of creativity.[18]

What Derrida removes from his critique of metaphor is the way in which experience, for each human being, can renovate metaphor. In the particular set of metaphors I have been looking at, the tongue in the mouth, bathed in saliva as the baby is bathed in the placenta in the womb, is (metonymically as well as metaphorically?) taken as an analogue for the speech which it produces, the writing that it leads to and which can be located in the 'house' of literature, which can be a 'good' environment, one that makes meaning out of life and induces creativity and individuation. The tongue in the mouth, thus in a safe and nurturing environment, is able to individuate and play (pursue itself through the forest, as in Dante, and be fed by words/milk by its nurse). And in its turn it becomes like the helm in a boat (the mouth, the body), a boat on the sea . . . The *container* – womb, sea, nurse – may be gendered, but in a special, almost neutral way, as Plato describes in *Timaeus* the receiver, the *chora*, that enables all things to be, 'the nurse of generation':

> the mother and receptacle of all created and visible and in any way sensible things, is not to be termed earth, or air, or fire, or water, or any of their compounds, or any of the elements from which these are derived, but is an invisible and formless being which receives all things and in some mysterious way partakes of the intelligible, and is most incomprehensible.[19]

What I am suggesting is that there can be metaphors of the womb as source of all life and trope of the condition for all creation which do not have to be gendered in the oppositional ways described by Derrida or Irigaray. The repeated unconscious human experience of beginnings (repeated in that all human beings go through it, being in the womb; human in that it has become archetypal) does not have to, cannot, equate the gender of childbearing women. The Mother (as Jung insists) is not to be equated with one's real mother, the 'fallible being' whose history is bound with ours. Live metaphors revive the archetype.

Cannot creativity be expressed by images/objects that do not have to be usury-making, do not have to be gendered?

Transitional Objects

And so, pursuing the tongue, in its sea, and the sea, I would like to dream for a few minutes about shells.

Seashells, by the seventeenth century, or so I've read, had become an emblem of the way in which art and nature might combine. Shells were beautiful, sculpturally perfect. They were one, and many. They had contained living creatures of the deep. They were their habitat, their architecture. And so does Socrates, in Valéry's *Eupalinos*, find them. Socrates is in hell, dialoguing with Phaedrus. He now regrets that in life he chose to be a thinker, not a maker. There was not enough body to his language, he mourns. And for a model of what he would have liked to make, he talks of his encounter, on a beach, with a strange white sculptural object, which he does not name and which the tide had left. Later, Phaedrus evokes a wondrous Phoenician whom he knew, who made ships, that were large bodies adapted to the sea. Shells or ships here, although you could liken them to wombs, are specifically not that: they are intermediary objects, that do not entail a hierarchy of male or female, or an erasure of the mother's body.

Francis Ponge, the author of poems called *Le Parti pris des choses*, literally 'things have made up their minds', but also 'taking the side of things', a poet I much liked in my youth, kept resurfacing while I was mulling over all this. His poems meditate on pebbles on beaches, molluscs, seashells, snails. The body of the sea creature is moored to its shell much as the tongue to the mouth in the Hélène Cixous passage. Ponge sings the good proportions of the shell. It is a model of what to Ponge is a good poem, one that is an appropriate house of language for man's tongue, and one that respects the alienness of the world. He imagines the animal inside the shell, its life in the sea – wishes that human beings, who share with seashells both fleshiness and the need for hard houses, were able to make dwellings for themselves that would be equally proportionate. He most admires measured writers – 'Malherbe, Horace,

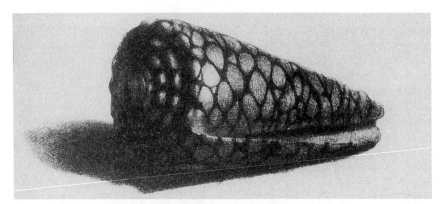

Rembrandt, *The Shell (Conus marmoureus)*, f. 1650, Private Collection

Balthasar van Ast, *Still Life with Shells*, Panel, 30 × 47 cms, collection Museum Boijmans Van Beuningen, Rotterdam

'Rare mussel and mollusc shells, brought back to Holland from exotic lands by the great trading companies, were popular collectors' items in the seventeenth century. ... On account of their beauty and value, these objects were seen to embody the transition from Nature (*Natura*) to Art (*Ars*) or their union. Conchylia (the shells of molluscs) and other natural objects were to be found alongside man-made works of art amassed by princes and displayed in a *Kunst-* or *Wunderkammer*.' From *Rembrandt: The Master and his Workshop: Drawings and Etchings*, ed. Holm Bevers, Peter Schatborn and Barbara Welzel (New Haven and London: Yale University Press, 1991, p. 248.)

Giovanni Bellini, *Allegory of Virtus Sapientia*, Galleria dell' Accademia, Venice

Mallarmé' – 'because their monument is made of the true common secretion of the mollusc man, the thing most proportioned and conditioned to his body, and yet the most different from his form that could be conceived – I mean SPEECH.'[20] Ian Higgins comments:

> There is a striking doubleness to language in [Ponge's] metaphors, a paradoxical coexistence of concrete and abstract. Language is a secretion, a substance, part of man and yet different from him, outside him, an exhalation floating round him. [Things, in Ponge] are often characterized by the meeting or 'intersection' of opposite ... qualities. The mollusc is such a thing, soft and boneless, yet secreting a hard shell which is part of it and yet so different from it. This doubleness makes it into a 'réalité des plus précieuses' ... So too, by analogy, man is a precious and privileged being because he is a paradox, a soft shapeless mass giving himself form – that is, difference, individuality – through his utterances, so different in form from himself.[21]

Here I am reminded of Winnicott:

> It is well known that infants as soon as they are born tend to use fist, fingers, thumbs in stimulation of the oral erotogenic zone, in satisfaction of the

Maruja Mallo, *Naturaleza viva*, photograph: Guillermo de Osma, Madrid, Private Collection

instincts of that zone, and also in quiet union. It is also well known that after a few months infants of either sex become fond of playing with dolls, and that most mothers allow their infants some special object and expect them to become, as it were, addicted to such objects.[22]

Thus does Winnicott introduce what he calls *transitional objects*. His claim is that, while it is true to say that the *'inner reality'* of an individual is constituted by his reaching the stage of 'being a unit with a limiting membrane and an outside and an inside', and that that inner world can be rich or poor, at peace or at war, there is a third area, an intermediate one, the 'area of *experiencing*, to which inner reality and external life contribute'. The transitional object corresponds to this intermediate state. It can be a bit of blanket, a bit of wool ... something 'between the thumb and the teddy-bear, between the oral eroticism and the true object-relationship'. It becomes for the infant a defence against anxiety, helps it go to sleep. Holding and mouthing, 'accompanied by sounds of mum-mum', babbling, anal noises, the first musical notes' occur. There is an implicit agreement with the mother that the baby has rights over the object. And – Winnicott underlines – *'there is no noticeable difference between boy and girl in their use of the original "not-me" possession*, which I am calling the original object.'[23]

It is true, Winnicott adds, that 'the piece of blanket (or whatever it is) is symbolical of some part-object, such as the breast. Nevertheless, the point of it is not its symbolic value so much as its actuality ... the term "transitional object" ... gives room for the process of being able to accept difference and similarity.'[24] It is part of a journey of progress towards experiencing, moving from subjectivity to objectivity.

At a poetic or painterly or more generally imaginary level, the shell could be read as an elaborate analogue to the transitional object. As the house of an animal, of an allegorical figure, it stands for the womb (or breast?). But it is so clearly an object, so distinct from the subsuming power of other womb metaphors, that it allows a writer like Ponge to make room for the *actuality* of the object, the acceptance of difference and similarity. Though in Ponge's poem the shell ends up standing for the hard structure of language that man, with his mollusc-like tongue, can secrete, there is never any doubt that this *is* an analogy: the 'is not' is present in the 'is'. This is not only a grown-up metaphor (unlike the Baudelaire or Rimbaud metaphors of the boat and sea I quoted earlier, full of longing for fusion with the sea-mother), it is also an ungendered metaphor: as an image of what language can do, it applies to a woman just as much as to a man. Doesn't Winnicott say that there is no difference between boy and girl in their use of the 'not-me' transitional object? The mother's body in this case is not elided, not taken for granted. Was it the mark of a wiser, a more grown-up culture when people (in the Caribbean, I believe) used shells for currency instead of coins? You do not *use*, wear out, make usury out of, shells: at best you might make music out of them, or listen to their sea sound?

Another transitional object comes to me as I write this: the orange, which both Colette and Hélène Cixous have written about. It comes to mind because I spent time writing about it.[25] No need to spell things out: the (breast-like) globe of the fruit, its juiciness ... you hold it, you suck it. In Colette's story 'Le Rendez-vous', while the characters pick and devour fruit in a Moroccan orange-grove, an April wind runs 'over a fresh desert of salt water, milky and clear like an Armorican sea' – 'laiteux et clair comme une mer armoricaine'.[26] The Brittany (= Armorican) sea that is here evoked, and that, in its milky transparency, reminds me of Vermeer (*The Milkmaid* ...) is made present through a pause, an internal rhyme ('laiteux et *clair* / comme une *mer*'): and, through that rhyming pause, the echo (mer = mère) is heard, while another echo ('Armoricaine' = 'Marocaine') connects the two alien seas, the northern and the Mediterranean one. In *Vivre l'orange*, Cixous celebrates the Brazilian writer Clarice Lispector, whose writing rejuvenated and inspired hers, was like a drink of orange in the desert for her. Clarice 'put the orange back into the desert hands of my writing ... And it was a whole childhood that came back running to get hold of the living orange.'[27] Links

between Brazil and Cixous's own childhood country, Algeria, with Oran, her native city, spring throughout the text like juice in the mouth, the taste of a recovered luminous childhood self: 'Oran-je' . . .
Transitional objects, oranges? Oh yes. Sometimes they are made to carry every form of anger and rejection (the child's rejection of the womb-world?): Jeanette Winterson's *Oranges Are Not the Only Fruit*, Anthony Burgess's *Clockwork Orange* . . . But in writers seeking for unity of self and world, for a reality based on experience and that would be, as Kristeva says of that of Proust *'all at once* cosmic, physical and significant', the metaphoric resources of the orange can be deployed with endless sensuousness. In her fine study of Proust, *Le Temps sensible*, Kristeva traces some of the vagaries of orangeade through *A la recherche du temps perdu*, from its association with Swann's vanishing love for Odette (as the squeezed fruit gets changed into juice, as the juice melts into 'jouissance' as it is being drunk?) to the fruit's capacity, through all its mutations, to sensuously survive in the most *mondaine* of situations. In the Guermantes after-dinner garden ritual, orangeade and orange *compote* are served. Kristeva quotes, and I translate (I imagine, never having had it, that orange *compote* is colourless but highly scented):

> Nothing wearies less than this transposition into taste of the colour of a fruit which, once cooked, seems to take us back to the season of the flowers. Purple as a spring orchard, or else colourless and fresh like a light breeze under the fruit trees, the juice lets itself be breathed in and looked at drop by drop.[28]

Under its two *'espèces'*, appearances – not bread and wine but *compote* and juice – the orange allows 'la communion sociale', social communion. Freshness and springiness incarnate, squeezed and diluted into water, its taste powerfully evocative of its ripening, its alien *'règne'*, its vegetal difference from the human realm, it becomes associated, in the narrator's love for Albertine, with the irreducible otherness of another human being. Whether it be in Hélène Cixous's endless variations with the name of the orange-giver, Clarice Lispector, that is made to mutate into all languages, or in Proust's metamorphoses, the globe-shaped fruit seems to be metaphoric abundance incarnate, juiciness, melting and spurting in the mouth: the ideal transitional object, what might console you but also not console you for the loss of the mother's breast? But then of course Proust is full of these: isn't the *petite madeleine* that, dipped in tea, recreates the first involuntary memory, *plump* (*dodu*) and tasty, but also shaped *like a shell*, the shell worn on their clothing by the pilgrims of Compostela to signify their pilgrimage?
    Winnicott stresses that there is already an element of play in the transitional object. And for him, the capacity to play is bound up with the capacity to be creative (= endlessly to reinvent metaphors?). It is not the

object that is transitional: it 'represents the infant's transition from the state of being merged with the mother to a state of being in relation to the mother as something outside and separate'.[29] What is striking about Colette's or Cixous's or Proust's writing about the orange is that, however charged with motherly connotations the orange can be (triggering the 'milky' sea image in Colette, summoning up childhood for Cixous, spring orchards for Proust's narrator), the orange remains very distinctly an orange.

'It is assumed', Winnicott also says, referring to Joan Riviere, 'that the task of reality-acceptance is never completed, that no human being is free from the strain of relating inner and outer reality, and that relief from this strain is provided by an intermediate area of experience ... which is not challenged (arts, religion, etc.).'[30] In a way then, the whole of literature, and our making for ourselves a house in it, our using it to make the world 'habitable', is like a relation to a huge transitional object: which is no more gendered, boy-specific, than the smaller transitional object, shell or orange. We can lose ourselves in it as the small child loses itself in the area of 'play' ... Which is not to say that when it comes to the choice of objects to play with, the difference between boys and girls might not enter. 'Boys to some extent tend to go over to use hard objects' (Winnicott again says), 'whereas girls tend to proceed to the acquisition of a family' by means of dolls, soft toys. Reading this I think that shells are hard indeed, and that the ideal of literature that Ponge outlines is very much made up of 'hard' poets (Malherbe, Mallarmé ...).

When Ponge writes about the orange (for he does too), he foregrounds the difference between skin – shell – and flesh. And the act of squeezing. One 'exprime', *expresses* the juice of an orange in French: as one expresses by means of language. This is, Ponge suggests, an *oppression*, the subsuming of the natural world: as the orange gets destroyed when it is *exprimée*, its fibres crushed and broken, so does the object when spoken, evoked through language – there is bitterness in the taste of pips, however much joy and light there may be in the colour and taste of the liquid. The poem ends with the pip, tiny, green, concentrating in itself all the qualities of the tree: 'the relative hardness and greenness ... of the wood, of the branch, of the leaf'. But also, the 'raison d'être du fruit'.[31] The fruit exists so that the tree can self-perpetuate by means of the pips. Which leaves humans, and what they do with oranges, whether they eat them or express their juice, up in mid-air ...

As against this, you can sink your teeth into an orange, be filled with its juice, smell, let sensation come to the fore. Is there also an element of sexual difference in that Cixous in particular, but also Colette, are inspired by the orange to 'babble', make music – to those sounds of desire for the mother's body which Kristeva has linked with the semiotic, but which might more properly be linked with what Winnicott says of the babble that accompanies the play with transitional objects? Are such areas more easily reactivated for girls, because they are of the same sex as their mothers, identify more readily with them? Are the male writers more intellectual, more analytical, more boundary conscious, the female writers keening for union? But then, sexual difference is something more complex than the sex you happen to be. But then, Proust writes of the 'jeux d'arrosage', the watering games that the squeezing of the orange allows, unveiling a hundred mysteries to the narrator's 'sensation', but none to his 'intelligence'.[32] But then, Michèle Roberts, in *Daughters of the House*, has her young girl protagonist Léonie work out her puzzlement at the reality of one and the riddle of two, at the gap between experience and analysis, as she juggles with oranges in a chapter called … 'The Oranges'. The gap that she worries about, which is between words and things, abstract operations and concreteness, wholeness and division, might be in Ponge's tradition. It is girlish one way (girls fear division), boyish another … Léonie is puzzling over magpies in the field, and the oranges she plays with play a transitional role in her puzzlement:

> Two was an odd word anyway. It did not express twoness. It was as short, round and compact as one. Léonie's formula was: one magpie in the same field as another magpie, both in view at once, makes two magpies. She preferred saying one-and-one to two. She knew what she meant. . . .
> She sat on the kitchen doorstep, knees wide apart, frowning. She was juggling with two oranges. They whirled through the air in front of her, an oval streak of orange. One. Then she made them slow down, and two oranges again spun between her hands.[33]

Whatever may be the case, whether the male writers tend to go more for boundaries, for hard containers, than the female writers, or whether it is a question of femininity or masculinity, shells are also there in Colette. As in Ponge … In *Le Blé en herbe*, the young adolescents, Phil and Vinca, find shrimps or lobsters in rock-pools on the Brittany – the 'Armorican' – coast. Their fishing is always written as a series of relationships, of people, perceptions, bodies, water, sea creatures. Vinca has drawn her playmate Phil's attention to the presence of some beautiful shrimps in a pool:

> She leant further forward, and her hair beat, like a short imprisoned wing, her companion's cheek. She moved further back, then came back, with an imperceptible motion, then back again. He seemed not to notice, but his free hand drew Vinca's naked arm, tanned and salty.
> 'Look, Vinca … The loveliest one, coming …'
> Vinca's arm, that she pulled back, slid as far as the wrist inside Phil's hand as in a bracelet, for he was not squeezing.
> 'You won't catch it, Phil, it's gone away again …'
> So as better to follow the shrimp's game, Vinca gave back her arm, as far as the elbow, to the half-closed hand. In the green water, the long agate shrimp was feeling the edge of the net with the tip of its paws, the tip of its antennae. A flip of the wrist, and … But the fisherman tarried, perhaps savouring the stillness of the docile arm inside his hand, the weight of a head veiled in hair that leant for an instant, conquered, on his shoulder, then fiercely pulled apart …
> 'Quick, Phil raise the net! Oh! it's gone! why did you let it go?'[34]

The shrimps are alive, they have their own movement. They can escape, as desiring girl escapes, or does not escape, boy, and as desiring boy escapes, or does not escape, desiring woman. Throughout the novel Colette keenly retains the boundaries, the distance, between character and character, between earth and sea. The metaphors make you feel and see, but ownness never subsumes alienness:

> The great August tide, bringing rain, filled the window. The earth ended there, on the edge of the sandy meadow. Just another effort of the wind, another upheaving of the grey field ploughed with parallel foams, and the house, no doubt, would float like an ark ... But Phil and Vinca knew the August tide and its monotonous thunder, the September tide and its white dishevelled horses. They knew that this tip of meadow remained unbridgeable, and their childhood had every year taunted the soapy thongs which danced, powerless, on the gnawed edge of the empire of men.[35]

The 'gnawing', as by rodents, gently deflates the uncharacteristic grandeur of 'l'empire des hommes'.

Colette is uncharacteristic. The confident sense of identity which her texts generate is not that frequent in women's fictions. It may have to do with her extraordinarily strong relationship with her mother. As if somehow the ability to let go of 'home', for the woman writer, had to do with having had it in the first place. That may be true, of course, for both sexes: Winnicott's work makes it clear that creativity has to do with having had 'good-enough' mothering. Wandering as I have through images of tongue and mouth, boat and sea, mollusc and shell – and oranges – as analogues for each other and for the self in literature, the self that creates in language, or as intermediaries between self and non-self, subject and world, I have come to see that, whatever 'white mythologies' metaphors may carry, there wasn't any necessary gendering of the 'holder', the container: neither the archetypal mother/womb/breast nor the transitional object need be other than neutral, open to the play of imagination of both sexes. Each writer gives it his or her configuration, and it expresses particular relations to the feminine or the masculine, but it is quite open. It is when we come to the contained – the animal inside the shell, the tongue, the *self* – that gendering becomes insistent.

Narrative and the Self at Sea

It is with the *subject* that gender trouble starts. With the subject of the author as embodied in narrative, explored through a protagonist. For with the subject, history – public and private, collective and individual – begins.

Who am I? How can I create a world of language which will make me be at home in the world? Those questions are even more difficult for women writers than for men. For a long time in the history of the Western world – perhaps since Lysistrata, or before – certainly in more recent periods, since the medieval *Querelle des femmes* through to *The Vindication of the Rights of Women* and beyond to the New Woman, the Suffragettes, *The Second Sex* and *The Female Eunuch*, generations of women have repeatedly questioned the organized systems of power which barred the door for them to financial or legal independence, political representation, education and access to the ritual and cultural positions – in religion, art or literature – that enable human beings to make meaning of who they are, give formal expression to being-in-the-world. No need to repeat or detail what has been so well said thousands of times, and which the early years of post-1968 feminisms were so eloquent in so variously stating. As well as that, for some of the reasons I have outlined above, women have felt divided in the creative act: both the maker of the sign and the sign, barred from, foreigners in, creation. Can you be both Pythoness and speaking God, muse and poet, dwelling-place and dweller? Yes, if you double up in some imaginary bisexuality as Hélène Cixous does in the passage quoted above, playing at being both tongue and mouth, actor and medium. Or if, like Dante, you are both labile, playful child and the nurse that feeds it words. But such happy doublings are not frequent.

The struggle to *be*, and the striving to be creative, have been made difficult for Western women at least, by living conditions and gender rules (I would venture to say, not only for Western women: indeed, things may be much worse for women in other parts of the world). Little girls being of the same sex as their mothers, and unconsciously conditioned to behave like their mothers, patterns have been passed on that make individuation difficult. Women may be less able to separate from an imaginary womb or containment within the real home, to take and accept the distance that is needed to seek for identity, to fashion a world which could be 'home' in the other, larger sense. If I turn again to sea images, to images of self as boat at sea, I am struck by how frequently themes of madness, drowning, going under, appear in modern women's writing: from Kate Chopin's *The Awakening* to Doris Lessing's *Briefing for a Descent into Hell* to Margaret Atwood's *Surfacing* to Janet Frame's *Faces in the Water* to the opening of Toni Morrison's *Tar Baby* ... Not that there isn't a plethora of male-authored fictions and poems that draw on the experience/image of boat at sea: from the Romantic trope to Poe's 'Descent into the Maelstrom' to Conrad ... But somehow as captains, sailors, voyagers, pirates, the men (who as far as I know since humans have gone to sea have alone had access to shipping) had experience of the realities of ships and voyages, of storms and shoals and charts, the formative processes of surviving dangerous journeys. Such experiences, over many generations, in many civilizations, created patterns for the discovery and strengthening of the self, which were then bequeathed to younger men as rites of passage and models of individuation (as

Conrad's Marlowe does with the young captain in *The Shadow-Line*). The combination of experience, access to the experience, and the separation from the world of women, that went with going to sea, meant that the self-on-a-ship or the self-as-boat found itself through surviving the trials of a cruel sea, learnt mastery, individuation – or, headstrong and manic like Captain Ahab in *Moby Dick*, tragically went under. Possibly for all the opposite reasons, because women until recently have had so little direct experience of sailing, of navigating, being at the helm, really or figuratively, because they have had few extreme tussles with, and chances to separate from, the sea/mother, again actual and figurative, the protagonists of female-authored fictions have, it seems to me, a much more mixed time of the sea.

For evil or for good.

Jean Rhys's *Wide Sargasso Sea* takes up the silenced history of Mr Rochester's mad wife from Charlotte Brontë's *Jane Eyre*. It chooses to give her the story. It lets her speak in her own voice. It seeks for the origins of the mad wife: childhood, Jamaica, the distant colonial world, one version or location perhaps of the 'dark continent' which Freud saw as femininity. For the first time in her fiction writing (for this is a late book, coming after a long silence) Rhys has found a protagonist distant enough (the mad wife comes from someone else's novel, remote in time; her ending, madness and death, is already written) and yet close enough to embody the divisions, the marginality, that plagued her life.

A white Creole, as Rhys herself was, Antoinette belongs to neither Jamaican community – she is neither black nor white: 'They say when trouble comes close ranks, and the white people did. But we were not in their ranks.'[36] 'Black nigger better than white nigger,' her poor black playmate Tia tells her in a dispute that involves Antoinette's ability to turn somersaults under water in the bathing pool at Coulibri, her impoverished mother's place.[37] Only in a waking fantasy of Eden can she use the few stable elements in her world to imagine herself held, contained: safe.

> I lay thinking, 'I am safe. There is the corner of the bedroom door and the friendly furniture. There is the tree of life in the garden and the wall green with moss. The barriers of the cliffs and the high mountains. And the barrier of the sea. I am safe. I am safe from strangers ...'[38]

The black people burn down Coulibri, the house of the 'white cockroaches'. Antoinette's mother goes mad. Later, Antoinette is married to Mr Rochester. Mr Rochester does see the loveliness of the bathing pool. 'I'd find myself thinking,' he writes, ' "What I see is nothing. I want what it hides – that is not nothing." '[39] Nietzsche or Derrida, had they been alive at the time of this fictional Caribbean 1840s world (the imaginary feminine to the colonizer, masculine Victorian England), they might have told him that he wanted the truth – the enigma – woman as truth or enigma. This he cannot have: it is his own fantasy. What the colonized world seems to conceal are the colonizers' projections and fears. What Mr Rochester thinks he would value if he could find it does not exist. What exists – Antoinette who is prepared to love him, the beauty of Coulibri – he counts as nothing. He is unfaithful to the wife who has brought him a fortune. He calls Antoinette out of her name: Bertha. He only listens to destructive hearsay, jealous denunciations. Antoinette breaks down under the strain of his non-recognition, his non-love. Mr Rochester gets to hate Coulibri; he ships his wife to England. There she'll go mad, roaming the passages of Thornfield, the Gothic mansion whose tower in *Jane Eyre* hosts and imprisons the animal-like madwoman.

Jean Rhys's novel reverses values and realities. In Charlotte Brontë's novel Jamaica was not represented, a convenient fantasy land, the source of unproblematic wealth, animality, intemperance, madness. Jamaica was a cardboard world, Thornfield a powerful Gothic presence. For Antoinette, Thornfield is not Gothic: it is a cardboard house. She finally sets fire to it, for only in the world of fire can she escape from non-being in a place that is not-home:

> They tell me I am in England but I don't believe them. We lost our way to England. When? Where? I don't remember but we lost it. Was it that evening in the cabin ... ? I smashed the glasses and plates against the port-hole. I hoped it would break and the sea come in. A ... man said drink this and you will sleep. I drank it and I said, 'It isn't like it seems to be.' – 'I know. It never is,' he said. And then I slept. When I woke it was a different sea. Colder. It was that night, I think, that we changed course and lost our way to England.[40]

Sargasso Sea. They say it is a moveable sea where the eels breed. It remains unnamed within the book but is the only one that can, as it were, represent Antoinette, forever unmoored and forever a foreigner. Rhys's book says something both deep and subtle about the difficulty of being a female subject – about processes of exclusion and repression: hence no doubt its appeal in the 1970s and 1980s. It also expresses a painfully ambiguous relation to a double sea: there is the sea of the real voyage that takes Antoinette to England – indeed, a double sea, first warm, then cold. There is the Sargasso Sea of the title, present through the rhythms and images of the writing, as a possibility of being: the true being, never reached. Antoinette herself never gets the mother's love that she longs for; repeats her mother's fate in her madness – reproduces the childhood house's fate by setting fire to Thornfield. Does she find herself when she finally jumps down over the parapet, hair streaming like wings, to join Tia whom she sees down there calling to her *by the pool*? Is this the somersault that will win Tia's approval, make white girl and black girl come together? Or does Antoinette simply repeat the most destructive episode in her childhood, since she also hears the call of the parrot – 'Qui est là?' – 'Who is there?' A *parrot's* call ... The parrot had burnt in the Coulibri fire, fallen down to its death burning, its clipped wings unable to bear it away. And her mother driven mad by the burning down of her house, her son's death, had taken up the parrot's call, 'Qui est là?' Is Antoinette's gesture of burning down the house, of jumping to her death, a parrot, a copycat death – or the discovery at last of *who is there*? The burning parrot had scared off the black Jamaicans who had set fire to the house: it was very unlucky to kill a parrot. They had gone away. Do we, as readers fascinated by the wonderful rhetoric of the passage, make Antoinette's death epiphanic? Is it unlucky to see her die? Are her wings clipped like the parrot's?

Belonging to two cultures and to neither need not be a curse. Foreignness need not be maddening or lethal. There is a passage, a navigable channel between two worlds in Michèle Roberts's *Daughters of the House* (evoked earlier about the orange). The book was short-listed for the Booker Prize in 1992. It tells the story of two cousins, Thérèse and Léonie. Léonie is half-French, half-English, as Michèle Roberts is herself. There is no doubt that Rhys and Roberts move me, that I am drawn to these two books, because I recognize in the double belonging of their authors, the dividedness of the heroines, aspects of my own dividedness, belonging as I feel I also do to two worlds. Mediterranean-born but now close to the North Sea, a writer in English as well as my own native French, of fiction as well as criticism, I warm up to the clash of shores and languages, the dream of a deeper language in this passage. Twelve-year-old Léonie is crossing the Channel, going from England to France:

> And now the boat, tiny on the black sea, slipped [Léonie] across towards [French]. She was hidden inside. She rode on a great crest of spittle, from one tongue, one watery taste, to another.
>
> For as they left England so they left the English language behind. Familiar words dissolved, into wind and salt spray, ploughed back into foam, the cold dark sea in whose bottomless depths monsters swam, of no known nationality.
>
> Halfway across, as the Channel became La Manche, language reassembled itself, rose from the waves and became French.... Léonie fought to keep awake, to know the exact moment when, in the very centre of the Channel, precisely equidistant from both shores, the walls of water and words met, embraced wetly and closely, became each other, composed of each other's sounds. For at that moment true language was restored to her. Independent of separated words, as whole as water, it bore her along as part of itself, a gold current that connected everything, a secret river running underground, the deep well, the source of life, a flood driving through her, salty breaker on her own beach, streams of words and non-words, voices calling out which were staccato, echoing, with promised bliss. Then the boat churned on. It abandoned English and advanced into French.[41]

In France what had been foreign becomes normal. Léonie's aunt exclaims, 'you look starved. Don't you have proper food in England?'

'Léonie climbed into the back of the car ... She'd forgotten how she liked its smell: leather, cigarettes, petrol. She thought: now I'm a foreigner again.'

Antoinette could say with Valéry's Pythoness, 'Who speaks me, in my very place?' Except she hasn't got a place, only a wandering voice. On the ship they've given her a bad drink. A bad mother? Her own lost mother was certainly that. Moving to England she's moved to a colder sea. By contrast, the restorative, lap-like properties of Léonie's sea are wonderful. They enable Léonie to make the passage, to cope with the repeated experience of being foreign. Her confident sense of identity, of the identity of things and people around her (the car with its smells of leather, cigarettes and petrol) is somehow connected with the strength and comfort of that motherly sea-presence. The sea is not a metaphor, but its buoying, watery abundance somehow guarantees the thingness of things, the peopleness of people. There is identity in language, as in the Colette, one that never loses sight of the simile, that does not appropriate.

But when Léonie comes to puzzling about magpies, oranges, oneness and twoness, trouble – dividedness – has started, even though there still are oranges to play with.

Léonie has her alter ego, her complement, Thérèse. They are cousins, their mothers are sisters. Indeed, as complex events surface, it turns out that they may be sisters, that their fathers may not be whom they thought. They are opposites, in looks, experience, temperament, the one thin, the other plump, the one Thérèse wholly French (apparently), the other Léonie mostly English, at least at the start. Léonie is the sensuous, the sexy one, Thérèse becomes religious, becomes a nun. When they are children, adolescents, they are twinned, intimates, part and parcel of each other. Later, they seem to exchange parts, even temperaments. Their fates cross over. Léonie marries the boy who might have been Thérèse's sweetheart, inherits what had initially been Thérèse's French house as Thérèse goes to the convent. There is deep animus also between them, rivalry, bitter resentment as the novel opens twenty years on, then goes back to piece together the narrative of the early years through a strikingly original list of household objects: the form of each of Michèle Roberts's novels is always innovative. The short, sharp little chapters are called 'The Soap Dish' or 'The Biscuit Tin'. It is like being faced with a collection of Proustian *petites madeleines*, a houseful of transitional objects through which memories surge and fan out. Both girls' childhoods become reconstituted, along with their love and hate, the family structure that makes up the house and made these particular daughters of the house, the repressed history that needs to resurface for both daughters to come to terms with themselves and with each other.

It is a highly female structure. As already noted, domestic objects make up the chapter headings. The two mothers, Antoinette and Madeleine, are more prominent and powerful than their husbands, as

Léonie, the one daughter who marries, also turns out to be. Each mother only has one daughter, therefore daughters are the inheritors of the house in every sense. They also inherit the house in that its past, as history and as a structure of power and powerlessness and suppression, possesses them. Bad things – as it turns out, the betrayal to the Germans of a Jewish family being hidden in the house – have been concealed, denied, and insist on returning. Thérèse's decision to become a nun has to do with a complex, masochistic desire to make up for her mother's suspected 'sin', or stain (Antoinette may have been raped by German soldiers; Thérèse's father may be German). Her leaving the convent twenty years on, when the novel starts, her returning to the house to face up to the past in turn forces Léonie to excavate it. To allow what is hidden by each object, each room from cellar to attic, to come to the fore.

The structure of the novel, as well as the two protagonists, Thérèse and Léonie, embody a particularly female predicament. I have quoted the long, beautiful, pre-Oedipal passage about Léonie's bliss on her sea crossing. It has its counterpoint in Thérèse's blissful breast-feeding by her wet nurse, Rose, her delight in what Rimbaud has called 'le murmure de lait du matin', the morning's milky murmur:

> Bliss. Feeding and being fed. Love was this milky fullness, Thérèse born a second time, into a land of plenty.... Rose was the world, the sky that curved above you when you first took a tottering step ... the water in which you lay and splashed and did not drown.[42]

For both cousins that is, there is a strong, early symbiotic, pre-language relation to a surrogate or archetypal mother. For a time, despite their rivalrousness, the two cousins, in their childhood games, reconstitute for each other a blissful, twinned, symbiotic relation, a bond in flesh. But division enters. It centres on one event. Léonie sees a beautiful, dark lady in red and gold at a shrine in the woods: a pagan apparition, some ancient goddess of the site perhaps, the projection of her awakening adolescent sexuality. Envious of the experience, jealous perhaps because of Léonie's theft of the boy she likes, longing for attention, for stardom, Thérèse makes up a lie: she claims that at this same site she has, like Bernadette at Lourdes, seen a lady in white and blue: the Virgin Mary. She manages to convince the bishop, makes a big splash in the church, joins the convent like St Thérèse of Lisieux, her namesake, whose *Histoire d'une âme* is one of the sources for the book. The two cousins' rival visions epitomize many things: the splitting up and alienation of the girls, the way women become divided, their desires censored; the way Christian shrines took over from pagan shrines, symbolizing perhaps the way in which a wholly patriarchal, Catholic establishment stole from earlier female, maternal sources of power. Thérèse courts the patriarchy in order to gain an advantage over her cousin: her sexuality is the price she has to pay. It also turns out, later on, that the theft is related to another betrayal: the shrine is the place where the Jews were murdered and initially buried, and the village priest was the betrayer.

At the end of the novel, when the puzzle has come together, when the truth is out, Thérèse goes into the local church where a statue of the virgin has been made ready for a harvest procession. Thérèse sets fire to the baskets of corn, the sheaves of straw that are offerings to the virgin. She burns the church down, fire making the white and blue lady back into a gold and red one. She herself burns down with the lady, a wing of flames sprouting on her back as she tries to flee. 'She flew with her one red wing. Her spine flared, one great red fin.'[43] Like Rhys's Antoinette, like the parrot, like a shark, like an angel ... Angels in pictures often have parrot's wings ... Léonie, released, prepares to denounce the priest. A new language has been born: the final chapter is called 'Words'.

The ending of *Daughters of the House* has striking echoes of the ending of *Wide Sargasso Sea*. The female protagonist's self is released through fire, the trope of flight appears twinned with the trope of fire, with all the sexual and erotic connotations each carry. In both novels, the ending couples the fates of imagined twins: Antoinette jumps towards Tia, her childhood playmate, by the pool at Coulibri. Burning the statue, and the church, and her lie, and herself with it, Thérèse rejoins her twin Léonie, enables her to become complete again, gives her the courage to face up to the past. She also burns down the patriarchal house of repression, the church, as Antoinette burns down Thornfield Hall, the Gothic mansion where patriarchal marriage had kept her imprisoned. Both releases are paid for by self-immolation. But *Daughters of the House* is much more hopeful: Léonie lives on. She at least has re-become one. And she has inherited the house. In the house of meaning, in the habitable house of fiction, perhaps today's women writers have a more secure hold than their mothers did. It is striking however that their narratives should link metaphors (of sea, of fire) in such similar patterns.

The sea voyage in Virginia Woolf's *To the Lighthouse*[44] is more elaborate and painful than Léonie's blissful crossing of the Channel. James, the eight-year-old boy who at the opening of the novel longs to go to the lighthouse the following day, is only taken there several years later, not by the mother who wished him to have his wish, but by the father who had told him the 'truth', given him a negative, told him that it would not be fine tomorrow, they could not go. Between the wish for the voyage and the voyage, time has passed; and the mother who, in the first section, through her open window, received the rhythmic beat of the lighthouse – the mother, Mrs Ramsay, who was another sort of lighthouse, who animated a hospitable house whose lights shone at dark, showing the way, the mother has died. Others have died also. The Great War has taken its toll. Women have died as well as men. Only three of the survivors make it to the lighthouse. One daughter, Cam, ambiguous as to her wish to mother her brother; James, the brother, obsessionally trying to negotiate a grown-up relationship with his father; and the father, who in his halting way is trying to make up for the lost mother. When their boat gets to the lighthouse, it's not a house of light. It's rock, it's very real, it's not an achievement. But the voyage has been made. James has had what he wanted from his father, words of approval. Lily Briscoe, the artist, who has loved Mrs Ramsay, and is haunted by Mrs Ramsay's shade, who needs that shade to finish her painting – Lily remains on shore. She chooses not to be a mother in life, but an artist. She chooses not to go to the lighthouse. And yet, her achieving her painting, her making it cohere thanks to the purple triangle that has appeared by the window where Mrs Ramsay sat, coincides with the voyage. It is at the moment when the boat reaches the lighthouse that in the process has ceased to be a lighthouse, that Lily, with 'a sudden intensity, as if she saw [the canvas] clear for a second, [draws] a line at the centre'.

Both expeditions, to the lighthouse and to the painting, require maximum effort. Both involve the disappearance of the house of light, the Mother. Mr Ramsay and his children only make the trip after the mother's death, perhaps to achieve what she wished them to achieve. The lighthouse in the process of being reached ceases to be what made it so profoundly attractive to James: a rhythmical beam shining in the night. Lily achieves her painting by killing the mother inside herself. She gives her all to art, not to the production, or should I say reproduction, of life. It is in the instant that follows the disappearance of Mrs Ramsay's ghostly presence that Lily draws the finishing line. It is vertical, dare I say phallic: just as the absences and lacks that turn out to make creative acts possible bespeak a phallic economy. It is Mr Ramsay, jumping like a young man, inscrutable to his children, who lands on the lighthouse, and it is his landing that Lily wills on. People often speak of the mother's overwhelming presence in this novel, but it is an amazing combination of male and female, presence and absence, that seems to enable the female creator to achieve her work. Though neither speaks nor appropriates the other.

There are two rhythms in this novel. The one is that of the sea, permanent, often muffled by the other noises of life. Mrs Ramsay hears it when she no longer worries. The 'monotonous fall of the waves on the beach' mostly beats 'a measured and soothing tattoo to her thoughts'. A 'cradle song', it murmurs 'I am guarding you' (rather, it occurs to me, as the child Antoinette dreams of being made safe by the sea). But at other times it beats the 'measure of life' 'like a [remorseless] ghostly roll of drums' making one 'think of the destruction of the island and its engulfment by the sea'.

If the sea, in this novel, is connected with an archetypal mother, it clearly is not Mrs Ramsay. The sea is as much a source of terror to her as to anyone else. The world of *To the Lighthouse* is not guaranteed by a stable motherly presence, as is that of Colette's *The Ripening Seed*, where the adolescents know that the tides will keep to their appointed bounds, will not engulf the land. Mrs Ramsay finds her own rhythm when she can be by herself, silent. 'Not as oneself did one ever find rest, in her experience ... but as a wedge of darkness. Losing personality, one lost the fret.' At such moments does Mrs Ramsay look out 'to meet that stroke of the Lighthouse, the long steady stroke, the last of the three, which was her stroke'. At such moments does she find the pantheistic state that in 'La Pythie' is achieved through divine male possession of a delirious female body: she becomes 'the thing she looked at – that light for example'. Ownness is found through becoming, not appropriation: through the dissolution of ego.

In an essay written in 1927, 'The Narrow Bridge of Art',[45] Woolf reflects on the limitations of lyric poetry. The 'lyric cry of ecstasy or despair', so intense, so overwhelmingly beautiful, is not enough, she feels:

> The mind is full of monstrous, hybrid, unmanageable emotions. That the age of the earth is 3,000,000,000 years; that human life lasts but a second; that the capacity of the human mind is nevertheless boundless; ... that science and religion have between them destroyed belief; that all bonds of union seem broken, yet some control must exist – it is in this atmosphere of doubt and conflict that writers have now to create.

Woolf goes on to dream of the novel of the future, that would take on itself some of the attributes of poetry. 'It will give the relations of man to nature, to fate; his imaginations; his dreams. But it will also give the sneer, the contrast, the question, the closeness and complexity of life.' It will dramatize those moments that

> play so large a part in life, yet have so far escaped the novelist – the power of music ... the emotions bred in us by crowds, the obscure terrors and hatreds which come so irrationally in certain places or certain people ... Every moment is the centre and meeting-place of an extraordinary number of perceptions which have not yet been expressed.

Woolf calls her novelist of the future a 'he' – a universal he, one must assume, since she is describing what she herself is trying to do in her fiction. It strikes me how profoundly Woolf's vision attempts to accommodate an ideal of the one and the many – a dream, but a vital necessity. Julia Kristeva writes about texts as Polylogues – many-tongued. We read for the many – we also read for the one. We also read for the moment of recognition. We read for those moments when we hear the one-two, or the one-two-three beat of a book, and know that the two beats are interwoven, male and female. It isn't just 'or', but and/or, as in the name Orlando. We read for when the beam strikes across our window, and we know it is our stroke. I suggested earlier that women writers embody their own quest for self through female protagonists, that this is where the subject of the author can be seen at play. It is true that in *To the Light-*

house Mrs Ramsay and Lily embody dilemmas and emotions that seem particularly pertinent to the author. It is also true that the whole fabric of the narrative, its whole cast of characters and interrelationships, and its high musicality, are what most truly embody it: many-tongued ...

To the Lighthouse proceeds to make Mrs Ramsay archaic. In 'Time Passes', the second, and middle, section, she dies. It is a death of the spirit, almost the death of a certain humanity, a certain England, a Europe that perished in the Great War. It is the world of ageing, of children growing up and dying and gone. The house is full of the ghostly noises and presences of 'how once ...' It is full of reflections, of the shadows of trees. Then a bark appears. It is Mrs McNabb, the cleaner:

> As she lurched (for she rolled like a ship at sea) and leered ... as she clutched the banisters and hauled herself upstairs and rolled from room to room, she sang. Rubbing the glass of the long looking-glass and leering sideways at her swinging figure a sound issued from her lips – something that had been gay twenty years before on the stage perhaps, had been hummed and danced to, but now ... was robbed of meaning, was like the voice of witlessness, humour, persistency itself, trodden down but springing again, so that as she lurched, dusting, wiping, she seemed to say how it was one long sorrow and trouble.[46]

To the Lighthouse is about a voyage. Multiple voyages. Relays of voyages by multiple characters, who are also the creator's multiple selves. The narrative, the multiplicity and the passing of time of the narration enable the various metaphors to become realized, and to be traversed. Traversed: the novel, crossing from Mrs Ramsay to Lily Briscoe courtesy of Mrs McNabb's hobbling bark and Mr Ramsay's boat, straining every nerve and sinew of its creator, invites its reader to travel from the position of reader to that of potential creator. Lily, struggling, not just against the reality that she sees, but against Charles Tansley's edict, 'Women can't paint, can't write,' struggling also against the temptation to be Mrs Ramsay, to take over from her; Lily, straining with, together with, in the tow of, the Mrs McNabbs and even the Mr Ramsays of this world, wrestling with the ghosts of time past, achieves her stroke. The painting's there. It amounts to very little. It will finish in some attic. It has taken everything she had. It leaves her gutted. 'Yes, she thought with extreme fatigue, I have had my vision.' What a strain, what effort, what calling upon the dead, the subsumed, the unconscious, for the woman creator to posit a many-voiced subject: not ownness; but multiplicity, but becoming ...

There is no woman in Angela Carter's *The Passion of New Eve*.[47] No book written in the last fifteen years so thoroughly deconstructs the term. Any hope of finding the subject of the author, the predicament of the woman writer, somehow embodied through the protagonist flounders from page one: the narrator-protagonist is an unsavoury man, whom enforced surgery will turn into a transsexual female. Parody, and a brilliantly omnivorous rhetoric, able to draw into its maw unbelievably diverse layers of references, chew myths, political, religious or feminist, into a pulp of apparently terminal absurdity. If there is a persona of the author here, it is transmogrification incarnate. The novel journeys through halls of refracting and broken mirrors, the images of women produced by centuries of high and low culture, carnivalizing each, making the protagonist painfully and disconcertingly traipse through his fantasies and fears of womanhood – through the mirage of femininity as both the construct of male desire and the experience of subjection and disempowerment.

Evelyn is a man. An Englishman in decadent Doomsday New York, where gangs of sharp-shooting female guerrillas run riot, Evelyn is in thrall to his feminine ideal, screen star Tristessa. While he worships the celluloid incarnations of his Diva (a parodic representation of the screen of the cavern, as reinterpreted by Irigaray?), he pursues and engrosses a black woman, Leila, and persuades her to have a (botched) abortion. He then flees into a parodic Western-style desert, and is captured by a cave-dwelling matriarchal tribe ruled over by a powerful Mother. Mother has neither milk nor lap-like comfort to give. She is an advanced plastic surgeon, and the tiers of breasts that she disports to give herself the archetypal mother-goddess look are implants. She operates on Evelyn, castrating him and making her into an exquisite female, his own archphantasm. Eve is a man's dream, and it is Evelyn's ultimate punishment to be made to embody in the flesh, and in his, now her, newly vulnerable body, his own fantasy of womanhood.

New Eve's punishment has only just begun. She now becomes the eighth wife of Zero, a Manson-style arch-patriarch, and learns femininity as humiliating subjection. With Zero and his wives Eve raids Tristessa's Hollywood mansion – only to discover, surprise surprise, that Tristessa the arch-female is a male in drag. In a burlesque double gender reversal, Eve consummates his passion for Tristessa as her passion for him.

The Passion of New Eve has been seen as a supremely postmodernist, deconstructionist text, propelled as it is by its picaresque carnivalization of womanhood. The women in this text are always artificial, the product of surgery or cross-dressing. Matriarchy as a dream of empowering female origins is savagely debunked. No Mother-Goddess here, but a parodic castrating Black Mamma with the head of Karl Marx's statue on her shoulders, literally armed with a Phallic knife in lieu of a surgeon's scalpel. Desire is self-deceit, both misguided as to its object, and narcissistic. There is no relation to the other. Ownness doubles in upon itself. Carter's Waste Land makes images of women, mother, virgin, whore, goddess, into a heap of broken images. Woman may seem many: all are false, and there is none. Eve has no innerness, no character, no identity. Though the novel adopts the format of the picaresque, the protagonist journeying from one situation to another, Eve barely travels, if travel is 'to' a place. She is passivity incarnate, remarkably unruffled in the midst of her many ordeals (rather like a parodic heroine of porn), never realistic enough to suffer or learn, despite the weirdly elegiac consummation of her passion for Tristessa. Unlike Valéry's *Eupalinos*, the text produces no object that could be an intermediary between nature and art, either shell or boat, whereby a human tongue might be born. As for oranges . . . You must be joking.

And yet . . . with all its savage debunking, the novel ends on a scheme of possible travel. On a desire for the one beyond the gutted shadows of the many. The possibility of the birth of a self, of a female self (beyond the deconstructions of femininity and masculinity), emerges from a pattern that strangely recalls Woolf's in *To the Lighthouse*. So that the figure of the woman creator, the question of self-creation, startlingly arises as the novel is about to end.

After the apocalyptic burning of the cities of California, Odyssean Eve re-encounters Leila, now Lilith. On a beach by the sea, an old crone, a compendium of doughty survivor, Medusa, witch and madwoman, armed in Beckett-like fashion with a folding garden-table, a can opener and a bottle of vodka, sings popular songs of the thirties. Eve has to crawl through the fissures of womb-like rocks, proceeding from cave to cave, tearing up her last illusions as she goes. 'For I know now that Mother is a figure of speech and has retreated to a cave beyond consciousness,' she says. Groping towards female creation, which is a process of self-engendering, not androgynous as in the Woolf yet carrying multiple genders within it, Mother, like Mrs Ramsay for Lily, has to disappear. Eve's 'coming home', on a shore by the sea, is a confirmation of exile. 'The destination of all journeys is their beginning,' she says. But there, on the shore, the old woman has a skiff. A light skiff. She lets Eve have it.

An old woman coming to the rescue, like Mrs McNabb? Both old women creaking, lurching, both singing 'something that had been gay twenty years before' . . .

'We start from our conclusions,' the last chapter begins. When you get old, Angela Carter was saying to her television interviewer (for Omnibus) shortly before the death she knew was coming, you return to your beginning. Childhood comes back to you. And beyond.

There is quotation, as always in Carter, but is there nothing but parody in Eve's last words, as she is about to embark on her skiff?

'Ocean, Ocean, mother of mysteries, take me to the place of birth.'

To a world that literature has made habitable?

And is that boat a transitional object?

I have wandered among metaphors of the sea, those that I remembered, those that came to me. My larger theme has been language; as two separate yet related entities, perhaps corresponding to what Jakobson called 'langue' and 'parole', language and speech. 'Langue', language as we

A Boat by the Sea at Twilight, photograph by Cathy Ward

find it, are immersed in it: the sea into which we are born, in which we try to find ourselves, which we somehow endlessly associate with the womb from which we come. 'Parole', speech, the tongue: the ways in which, as speaking subjects, we attempt to make meaning of the world we inhabit. The sea-as-language, 'la mer' suggests 'la mère', mother. Metaphors also spring from the tongue, 'langue' as speech: boat, bark, helm, mollusc in its shell, and even the orange, juicy in its gloriously safe luminous pitted skin.

Since the mother, I asked, is so mixed in with images of the sea, since the tongue that speaks never ceases to renegotiate its relation to the mother, what does this do to gender? Does it mean that in creation the female as mother is always being subsumed? What does that do to the female creator?

Two answers have appeared. The first concerns metaphors. I was helped to this answer by both Ricoeur's notion of metaphors as alive, and by Winnicott's reflexions on transitional objects. When metaphor occurs, I came to see, both male and female creators are similarly positioned. Despite the greater bodily closeness of females to the mother, the imaginary relation to the womb exists for both sexes, and is archetypal. The power to create is in both sexes. This shows particularly with metaphors that act as transitional objects: more mature metaphors, as it were, metaphors that do not express a longing for the womb, but negotiate a relation between subject and world. Differences can be found between male and female writers, but then it also turns out that each sex can produce a variation of what the other does. Colette, or Michèle Roberts, may each in her way be as preoccupied with thingness, with the 'ownness' of things, as Ponge, Proust as deeply immersed in sensuousness as Cixous.

Metaphors, I came to see, are about moments. Moments of being. Moments of oneness – of transport – of joy. They are temporary, they surface and dissolve, whether in the flow of prose or in verse, however much they may expand over sentences, stanzas, sometimes the book itself: like the involuntarily remembered taste of Proust's *petite madeleine*, a frail impalpable 'droplet' bearing up 'the immense edifice of memory' – like Marvell's 'drop of dew' reflecting the sky in its tiny globe. Moments of oneness, made archetypal sometimes through long association with human experience: as boat, as shell, as golden fruit . . . Unburdened by sexual identities, however much they can come to bear the signs of gender.

The second answer concerns larger units than metaphors: narratives, quests of the self through pattern, rhythm, plot. In these, I have suggested, the subject of the author with his or her history is at stake. That history carries more than psychic or archetypal dimensions. It carries race and class (though I have spoken little about those). It carries economics, gender roles and values and the range of experiences that being of a particular gender (class, race, degree of wealth, ethnic group) both prescribes and allows. It carries sexual identifications, cultural norms: permitted or forbidden access to education, sexual licence or censorship, actual and ideological relations to power. A male subject would not have the experience of becoming Zero's eighth battered wife, like Eve; would not dream of ingratiating himself with the clergy by pretending to have seen the virgin, like Thérèse; would not lose all rights to his money upon marriage, like Antoinette; would not be told that by virtue of his sex he is not allowed to either write or paint, like Lily Briscoe (though, if he were a slave from the American Deep South, he might be told that by virtue of his race). The attempt to make meaning of his life through narrative representation of imaginary people's lives, for a male author, would take different forms. This is where, it seems to me, gender differences are formally at work. It may be because, as Kristeva has contended, 'women's time' is different from men's time, that the time of narrative is occupied by women writers in different ways. It may also be that because (some?) women have a different relation to the pre-Oedipal, a greater nostalgia for, and desire for symbiosis with, the womb or the breast, because for women *apparently* at least to individuate there is not so keen an obligation to separate from the mother's body as there is for men, sexual difference is also there at work. I can think of no male-authored passages that seek the maternal body with the keenness and confidence that can be found in Colette or Michèle Roberts. On the other hand, if Eve's experience at Mother's knife-wielding hands is anything to go by, women, like men, need to run a mile from the mother's body . . .

Individuation. I think of the Jungian model, which is one among many, but which has an immediate relevance: it is about the dissolution of ego so that the self can be born. The four novels I have looked at share not only sea voyages and sea rhythms but the function of those voyages and rhythms: they are part of, as well as symbolize, the heroines' search for their real selves, and this search comes to some degree of (imagined or real) fruition through a process of destruction. Antoinette dies in the fire lit to free her entrapped self. Thérèse's death through a fire she has lit to destroy another patriarchal house and a patriarchal female image (the Virgin) frees Léonie to at last utter 'Words'. Mrs Ramsay's death is bound up with Lily's painting. As for New Eve . . . the cities of the plain have gone up in flames and all 'false' images of woman have been imploded by her narrative: what there is to be born is to say the least uncertain, but a voice *is* asking to be taken 'to the place of birth'.

At first glance, these are all tales of individuation: the painful birth of the self, separate, individual, containing and in touch with inner contradictory forces, previously unknown parts of the self. Jung distinguished the ego from the self. 'The ego is only the subject of my total psyche, which also includes the unconscious.'[48] The point of individuation, ultimately, is to become one's self. Ego, that was master in its own house, or was under the illusion that it was, must, for wholeness to happen, almost reach the point of extinction.[49]

Does this apply to the novels I have considered? Demaris S. Wehr, in her interestingly balanced *Jung and Feminism*, criticizes the, to her, gen-der-ridden assumption that ego starts from the belief that it is 'master in its house'. 'Jung's understanding of ego is more appropriately applied to men than to women, many of whom do not feel their ego's mastery in the first place.' Jung, she feels, shares unconsciously male-based premises with the traditional religions. She continues:

> Traditionally in patriarchy, males seem to have a stronger sense of self (firmer ego boundaries) than do females, and male agency and authority are constantly validated. Let me be clear: I believe that everyone needs a per-spective beyond the necessarily limited one of the personal ego or self. Yet I wonder about urging this vision of self-development on people who are not strongly based in the ego in the first place. Such is the condition of most women in patriarchy, whose egos are not validated by their context.[50]

She then goes on to quote Jean Baker Miller:

> Prevailing psychoanalytic theories about women's weaker ego or super-ego may well reflect the fact that women have no ego or super-ego at all as these terms are used now. Women do not come into this picture in the way men do. They do not have the right or the requirement to be full-fledged repre-sentatives of the culture.

('Can't paint, can't write' . . .)

> Nor have they been granted the right to act and to judge themselves in terms of the direct benefit to themselves. Both of these rights seem essential to the development of ego and super-ego.[51]

If Miller is right, Wehr concludes, some doubt is cast 'on the advisability, for women, of undergoing a crucial stage in the Jungian individuation process – "annihilation of the ego" '. Wouldn't the required annihilation simply reinforce the 'self-abnegation in which women already engage, to their detriment'? Wouldn't this be closer to 'socially prescribed masochism'?[52]

This very much applies to the four novels I have been discussing. Antoinette's gesture of annihilation quite simply kills her. Thérèse dies as she burns the statue of the Virgin, the false image that she has made of her ego (or super-ego?). Their liberation gestures are masochistic – suici-dal. Even more strikingly, none of the protagonists considered has an ego that could remotely be regarded as 'master of the house'. Lily is a guest, almost a poor relation in the Ramsay household. Antoinette has no safety of tenure in her mother's house, her ego is made up of bits and pieces, mostly the outdoors: 'the golden ferns and the silver ferns, the orchids, the ginger lilies and the roses, the rocking-chairs and the blue sofa, the jasmine and the honeysuckle, and the picture of the Miller's daughter'.[53] Of that nothing is left but 'blackened walls and the mounting stone' when Coulibri burns down. And Antoinette's alter ego, her complement and only childhood friend, Tia, rejects her. Tia (understandably, but sadly) sides with *her* lot, joins Antoinette's black persecutors. She casts a stone at her – and then cries, for she too has lost a self-image, a childhood friend who was part of herself: 'We stared at each other, blood on my face, tears on hers. It was as if I saw myself. Like in a looking-glass.'[54] The heroine's ego, that is, unsafe from the start, tries to make itself safe through a twin, an alter ego: and fails. Race and class here split them apart. The suicide is an attempt to meet an imaginary Tia beckoning by the pool, join up again, that is, with a lost part of the potential self, *not to dislocate a strong ego in order to individuate*.

Though *Daughters of the House* is a thoroughly different kind of novel, the same pattern is at work. Léonie and Thérèse form a loving dyad that makes up for their mothers' inadequacies. It is not ego, it is pre-Oedipal. Rivalry, and rival projections, split them asunder. From then on both are suspended in time, incomplete. Something like ego – or is it self? – is restored to Léonie through Thérèse's self-destruction. The process, again, is not from strong ego to annihilated ego. If something like self is found, it is through twinning and division and destruction of the *double*.

Is the double that needs to be destroyed (Thérèse, Antoinette, Mrs Ramsay) the patriarchally defined, 'feminine' woman? Theologian Carol Christ, again quoted by Demaris Wehr, claims that 'the spiritual quest of a modern woman begins in the experience of nothingness, the experience of being without an adequate image of self.'[55] Are woman's sins, as another feminist theologian, Valerie Saiving, argues, 'lack of an organizing center or focus; dependence on others for one's self-definition; . . . in short, underdevelopment or negation of the self'?[56] Is this why it is so brave, so self-creative of Lily to refuse both Mrs and Mr Ramsay's demands – that she'll marry, that she'll mother the man? Or is the double a displaced or fantasized figure of the mother from whom the protagonist dreams of never having to separate, and from whom she is forced to separate (or whom she is forced to find) through the ultimate act of destruction? It is at the moment when the shade of Mrs Ramsay disappears that Lily completes her painting. If so, individuation for a woman is bound up with separation from the mother. It does not travel through mastery, never achieved in the first place, at least not in the texts under consideration. They testify to the power of gender, they don't just bear its marks . . . Reading Carol Christ I was thinking of contemporary *male* quests: of how strong are the egos of Bloom and Stephen in Joyce's *Ulysses*, despite the originality of their personalities, the 'feminine' elements in Bloom. How strong the identity of Proust's narrator, despite his sexual ambiguity, the strength of his bond to the mother, in love and hate . . .

Is it because of the strength of the male ego that the source of Angela
Carter's New Eve is ... a man? An initially male voice? Never given the
remotest chance to fuse with Mother. Mother is, of course, the first character Evelyn meets on his way to becoming woman. But the grotesque
phallic and castrating mother figure never provides poor Eve with the
slightest opening towards dyads, symbiosis or womb-like safety ...
Angela Carter might be a usefully caustic reminder of the dangers of
generalization. Or else she might point the way to what could be female
individuation, since being very much 'master of the house' to start with,
Evelyn on his way to being-woman has every notion of femininity he
might have annihilated. From ego to self? Aye, but (s)he has no self, no
inner contradictions, no unsuspected depths or drives ... One is left with
the conclusion that the only proper way to be a reconstructed, a 'new'
woman, is to be a man to start with. Which apart from anything else
leaves those of us who were born and want to remain women nowhere
to go.

There are, it seems to me, other solutions. One is to question the male
model that Jung offers, to celebrate the inventiveness of the human spirit
that makes the women novelists explore other ways to selfhood than
Jung's. I have only discussed four novels – because of their metaphoric
connections – but how much there would be to say here about Toni Morrison or Clarice Lispector! The way to selfhood is out of and through
what we actually are, what everything in our history has made us, not
through a model, however deeply inspired. Another is to suggest that
'underdevelopment or negation of the self' are not feminine *fate*, they are
the product of all sorts of genderized acts and contexts that can be
changed. Marie Louise von Franz, for instance (again quoted by Wehr),
writes about the 'entanglement of men's anima projections and women's
sense of themselves':

> If [man] only likes her as an anima figure, she is forced to play the role of
> the anima. This interaction can be positive or negative, but the woman is
> very much affected by the man's anima figure, which brings us to a very
> primitive and simple and collective level where we cannot separate the fea-
> tures of the anima and real women.[57]

Thus does Thérèse fulfil church expectations of the Virgin Mary. Thus
does Tristessa embody male fantasies of masochistic femininity. Michèle
Roberts's or Angela Carter's novels precisely set about disentangling
men's projections from women's anima: showing, passionately or parod-
ically, that they can be disentangled. If the shape of so many women's
novels is gender-marked, if women-authored heroines' trajectories are
different from men's, it is because they express how different matters can
be for the two sexes. Not that it need remain so. We are evolving human
beings, both men and women. We are only trapped in certain scenarios if
we wish that it be so. As gender evolves at the hands of human beings,

who knows what narratives of the self male and female writers of the future may not create?

Postscript

As I was mulling over the end of this chapter, I felt I should have said more. I should have stressed how precarious was the selfhood gained at the end of each of the novels I had looked at. Antoinette's and Thérèse's flights are a drowning in flames, Lily's moment of vision achieves so little, new Eve has not even been born as the book closes. I should have said, I thought: look at how hard it is for twentieth-century women to achieve selfhood. Think how many went mad or lived in the shadow of madness and depression: Charlotte Perkins Gilman, Dorothy Richardson, Virginia Woolf, Janet Frame, Sylvia Plath, Jean Rhys . . .

Whereupon – life plays such tricks – I came upon a series of articles about how it had been demonstrated that a huge percentage of male writers had been mentally unbalanced. The studies were all about male authors, don't ask me why . . . The *Guardian* reported that a psychiatrist, Dr Felix Post, had found that, against expectations, playwrights and novelists fared worse than poets in a league table ranking them from 0 to 6 for severity of psychopathology. Only 31 per cent of poets suffered from alcoholism compared with 54 per cent of playwrights. 'In terms of mental illness such as manic depression, severe depression and mood swings . . . 80 per cent of poets had symptoms compared with 87 per cent of playwrights.'[58]

The *Sunday Times* described the work of a US psychiatrist at Johns Hopkins University in Baltimore, Dr Kay Jamieson, the author of *Touched with Fire*, which Anthony Clare, another psychiatrist, described as

> a stunning book on the relationship between manic-depressive illness and the artistic temperament . . . Drawing on recent advances in genetics, neurochemistry, psychopharmacology and psychology, she re-examined the constellation of afflicted artistic giants and concluded that the suspected association between mood disorder and creativity is indeed a reliable one. In some families – most notably those of Tennyson and Byron – she was able to trace the genetic transmission of the disorder more than 150 years.[59]

Poor old me, I thought, who imagined that strain and depression had something to do with life experiences, and who laboured so hard at disentangling the strands of gender and creativity! All so simple really: the women who were mentally unstable, and artists (and so few, really, that they don't need to be even mentioned along with such giants as Tennyson and Byron), were just fortunate enough to have inherited ancestral genes that predisposed them that way. Lucky them, and silly me: there are more male artists than female simply because the genes are more inclined to the male part. They spot a little Y in there alongside the X and say, miam, miam, gobble gobble gobble, let's get in there, it'll be more fun. My only comfort is that Dr Post, also a psychiatrist, but perhaps less *au fait* with recent developments in geneticism, pharmacology, etc., than Dr Jamieson and Dr Clare thinks that 'instead of genius being caused by "madness", it is the intense mental efforts required for verbal creativity of the highest order that cause changes in the neural pathways of the brain.'[60]

Where does that leave the women? Many of those that were foolhardy enough to try for creativity of the highest order sure got it in the neural pathways. And Shakespeare and Dante, who were not psychopaths? In the olden days brains were made of tougher stuff. Do such studies ever go beyond the eighteenth or nineteenth centuries, when madness became romanticized, when the strains of living grew worse, when masculinity and femininity became more polarized, when neurasthenia came centre-stage? Anyway – what a lucky escape I've had, I thought on reading the articles. Just think I might have been waxing eloquent over the difficult birth of the self for women, when it was all a question of genes and brainwaves ...

Notes

1 Paul Ricoeur, *Du Texte à l'action: Essais d'herméneutique*, vol. 2 (Paris: Seuil, 1986), p. 116.
2 Ibid., p. 117.
3 Gayatri Spivak, 'Displacement and the Discourse of Woman', in *Displacement: Derrida and After*, ed. Mark Krupnick (Bloomington: Indiana University Press, 1983), pp. 169–95.
4 In Paul Valéry, *Oeuvres* (Paris: Gallimard, 1965), vol. 1, p. 131.
5 J. Lacan, *Écrits I* (Paris: Seuil, 1966), p. 167.
6 Hélène Cixous, *La* (Paris: Gallimard, 1976), pp. 112, 113.
7 Luce Irigaray, *Speculum of the Other Woman*, tr. G. C. Gill (Ithaca: Cornell University Press, 1985).
8 Charles Baudelaire, 'L'Homme et la mer', in *Les Fleurs du mal*, ed. Georges Blin and Claude Pichois (Paris: José Corti, 1968), p. 49.
9 Valéry, *Oeuvres*, vol. 1, p. 151.
10 J. Derrida, *Margins of Philosophy*, tr. Alan Bass (Brighton: Harvester, 1982), p. 213.
11 Ibid., p. 225.
12 Ibid., pp. 242–4.
13 Ibid., p. 226.
14 Hélène Cixous, 'Sorties' (1975), in Hélène Cixous and Catherine Clément, *The Newly Born Woman*, tr. Betsy Wing (Manchester: Manchester University Press, 1987).
15 Martin Sorrell, (ed.), *Elles: A Bilingual Anthology of Modern French Poetry By Women* (Exeter: Exeter University Press, 1995), p. 251.

16 Dante, *De vulgari eloquentia*, my translation from a French edn. I found the passage in Jacqueline Chenieux-Gendron's 'Epilogue', in Sorrell, *Elles*, p. 241.
17 Paul Ricoeur, *La Métaphore vive* (Paris: Seuil, 1975), pp. 368–74.
18 D. W. Winnicott, *Playing and Reality* (Harmondsworth: Penguin, 1971), pp. 83–4.
19 Plato, *Timaeus*, in *The Dialogues of Plato*, tr. B. Jowett, vol. 3 (Oxford: Oxford University Press, 1964), pp. 637–8.
20 Francis Ponge, *Le Parti pris des choses* (London: Athlone, 1979), p. 65.
21 Ian Higgins, *Francis Ponge* (London: Athlone, 1979), p. 48.
22 Winnicott, *Playing and Reality*, p. 1.
23 Ibid., pp. 2–5.
24 Ibid., pp. 6–7.
25 Nicole Ward Jouve, 'Oranges et sources: Colette et Hélène Cixous', in F. van Rossum-Guyon and M. Diaz-Diocaretz, (eds), *Hélène Cixous: Chemins d'une écriture* (Paris: Presses Universitaires de Vincennes, 1990), pp. 55–73.
26 Colette, 'Le Rendez-vous', in *Oeuvres complètes*, vol. 11 (Paris: Flammarion, 1950), p. 233.
27 Hélène Cixous, *Vivre l'orange* (Paris: Éditions des Femmes, 1979), p. 17.
28 Julia Kristeva, *Le Temps sensible: Proust et l'expérience litteraire* (Paris: Gallimard, 1994), p. 255.
29 Winnicott, *Playing and Reality*, p. 17.
30 Ibid., p. 15.
31 Ponge, *Le Parti pris des choses*, p. 44.
32 Kristeva quoting, in *Le Temps sensible*, p. 256.
33 Michèle Roberts, *Daughters of the House* (London: Virago, 1992), p. 97.
34 Colette, *Le Blé en herbe* (Paris: Flammarion, 1923), pp. 9–10; my translation.
35 Ibid., pp. 35–6.
36 Jean Rhys, *Wide Sargasso Sea* (Harmondsworth: Penguin, 1968), p. 15.
37 Ibid., p. 21.
38 Ibid., p. 23.
39 Ibid., p. 73.
40 Ibid., p. 148.
41 Roberts, *Daughters of the House*, pp. 35–6.
42 Ibid., p. 33.
43 Ibid., p. 166.
44 Virginia Woolf, *To the Lighthouse* (London: Grafton, 1977).
45 *New York Herald Tribune*, 14 Aug. 1927.
46 Woolf, *To the Lighthouse*, pp. 121–2.
47 Angela Carter, *The Passion of New Eve* (London: Virago, 1982).
48 C. G. Jung, *Collected Works*, ed. Herbert Read, Michael Fordham and Gerhard Adler (Princeton: Princeton University Press; London: Routledge, 1959), vol. 7, p. 238.
49 Ibid., vol. 16, p. 263.
50 Demaris S. Wehr, *Jung and Feminism: Liberating Archetypes* (London: Routledge, 1988), pp. 100–1.
51 Ibid., p. 101.
52 Ibid., pp. 101, 102.
53 Rhys, *Wide Sargasso Sea*, p. 38.
54 Ibid.
55 Wehr, *Jung and Feminism*, p. 103.
56 Ibid., p. 141.
57 See ibid.

58 Chris Mihill, 'Poets "Least Mad of the Literati": Psychiatrist's Study Gives the Lie to Lord Byron', *Guardian*, 1 May 1996, p. 3.
59 Anthony Clare, 'Retrieving your Sanity', review article of *An Unquiet Mind* by Kay Jamieson, *Sunday Times*, 5 May 1996, p. 8.
60 Mihill, 'Poets "Least Mad of the Literati" ', p. 3.

Conclusion

New Directions

9
The Name of the Father

When you're no longer in the midst of the trees – are writing your conclusion – you begin to see the wood. I look at my wood, and am struck
by some of its oddities. Three of them in particular. The first is, that
while I have, in my introduction, mapped out ideas about the balance of
male and female in creativity, my essays are about what goes wrong in
this ideal balance: wrong with fatherhood, askew with motherhood. The
second: the essays on motherhood return again and again to the question
of the girl's separation from the mother. I confess myself still torn by the
pull of contrary arguments: those which (along with Fouque, Cixous,
Kristeva, Irigaray, some anthropologists ...) see the stress on separation,
repudiation of the mother as patriarchally induced, and are drawn (like
Jung) to possibilities of a continuing or renewed union with the mother;
and those which claim that only through separation, loss, castration, a
kind of death (the models are countless) can growth and a relation to the
Other come. I am not going to solve that one today any more than I have
done above, so let it be. The third concerns the father.

Calling my second section 'In Father's Lack' was, of course, among
other things, a 'pied-de-nez', a dig at, Lacan. 'You say that women are
lacking? Well – look at those men! look at fatherhood!' But, without realizing it at the time, I was also inscribing my own extraordinary lack of –
knowledge of? interest in? capacity to portray? – fathers. None of these
essays is about, say, the Author (dead or alive), powerful father figures,
detailed relations between fathers and daughters such as the fascinating
Virago collection *Fathers by Daughters* portrayed.[1] The father has been as
lacking from this book as Monsieur Lancelin from his household. I feel I
cannot leave off without making a gesture in the direction of what lies
beyond my ... let's call it ignorance.

All the more so as, since the questions 'what is a father for?' began to bother me, I came to notice that the father had moved centre-stage: in men's angry indictments, anguished or defiant self-searchings or brave bodies of reflexion, from Neil Lyndon and David Thomas to Robert Bly to Men's Studies to Family Studies; in feminists' growing preoccupation with masculinity . . . Noting that 'without much care for nuance, people herald the twilight of the fathers, or their renaissance,'[2] Elizabeth Badinter footnotes reams of sociological and psychological and analytic enquiries conducted over the past fifteen years. It is an expanding field.

To start from a large perspective: a special issue of the French *Cahiers Jungiens de Psychanalyse, Au Défaut des pères* (1991), produced a brief survey by Bernard Vasseur of the attributes of the Indo-European father, from which the Germanic, Roman and Greek models issued. The Indo-European father was above all the chief of the 'great family' (his role as begetter was secondary). He gave it his name, was the warrant of its rank and ensured its well-being. His status survived in the Roman *pater familias*, and into 'tyrannical medieval fathers and nineteenth century bosses'.[3] His name could also be 'dems-pot', the Greek 'despot' and Roman 'dominus': the master of the house. The father of the Gods, 'dyeus peter', the father in heaven, is Zeus pater, Jupiter. Much of this tradition has survived in the Christian address to the Eternal Father, 'Pater qui es in coelis', and in the hierarchies of the Christian churches. 'The symbolic power of the Judaeo-Christian God has reinforced the status of the Indo-European father', 'leaving indelible traces on our genetic memory'.[4] Vasseur stresses that Greek myths, as has been much argued in recent years (for instance by Marie Delcourt on the Oedipus myth), may mark various shifts from matrilinear societies to patriarchal societies, thus expressing the collision of two cultures. The individualism brought about by Christianity, along with 'the dislocation of the modern family' tends to weaken and invalidate these patterns, 'if not their functions'.[5]

Another writer, Viviane Jullien-Pelletier, analyses what it is that we call 'father': there are, she lists, the 'biological father' (who may or may not live with the child), the 'educating father', who lives with the child (the two may be one), the 'genealogical father' (who gives his name to the child), but also, on the psychic level, the 'symbolic father', the one who differentiates and carries the law (Freud would say, symbolizes or enacts the castration threat; Lacan would say, he is the one who says no, who embodies the Law). He is, Viviane Jullien-Pelletier adds, the source of the 'paternal principle'.[6] Other (psychoanalytic) theorists might add that the father is the larger or outer container to the mother's inner one. Or he who negotiates the relations between the family and the outside world. What I wish to retain from Jullien-Pelletier are two kinds of functions for the father: the real ones (as biological or educator), involving particular forms of behaviour, and the symbolic ones (as genealogical or what Jullien-Pelletier and others call symbolic), having to do with structure. I shall be using these terms in the following discussion whenever wanting to make the distinction.

Another writer from that same issue of the *Cahiers*, Aimé Agnel, reflects on both Freud's and Jung's faulty fathers and how they, the sons, came to terms with their disillusion or contempt.[7] He remarks that Freud's high-minded vision of the 'great man', seen as embodying the 'paternal persona' in *Moses and Monotheism*, ' "Firm in his ideas, full of will-power, resolute in his acts" ', ' "filled with self-confidence, the divine conviction to be always in the right" ', etc., is an idealizing imago, the projection perhaps of a future self, meant to compensate for the disappointing reality of Freud's real father. This is a crucial reminder of how analytic and other theories of the father are coloured by the theorist's own relation to his or her father.

From all this there emerges an at least triple reality: a powerful and ancient set of religious and cultural imagos; the father as serving various functions, social, relational and symbolic; the human father, pitched between idealizing images and his own, it seems today often bewildered, humanity.

In a rich body of reflection on fathers, what they do, which concludes with a section called 'healing the father', Andrew Samuels points out that there are acute gaps in our understanding of both symbolic and real fathering. 'There is very little description of ordinary, devoted, good-enough fathering'; we 'lack an adequate account of the early, direct, "pre-Oedipal" relationship of father and infant'.[8] We would not need it, would we, the thought occurs to me, unless relationships between fathers and children had changed a great deal in recent years, at least in the European upper and middle classes: it wouldn't have occurred to Dickens's Mr Dombey, or even to Proust's father, even to take up their sons in their arms. Though it might be a question of class: in *Great Expectations* it is Jo, not Mrs Jo, who is tender to Pip . . .

Andrew Samuels then goes on to express creative dissatisfaction with the various accounts of fatherhood available. He identifies four models. The 'insertion metaphor', from Margaret Mahler, which represents 'a present day consensus of opinion concerning father–child relating', according to which the father, 'like a huge penis', 'inserts himself between baby and mother so as to break up the symbiosis or fusion of which they are supposed to be unconscious'. Samuels does not much like the notion that the father's first appearance in the child's life should be '*to deprive the child*'.[9] The second model is Winnicott's: 'the father holds the mother who holds the baby' (akin, it seems to me, to the notion of the father as the larger container which I have found in some Jungian studies of myth). Samuels points out that the notion that the father's access to the baby is via the mother is contradicted by researchers into 'infant attachment patterns' which show that the father–infant relation is independent of the infant's relation to the mother, depending instead on the qualities the father brings into the relationship – and that Winnicott's ideas reflect the family pattern and habits of the period in which he was writing.[10] I personally think that the idea of the larger container is not incompatible with an independent father–infant relationship, and that, yes, Winnicott's ideas bear the imprint (and limits) of his time – but then, so surely do ours.

The third model is Lacan's. The father here 'crops up' 'solely as a metaphor, just a name or Name', 'a third term'. This approach 'lacks a sustained recognition of the interplay between father's concrete, literal presence and his metaphorical function'. Samuels doubts that you can disassociate the fleshy penis from the phallus, as Lacan claims. In identifying, 'more or less' 'language and the father', Lacan fails to notice that there *is* a real as well as a symbolic father, and that the real father is both constrained by society (as his child is) and makes his own choices (that is, could be a 'subversive and radical' father).[11] Samuels reiterates his dissent from the notion that there is an early state of symbiosis with the mother, on which the need for the symbolic intervention of the father (the triadic Oedipus complex) depends. In fact, 'babies *themselves* desire to grow and separate from their mothers as well as to rest in permanent oceanic bliss.' Furthermore 'what is nowadays being noted is the existence of an intense conversation or proto-conversation between mother and infant, and, where this can be observed, between father and infant as well. The extent of mutual communication is massive.' In fact, Samuels concludes, quoting Page du Bois, both Lacan and Lacan's followers ' "perpetuate a metaphysics of wholeness, presence, deism and worship of the symbolic father. . . . Such an ideology supports relations of male dominance, class and racial hierarchy . . ." '[12]

But – and this is the fourth model of fatherhood Samuels is critical of – Jung is tarred with the same brush as Lacan. Jung also conflates 'the specific or cultural moment and what is claimed to be eternal or universal'. He 'ignores the *cultural* construction of the father–child relationship as he seeks to identify its essential and universal features.' Precisely because, Samuels argues, the father–infant relationship is culturally constructed, depends on two other bonds, the mother–infant and the man–woman, it is open, full of 'exciting possibilities'. The father's role can change, it is historically mutable: wholly cultural. '*The archetypal element is that there is no father archetype*; the father relation features a lack of innate features.'[13]

Brilliant, I thought when I first came upon this. When I grouped my first set of chapters under the title 'In Father's Lack', it seems that I had stumbled by sheer luck into what it takes all of Samuels's considerable nous to establish. I was all the more cheered as Samuels goes on to show that the mother and the father are *not* complementary, that our habit of thinking in binary pairs keeps leading us astray. This is also what made itself manifest to me, I thought: that there was no parallelism, that what I had written about the mother was not in any way symmetrical with what concerned the (lacking) father.

Samuels proceeds to interrogate paternal realities as well as the range of mythical images and possible roles open to 'the father (of whatever sex)'. At which point, while still fascinated, I began to take my distance: take stock of where I myself had been led to.

It was not because of the lack of a father archetype, I reflected, that I had felt the need to call my first section 'In Father's Lack', but because of the lack of real and cultural fathers: absences, bad behaviour, dereliction of duty, and in the First World War appallingly deficient leaders, old men using young ones as cannon-fodder ... My 'lack' implied there could have been a fullness. Mature ministers or generals, for instance, caring about young men's lives. A Gustave Papin who would have behaved well to his wife and daughters ... I'm not sure what 'well' might have meant, but it certainly would not have included seducing his elder daughter or disappearing into the great beyond, leaving his wife to fend for herself and put the girls in an orphanage. In this dream scheme of things, Lawrence's father would have been self-confident, and Woolf's not so childishly self-centred. There may not be a father archetype, but there have been varieties of patriarchal family structures around for at least two-and-a-half to three thousand years, creating culturally varied and mutable but still enduring expectations that a father ... well, a father would make you safe, for a start. Would look after you. Would care for your greater good, and have some *vision* of that: 'Our Father, Which art in heaven...' He would be trustworthy. I am sorry, Mr Samuels, I do concur with you about recognizing how 'culturally mutable' the father is, how freeing the recognition is – for it means fatherhood can change for the better – and I am even prepared to let go of the archetype. But the image, the need for what the image signifies, what it can do, even apart from whether it signifies language or not, a need developed in a thousand and one forms over millennia – that is not empty. If he (of whatever sex?) is not there, if s/he behaves predatorily, selfishly – that makes a hell of a lot of difference. But also, what the father has come to symbolize – this is so deeply embedded, it has to be taken into account.

And so while wanting to applaud the ways in which the father, the 'Cinderella-child of development psychology',[14] is beginning to be properly researched today, and the opening up of the roles of mother and father (of whatever sex), I find myself seeking in yet other directions. Is there no model of fatherhood that would be positive, lasting despite mutability, and that would retain its link with the symbolic? There may be, as Samuels claims, no archetype of the father. Progress, in terms of good-enough, or better, fathering, is to be sought in practical research, openness and exploration. Yet the symbolic role of the father still seems to me to be paramount, to need to make itself felt, to be active, through and beyond the day-to-day father–child relationship.

I do agree with Joyce's Stephen Dedalus when he talks about the 'fiction of paternity', its mystery and the creative power of that mystery. I will not repeat myself: I quoted the passage when discussing Angela Carter. I also think that Lacan, whatever his excesses and shortcomings, is on to something important when he stresses the value of 'the Name-of-the-Father, the only defence' against acute paranoia of the kind suffered by Freud's famous patient President Schreber – against, Lacan says, 'a Schreber-type delirium', the 'fourth element which holds together the Real, the Imaginary and the Symbolic'.[15]

Lacan however is an infuriating ally. For, as Marini, after Irigaray, points out, by bracketing, downgrading or downright eliminating the mother, he closets father and son in a love–hate state of 'hainamoration', haunted by infanticide and parricide, more rigorously all-male than the Judaeo-Christian God he regards as dead, and still remains fascinated by.[16] I still think he is right in his commentary on Victor Hugo's poem, 'Boaz endormi', to point out that the Old Testament God, 'the Lord with the unpronounceable name' makes his chosen people propagate 'through post-menopausal women and old men past begetting', like Booz, and that this is highly significant. However, Lacan's misreading of the Ruth story is, to my mind, rooted in his own unconscious projections and prejudices. There must have been deep down things in him that made the father–son relationship exclusive: just as Freud praised Moses's 'paternal' virtues in compensation for his own father's deficiencies. I want to spend a little time looking at Lacan's misreadings, because I think it reveals how modern rereadings of the Bible can end up in patriarchal reductionism – and this further distorts our images (archetypal or not) of the father.

The Book of Ruth is one of the three Old Testament books that bear the name of a woman (the others being Judith and Esther). It is the story of Naomi, driven by famine to the fields of Moab with her husband and two sons. The sons marry Moabite women. Then they die, as well as Naomi's husband. A famine in Moab drives Naomi back to her own land, around Bethlehem. About to leave Moab, she bids good-bye to her two daughters-in-law, telling them she is now too old to produce sons for them: they should fend for themselves, find new husbands, stay in their own land. One daughter-in-law does just that. The other, Ruth, in a beautiful speech, tells Naomi that she will follow her wherever she goes: Naomi's God will be her God.

Once in Naomi's land, Ruth, inspired, goes to glean barley and wheat in the fields of a wealthy kinsman of Naomi's, Boaz. Boaz is kind to the gleaner, whom he honours for her love for Naomi. He makes sure Ruth is kindly treated by his reapers, given food and drink; that plenty of ears should be left about for her. Ruth reports this to Naomi, who tells her to wait for Boaz to have fallen asleep after the day's threshing, then, handsomely dressed and scented, go and lie at his feet, and *uncover them*. When Boaz wakes he will tell her what to do. There was a law of Moses according to which a widow could ask her dead husband's closest kinsman to redeem her by marriage, so that the dead man should have a descendance. Ruth does as she has been told. Boaz on waking covers her with his cloak as a pledge, but says there is a kinsman with a prior claim:

if that kinsman gives up his claim, then Boaz will redeem Ruth. He then promptly and cannily gets the kinsman to give up his claim. Boaz marries Ruth. They have a son. Naomi brings up the child.

Hugo's poem occurs at the moment of night when Boaz is asleep in his field. There is a crescent of moon in the starry sky. Ruth has come to lie at Boaz's feet, 'le sein nu', having bared her breasts. As in the biblical story, Hugo's Boaz is full of generosity. But Hugo, an ageing man, in his sixties when he writes *La Légende des siècles*, and a randy one, makes Boaz a very old man, *past childbearing*, yet attractive as *old men are*, Hugo tells us: if there is flame in young men's eyes, there is light, 'de la lumière', in old men's. Read: I may be old but my attractiveness is only enhanced thereby: witness Boaz and how that young woman is behaving to him. Indeed, a fine mixture of heaven-bound reverie and erotic charge develops at the end of the poem:

> Booz ne savait pas qu'une femme était là
> Et Ruth ne savait pas ce que Dieu voulait d'elle ...

Boaz does not yet know a woman is there, lying at his feet; Ruth does not know what God wants from her ... She has – a Hugo, a nineteenth-century touch, not a biblical one – bared her breasts, so she must have some idea (in the Bible she bares *his* feet). There is no suggestion in the biblical story that Ruth has come to seduce. Indeed, Boaz says 'all the city of my people doth know that thou art a virtuous woman' (Ruth 3:11). She has made herself beautiful, yes: she is after marriage, after security, after recreating a place in society for the two outcasts she and Naomi have become through poverty, exile and widowhood. She is doing as Naomi, whom she loves, has bid her. She is appealing to a law.

Another twist: Hugo gives Boaz biblical Jesse's dream. Boaz dreams that the trunk of a huge oak-tree is sprouting from his midriff: he asks God, how can that be, since I am old? Poetic licence: in the Bible Jesse is Boaz's grandson. He is often represented in medieval stained glass and elsewhere with a tree issuing from his belly, leading as it does through David his son all the way to Christ. The Jesse story is about Christ's ancestry, Christ's coming through God's chosen people. So is the Ruth story, it seems to me. It prefigures the birth of Christ. It takes place in Bethlehem. Ruth is full of loving fidelity: she does Naomi's bidding without ever questioning what is being asked of her. She has Mary's startling readiness: 'I am the handmaid of the Lord ...' Twice Ruth says to Boaz, 'I am Ruth thine handmaid.' Boaz tells Ruth that she has come to trust 'under the wings' of the Lord of Israel: 'Blessed be thou of the Lord,' he repeatedly says to her.

The biblical Boaz is a marvellous figure, prompt to act, bountiful, manly, honourable. The focus however is on Ruth and Naomi, *and it is Naomi who says, 'I am too old to have an husband.'* Hugo's Boaz is so ancient he becomes another Abraham, an old man whose wife was well past childbearing. The poem's images of a sky full of stars evokes God's promise to Abraham to give him a descendance as numerous as the stars of heaven. This has some correspondence to the Book of Ruth in that Boaz's striking generosity with the poor reaper is rewarded by marriage to her, the birth of a son and a miraculous descendance. The biblical Boaz is certainly not young: he congratulates Ruth for not being after young men. He is an honoured, a wealthy landowner, yes. But nothing indicates that age is a problem that might interfere with his begetting children. The one who is old – *the one to whom God gives a miraculous child* – is Naomi, Ruth's mother-in-law:

> And the women said unto Naomi, Blessed be the Lord, which hath not left thee this day without a kinsman, that his name may be famous in Israel.
> And he shall be unto thee a restorer of thy life, and a nourisher of thine old age: for thy daughter in law, which loveth thee, *which is better to thee than seven sons*, hath borne him.
> And Naomi took the child, and laid it in her bosom, and became nurse unto it. (Ruth 4: 14–16)

Lacan, it seems clear to me, never bothered to reread the Book of Ruth. He uses Hugo's poem as evidence for the Bible, since he says that 'the Lord with the unpronounceable name' makes fruitful old women and men past childbearing. Here he refers to Boaz, asking, according to Lacan, 'How can a descendance spring from me, an old man?', when in the biblical story the descendance is miraculously sprung, both to an old woman, Naomi, through Ruth, as in the above passage, and to her dead son. Boaz has it witnessed by elders:

> Ruth the Moabitess, the wife of Mahlon, have I purchased to be my wife, to raise up the name of the dead upon his inheritance, that the name of the dead be not cut off from among his brethren, and from the gate of his place. (Ruth 4: 10)

In other words, what is mysterious, fictional, symbolic or whatever here about the Name-of-the-Father does have to do with biological paternity being subsumed by the larger law of the clan, the Mosaic law, and by the miraculous operation of God's mercy: He has taken Ruth under his wing, rather as Boaz symbolically covers her with his cloak. God, through Boaz, produces a descendance through the women for a dead man (as Mary will bear God's son thanks to Joseph). Boaz plays a major part. Indeed, his qualities will make a marvellous father. But Ruth and Naomi play an even larger part. They are those whose love and faith enable incarnation to take place.

But what Lacan regards as most significant in Hugo's poem is the concluding image. Hugo's Ruth wonders

Quel Dieu, quel moissonneur de l'éternel été
Avait, en s'en allant, négligemment jeté
Cette faucille d'or dans le champ des étoiles.

Looking at the crescent of moon in the star-studded sky, lying in fields recently harvested, Ruth wonders here, 'What God, what reaper of eternal summer / Had, as he was leaving, negligently thrown / This sickle of gold in the field of the stars.' For Lacan, who has just praised the bountifulness of Hugo's Boaz, this is an evocation of the sickle Jupiter used 'to flood the world with Chronos's blood'.[17] It is hard to disentangle the paradoxes that Lacan's associational reading of the metaphor produces: for seeing in Hugo's image of the sickle 'the hidden dimension of the poem', Lacan visualizes Jupiter, the Roman *Zeus pater*, where the Bible and Hugo have the Hebrew God. Does this imply that Boaz, now supposed to be impotent because too old, is bountiful while Jahweh leaves a 'negligent' clue to his being a father-castrator, a *son* therefore, not a father threatening his son with castration as in the Freudian model? And the castrator of an *old* father, to boot – just when He is about to make an old man fruitful ... I had always read the poem's closing wonder about what God, 'what reaper of eternal summer' had thrown his sickle into the field of stars as both an image of covenanting, prolific abundance, with the reference to Abraham that I described above ('your posterity will be as many as the stars in heaven': circumcision becomes the sign of the covenant), and a reminder that God is also the Great Reaper, the master of life and death. This is Hugo's closing image, of course: not that of the Book of Ruth, which finishes with Obed, Ruth's son, being the father of Jesse, who is the father of David. Hugo's God, by promising Boaz a son through the Jesse dream, renews his covenant, first made fast by Abraham's readiness to sacrifice his son Isaac. God in his turn, for Christians at least, will later sacrifice his own son for man. In my reading, it was the sons whose blood was threatened, whose sacrifice had happened, or would happen. In Lacan's, with the evocation of the Greek myth of Chronos, it is a *previous* father. Jahweh slides into father-castrating Jupiter, bizarrely rejuvenated, to me rather out of character. Impossible of course to tell which myths Hugo himself was thinking about. This is a case for accepting the opennness of the text. But yes: parricide, infanticide, Marini is right. Peculiar father–son dramas enact themselves throughout Lacan (and possibly Hugo).

Lacan may be perceiving something insightful about Hugo here, an ambiguity, an area where the metaphor takes over, creating meaning in excess of what is intended. But what I find pernicious about such a reading is that Lacan assumes, without a shadow of doubt or its even occurring to him that he'd better check the biblical text, that what his hunch is about Hugo is bound to be right about the Bible, and *all* father–sons relationships (a Greek myth will be just as appropriate as the Hebrew one). He neither bothers to notice that particular, and to us twentieth-century

Westerners strange, rules regulated fatherhood in that place and those days, nor that this Book bears the name of a woman, has two women at its centre, prefigures Mary's faith and miraculous *motherhood*. He is being infinitely more patriarchal than the Bible. Everything that pertains to the specifics of place and time, *and* to women/the mother, is eradicated from the story/poem so that Father-killing and castration can 'flood the world' with their blood (to use his own terms). So that yes: Andrew Samuels is quite right to complain that the real father is excised by Lacan from his symbolic teasing out of the meaning of fatherhood. But Irigaray and Marini are right as well: it is by erasing woman/the mother from the scene, as both body and agent and carrier of symbolic/spiritual meaning, that Lacan leaves his father so nakedly face-to-face with the son, ignoring the fact that the women tell Naomi that Ruth is better to her *than seven sons* ... Ruth, whose name means 'friendship', is gone – and what is left in her place?

Is Lacan then speaking of the laws of meaning in language, or of his own sleights-of-hand when he writes about *metaphor*, alluding to the Boaz story and God's predilection for post-childbearing-age genitors:

> The fundamentally transbiological character of paternity, introduced by tradition into the destiny of the chosen people, has something in it that is originally repressed, and which always resurfaces in the ambiguity of limping, of stumbling, and of the symptom, the non-encounter, *dustuchia*, with the meaning that remains hidden.[18]

Isn't the meaning that is repressed, that remains hidden here, Ruth and Naomi? Faith and friendship? But what Lacan is being accurate about is what he himself does when he reads metaphors: when he interprets Hugo's God's sickle as Jupiter's, a non-encounter occurs. There is a transfer of father to son and son to father – and the meaning (be it but that Ruth in Hugo is the one who is half awake, who wonders while the man, Boaz, sleeps) remains hidden. Where you had fatherless Jewish God establishing a descendance, suddenly at Lacan's hands you have father-castrating Jupiter 'negligently' displaying the instrument of his crime, and where does that leave father-to-be Boaz? It has been said that where Freud wrote interpretatively, Jung's method was amplification, and that made him hard to discuss. Lacan's method is slippage, twisting, obliquity, *prestidigitation*: while you watch his hands the object disappears, and an often startling one appears in its place. That makes him even more difficult to think about than Jung. The linguistic dexterity conceals the odds, the projections which might be there: like this father–son business, sprung, Marini claims, from Lacan's own wished-for filiation from Freud, and from his own difficulties at having slid in later years into a father position in relation to his followers.

And *yet* I think there is a truth beyond Lacan's own projections here. I go along with his claim that the 'hidden' nature of paternity has a deep and puzzling connection with how human beings make meaning.

One of the functions of the father in Lacan is to introduce the Other into the child's psychic life. Kristeva agrees about this. But she also provides the combination of practicality and symbolism which I was hankering for: her *Histoires d'amour* is preoccupied with the symbolic function of both real, and ideal fathering. It does not subsume the mother. It does not relegate the father to a negative or supplementary or purely symbolic role.

Kristeva praises Freud for having dissociated 'idealization (and with it the love relation) from the mother–child bodily symbiosis', and introduced a Third ('le Tiers') – the father – as 'the condition of psychic life in so far as it is about love'.[19] If the mother goes on too long caring for and glued to the child, being a 'mère soignante et collante', the girl-child in particular may fall a prey to hysteria. And both children may become 'schizoid, phobic or *borderline*'.[20] The truly loving mother 'is someone who has an object of desire, and beyond, an Other in relation to whom the child will be an intermediary'. 'It is in relation to a Third that the child will become constituted as "beloved" by its mother,' that it will become a ' "he" ' (or a she). Otherwise the 'corps à corps', the dyad, becomes 'an abjection or a devouration'.[21] In this perspective, the father (one could presumably add with Andrew Samuels, 'of whatever sex') is he who is the object of the mother's desire. He who makes love to the mother, has a loving relation to the mother. It is not because he threatens the child with castration that he intervenes in the Oedipus complex, cuts the bond with the mother, but because his being the mother's lover will compel the child to relinquish its desire for the mother, to take its place in the family unit as a child and not the possessor/possessed of the mother. The father does not so much symbolize language as stand for a relationship which allows the child to find its place, and enter language.

What Kristeva argues is not exclusive of what Samuels argues. I see them more as complementary. The symbolic role, the role of the Third that Kristeva ascribes to the father, and that serves to introduce the Other into the child's life, is fully compatible with a child–father relationship. But there is another territory of the father into which Kristeva ventures, which was also Lacan's territory: a spiritual or even religious, mystical one. Strange, because neither is a believer. But then, as analysts both, they do have experience of what people bring up from the depths. And it has to do with the 'Nom-du-Père'.

Histoires d'amour discusses God as *agape*, love, and the believer's relation to the Father through the Son: through the Son's passion. It is an ideal identification with the Other, but also one that does not remain trapped in narcissism, that goes beyond:

Inhabited by Christ, 'adopted' by the Father, the believer only dies to his body of sin, on the way that leads to *agape*. The putting to death therefore is one moment in the *adoption* process – a theme that is essential if we want to understand *agape*, for it sets forth a paternity which is not in the flesh, but in the name.[22]

Kristeva quotes St Paul: ' "ye have received the Spirit of adoption, whereby we cry, Abba, Father!" ' (Romans 8: 15) and ' "nevertheless I live; yet not I, but Christ liveth in me; and the life which I now live in the flesh I live by the faith of the Son of God, who loved me, and gave himself for me" ' (Galatians 2: 20). She comments:

> Christian love is an idea that transforms my body into an adored Name. The putting to death of the body will be the way through which the I-body will gain access to the Name of the Other who loves me and makes of me a Subject immersed (baptised) in the Name of the Other.[23]

This leads to love of one's neighbour – one's brother. The sign of agape is the Christian meal, the Eucharist, in which orality is turned, through the eating of the Word, towards the Father. 'Christian love: a more-than-hunger in the Father's breast.'[24]

Au commencement était l'amour: Psychanalyse et foi, Kristeva's next, short but pithy book, develops what is implicit in this image of an orality transferred to the Father. Kristeva presents faith as a primary identification with a loving, protective presence:

> Beyond the perception of an irredeemable separation, Western man re-establishes, with 'semiotic' rather than 'symbolic' means, a continuity and a fusion with the Other, an Other that is no longer substantial or maternal but symbolic and paternal. Saint Augustine goes so far as to compare the Christian's faith in his God with the infant's relation to its mother's breast: 'This complete dependence, this intimate participation in everything which, good or bad, flows from this unique source of life.' A fusion with the carrying, nourishing, loving and protective womb/breast [le sein], but one which henceforth would be transposed from the maternal body to an invisible presence beyond.[25]

For Kristeva, a non-believer, it is through language – the 'talking cure' – through playfulness and creative acts that a similar result can be achieved: separation from the mother, and the 'jump' towards the Other which the Father's presence makes possible. I do not know whether this is because I myself am a believer, but the above passage finds a huge echo in me. For this conception of the Father as absolute love, as what we travel towards once we've let go of the Mother, accepted that 'il y a de l'Autre', that the Other exists, as the *terminus ad quem* to the Mother's *terminus a quo*, is the only conception of reality I have come across that squares what otherwise is to me the circle of needing fusion with the mother, and recognizing that separation from her *has* to occur. I wrote above that this remained for me *the* unsolved question in relation to the mother, that the chapters in my second section all somehow stemmed from that insolubility. There is a profound appeal to me in the Christian conception that Kristeva outlines. She can present it in the terms she does *because* she has done so much work on the maternal, because, unlike Lacan, she makes room for the semiotic, for non-symbolic meaning. Because she recognizes the enduring importance of the mother's body. It is a conception in which room is made for the Father, for the Father's symbolic role as essential (which neither most feminisms, French or Anglo-American at any rate, nor Andrew Samuels will accept, or be interested in). But, unlike a lot of other approaches, Lacan's in particular, symptomatically eliminating the mother from the Ruth and Boaz story as we have seen, the Mother here is fully integrated. Her love, the kind of union which being in the womb, or at the breast, can represent (with its loving and its hating impulses – 'good or bad'), becomes what has to be lost, what has to die so that the same source of bliss can be born at the other end (on the other side of the Passion, of death, of the death to sin, and of all the losses and deaths we experience through our lives). The Mother is where we come from. The Father is where we are going, He whose beloved child we can become. It is because the transfer from the Body to the Name has to occur that the Spirit can enter. But unless we have love for the Body – the Mother – unless what pertains to the semiotic, meaning rooted in the whole of the body, is alive and active in us, we cannot find love at the other end: we have nowhere but language to travel to. We become locked in cleverness, in Lacan's Father–Son confrontation, in infanticide and parricide.

What have I been saying?

First, that our conception of fatherhood is changing. There is an ongoing search for new ways of fathering, adapted to what we are today, what we are becoming. I have used Andrew Samuels as one impressive example of this. The task is crucial. After all, the fate of the world depends on the quality of the next generation, not on our ability to further split the atom or go to Mars. Better parenting can make the difference.

Second: though this task is of paramount importance, its practicalities do not exhaust the dimensions of fatherhood. There is a symbolic as well as a real father. Joyce, Lacan, Kristeva are right: there is a mystery in paternity, bound up with or manifested by its invisibility. It is through the dominance of fatherhood, through familial formations, that Indo-European, Judaeo-Christian notions of the godhead have become manifest. The twists to biology, the sets of rules that Western civilization has evolved, which Lacan connects with language and others to discourse are bound up with the Name-of-the-Father – with genealogy. In the case of the Jewish people, genealogy, the sign of the covenant, is one extraordinary but effective way of having a certain form of spiritual identity survive through time, in excess of the sheer survival of a society. The result is paradoxical. On the one hand, patriarchies have produced and keep producing monstrous excesses of power. On the other, it is through the father that the spiritual dimension of humankind has been revealed.

Thirdly: it is to the extent that the savage dimension of the symbolic father (the cutting, the separating, the power) is not allowed to downgrade or erase the early relational, symbiotic, loving dimension of the mother that fatherhood does not become predatory. It is also to the extent that identification with the father does not become a pretext for domination, a means to power, but a means to a higher, or deeper, selfhood (as in the Christian model of agape that Kristeva outlines) that the father ceases to be a means to division and conflict (binaries) and becomes instead a means to evolution, to inner growth. The higher one rises, the fewer antagonisms there are. 'What opposes spiritualities is their lowering. If you go down the slope, everything is in opposition to everything else; if you climb it, everything becomes reconciled.'[26]

Kristeva is a semiotician and an analyst. She has wrought her own, rich meaning of the word 'semiotic', laden with the pre-Oedipal. It is by evoking the semiotic dimension in us that she manages to make room for the mother beside the father – to suggest how we might, and sometimes do, balance the mother and the father in us. But there are other words to allude to what lies beyond, beneath, around, the intellect: what in us is attuned to the movement of life. Philosophies and spiritualities, especially Eastern, have evolved many ways of accessing it. Bergson in *L'Évolution créatrice* wrote about intuition, 'disinterested instinct' that can lead us to the 'innerness of life'.[27] There is, appropriately to my discussion of the Name of the Father, a great Orthodox Christian tradition of invoking the *Name*, the Hesychastic prayer, meant to pass through the heart, not the head: only through the heart can the initial, the Edenic love of God and man be found again. In Eden, the Hebrew text of Genesis says, Adam and Eve lived 'mouth to mouth' with God. Cain's crime ruptures the early (symbiotic, maternal?) intimacy with God. From then on, Cain wanders East of Eden, constructing cities and civilizations. Wordly success attends upon Cain. But Seth, Adam and Eve's third son, renews the alliance with God by *calling upon him*. The Name becomes the sign of a new covenant: 'Then began men to call upon the name of the Lord' (Genesis 4: 26).

A fine introduction to the 'prayer of the heart' by Alphonse and Rachel Goettmann describes how, at every manifestation in the Old Testament, God named himself: Elohim (God) to Noah; El-Shaddai (He of the Mountain) to Abraham; Yahweh to Moses. Only those who 'love the name of the Lord' (Isaiah 56: 6) will be brought to the holy mountain. But also, the name of Yahweh ('the Lord with the unpronounceable name', Lacan would say) is so awesome that only the great priest can call upon him once a year, that it is replaced by Elohim or Adonai, and in the Greek translation of the Bible, by Kyrios, which becomes in its turn sacred.[28] Not taking the Name of the Lord in vain is the third commandment. 'Hallowed be Thy Name,' in the prayer given by Christ to his apostles, follows immediately from 'Our Father Which art in Heaven'. Difficult for us, who take both the names of God and Christ in vain at every turn of phrase in a *vain* attempt to find words strong enough to express anger or force of feeling, to have even a minimal understanding of what such injunctions mean . . .

With the advent of Christ, the Word, comes the Incarnation of the Name. To invoke the name of Christ is to invoke the name of the Father. 'All that you will ask the Father in my name, He will give to you.' It is through the invocation of an embodied, crucified and resurrected Christ that, as Kristeva says, an 'ideal identification' with the Father can take place. It is not something that intelligence can understand. It is something that the heart can experience if the body is involved: a kind of incarnation then takes place. The parable of the Good Sower shows that nothing much happens to the man who has 'no depth of earth' (Mark 4: 5), and the Fathers of the Church talk about God's law being 'in the middle of the belly'.[29]

There are, however, things which the intelligence can to a certain degree perceive in relation to . . . the gender of God.

Notes

1 *Fathers by Daughters*, ed. Ursula Owen (London: Virago, 1984).
2 Elizabeth Badinter, *XY: De l'identité masculine* (Paris: Odile Jacob, 1992), p. 252.
3 Bernard Vasseur, 'Le Père Indo-européen', *Cahiers Jungiens de Psychanalyse*, no. 69 (1991), pp. 61–7, at pp. 62–3.
4 Ibid., p. 67.
5 Ibid., pp. 66–7.
6 Viviane Jullien-Pelletier, 'De Père en fils', *Cahiers Jungiens de Psychanalyse*, no. 69 (1991), pp. 27–39, at pp. 27–9.
7 Aimé Agnel, 'La Défaillance paternelle et sa compensation chez Freud et chez Jung', *Cahiers Jungiens de Psychanalyse*, no. 69 (1991), pp. 5–17.
8 Andrew Samuels, *The Political Psyche* (London: Routledge, 1993), pp. 135, 137.
9 Ibid., pp. 138, 137.
10 Ibid., p. 138.
11 Ibid., pp. 138, 140.
12 Ibid., pp. 140, 141.
13 Ibid., pp. 141, 143.
14 Ibid., p. 163.
15 Marcelle Marini, *Lacan* (Paris: Belfond, 1986), pp. 82–3; my translation.
16 Ibid., pp. 83–5.
17 Jacques Lacan, 'Le Champ de l'Autre', in *Le Séminaire livre XI: Les quatre concepts fondamentaux de la Psychanalyse* (Paris: Seuil, 1973), p. 224.
18 Ibid., p. 224.
19 Julia Kristeva, *Histoires d'amour* (Paris: Denoel, 1983), p. 48; my translation.
20 Ibid., pp. 70–1, 49.
21 Ibid., pp. 48–9.

22 Ibid., p. 183.
23 Ibid., p. 185.
24 Ibid., p. 189.
25 Julia Kristeva, *Au commencement était l'amour: Psychanalyse et foi* (Paris: Hachette, 1985), p. 37.
26 M. D. Molinié, *Le Courage d'avoir peur* (Paris: Cerf, 1994), p. 121.
27 Henri Bergson, *L'Évolution créatrice* (Paris: Félix Alcan, 1920), pp. 177–80.
28 Alphonse Goettmann and Rachel Goettmann, *Prière de Jesus, prière du coeur* (Paris: Albin Michel, 1994), pp. 33–41.
29 Ibid., p. 86.

10
Male and Female Made They Them

Kristeva's venture into *agape*, her reflections on the links between psychoanalysis and faith make room, as I have underlined, for the mother as the starting-point for the experience of love. But the Judaeo-Christian God, despite the strong patriarchal stresses through which we are accustomed to see 'Him', has more of the mother in 'them' than meets the eye (and, as I hope to have shown, than the likes of Lacan are prepared to grant). Alphonse and Rachel Goettmann repeatedly show that the word 'mercy', which turns up constantly as God's main attribute in both the Old and the New Testament, is from the Hebrew 'rehem', or 'rahum', and comes from a root which signifies the matrix, the maternal womb, the entrails of love. 'In his merciful tenderness, God shows himself in turns like a Father, a Husband, a Mother who exclaims, "My heart turns inside me, my entrails shiver" [Hosea 11: 8].' Another Hebrew scholar, André Neher, talks about the 'love-matrix evoked by "rahamin"' as one which presides over an 'untearable union, a co-presence'.[1] Christ as the beginning and end of all things is 'the matrix' as well as '"the New Man"' who, according to St Paul, makes all things new. The powerful emotions of compassion at the sight of pain that the Gospels describe Christ as experiencing, 'down to his entrails', are also those of the Father of the Prodigal Son. The father, in that parable, puts a ring on his newly returned son's finger as if he were a bride ... Father–son, but also, in love, man and wife. And St Paul says that Christ loves the Church as a husband loves his wife. In the Trinitarian dynamic of love, that is, and the dynamic of its incarnation, the God-persons occupy all the gender roles.

But of course they do. Hebrew scholar and Orthodox theologian Annick de Souzenelle, offers a 'Christian' reading of the Hebrew text of Genesis that traces every word, indeed every letter and sign making up every word of every verse, down to original meanings. Every word is compact with an amazing range of meanings, which in turns involves continuous gender shifts. Souzenelle explains how the word 'Bara', 'to create' 'is essentially a work of separation so that a union between the two separated terms might come about: a union that would be a source of fecundity'.[2]

Elohim (which is how God is named, although S/He is also named in the word for 'In the beginning') is the principle of the unity of fire and water. Yam is 'the sea', Em is 'the mother':

> Elohim Father is also Mother. Elohim is beyond any human category. The principle of all that is, He is the archetype of all maternity as well as of all paternity ... Woman is biologically the mother, but both man and woman have an essential maternal vocation: to give birth in themselves to the dimension of Son [Hebrew character], of which Yah is a contraction. This essential maternity is one of the aspects of the image of Elohim to which Adam obeys since his own name is constituted by the same structure. Adam, as we shall see, is humankind, men and women.[3]

The divine man Elohim is *in itself a plural*. As the subject of a verb, when 'They' speak, it is singular: They *speaks*. When Elohim *talk* about Themselves, *refer* to the Three Persons in the Trinity, then the verb is plural.

In the name Adam, unbelievably rich in semantic associations, Annick de Souzenelle reads 'mother' (he is his own mother), door, son, seed of wheat in the earth, wheatgerm as yet not come unto fulfilment. His maternal vocation defines him from the start. He is symbolically the salt in the sea, the taste of salt, water ('ed'), vapour and blood ('Dam').[4] The phrase 'Male and female' does not mean man in front of woman. Adam is 'the whole of humankind, men and women'. He 'is male when he remembers who he is, when he remembers the ... reserve of energies which he is inside the Adamah, itself revealed in the word "female" ':

> I, a woman, can be male when I plunge into the memory, not of my historic past, but of what will on the contrary be my becoming, i.e. by remembering the potentiality which lies hidden in the depths of my being.[5]

> Male is connected with accomplished-dry-light-purity. Female is connected with inaccomplished-wet-darkness-impurity.[6]

Pure and impure are not moral terms: they refer to what is finished and what is not. Female is from the root Naqob, meaning to make a hole, but also to name. It points to a container. 'The "female" is the secret place in Adam where Elohim has deposited the secret of the NAME,' that is, the content. 'Adam can only discover his Name by penetrating this belly, by marrying his own femininity and getting to "name" the energies that constitute it.' With Christ, 'humankind acquires consciousness of the Name.' 'Christ himself, paradoxically born of a biologically single woman, calls himself the son of Man for through Mary conscious humankind becomes male.' 'Male Man is he who remembers his own femininity in which the *Name* is deposited.'[7]

I may seem to have flown into the stratosphere. But what Annick de Souzenelle describes are truths which have been observed on a practical level by analysts, art critics and art therapists. In her essays on creativity, Rosemary Gordon points out how the 'passive' or 'feminine' elements, the stages of 'preparation', 'incubation' or 'muddled suspense', and 'illumination' or 'creative emptiness' have been portrayed by Herbert Read, A. N. Whitehead, Harold Rugg and others in terms reminiscent of motherly conception and gestation (also there, as Souzenelle shows, in the early verses of Genesis) and how countless others (she names Freud himself, Jung, Michael Balint, Milner, Winnicott and others)[8] have mapped out the combination of forces or areas in the self which enter into the creative act:

> Creativity involves play and paradox and depends on a person's capacity to tolerate contradictory – yet also complementary – qualities or processes, such as, for instance, activity and passivity; receptivity and productivity; consciousness and unconsciousness; masculinity and femininity. It might also involve the capacity to balance surrender and control, effort and passivity, waiting and forging ahead, solitude and communication.[9]

The truths which Annick de Souzenelle elicits from her reading of Genesis are available to the practical explorer. Indeed, those truths only gain their meaning when they are made real – when they become embodied, incarnated, in daily living. An example of how this can be is a modest and profound book, Marion Milner's *A Life of One's Own*. A young woman, barely in her twenties, publishing under the pseudonym Joanna Field, she proceeded to discover, by her own lights, what Souzenelle explores through Hebrew etymologies – and what wisdoms and religions throughout the world have also explored. Marion Milner wanted to know what made her happy. She watched herself feeling, thinking, relating, turning inwards Robinson Crusoe's capacity to observe the outward things: Defoe's text about how to survive on a desert island after a shipwreck provides several of the epigraphs, and a straightforward model of style.

Marion Milner gradually discovers that delight comes to her when she can 'spread wide the invisible feelers of mind', push herself 'out into the landscape or the movements of a flying bird', or music.[10] She then discovers that she can also 'spread them round people'. Finding sources of happiness, she writes, 'seemed to depend upon the capacity to relax all straining, to widen my attention beyond the circles of personal interest, and to look detachedly at my own experience'.[11] It meant accepting a great sense of insecurity, an 'utter giving in', 'being prepared to accept annihilation'. Only when this had occurred could a new security be found. Later, she found other words for what she had discovered. In biology, where one text spoke of ' "sexual multiplication" ' as involving the ' "egg cell or female gamete, slow-moving, placid, enduring, receptive ... in a word, introverted; and the male gamete, active, impetuous, courageously self-sacrificing ... in a word, extraverted" '.[12] She also found a book on *Bisexuality*, by T. J. Faithfull, that described sex equality as ' "no myth, for we are each of us essentially whole" '. ' "Below a complete surface femininity" ', however deep we have to dig, ' "we find a complete male striving for expression," ' and vice versa: in the depths of the psyche of ' "the painfully self-assertive male" ', there is the woman, ' "seeking for outlet" '.[13]

Marion Milner comes to see that she had first discovered delight by letting go, putting out feelers, when she had begun to understand 'real femininity'. She further reads Eastern sages, Lao-tze's ' "He who, being a man, remains a woman, will become a universal channel." ' She comes to appreciate the depths of Western fear of the female attitude: 'I had unknowingly accepted the male assumption that the purpose of life was to have purposes and get things done.' It was fear of the loss of her individuality in the necessary surrender that the female attitude required, fear that 'the satisfaction of the female meant the wiping out of the male for ever', which had caused such a fear of the loss of safety. 'And in its terror of losing the male in the female it had in fact lost both.'[14] She ended up thinking that maleness and femaleness, 'not necessarily correspond[ing] with the sex of the body', can be 'utterly distorted' in children, that in particular the 'female response', an 'inopportune femininity' can be overdeveloped and arouse anxiety and passivity, and that only a 'subtle balance of male and female activity', 'a male-female rhythm' would do: ' "Duality is necessary for observation and comprehension." '[15] For Marion Milner as for Annick de Souzenelle's reading of Genesis, that is, in the act of self-creation which is also the pursuit of happiness, in men as in women, the female part can be so lost that no birth of the true self is possible. Conversely, to be born the male part requires courage, necessitating as it does separation, a kind of 'annihilation', with attendant fear.

Contemporary reviews saw Milner's book as attempting a reconciliation of Eastern and Western approaches, 'a marriage between the two protagonists, not an either/or solution'. Olga Martin wrote: 'if the bisexual nature of man (admitted by Freud ...) were generally recognized, then the values appropriate to the suppressed feminine urge would be given their proper place in society and our problems would be tackled in a more peaceful and understanding spirit.'[16] A later book emphasized the distinction between 'the narrow focus, seeing life as if with blinkers and from the head', and the wider one which is 'knowing with the whole of the body'. Marion Milner comments, in words strongly reminiscent of the Genesis notion of female as container, male as penetrating: 'it was here that my attempt to define the way I have been using the terms male and female came in useful, for surely the wide knowing is a containing act, as against a male penetrating one.'[17]

Another reviewer, Olaf Gleeson, claiming that Marion Milner had rediscovered ' "the secret of that universal symbol" ', ' "embodied in the *Ankh* and included in the mystery of the Pythagorean Tetractys" ' (which means ' "the marriage of four" '), wrote: 'It is likewise in the unsuspected meaning of the phrase, "Male *and* Female created He them." '[18]

It seems that the phrase ought to be rewritten to 'Male and female created They Them.' That an in-depth rereading of Genesis, loaded as it is with ancient wisdom, earlier civilizations, reveals the female which is in the Godhead as well as the male, and which later readings, privileging the male and subsuming or erasing the female, have concealed. From early times to recent ones there travels a call to sexual, or gender, *inclusiveness*. To a bisexuality more fundamental than the sex/gender of whom we desire. A call to wholeness, which can only be answered when the *female* has been reintroduced into Genesis. When 'she', woman, femininity, the femaleness that can go by the name of Ruth, is put back in there.

Notes

1 Quoted by Alphonse Goettmann and Rachel Goettmann, *Prière de Jesus, prière du coeur* (Paris: Albin Michel, 1994), p. 216.

2 Annick de Souzenelle, *Alliance de feu: Une lecture chrétienne du texte hébreu de la Genèse*, rev. edn (Paris: Albin Michel, 1995), p. 227; all translations mine.

3 Ibid., pp. 54–7.

4 Ibid., pp. 343–61.

5 Ibid., p. 385.

6 Ibid., p. 388.

7 Ibid., pp. 389, 388–9, 393.

8 Rosemary Gordon, *Bridges: Psychic Structures, Functions, and Processes* (London: Karnac Books, 1993), pp. 324–7.

9 Ibid., p. 339.

10 Marion Milner (alias Joanna Field), *A Life of One's Own* (1934; London: Virago, 1986), p. 190.

11 Ibid., pp. 192, 193.

12 Quoted ibid., pp. 210–11.

13 Ibid., p. 211.

14 Ibid., pp. 213, 214, 215.

15 Ibid., pp. 216–17.

16 Ibid., pp. 223, 222.

17 Ibid., p. 224.

18 Ibid., p. 223.

Index

Abel, Elizabeth 120, 127
abjection 13
Abraham, Karl 128
Abraham, Nicolas 92
Abraham's sacrifice 92–3, 94
Adam 1–3, 189, 246
adultery 37, 38, 41, 55
agape 239–40, 245
Agnel, Aimé 231
Agoult, Marie d' 40
Akhmatova, Anna 89
Alcoff, Linda 16
alcoholism 223
Aldington, Hilda *see* H.D.
Aldington, Richard 90, 95, 96, 111, 134
androgynes 3–4, 165
androgyny 22, 23, 56, 101, 125, 135, 170
'Angel in the House', killing the 3, 153, 156, 166
Angelou, Maya 188
Angenot, Marc 60
anima 3, 22, 24, 97, 117, 134, 177–8, 222
animus 3, 22, 23, 97, 134, 177–8
aphanisis 98, 99
Apollonialism 21
archetypes 135, 150, 180, 196, 218
   lack of father 232–3
   of mother 29, 173–6
   of the unconscious 177–8
Aristotle 2, 12, 187, 189
Artaud, Antonin 170

artifice 147–8, 215
Asquith, Lady Cynthia 108
Athena 22, 70, 164, 165
Atwood, Margaret 205
Auffret, Séverine 100
Aurevilly, Barbey d' 43
Austen, Jane 44, 130, 161
author, as embodied in
   narrative 204–23

Badinter, Elizabeth 18, 165, 230
Balint, Michael 247
Balzac, Honoré de 3, 4, 9, 23, 26, 28
   A Daughter of Eve 35–63
Barker, Pat 92–3, 94, 100
Barthes, Roland 46, 142
Bataille, Georges 71, 81, 82, 155, 166, 170
battle of the sexes 28
   and World War I 85–137
Baudelaire, Charles 21, 60, 132, 191
Beauvoir, Simone de 5, 12, 18, 19, 64, 66, 77, 78, 79, 83, 142, 153, 164, 189
becoming 187–9
being, and doing 25–7, 28
being-in-the-world 205
Bergson, Henri 242
Berny, Madame de 39, 52
Bhatt, Sujata 174, 175
Bible 1–3, 234
binaries 5, 8, 10, 12, 73, 232
biography 218–19

biological essentialism 153–4
biology, divorced from
    mothering 154–5
bisexual studies 6
bisexuality 23, 25–7, 55, 135, 248–9
    Salome's theory of 97
black community, exclusion of 14–15
black feminism 6
Blake, William 99, 168
Blixen, Karen 83
Bloomsbury 127–8
Bly, Robert 230
boats 184, 205–6, 217
Bobbitt case 144
body 7, 9, 10–11, 94, 155–7, 241
    see also female body
Bolognini-Visconti, Countess 39
Bonald, Louis 41
Bonaparte, Marie 98
Bonaparte, Napoleon 36
boundaries 10–11, 13
bourgeoisie 41–2
    domestic tyranny 65, 66
Bowlby, Rachel 120, 128
Braidotti, Rosi 16
Brancusi, Constantin 24, 25, 30–1n
breast 29, 113, 172
    as the primary object 26
breastfeeding 43
Breton, André 4, 67, 70, 71
Breuer, Josef 88
Bricard, Isabelle 43, 45
Brittain, Vera 90, 92
Brontë, Charlotte 130, 206, 207
Brontë, Emily 165, 170
Brooke, Rupert 89
Browning, Elizabeth Barrett 165
Bryher 127
Buffon, Georges-Louis Leclerc, comte
    de 35
Buñuel, Luis 81
Burgess, Anthony 201
Butler, Judith 5, 10–13, 21, 22
Byron, George, Lord 223

Cahiers Jungiens de Psychanalyse 230–1
Campan, Madame 43
Capelle, Marie 37
Carrington, Charles 88
Carswell, Catherine 107
Carter, Angela 3, 19, 27, 141–62, 166,
    214–16, 222
castration 81, 115

Castries, Madame de 52
cave, Plato's 190–1, 193
Céline, Louis-Ferdinand 170
Charcot, Jean Martin 23, 88
Chasseguet-Smirgel, Janine 97–9, 100,
    114, 115, 131, 136
child abuse 76
Chirico, Giorgio de 90
Chodorow, Nancy 155, 179
Chopin, Kate 164, 205
chora 195
Christ 18, 221, 246–7
Christianity 2, 105–6, 230, 239–41,
    242–3
Citron, Pierre 53, 54
Cixous, Hélène 5, 16, 35, 55, 73, 156–7,
    158, 164, 170, 172, 189, 190, 192,
    193, 200, 202, 205, 218
Clare, Anthony 223, 224
class dimension of gender 130, 144,
    165
Claudel, Paul 168
Clément, Catherine 52
Colette, Sidonie Gabrielle 9–10, 89, 92,
    135, 146, 147, 158, 164, 200, 202,
    203–4, 212, 218, 219
Collins, Joan 144
complexities 7, 8
Conrad, Joseph 188, 205, 206
contradictions 7, 23, 45–9
convent schools 43–4
courtesan, and the Madonna 55–61
Cowan, James C. 114, 115
Cozlan, Leon 53
creation, gender and the
    imaginary 183–225
creativity
    female 3, 140–82, 247–9
    male 4
    maleness of 165
    and manic-depressive illness
        223–4
    masculine and feminine in 23–5
    and play 201–2
    and self 25–7
Crich, Gerald 110
Culler, Jonathan 100
cummings, e.e. 95
Cuvier, Georges 35
cyborg 16–18, 19

Dali, Salvador 81
Dante Alighieri 50, 194, 205

'dark continent of femininity' 96, 116, 190, 206
Darwin, Charles 94
daughters
  anger of 153
  good/bad 33–84
De Lauretis 19
De Quincey, Thomas 132
death 121, 193
death principle 105
deconstruction 151, 153, 214–16
Defoe, Daniel 247
Defromont, Françoise 119
Delaney, Paul 107, 113, 114
Delcourt, Marie 230
Deleuze 5
dependence, relative and absolute 19
depression 223
Derrida, Jacques 5, 73, 188–9, 206
  'White Mythology' 192–6
DeSalvo, Louise 134
desire 101, 120, 215
  the mother's 158–9
Deutsch, E. O. M. 98
Dickens, Charles 132, 188
Dickinson, Emily 164, 165, 168, 170
différance 5
difference 6, 10–11, 200
differences, exaggeration of 10–14
Dinnerstein, Dorothy 180
discourse
  becomes structure 11–13
  repressive 11
Djikstra 92
doing, and being 25–7, 28
Dorval, Marie 92
Douglas, Mary 10–11, 13
du Bois, Page 232
Dumas, Alexandre 53
Dupré, Francis 72–3, 74, 76

Eder, David 106
education for girls 38, 43–5, 46–8, 55
ego 219–20
either/or 23
Eliot, George 130
Eliot, T. S. 88, 90, 168, 186
embodiment 9
emotional issues 6
empowerment 16
environment 26, 195
Epictetes 185
eroticism, and pornography 144, 155

ethics, and poetry 181
Euridice 168–9, 171
Eve 1–3, 189, 214–16
exclusion 11–12, 13–15, 206
experience 29, 195–6, 199, 247
eye 71, 81–3, 193

Fairbairn, W. A. D. 114
faith, and psychoanalysis 239–43, 245
Faithfull, T. J. 248
Faludin, Susan 136
family, ethics of the 41
family studies 230
fantasy 148
  and separation 150–1
fashion 19–20
father 4, 15, 151
  absent 28, 134
  biological 230
  educating 230
  genealogical 230
  'good enough' 123
  the name of the 229–44
  symbolic 230, 233, 239, 241–2
  see also Freud, on the father
father-child relating, insertion
  metaphor 231
fatherhood
  changing conception of 241
  crisis of 28
  models of 231–3
Fathers by Daughters 229
fear 146–7
Feinstein, Elaine 104, 174, 175
female
  etymology of word 246
  gendering the 33–84
female attitude, Western fear of 248
female body 190–1
female castration 74
female creativity 3, 140–82, 247–9
female myth 163–4
female sexuality 96–101
femininity
  construction of 4
  gendered 23
  refusal of 19–20
  see also Freud, on femininity
feminism 17
  black 6
  and psychoanalysis 27
  second wave 5, 194

feminisms 4–8
Fénélon, François de Salignac de la
    Mothe 37, 44
Field, Joanna *see* Milner, Marion
fire 211
Fitz-Jameses 52
Flavigny, Marie de *see* Agoult, Marie
    d'
Ford, Ford Madox 88
Foucault, Michel 5, 6, 10, 11, 12, 18, 25,
    112, 142
Fouque, Antoinette 18, 19–20
Frame, Janet 205, 223
Franz, Marie Louise von 222
Freud, Sigmund 4, 13, 14, 25, 29, 72,
    73, 76, 94, 98, 104, 164, 234, 247
    on bisexuality 23
    on the father 231, 238, 239
    on female sexuality 96–7
    on femininity 2, 7, 22, 116
    on hysteria 88, 96
    on penis envy 96–7, 127, 130
    on the pre-Oedipal stage 121, 156,
        231
    theory of the phallus 20, 99, 136
    on unconscious drives 105, 106,
        114
Frieda (D. H. Lawrence's wife) 103,
    105, 109, 113

Garnett, Edward 106
Gaskell, Mrs Elizabeth 166
Gauthier, Théophile 53
gay studies 6
gaze 9, 60, 119
gender 6, 23
    class dimension of 130, 144, 165
    creation and the imaginary 183–225
    as a repressive act 11
    social construction of 9, 28
    see also God, gender of
gender confusion 9–10, 15
gender rules 205
gender trouble 8–15, 204–23
genealogy 18, 241
genes 223–4
Genesis 1–3, 245–7, 249
Genet, Jean 77–9, 81–3
Genlis, Madame de 37
Ghea 174, 175–6
Gilbert, S. 88
Gilman, Charlotte Perkins 223
Gleeson, Olaf 249

God 242–3
    as *agape* 239–40
    the disappearance of 28
    gender of 1–29, 243, 246, 249
goddesses 2, 13, 164
Goethe, Johann Wolfgang von 18, 30
Goettmann, Alphonse and Rachel 242,
    245
Gordon, Rosemary 247
Grandville, J.-J. 81–2
Greece 2, 164
Greek myths 21, 230
Groot, Jeanne Lampl-de 98
Gross, Otto 106
Gubar, S. 88
Guizot, Madame 37

Halley, Anne 178–9
Hanska, Madame 36, 54
Hanson, Clare 119
happiness 37, 248
Haraway, Donna 16–18, 22
Hartmann, Heinz 114
H.D. 90, 91, 104, 164, 165, 168
Head, Bessie 111
Hegel, Georg Wilhelm Friedrich 163,
    189, 193
Heidegger, Martin 187
heterosexuality, compulsory 6, 11
Higgins, Ian 198
Hoffmann, E. T. W. 59, 61
Holtby, Winifred 91, 131
Homer 163, 164
homophobia 11–12
homosexuality 11–12
    in artists 23
Hopkins, Gerald Manley 168
Horney, Karen 97, 98, 110
Houdyer, Paulette 74–6, 77, 83
Hugo, Victor 234–8
husbands, school for 38–42
Husserl, Edmund 167
hysteria 88
    female 96
    male fear of 96

Ida, Mademoiselle 53
imaginary, creation and gender and
    the 183–225
incest 11, 76, 106, 113, 169–70
individuation 19, 219, 221–2
inequalities 5
infant attachment patterns 231

inner reality 199–200, 202
interdisciplinarity 7
intuition 242
Irigaray, Luce 5, 13, 19, 73, 94, 96, 97,
    115, 157, 158, 190–1, 193, 194, 234,
    238

Jackson, Rosie 180
Jakobson, Roman 216
James, St 185–6
Jamieson, Kay 223
Jan, Laurent 53
Jews 241
Jones, Ernest 97, 98, 106, 128, 132
jouissance 116–17, 149
Joyce, James 23, 101, 132, 151, 154, 158,
    170, 221
Jullien-Pelletier, Viviane 92, 230
July Revolution 42
Jung, Carl Gustav 21, 26, 27, 161, 219,
    220, 231, 238, 247
  anima and animus 3, 97, 222
  archetypes of the unconscious 150,
    156, 177–8, 232
  on hostility to the mother 18–19,
    156
  on the unconscious 14, 105–6

Kafka, Franz 10, 12
Keats, John 92
Keegan 87
kinship systems 2
Kipling, Rudyard 28, 92, 124
Kiyoko, Nagase 177
Klein, Melanie 25, 26, 27, 29, 97, 98,
    113, 122, 128, 132, 172
knowledge of good and evil 35–63
Kohut, Heinz 114
Kristeva, Julia 5, 11, 13, 14, 16, 117,
    157, 158, 169–70, 173, 176, 179,
    201, 202, 213, 219, 239–41, 242,
    243, 245

Labbé, Louise 165, 169, 171
Lacan, Jacques 4, 7, 26, 66, 67, 73, 74,
    77, 78, 79, 81, 83, 97, 114, 116–17,
    123, 136, 189, 229–44
Laclos, Pierre 37
Lacoue-Labarthe, Philippe 79
Lancelins 64
language 140, 169–70, 173, 216–18
  the naming power of 175
  source of 172

langue 186–7, 216–18
Lao-tze 248
Lauretis, Teresa de 16
Lautréamont, comte de 70
Lawrence, D. H. 4, 26, 27, 93–4, 96, 97,
    99, 100–1, 103–18, 119, 124, 132,
    134, 135
lesbian studies 6
lesbian thinking 16, 120
Lessing, Doris 205
Lévi-Strauss, Claude 12, 51, 170
libido 105
Light, Alison 126
Lispector, Clarice 188, 200, 222
Liszt, Franz 40
literature 9, 186
London Psycho-analytic Society 128
Lorde, Audre 16, 17
love 175
Low, Ivy 106
Lowe, Barbara 106
Lowell, Amy 105
Lowell, Sarah *see* Bolognini-Visconti,
    Countess
Lyndon, Neil 230
lyric poetry 168, 213

madness, creativity and 223–4
Madonna
  and the courtesan 55–61
  the mother as 176
Maffei, Countess Clara 54, 56
Mahler, Margaret 231–2
Mailer, Norman 99, 100
Maistre, Joseph de 43
male, privileging of the 2, 17
male creativity 4
male and female 1–31, 245–9
male myth 163
maleness 64–83
Mallarmé, Stéphane 186
man's sentence 119–37
Mansfield, Katherine 103, 104–5,
    106, 109, 112, 113, 115, 117, 119,
    173
Marcadé, Bernard 30–1n
Marini, Marcelle 234, 237, 238
marriage 35–8, 48–52
Martin, Olga 248
Marvell, Andrew 218
Marx, Karl 163
masculine and/or feminine 22–5,
    85–137

masculinity 230
    crisis in 97, 136
    in differentiation from the maternal
        feminine 18–19
masculinity studies 6
masochism, feminine 176, 220
maternity, the fiction of 151–5
matrilinear societies 2, 13, 230
matrix 13, 18, 160, 245
maturation 161
Mauss, Marcel 52
Memoir Club, Bloomsbury 127–8
men
    envy of women and childbirth 20
    missing 87–102
men's studies 230
metamorphosis 168
    of woman 192
metaphors 4, 23, 28, 135, 168, 187
    derivation of word 192
    live 194–6, 218
    as moments 218
    and narrative 185–225
metaphysics 193
Michel, Arlette 45
Miller, Alice 74, 76
Miller, Henry 94, 99, 190
Miller, Hillis 28
Miller, Jean Baker 220
Millett, Kate 100, 109–10, 115
Milner, Marion 9, 247–9
Minow-Pinkney, Makiko 119–20
mirror 72, 121, 172, 191
misogyny 19, 22, 90
misreadings 143–9, 234–8
Mitchell, Juliet 97
Molière 37, 44, 50
Montmignon, Abbé de 44
mood disorder, and creativity 223
moon, and womb 111–12
Moravia, Alberto 144
Morejon, Nancy 177
Morrell, Ottoline 103, 108, 109
Morrison, Toni 14–15, 156, 205, 222
Moses 25
Moskowitz, Cheryl 178
mother
    absence of the 28–9
    Amazon 177
    archetypal 29, 173–6
    the bad 177
    body of the 94, 241
    as darkness 172

    and death 121
    desire of the 158–9
    as a figure of speech 141–62
    'good enough' 25–7, 204
    hostility to the 18–20
    the ideal 180
    as Madonna 176
    murder of the 94–6
    as object of desire 169–72, 173
    Oedipal 99
    the real 29, 177–81
    relation to the 4, 15
    separation from the 221–2
    as source of care 172
    troublesome 140–82
    writing and the 155–8
mother-centred societies, see
        matrilinear societies
mother-daughter relationship 157–8
mother-incest 106, 113
motherhood
    and poetry 163–82
    women and 155–8
mothering 155–6
    biology divorced from 154–5
    double identification in 179–80
Murasaki, Lady Shikibu 188
murder, fascination with 64–83
Murry, Jack Middleton 103, 104, 113,
        114
mythology
    Indo-European 192–6
    of the perfect mother 180
myths 2, 159
    of creation 13
    male and female 163–4

name, the proper 193
Namjoshi, Suniti 177
narcissism 20, 72
Narcissus 168, 170
narrative
    and metaphors 185–225
    as quest for the self 218–20
    and the self at sea 204–23
nature, idealizing or demonizing 21–2
Navarre, Marguerite de 165
Neher, André 245
Newman, John 41
Nichols, Grace 174–5
Nietzsche, Friedrich 189, 206
Nin, Anaïs 94
not-me 13–14, 11

ocean 155
ocularcentrism 81
Oedipus complex 99, 113, 115, 128, 136
offensive à outrance 87, 99
Olsen, Tillie 155, 156, 165–6, 181
orality 115, 240
oranges 200–1, 202–3, 218
Orpheus 168–9, 170, 171
Other, the 5, 239–40
Owen, Wilfred 92, 107

Paglia, Camille 21, 22, 23–4, 26, 94,
    144, 165, 166, 170
Pan 171
Papin sisters 28, 64–83
paranoid delirium 65, 67
parole 216, 218
Pascal, Blaise 186
Pasolini, Pier Paolo 142
passivity 42, 55, 56
paternal principle 230
paternity
    fiction of 23, 152–3
    hidden nature 238–9
patriarchy 5, 28, 93, 194, 220, 230, 233,
    241–2
Paul, St 240, 245
penis envy 4, 20, 96, 119–37, 132, 136
Péret, Benjamin 67, 70, 71
Perse, St John 168
phallic sexual monism 97–9, 114, 136
phallocracy 156
phallogocentrism 5, 6, 73
phallus 5, 20, 99
    see also Freud, on theory of the
        phallus
philosophy 2, 5
Picasso, Pablo 90
Planche, Gustave 53
Plath, Sylvia 165, 166, 172, 175, 178,
    223
Plato 3, 12, 13, 18, 189, 190–1, 193,
    195
play 148, 159–61
    and creativity 201–2
plurality 187–8
Poe, Edgar Allan 205
poetry
    and ethics 181
    lyric 168, 213
    and motherhood 163–82
    realms of 168
politics 5

pollution 10–11, 13
Ponge, Francis 4, 27, 196, 200, 202,
    218
Pope, Jessie 95
pornography
    and eroticism 144, 155
    using to make the reader think 148,
        150–1
Portalis, Jean Etienne Marie 36
Post, Felix 223, 224
post-colonial studies 6
postmodernism 149
Poubelle 57
Pound, Ezra 93, 168
power 5, 10, 23
    domestic 78
    and exclusion 14–15
    women and organized systems
        of 205
    see also empowerment
powerlessness, enforced 88–91
Praz, Mario 92
pre-Oedipal stage 119, 121, 156, 219,
    231, 242
projections 29, 177–8, 180
    and subtexts 52–5
prostitute 60, 93
Proust, Marcel 164–5, 201, 202, 203,
    218, 221
psychoanalysis 7–8, 12, 14, 72,
    96–101, 106, 127–9
    and faith 239–43, 245
    and feminism 27
psychopathology 223
Pythoness 189

queer theory 6

racism 11–12
Read, Herbert 247
reading 188
Récamier, Madame 52
relations between the sexes 22–5, 28;
    see also battle of the sexes
religions 2
Rémusat, Madame de 37
representations 7
repression 14, 106, 206
Rhys, Jean 206–8, 223
rhythms 219
Rich, Adrienne 2, 18, 22, 155, 163,
    164, 167, 168, 180
Richardson, Dorothy 223

Ricoeur, Paul 27, 187, 188, 194–5, 218
Riley, Denise 16
Rimbaud, Arthur 191
Rivière, Joan 202
Roberts, Michèle 27, 28, 156, 160,
    175–6, 203, 208–11, 218, 219, 222
Rochester, Earl of 190
Roman de Renart 2
romance 146
Romanticism, German 57
Rose, Jacqueline 97, 156
Rosenberg, Isaac 93
Rossetti, Christina 125–6
Rousseau, Jean-Jacques 18, 36, 37, 43,
    45
Rugg, Harold 247
Rushdie, Salman 186
Russell, Bertrand 107
Ruth, The Book of 234–8

Sackville-West, Vita 133
Sade, Marquis de 90, 141–2, 143, 148,
    159, 170
sadism 71
Sage, Lorna 141
Saint-Hilaire, Geoffroy 35
Saiving, Valerie 221
Salome, Lou Andreas 97
Samuels, Andrew 9–10, 23, 26, 231,
    232–3, 238, 239
Sand, George 37, 43, 45, 53, 56, 92, 166
Sappho 163–4, 165, 169, 171–2
Sartre, Jean-Paul 65, 66, 70–1, 73, 78,
    79–80, 83
Sassoon, Siegfried 88, 92, 95
scapegoats 65
schizophrenia 72
Schreber, President 72, 234
Scott, Sir Walter 46
sea 29, 105–6, 184, 191–2, 204–23
sea mother 192–6
second sex 5, 189
self
    at sea, and narrative 204–23
    and creativity 25–7
    in literature 204
    in the making 187–9
semen 2
semiotic 157, 169–70, 173, 202, 242
separation 160, 164, 229
    and fantasy 150–1
    from the mother 221–2
serial killer, female 144–5

sexual vision 81
Shakespeare, William, hypothetical
    sister 129
shells 196–8, 200, 203
Showalter, Elaine 89
Smart, Elizabeth 141
socialization 14
Socrates 191
soul 11
Souzenelle, Annick de 245–7, 248
Spivak, Gayatri 188–9
Staël, Madame de 36, 45
Stendhal 36
Stephen, Adrian 128
Stevenson, Anne 179–80
Stott 92
Strachey, James and Alix 128
Strachey, Lytton 128
subject
    construction of the self as 187–9
    and gender trouble 204–23
    western 5
subversion 14–15
sun 193
Surrealists 67, 70, 73, 78, 79–80, 81, 83,
    90, 91
Symbolists 27
symmetry, lack of 26
Syrinx 168, 169, 170, 171

taboos 2, 10–12, 155
Tennant, Emma 141
Tennyson, Alfred, Lord 94, 125, 223
texts
    as Polylogues 213
    and self-in-the-making 187–8
Thackeray, William Makepeace 132
Tharaud, Jérôme and Jean 66–7
Thomas, David 230
Thomas, Keith 21
time, women's 218–19
tongues 185–90, 190, 218
Torok, Maria 92, 132, 134
transitional objects 196–204, 209, 218
Tuchman, Barbara 87

unconscious 14, 18–19, 105, 157, 160
    archetypes of the 150, 156, 177–8,
    232
    see also Freud, on unconscious
    drives; Jung, on the unconscious
Unheimlich 164
usure 192–6

Valéry, Paul 71, 189, 191–2
Vasseur, Bernard 230
Vigny, Alfred Victor, comte de 92
violence 106, 136
Vivien, Renée 164
voice, personal 29
voyages 29, 214, 219

Walker, Alice 17
war 4, 121, 124–7
   and male writers 106–11
war poets 4
Warner, Marina 2
Wehr, Demaris S. 220, 222
West, Rebecca 91
Whitehead, A. N. 247
Whitman, Walt 168
whore/madonna 60
Wille zur Macht 108, 110
Winnicott, D. W. 14, 19, 20–1, 25–7,
   28, 114, 123, 204, 231–2, 247
   transitional objects 198–200, 201–2,
   218
Winterson, Jeanette 201
Wittig, Monique 16
wives, the school for 43–5
Wolf, Christa 156
Wollstonecraft, Mary 165
woman
   metamorphosis of 192

as the metaphor for truth 189
as the unacknowledged mother 19
use of the word 15–22
'womanism' 17
woman's body, reclaiming of 155–7
womb 13, 18, 96, 172, 190–1, 195–6
womb envy 4, 103–18, 110, 136
women
   men's sense of awe before 99–100
   and motherhood 155–8
   as objects of exchange 49–52
women writers 204–23
women's sentence 87–102
Woolf, Leonard 127, 128
Woolf, Virginia 3, 26, 89, 91, 101,
   119–37, 153, 156, 163, 188, 194,
   211–14, 223
Wordsworth, William 22
World War I 28, 135
   and battle of the sexes 85–137
writing 16, 188
   and the mother 155–8

Yealland, Lewis 88–9
Yeats, William Butler 152, 168
Yorkshire Ripper case 22, 144

Zola, Emile 60
zoology 35